Leading Professional [
in Education

This reader is part of a course: Leading Professional Development in Education, that is itself part of the Open University MA programme.

The Open University MA in Education

The Open University MA in Education is now firmly established as the most popular postgraduate degree for education professionals in Europe, with over 3,000 students registering each year. The MA in Education is designed particularly for those with experience of teaching, the advisory service, educational administration or allied fields.

Structure of the MA

The MA is a modular degree, and students are therefore free to select from a range of options the programme that best fits in with their interests and professional goals. Specialist lines in management, applied linguistics and lifelong learning are also available. Study in the Open University's Advanced Diploma can also be counted towards the MA, and successful study in the MA programme entitles students to apply for entry into The Open University Doctorate in Education programme.

OU Supported Open Learning

The MA in Education programme provides great flexibility. Students study at their own pace, in their own time, anywhere in the European Union. They receive specially prepared study materials, supported by tutorials, thus offering the chance to work with other students.

The Doctorate in Education

The Doctorate in Education is a part-time doctoral degree, combining taught courses, research methods and a dissertation designed to meet the needs of professionals in education and related areas who are seeking to extend and deepen their knowledge and understanding of contemporary educational issues. The Doctorate in Education builds upon successful study within the Open University MA in Education programme.

How to apply

If you would like to register for this programme, or simply find out more information about available courses, please write for the *Professional Development in Education* prospectus to the Course Reservations Centre, PO Box 724, The Open University, Walton Hall, Milton Keynes, MK7 6ZW, UK (Telephone 0 (0 44) 1908 653231). Details can also be viewed on our web site http://www.open.ac.uk

Leading Professional Development in Education

Edited by Bob Moon, John Butcher
and Elizabeth Bird

 in association with

London and New York

First published 2000
by RoutledgeFalmer
11 New Fetter Lane, London EC4P 4EE

Simultaneously published in the USA and Canada
by RoutledgeFalmer
29 West 35th Street, New York, NY 10001

RoutledgeFalmer is an imprint of the Taylor & Francis Group

© 2000 Compilation, original and editorial matter, The Open University

Typeset in Garamond by Steven Gardiner Ltd, Cambridge
Printed and bound in Great Britain by Biddles Ltd, Guildford and King's Lynn

British Library Cataloguing in Publication Data
A catalogue record for this book is available from the British Library

Library of Congress Cataloging in Publication Data
Leading professional development in education / edited by Bob Moon,
John Butcher, and Elizabeth Bird.
    p.   cm.
Includes bibliographical references and index.
1. Teachers – In-service training. 2. Educational leadership. 3. Educational change.
I. Moon, Bob, 1945– II. Butcher, John, 1956– III. Bird, Elizabeth, 1958–
LB1731.L424 2001   00-055224
371.2—dc21

ISBN 0-415-24382-3 (PB)
ISBN 0-415-24381-5 (HB)

Contents

SECTION 5
Education, communication, information and the
future of professional development

Figures

Tables

Preface

The significance of the leadership of professional development in education is widely recognised. Demanding international agendas for school reform and improvement are creating equally ambitious challenges for teacher development. These new forms of public expectations and accountability go beyond schools to embrace an increasingly diverse range of educational institutions.

Leaders in professional development take many forms: there are the formal positions of headteacher, principal, deputy or depute, subject coordinator or head of department adviser and inspector, or the less formal leadership roles that occur in a more informal way as a consequence of the autonomies and collegiality that characterise any professional group. This collection of articles provides a set of sources that we hope will be of value to anyone preparing for, or involved in, such a task. They are clustered under a number of broad headings. An introductory chapter sets out a number of themes for the future of professional development and relates these to subsequent sections of the book. **Section 1 Orientations** focuses on the nature of professional learning and the policy context in which educational reform takes place. **Section 2 Models of leading professional development** explores the forms of leadership relevant to the differing contexts of professional development. **Section 3 Skills and processes in the leadership of professional development** considers mentoring, peer coaching, team and group work. These processes are examined through international experience and by reference to work in other professions. **Section 4 Evidence in the development of professional knowledge** provides an analysis of the potential of applying the experience of evidence-based work in medicine and the health service to education. The section reviews contested views on this theme. The final section, **Section 5 Education, communication, information and the future of professional development**, looks specifically at the potential role that interactive technologies can play in the professional development. In doing this a number of contemporary case studies are explored and critically analysed within the emergent theoretical models being developed around information and communication technologies.

The classification of this Reader is directed towards an Open University MA/MEd course with the same title as this book E843 *Leading Professional Development in Education*. The book is one of a range of text and on-line resources used by students.

In choosing the articles and arriving at the classification, the editors benefited enormously from the advice of colleagues within the Centre for Research and Development in Teacher Education (CRETE) and those working on the Open University/Research Machines Learning Schools Programme.

In selecting from an increasingly rich literature, we have sought to identify themes that we see as central to the leadership of professional practice in the first decade of a new century. New ideas and new examples of policy and practical implementation will develop whilst this book is in print. The editors would welcome further ideas and comment on any of the issues raised.

Bob Moon (r.e.moon@open.ac.uk)
John Butcher (j.s.butcher@open.ac.uk)
Elizabeth Bird (e.bird@open.ac.uk)
See also http://soe.open.ac.uk/CRETE/index.htm
The Open University
Milton Keynes
April 2000

Acknowledgements

While the publishers have made every effort to contact copyright holders of previously published material in this volume, they would be grateful to hear from any they were unable to contact.

Chapter 2 Putnam, R. T. and Borko, H. (2000) 'What do new views of knowledge and thinking have to say about research on teacher learning?' in *Educational Researcher*, 29, 1: 4–15. Copyright 2000 by the American Educational Research Association. Reprinted (or adapted) by permission of the publisher.

Chapter 3 Elmore, Richard F. *Harvard Educational Review*, 66, 1.

Chapter 4 Fidler, Brian. (1997) *School Leadership & Management*, 17, 1.

Chapter 5 West-Burnham, John. (1997) *School Leadership & Management*, 17, 2.

Chapter 6 Busher, Hugh and Harris, Alma. (1999) *School Leadership & Management*, 19, 3.

Chapter 8 Swafford, Jeanne. (1998) 'Teachers supporting teachers through peer coaching' in *Support for Learning*, 13, 2: 54–8. Copyright 2000 by NASEN.

Chapter 9 Khan, K. S. and Gee, H. (1999) 'A new approach to teaching and learning in journal club', in *Medical Teacher*, 21, 3: 289–93. http://www.tandf.co.uk/journals/carfax/0142159x.html

Chapter 10 Estebaranz, Araceli, Mingorance, Pilar and Marcelo, Carlos. (1999) *Teachers and Training: Theory and Practice*, 5, 2.

Chapter 11 West-Burnham, John. (1992) *Managing Quality in Schools*, Harlow: Longman, with permission from Pearson Education.

Chapter 12 Russell, Sheila. (1996) *School Organisation*, 16, 3.

Chapter 13 Alkin, Marvin C. (1975) 'Evaluation, Who Needs it? Who cares?' in *Studies in Educational Evaluation*, 1, 3: 314–29, with permission from Elsevier Science.

Chapter 14 Barth, Britt-Marie. (1991) 'From practice to theory: improving the thinking process' in Maclure, S. and Davies, P. (eds) *Learning to Think: Thinking to Learn*, pp. 115–26, Oxford: Pergamon Press, with permission from Elsevier Science.

Chapter 15 Hargreaves, David H. (1996) Teacher Training Agency annual lecture.

Chapter 16 Hammersley, Martyn. (1997) *British Educational Research Journal*, 23 (2).

Chapter 17 Hargreaves, David H. (1999) 'The knowledge-creating school' in *British Journal of Educational Studies*, 47(2), pp. 122–44. Copyright 2000 by Blackwell Publishers Ltd.

Chapter 19 Davies, Philip. (1999) 'What is evidence-based education?' in *British Journal of Educational Studies*, 47 (2), pp. 108–21. Copyright 2000 by Blackwell Publishers Ltd.

Chapter 21 Marx, Ronald W, Blumenfeld, Phyllis C., Krajcik, Joseph S. and Soloway, Elliot. (1998) 'New technologies for teacher professional development' in *Teaching and Teacher Education*, 14 (1), pp. 33–52, with permission from Elsevier Science.

Chapter 22 Moonen, Bert and Voogt, Joke. (1998) *Journal of In-service Education*, 24(1), February.

Introduction

Chapter 1

The changing agenda for professional development in education

Bob Moon

Commissioned for this volume (2000).

Globally increased emphasis is being placed on teachers' professional development. Policy processes and systems are moving from a preoccupation with universal pre-service education, one of the great achievements of the twentieth century, to the challenges of creating opportunities for career-long education and training in the twenty-first. Such a reorientation recognises:

- changing forms of economic and social organisation, most notably the shift from manual to knowledge-based forms of employment;
- increasingly rapid changes in the knowledge base of many parts of the curriculum;
- rising public expectations about the standards that schools and other educational institutions should achieve;
- new forms of public accountability at all levels of the public education system; an accountability often enforced by regulatory and statutory mechanisms;
- the availability of new forms of technologies with the potential for significantly enhancing access to personal and communal professional development programmes of a formal and informal nature.

These interrelated processes present opportunities and challenges to all levels of an education system. Some countries have established very explicit professional responses. South Africa, for example, following a period of extensive consultation, is driving professional development reform through an agreed set of socio-political and pedagogical values: democracy, liberty, equality, justice and peace for the former, relevance, learner centredness, professionalism, co-operation and collegiality and innovation for the latter (Moon, 2000).

In England and Wales a consultation paper (DfEE, 2000) on professional development set out ten principles upon which new systems and structures could be based: teacher ownership, equality of opportunity, and learning from the best are three examples. David Blunkett, the Minister responsible for introducing the paper, said:

> I intend to support individual teachers, whole schools and the whole profession in a partnership of commitment to inclusive, high quality professional development.

> Nobody expects a doctor, accountant or lawyer to rely for decades on the knowledge, understanding and approach which was available when they began their career . . . commitment to professional development is crucial.
>
> (p. 1)

The advocacy of career-long professional development is not new. The turn of the century, however, often provides moments of review and fresh thinking and a number of themes appear to be creating more strongly conceptualised models of professional development than hitherto have been possible. In particular:

- new understanding of the learning process;
- more explicit acknowledgement of the role of leadership in professional development;
- the moves to provide a stronger knowledge and evidence base to teaching and school organisation;
- the recent, rapid deployment of new forms of interactive technologies.

New understandings of the learning process

There is a growing recognition that successful professional development programmes articulate well thought through ideas about the learning process. What has been dubbed the cognitive revolution (Bruner, 1996), the move towards a more psycho-cultural approach to education, is every bit as relevant to professional learning as it is to the nursery play area or classroom. Attention to the forms and contexts in which the development activity is played out is increasingly occupying the attention of policy makers and those implementing practice.

In the next chapter of this book, Ralph Putnam and Hilda Borko explore the links between teacher learning and the conceptualisation of learning as situated, social and distributed. In other words, that context critically defines the nature of learning, that interaction and discourse provides the necessary conditions for learning and that effective learning can be understood in terms of the achievement of groups of individuals (including groups of individuals with other materials and artefacts).

This focus on learning reflects the influential work of Jerome Bruner. The insights that Bruner has brought to bear on learning in general are relevant to the task of building professional communities. In a fascinating summary of his ideas, Bruner has set out a number of tenets that he sees as guiding the psycho-cultural approach to education (Bruner, 1996). He talks, for example, of the externalisation tenet whereby the main function of all collective cultural activity is to produce *oeuvres* (he quotes the French psychologist Ignace Megerson) or 'works'. The benefits of externalising joint products, he suggests, has been overlooked. Collective works help *make* a community, communities of mutual learners. And the products are *records* of our mental efforts that go beyond individual or collective memory.

A second tenet Bruner terms institutionalisation. Cultures embrace institutions that specify roles, status and respect. Pierre Bourdieu is quoted as suggesting that institutions provide the markets where people trade their acquired skills, knowledge and ways of constructing meaning for distinctions or privileges. Such privileges exist in various shades of subtlety, financial reward, personal acclaim and local respect.

This links directly to a third tenet, that of identity and self-esteem. Our successes and failures, Bruner argues, are the principal nutrients in the development of selfhood.

> The management of self-esteem is never simple and never settled, and its state is affected powerfully by the availability of supports provided from outside. These supports are hardly mysterious or exotic. They include such homely resorts as a second chance, honour for a good if unsuccessful try, but above all the chance for discourse that permits one to find out why, or how things didn't work out as planned.
>
> (Bruner, 1996, p. 37)

And then there is the narrative tenet, or the mode of thinking and feeling that helps us create a version of the world in which psychologically we can envisage a place for ourselves. Feeling at home in the world, knowing how to place oneself, is at the core of the personal confidence and security that allows us to find an identity within our culture. Without it we stumble in our efforts for meaning.

The tenets that Bruner sets out interrelate. Collective externalised endeavour, institutional supports, identity and self-esteem all build to *envisaging a place for ourself*. This is true of all ages and many contexts and embraces personal and professional life. Each has relevance to the ongoing learning that is required of professional communities.

These same themes are taken up in Chapter 3. Richard Elmore explores the policy context of educational reform, particularly in the USA. For Elmore, development that seeks to change practice must *embody an explicit theory about how human beings learn to do things differently.*

The role of leadership in professional development

Leadership represents a theme that has become increasingly important in professional development. Traditionally, to follow Bruner's analysis and as a number of contributors to this book argue (Putnam and Borko, Chapter 2, Leach, Chapter 23, for example), most professional development activity has been focused through individuals. And yet the focus on networks and knowledge creating educational communities points to the importance of more collective approaches to improvement. Section 3 of this book explores a number of different conceptions of the role that leaders play in professional development. Leadership takes many forms and many government policies now abound that focus on the roles of principals and head-teachers, middle managers or inspectors. These are important and yet there are other more complex ways in which leadership is exercised in all professional communities.

Confident, knowledge-based professional development will generate multifarious leadership roles that provide inspiration and personal gratification, irrespective of formal statuses. Mature types of institutional structure are required if the demands of formal structures are to be reconciled with the rewards of genuinely collegial activity. How these evolve, and the extent to which they break free from the assumptions that have characterised professional development and professional learning in the past, is at the core of many of the contributions to this volume.

Developing a stronger knowledge and evidence base to teaching and school organisation

A third related theme is the need to give a stronger evidence or knowledge base to the professional development practice of teaching. In an important sense this theme has a history. The quest to deepen professional knowledge is represented in an extensive literature over a long period. The 'teacher as researcher' movement would be one example (Elliott, 1991). The advocacy for developing teachers' pedagogical content knowledge (Shulman, 1996) and the way this has been utilised to construct a model of teachers' professional knowledge (Banks *et al.*, 1999) represents a parallel example. In Section 2 of this book a selection of articles explore the processes by which professional knowledge can be extended. The choice of articles reflects the broad focus set out by Putnam and Borko in Chapter 2. An international case study from Andalusia and the account of the 'journal clubs' of the medical profession are illustrative of the types of communities of practice and discourse that can underpin professional development.

In recent years a debate has begun about the forms of evidence that teachers, and other educational professionals, should draw on in developing their practice. Section 4 explores this debate in some detail. David Hargreaves has been a leading advocate of the move towards a more structured analysis of evidence, and a public speech on the issue is transcribed in Chapter 15. He has also argued the case for the knowledge-creating school (Chapter 17). He suggests that some of the models of knowledge creation in high technology businesses are suggestive of the conditions under which the creation of professional knowledge in education, and its more rapid dissemination throughout the whole education service, might flourish. Hargreaves is particularly impressed with a model formulated by Nonaka and Takeuchi (1995). They argue that knowledge is created from the interaction of explicit and tacit knowledge and they go on to postulate four modes of knowledge conversion:

> *Socialisation* concerns the shared experience through apprenticeship and on-the-job training which generates tacit knowledge. Dialogue and collective reflection among members of the community trigger *externalisation* by which tacit knowledge is articulated into explicit knowledge. Learning by doing stimulates *internalisation*, by which explicit knowledge is converted into tacit knowledge; as in skill acquisition, what is initially explicit becomes tacit through experience. People with different knowledge coming together through networking results in

combination, a process of systemising and elaborating explicit knowledge by combining different bodies of knowledge.

(see below, p. 228)

This viewpoint is explored in depth in Chapter 17, but it is briefly summarised here to illustrate the strong resonance, even some overlapping of terms, with the examples of Bruner's tenets.

Hargreaves goes on to argue that the model offers only a suggestive bridge from the industrial to the educational. Overall he sees education as lacking sophisticated theories and models of knowledge creation because such activity has not been seen as a key to educational improvement. Hargreaves, along with others, describes the evidence-based models to development that in recent years have become influential in the worlds of health and medicine. He points out the limitations of trying to transpose such ideas from one professional context to another, but he sees potential in a more rigorous and grounded approach to research and evidence accumulation in education. Section 4 critically explores the sometimes contested views in this important area and, in the chapters by Hill and Davies (Chapters 18 and 19 respectively), looks at the form that debate has taken on medicine and health.

Interactive technologies

The new forms of technologies are making the search for evidence both easier (electronic access to data in ways previously unthought of) and more complex (the sheer extent of the data that can now be found). It is clear that technologies have the potential to influence profoundly the way professional development evolves. Most significant is the interaction modes of working that distinguish the contemporary situation from earlier periods of technological innovation. The advent of interactive technologies in the 1990s created the potential to bring together the more school-based and focused approaches with the rich and varied resources and support that might previously have existed in difficult-to-access teachers' centres, universities or other 'bricks and mortar' institutions. In the English and Welsh consultation paper referred to earlier this potential was recognised with one of the principles of provision, suggesting that Information and Communication Technologies (ICT) should play a central role in promoting self-learning at times and places to suit individuals.

The individualised way in which that principle was set out represents however a rather old-fashioned representation of the new technologies. Increasingly the virtual environments now developing strive to evolve as communities of practice (Leach, Chapter 23). The more imaginative uses of the technologies described in Section 5 centrally address the dangers of isolation and individualism through which they were so often parodied. In this sense the emphasis on co-operation and collegiality, working in teams (some of the traditional virtues of good professional development), goes with the grain of the new forms and uses of technological activity.

Hence the emphasis, in each of the chapters that make up Section 5, on the social dimensions of new forms of communication. Leaders of professional development now have available significantly enhanced modes of working and interaction. As the authors in this section and others (Epstein, 2000) have demonstrated, this is a moment of transition, requiring rigorously grounded models and conceptualisations of professional learning, if a measure of the potential for improvement is to be realised.

References

Banks, F., Moon, B. and Leach, J. (1999) 'New understandings of teachers' pedagogic knowledge', in Leach, J. and Moon, B. (eds), *Learners and Pedagogy*, London: Paul Chapman.

Bruner, J. (1996) *The Culture of Education*, Cambridge, MA: Harvard University Press.

Craft, A. (2000) *Continuing Professional Development*, London: Routledge.

DfEE (2000) *Professional Development: Support for Teaching and Learning*, London: DfEE.

Elliot, J. (1991) *Action Research for Educational Change*, Buckingham; Open University Press.

Epstein, J. (2000) 'The rattle of pebbles', *New York Review of Books*, **XLVII** 7, 55–9.

Moon, B. (2000) *International Experience in Initial Teacher Education and Training*, UCET.

Nonaka, I. and Takeuchi, H. (1995) *The Knowledge Creating Company: How Japanese Companies Create Dynamics of Innovation*, Oxford: Oxford University Press.

Shulman, L. (1996) 'Those who understand: knowledge growth' *Teaching Educational Research Review*, **57**(1), 4–14.

Section 1

Orientations

Chapter 2

What do new views of knowledge and thinking have to say about research on teacher learning?

Ralph T. Putnam and Hilda Borko

The education and research communities are abuzz with new (or at least re-discovered) ideas about the nature of cognition and learning. Terms like 'situated cognition', 'distributed cognition', and 'communities of practice' fill the air. Some have argued that the shifts in world view that these discussions represent are even more fundamental than the now-historical shift from behaviourist to cognitive views of learning (Shuell, 1986).

These new ideas about the nature of knowledge, thinking and learning – which are becoming known as the 'situative perspective' (Greeno, 1997; Greeno *et al.*, 1996) – are interacting with, and sometimes fuelling, current reform movements in education. Most discussions of these ideas and their implications for educational practice have been cast primarily in terms of students. Scholars and policy-makers have considered, for example, how to help students develop deep understandings of subject matter, situate students' learning in meaningful contexts, and create learning communities in which teachers and students engage in rich discourse about important ideas.

Less attention has been paid to teachers – either to their roles in creating learning experiences consistent with the reform agenda or to how they themselves learn new ways of teaching. In this article we focus on the latter. Our purpose in considering teachers' learning is twofold. First, we use these ideas about the nature of learning and knowing as lenses for understanding recent research on teacher learning. Second, we explore new issues about teacher learning and teacher education that this perspective brings to light. We begin with a brief overview of three conceptual themes that are central to the situative perspective – that cognition is (a) situated in particular physical and social contexts; (b) social in nature; and (c) distributed across the individual, other persons, and tools.

Cognition as situated

Early cognitive theories typically treated knowing as the manipulation of symbols inside the mind of the individual, and learning as the acquisition of knowledge and skills thought to be useful in a wide variety of settings (Greeno *et al.*, 1996). Situative theorists challenge this assumption of a cognitive core independent of context and intention (Brown *et al.*, 1989; Greeno and The Middle School Through Applications Project Group, 1998; Lave and Wenger, 1991). They posit, instead, that the physical and social contexts in which an activity takes place are an integral part of the activity, and that the activity is an integral part of the learning that takes place within it. How a person learns a particular set of knowledge and skills and the situation in which a person learns become a fundamental part of what is learned. Further, whereas traditional cognitive perspectives focus on the individual as the basic unit of analysis, situative perspectives focus on interactive systems that include individuals as participants, interacting with each other as well as materials and representational systems (Cobb and Bowers, 1999; Greeno, 1997).

A focus on the situated nature of cognition suggests the importance of *authentic activities* in classrooms. J. S. Brown and colleagues (1989) defined authentic activities as the 'ordinary practices of a culture' (p. 34) – activities that are similar to what actual practitioners do. They claimed that 'school activities', which do not share contextual features with related out-of-school tasks, typically fail to support transfer to these out-of-school settings. A. Brown and colleagues (1993) offered a different definition of authentic classroom activities – derived from the role of formal education in children's lives. If we consider the goal of education to be preparing students to be lifelong intentional learners, then activities are authentic if they serve that goal. Authentic activities foster the kinds of thinking and problem-solving skills that are important in out-of-school settings, whether or not the activities themselves mirror what practitioners do. Our discussion of authentic activities for teacher learning adopts a position similar to that of A. Brown and colleagues; that is, we consider the kinds of thinking and problem-solving skills fostered by an activity to be the key criterion for authenticity.

Cognition as social

Dissatisfied with overly individualistic accounts of learning and knowing, psychologists and educators are recognising that the role of others in the learning process goes beyond providing stimulation and encouragement for individual construction of knowledge (Resnick, 1991). Rather, interactions with the people in one's environment are major determinants of both what is learned and how learning takes place. This *sociocentric* view (Soltis, 1981) of knowledge and learning holds that what we take as knowledge and how we think and express ideas are the products of the interactions of groups of people over time. Individuals participate in numerous *discourse communities* (Fish, 1980; Michaels and O'Connor, 1990; Resnick, 1991), ranging from scholarly disciplines such as science or history, to groups of people sharing a common interest, to particular classrooms. These discourse communities provide the cognitive tools – ideas, theories and concepts – that individuals appropriate as their own through their personal efforts to make sense of experiences. The process of learning, too, is social. Indeed, some scholars have conceptualised learning as coming to know how to participate in the discourse and practices of a particular community (e.g. Cobb, 1994; Lave and Wenger, 1991). From this perspective, learning is as much a matter of enculturation into a community's ways of thinking and dispositions as it is a result of explicit instruction in specific concepts, skills, and procedures (Driver *et al.*, 1994; Resnick, 1988; Schoenfeld, 1992). It is important to note that this learning is not a uni-directional phenomenon; the community, too, changes through the ideas and ways of thinking its new members bring to the discourse.

One important idea emerging from a social perspective is that a central goal of schooling is to enculturate students into various discourse communities, equipping them with competence in using the concepts and the forms of reasoning and argument that characterise those communities (Lampert, 1990; Michaels and O'Connor, 1990; Resnick, 1988). This perspective leads to the question of what kinds of discourse communities to establish in classrooms. In parallel to their position on authentic activities, some scholars argue that classroom communities should be modelled after disciplinary communities of mathematicians, scientists, historians and so on (J. S. Brown *et al.*, 1989). Others argue that – rather than preparing students to participate in the professional cultures of mathematicians and historians – 'schools should be communities where students learn to learn' (A. Brown *et al.*, 1993, p. 190). Their assumption is that by participating in activities designed to question and extend their own knowledge in various domains, students will become enculturated into ways of learning that will continue for the rest of their lives. In either case, the discourse communities being envisioned are significantly different from those traditionally found in public school classrooms.

Cognition as distributed

Rather than considering cognition solely as a property of individuals, situative theorists posit that it is distributed or 'stretched over' (Lave, 1988) the individual, other persons and various artifacts such as physical and symbolic tools (Salomon, 1993a). For example, Hutchins (1990, 1991) described the navigation of a US navy ship, where the knowledge for successfully piloting the ship was distributed throughout the entire navigational system. Six people with three different job descriptions and using several sophisticated cognitive tools were involved in piloting the ship out of the harbour. The distribution of cognition across people and tools made it possible for the crew to accomplish cognitive tasks beyond the capabilities of any individual member (Hutchins, 1990).

School learning environments typically do not emphasise such sharing of learning and cognitive performance, focusing instead on the importance of individual competencies. But, as Resnick (1987) wrote, 'as long as school focuses mainly on individual forms of competence, on tool-free performance, and on decontextualized skills, educating people to be good learners in school settings alone may not be sufficient to help them become strong out-of-school learners' (p. 18). Pea (1993) made a similar point: 'Socially scaffolded and externally mediated, artifact-supported cognition is so predominant in out-of-school settings that its disavowal in the classroom is detrimental to the transfer of learning beyond the classroom' (p. 75). Admittedly there are disadvantages to incorporating tool-aided cognition and socially shared cognitive activities in classrooms; it seems clear, however, that to prepare students for successful participation in society, schools must achieve a better balance between activities that incorporate ideas of distributed cognition and those that stress only individual competence.

These three themes – learning as situated, social, and distributed – are fairly recent arrivals on the educational research scene in North America, although they have roots in the thinking of educators and psychologists as early as the late nineteenth century (e.g. Dewey, 1896; Vygotsky, 1934/1962). Greeno and colleagues (1996) wove these themes together in characterising the situative perspective:

> Success in cognitive functions such as reasoning, remembering, and perceiving is understood as an achievement of a system, with contributions of the individuals who participate, along with tools and artifacts. This means that thinking is situated in a particular context of intentions, social partners, and tools.
>
> (p. 20)

As well as providing new perspectives on teaching and learning in K-12 classrooms, the situative approach has important implications for research on the learning of teachers. In the remainder of this article, we consider these implications. We focus on three issues: (a) where to situate teachers' learning experiences; (b) the nature of discourse communities for teaching and teacher learning; and (c) the importance of tools in teachers' work. (For a more comprehensive discussion of the three themes and there implications for classroom practices and teacher education, see Putnam and Borko, 1997.)

Where should teachers' learning be situated?

Teacher educators have long struggled with how to create learning experiences powerful enough to transform teachers' classroom practice. Teachers, both experienced and novice, often complain that learning experiences outside the classroom are too removed from the day-to-day work of teaching to have a meaningful impact. At first glance, the idea that teachers' knowledge is situated in classroom practice lends support to this complaint, seeming to imply that most or all learning experiences for teachers should take place in actual classrooms. But the situative perspective holds that all knowledge is (by definition) situated. The question is not whether knowledge and learning are situated, but in what contexts they are situated. For some purposes, in fact, situating learning experiences for teachers outside the classroom may be important – indeed essential – for powerful learning.

The situative perspective thus focuses researchers' attention on how various settings for teachers' learning give rise to different kinds of knowing. We examine here some of the approaches that researchers and teacher educators have taken to help teachers learn and change in powerful ways, focusing on the kinds of knowing each approach addresses. We begin by considering professional development experiences for practising teachers.

Learning experiences for practising teachers

One approach to staff development is to ground teachers' learning experiences in their own practice by conducting activities at school sites, with a large component taking place in individual teachers' classrooms. The University of Colorado Assessment Project (Borko *et al.*, 1997; Shepard *et al.*, 1996) provides an example of this approach. The project's purpose was to help teachers design and implement classroom-based performance assessments compatible with their instructional goals in mathematics and literacy. As one component, a member of the research/staff development team worked with children in the classrooms of some participating teachers, observed their mathematical activities and then shared her insights about their mathematical understandings with the teachers. Teachers reported that these conversations helped them to understand what to look for when observing students and to incorporate classroom-based observations of student performances into their assessment practices (Borko *et al.*, 1997).

Another approach is to have teachers bring experiences from their classrooms to staff development activities; for example, through ongoing workshops focused on instructional practices. In the UC Assessment Project (Borko *et al.*, 1997), one particularly effective approach to situating learning occurred when members of the staff development/research team introduced materials and activities in a workshop session, the teachers attempted to enact these ideas in their classrooms and the group discussed their experiences in a subsequent workshop session. Richardson and Anders's (1994) practical argument approach to staff development provides another example. These researchers structured discussions with participating elementary teachers to examine their practical arguments – the rationales, empirical support and situational contexts that served as the basis for their instructional actions – often using videotapes of the teachers' classrooms as springboards for discussion.

These approaches offer some obvious strengths when viewed from a situative perspective. The learning of teachers is intertwined with their ongoing practice, making it likely that what they learn will indeed influence and support their teaching practice in meaningful ways. But there are also some problems. One is the issue of scalability: having researchers or staff developers spend significant amounts of time working alongside teachers is not practical on a widespread basis – at least not given the current social and economic structure of our schools. A second problem is that, even if it were possible in a practical sense to ground much of teachers' learning in their ongoing classroom practice, there are arguments for not always doing so. If the goal is to help teachers think in new ways, for example, it may be important to have them experience learning in different settings. The situative perspective helps us see that much of what we do and think is intertwined with the particular contexts in which we act. The classroom is a powerful environment for shaping and constraining how practising teachers think and act. Many of their patterns of thought and action have become automatic – resistant to reflection or change. Engaging in learning experiences away from this setting may be necessary to help teachers 'break set' – to experience things in new ways.

For example, pervading many current educational reform documents is the argument that 'school' versions of mathematics, science, literature and other subject matters are limited – that they overemphasise routine, rote aspects of the subject over the more powerful and generative aspects of the discipline. Students and teachers, reformers argue, need opportunities to think of mathematics or science or writing in new ways. It may be difficult, however, for teachers to experience these disciplines in new ways in the context of their own classrooms – the pull of the existing classroom environment and culture is simply too strong. Teachers may need the opportunity to experience these and other content domains in a new and different context.

Some professional development projects have addressed this concern by providing intensive learning experiences through summer workshops housed in sites other than school buildings. Such workshops free teachers from the constraints of their own classroom situations and afford them the luxury of exploring ideas without worrying about what they are going to do tomorrow. The SummerMath for Teachers programme (Schifter and Fosnot, 1993; Simon and Schifter, 1991), for example, included a two-week summer institute, during which teachers learned mathematics by participating in activities designed according to constructivist principles. A key goal of the institute was for teachers to experience the learning of mathematics in new ways. The Cognitively Guided Instruction (CGI) project (Carpenter *et al.*, 1989) also included a summer institute, during which teachers were introduced to research-based ideas about children's learning of addition and subtraction through a variety of experiences situated primarily in children's mathematics activities. In both projects, participants' beliefs and knowledge about teaching and learning mathematics shifted towards a perspective grounded in children's mathematical thinking.

Although settings away from the classroom can provide valuable opportunities for teachers to learn to think in new ways, the process of integrating ideas and practices learned outside the classroom into one's ongoing instructional programme is rarely simple or straightforward. Thus we must consider whether and under what conditions teachers' out-of-classroom learning – however powerful – will be incorporated into their classroom practice. There is some evidence that staff development programmes can successfully address this issue by systematically incorporating multiple contexts for teacher learning.

One promising model for the use of multiple contexts combines summer workshops that introduce theoretical and research-based ideas with ongoing support during the year as teachers attempt to integrate these ideas into their instructional programmes. The intensive two-week summer institute in the SummerMath programme, in addition to providing opportunities for teachers to participate in mathematics learning activities, engaged them in creating similar instructional sequences for their own students. Throughout the following school year, staff members provided feedback, demonstration teaching and opportunities for reflection during weekly visits to the teachers' classrooms, as well as workshops for further exploring issues related to mathematics, learning and teaching. This combination of experiences helped the teachers to develop different conceptions of mathematics and deeper understandings of mathematical learning and teaching and to incorporate strategies such as group problem solving, use of manipulatives and non-routine problems into their mathematics instruction.

The CGI project provided a similar combination of experiences for some of its participants (Fennema *et al.*, 1996; Franke *et al.*, 1998). In addition to the summer workshops, these participants received support during the school year from a CGI staff member and a mentor teacher that included observing in the teacher's classroom and discussing the children's mathematical thinking, planning lessons together and assessing children together. At the end of a four-year period, most teachers had shifted from a view of teaching as demonstrating procedures and telling children how to think to one that stresses helping children develop their mathematical knowledge through creating learning environments, posing problems, questioning children about their problem solutions and using children's thinking to guide instructional decisions. These two projects thus used a series of settings to introduce teachers to new ideas and practices and to support the integration of these learnings into classroom practice.

We have described in this section a variety of ways to situate experienced teachers' learning, ranging from staff developers working alongside teachers in their own classrooms; to teachers bringing problems, issues and examples from their classrooms to group discussions; to summer workshops focused on the teachers' own learning of subject matter. Research on these projects suggests that the most appropriate staff development site depends on the specific goals for teachers' learning. For example, summer workshops appear to be particularly powerful settings for teachers to develop new relationships to subject matter and new insights about individual students' learning. Experiences situated in the teachers' own classrooms may be better suited to facilitating teachers' enactment of specific instructional practices. And, it may be that a combination of approaches, situated in a variety of contexts, holds the best promise for fostering powerful, multidimensional changes in teachers' thinking and practices. Further research is needed for a better understanding of the complex dynamics of these multifaceted approaches to teacher learning.

Case-based learning experiences for teachers

Teachers' learning experiences in university classrooms typically entail reading about and discussing ideas; their learning experiences in K-12 classrooms usually involve actually engaging in the activities of teaching. Case-based teaching provides another approach for creating meaningful settings for teacher learning (Doyle, 1990; Leinhardt, 1990; Merseth, 1996; Sykes and Bird, 1992). Rather than putting teachers in particular classroom settings, cases provide vicarious encounters with those settings. This experience of the setting may afford reflection and critical analysis that is not possible when acting in the setting.

Some proponents suggest that cases have several advantages over other activities used in preservice and inservice teacher education. As with actual classroom experiences, they allow teachers to explore the richness and complexity of genuine pedagogical problems. Cases, however, provide shared experiences for teachers to examine together, using multiple perspectives and frameworks (Feltovich *et al.*, 1997; Spiro *et al.*, 1988). They also afford the teacher educator more control over the situations and issues that teachers encounter and the opportunity to prepare in advance for discussion and other activities in which the case materials are used (Sykes and Bird, 1992). For preservice programmes, cases avoid the problem of placing prospective teachers in settings that do not embody the kinds of teaching advocated by university teacher educators.

Although all cases limit the information provided, they vary in the richness or complexity of classroom life portrayed. Some media, such as videotape, can convey more of the complexity of classroom events than written cases. Interactive multimedia cases and hypermedia environments have the potential to provide even richer sets of materials documenting classroom teaching and learning. Lampert and Ball (1998), for example, developed a hypermedia learning environment that combines videotapes of classroom mathematics lessons, instructional materials, teacher journals, student notebooks, students' work, and teacher and student interviews, as well as tools for browsing, annotating and constructing arguments. The non-linearity of such hypermedia systems, the ability to visit and revisit various sources of information quickly and easily, and the ability to build and store flexible and multiple links among various pieces of information, allow users to consider multiple perspectives on an event simultaneously (Feltovich *et al.*, 1997; Spiro *et al.*, 1988). Further, the extensiveness of the databases and ease of searching them enable teachers to define and explore problems of their own choosing (Merseth and Lacey, 1993). Like traditional cases, these multimedia and hypermedia materials provide a shared context for the exploration of pedagogical problems. They can come much closer, however, to mirroring the complexity of the problem space in which teachers work.

Despite vocal advocates and an increased use of cases in recent years, there is much to learn about their effectiveness as instructional tools. Commenting on this 'imbalance between promise and empirical data', Merseth (1996) noted, 'the myriad claims for the use of cases and case methods far exceed the volume and quality of research specific to cases and case methods in teacher education' (p. 738). Questions for research include differences in what is learned from the rich and open-ended experiences provides by hypermedia cases versus more structured and focused written and videotaped cases, as well as comparisons of cases and case methods with other instructional materials and approaches. In addressing these questions, it will be important to understand and take into account the variety of purposes and uses of case-based pedagogy. We may learn, for example, that considerable limiting of complexity is desirable for some purposes, such as illustrating particular teaching concepts or strategies. For other purposes such as reflecting the confluence of the many constraints on a teacher's problem solving, complex open-ended case materials may be important.

Discourse communities for teachers

Just as a situative perspective shifts our attention to establishing and participating in discourse communities in K-12 classrooms, so too it draws attention to the discourse communities in which teachers work and learn. These discourse communities play central roles in shaping the way teachers view their world and go about their work. Indeed, patterns of classroom teaching and learning have historically been resistant to fundamental change, in part because schools have served as powerful discourse communities that enculturate participants (students, teachers, administrators) into traditional school activities and ways of thinking (Cohen, 1989; Sarason, 1990). In this section, we explore existing research and unresolved issues concerning the role of discourse communities in supporting teachers learning to teach in new ways.

Discourse communities for experienced teachers

A number of educational reformers have argued that for teachers to be successful in constructing new roles they need opportunities to participate 'in a professional community that discusses new teacher materials and strategies and that supports the risk taking and struggle entailed in transforming practice' (McLaughlin and Talbert, 1993, p. 15). Further, the notion of distributed cognition suggests that when diverse groups of teachers with different types of knowledge and expertise come together in discourse communities, community members can draw upon and incorporate each other's expertise to create rich conversations and new insights into teaching and learning. The existing cultures and discourse communities in many schools, however, do not value or support critical and reflective examination of teaching practice. Ball (1994) characterised the discussions in many staff development sessions as 'style shows' that provide few opportunities for meaningful reflection and growth:

> The common view that 'each teacher has to find his or her own style' is a direct result of working within a discourse of practice that maintains the individualism and isolation of teaching. This individualism not only makes it difficult to develop any sense of common standards, it also makes it difficult to disagree. Masking disagreements hides the individual struggles to practice wisely, and so removes an opportunity for learning. Politely refraining from critique and challenge, teachers have no forum for debating and improving their understandings. To the extent that teaching remains a smorgasbord of alternatives with no real sense of community, there is no basis for comparing or choosing from among alternatives, no basis for real and helpful debate. This lack impedes the capacity to grow.
>
> (p. 16)

Several recent professional development programmes provide existence proofs for the kind of critical, reflective discourse community envisioned by Ball (1994) and by McLaughlin and Talbert (1993). In the Community of Learners project (Wineburg and Grossman, 1998; Thomas *et al.*, 1998) high-school teachers of English and history gathered with university-based educators to read books, discuss teaching and learning, and design an interdisciplinary humanities curriculum. Central to this work was the idea that each participant brings unique knowledge and beliefs to a professional learning community:

> The individual teachers . . . bring with them very different areas of expertise; some are extremely knowledgeable about the subject matter, whereas others bring specialized knowledge of students, including linguistic minority students and students enrolled in special education programs. Teachers also bring different pedagogical understandings and expertise to the group discussions. By drawing on each individual's private understandings, which represent these different degrees of pedagogical and disciplinary expertise, the collective under-standing of the group is thus advanced.
>
> (Thomas *et al.*, 1998, p. 23)

Preliminary findings indicate that an intellectual community for teachers developed within the high school, collegiality among faculty within and across departments was enhanced and the curriculum of the school was affected. Members of the university team gained new insights about the time, effort and trust required to reform the pro-fessional culture of teaching (Thomas *et al.*, 1998).

In another project, Goldenberg and colleagues (Goldenberg and Gallimore, 1991; Saunders *et al.*, 1992) worked with a group of teachers to elaborate the concept of instructional conversation – a mode of instruction that emphasises active student involvement in goal and meaning-oriented discussions. Together, participants developed principles of instructional conversations for elementary classrooms as they engaged in instructional conversations themselves. Goldenberg played a critical role in guiding instructional conversations with teachers, while the teachers brought intimate knowledge of their own classrooms and teaching practices to the con-versations (Saunders *et al.*, 1992).

Richardson and Anders's (1994) practical argument approach to staff develop-ment (see previous discussion) also used new forms of discourse among teachers as a professional development tool. Their staff development team brought research-based ideas about learning and instructional practices to the task of developing and examining practical arguments. Teachers provided knowledge about their students, the particular settings in which they taught and their own teaching practice.

Although these three projects differed in their goals, they all illustrate the bringing together of teachers and university-based researchers or staff developers into new forms of discourse communities focused on teaching and learning. University participants can bring to these communities the critical and reflective stance and modes of discourse that are important norms within the academic community. In addition, they bring research-based knowledge, including 'conceptual inventions, clarifications, and critiques' (Shulman, 1986, p. 27) that can contribute to the improvement of teaching. Teachers, in turn, can bring to such discourse communities craft knowledge about pedagogical practices, their own students, and the cultural and instructional contexts of their classrooms. Together, these two groups of participants can learn new ways of thinking about their practices and simultaneously create new forms of discourse about teaching.

New kinds of discourse communities for teachers, while potentially powerful tools for improving pedagogical practice, also may introduce new tensions into the professional development experience. For example, the university teams in all three projects struggled with the question of how much guidance and structure to bring to the conversations, seeking an appropriate balance between presenting information and facilitating teachers' construction of new practices. In considering these issues of balance, we are reminded of what Richardson (1992) labelled the *agenda-setting dilemma*: the staff developer wants to see teachers' practice change in particular directions while empowering the teachers themselves to be meaningfully involved in determining the changes. This dilemma is analogous to one faced by the classroom teacher who wants to empower children to build upon their own thinking while simultaneously ensuring that they learn expected subject-matter content. Staff developers, like teachers, must negotiate their way between the learners' current thinking and the subject matter or content to be learned. In the case of staff development, the 'learners' are teachers and the 'content' is typically new teaching practices and forms of pedagogical thinking.

The university teams in all three projects addressed these issues of balance by avoiding the extremes of either viewing teachers as merely implementing someone else's pedagogical approach or attempting to empower them without introducing new pedagogical ideas. Instead, they drew upon the unique sets of knowledge and skills offered by researchers and teachers. As a result, the ideas that emerged in the discourse communities created within the projects were 'joint productions' that furthered the understanding of all participants. Researchers, as well as teachers, came away with new insights about teaching and learning.

The importance of tools

In the world outside of school, intelligent activities often depend upon resources beyond the individuals themselves such as physical tools and notational systems (Pea, 1993). Many of these tools do not merely enhance cognition, they transform it; distributing cognition across persons and tools expands a system's capacity for innovation and invention. For example, productivity tools such as word processors, spreadsheets and database management systems have fundamentally changed many tasks of the business world. Numerous writers have argued that computers and other new technologies have the potential to transform teaching and learning in schools as well (Means, 1994; Office of Technology Assessment, 1995).

Most research on the use of technology by teachers, however, has focused on availability of new technologies, frequency of use and attitudes towards computers. The situative perspective provides lenses for examining more thoughtfully the potential of new technologies for supporting and transforming teachers' work and learning.

In discussing the use of computers in education, Salomon (1993b) made a distinction between *performance tools*, which enhance or change how a task is accomplished (e.g. a calculator or a word processor), and *pedagogical tools*, which focus primarily on changing the user's competencies (e.g. a simulation designed to change a teacher's understanding of a mathematical concept). Although this distinction oversimplifies the complex interweaving of performance and pedagogical functions, it is useful for organising our discussion. We first consider tools that can support, enhance, or transform teachers' work and then focus on those explicitly designed to support teachers' learning.

Performance tools to enhance and transform the work of teaching

Despite claims about the power of new technologies to transform education, the actual use of computers in schools has been rather limited (Becker, 1993; Peck and Dorricot, 1994). The most widely adopted tools are those that fit easily within the existing conceptual and social organisation of classrooms – drill and practice programmes that can be used by individual students without interfering with whole-class activity, word-processing tools for preparing instructional materials, presentation tools that can replace overhead projectors and tools for keeping attendance and grades. Such tools can support teachers in doing what they already do, but have little potential for transforming the work of teachers or the nature of teaching and learning in classrooms (Marx *et al.*, 1998; Means, 1994).

More recently, however, researchers and teacher educators have developed computer-based technologies with considerable potential for supporting and trans-forming teachers' work. One example is the Project Integration Visualization Tool (PIViT; Marx *et al.*, 1998), a productivity tool designed to aid teacher planning. Using PIViT, teachers can create, elaborate and revise 'project designs' – graphical representations of projects that include central questions, curricular objectives, concepts, student investigations, teacher activities and artifacts. This tool was developed to be consistent with how teachers actually plan, while helping them think about curriculum and instruction in new ways. Teachers who used PIViT to develop and adapt curriculum for their classrooms were able to create multiple representations of their project designs that would not have been possible had they used linear planning.

In theory, teachers should be able to use computer-based planning tools such as PIViT to design projects for any grade level or subject area. Marx and colleagues (see Chapter 21 of this volume) have revised PIViT based on studies of how teachers use it and the supports they need, and have shown it to be applicable to multiple areas of science (Marx *et al.*, 1998). Additional research is needed to determine what adjustments are required to ensure its applicability to other subject areas. Future research might also explore the possibility, suggested by Marx and colleagues, that planning tools such as PIViT can be used to create communities of practice in which teachers learn from each other by sharing common templates and models of instructional innovations.

Computers and new communication technologies also have the potential to transform teaching and learning in classrooms and the work of teachers by providing new avenues to access distributed expertise. As Marx and colleagues (1998) noted, teachers' access to the expertise of others has traditionally been limited primarily to printed materials and face-to-face interactions (e.g., through inservice activities, workshops, and conferences). Electronic mail, users groups and other on-line forums, however, open up a myriad of possibilities for interacting with colleagues and experts in various fields. Information systems such as the World Wide Web provide access to digital libraries and vast amounts of information in print, visual and video form.

At the same time, these new communication opportunities raise a number of questions and concerns. For example, just as Ball (1994) noted the lack of critical reflection in many teacher discourse communities, there is some evidence that teachers' network-based communication may not be particularly substantive (DiMarco and Muscella, 1995; McMahon, 1996). Given our understanding of discourse communities, informed in part by the situative perspective, this should come as no surprise. As Cuban (1986) observed, it is tempting to assume that simply introducing new technologies into schools will transform educational practice. But just as the existing norms and practices of teachers' discourse communities shape their face-to-face interactions, they will shape and limit teachers' electronic interactions. Simply providing new media and access to communication with a much wider circle of colleagues and experts is, in itself, unlikely to change the nature or form of teachers' professional interactions.

Further complexity is added to the picture because conversations over email and listserve forums typically take place over time, with participants reading what has come before and adding their contributions. Such *asynchronous communication* may afford a different sort of reflection and analysis than face-to-face discourse, but also requires the establishment of new norms and strategies for interacting.

Given these features of communication technologies, it is not surprising that teachers need guidance and support to engage in productive technology-based discourse about teaching and learning (Ruopp *et al.*, 1993; Watts and Castle, 1992). Additional research is needed to determine how such guidance should be designed and made available, to maximise its potential for fostering educationally worthwhile conversations among teachers. Further, we need a better understanding of the impact of virtual communities of practice and on-line conversations on teachers' relationships with their colleagues. Do virtual professional communities detract from school-based communities? Do teachers shift to participating in on-line conversations at the expense of face-to-face conversations with other teachers in their buildings?

Pedagogical tools to support teachers' learning

In addition to transforming the tasks of teaching, new computer technologies can support the learning of novice and experienced teachers in ways that build on assumptions about the social, situated and distributed nature of knowledge and learning. As we discussed earlier, multimedia systems, with their new and flexible ways of representing and connecting information, can enable teachers to explore unfamiliar pedagogical practices and various problems of pedagogy.

The Student Learning Environment (SLE; Lampert and Ball, 1998), described briefly in our discussion of case-based teacher education, provides one image of the possible (Shulman, 1983). Within this environment teachers investigate pedagogical problems that arise as they view and read about Ball's teaching of mathematics in a third-grade classroom and Lampert's in a fifth-grade classroom, simultaneously becoming familiar with new technological tools and exploring new ideas about teaching and learning. Lampert and Ball examined 68 investigations conducted by teacher education students and identified several patterns. Most students saw teaching and learning through pedagogical and psychological lenses, exploring features of the classrooms such as teacher–student relationships, instructional strategies, classroom management and student participation, rather than mathematical content or curriculum. The students' investigations in this multimedia environment some-times pushed their thinking beyond where it was when they started. For example, after carefully examining the empirical evidence, some students changed their minds about particular features of classroom life, such as whether boys were being called on more than girls, or whether students were understanding fractions. In contrast, the investigations sometimes reinforced beliefs that the students brought with them into the teacher education programme. The initial questions these teacher education students posed when conducting their investigations were typically based on strong normative assumptions such as their notions about a 'good' classroom environment or 'helpful' teacher. These assumptions framed the students' inquiry and were rarely challenged by doing the investigations. Rather, the collection and interpretation of records of practice simply reinforced the students' entering assumptions.

Conclusion

In this article we set out to consider what the situative perspective on cognition – that knowing and learning are situated in physical and social contexts, social in nature, and distributed across persons and tool – might offer those of us seeking to understand and improve teacher learning. As we pointed out earlier, these ideas are not entirely new. The fundamental issues about what it means to know and learn addressed by the situative perspective have engaged scholars for a long time. Almost a century ago, Thorndike and Dewey debates the nature of transfer and the connections between what people learn in school and their lives outside school. These issues, in various forms, have continued to occupy the attention of psychologists and educational psychologists ever since (Greeno *et al.*, 1996).

Labaree (1998) argued that this sort of continual revisiting of fundamental issues is endemic to the field of education Unlike the *hard* sciences, whose hallmark is replicable, agreed-upon knowledge, education and other soft knowledge fields deal with the inherent unpredictability of human action and values. As a result, the quest for knowledge about education and learning leaves scholars

> feeling as though they are perpetually struggling ti move ahead but getting nowhere. If Sisyphus were a scholar, his field would be education. At the end of long and distinguished careers, senior educational researchers are likely to find that they are still working on the same questions that confronted them at the beginning. And the new generation of researchers they have trained will be taking up these questions as well, reconstructing the very foundations of the field over which their mentors labored during their entire careers.
>
> (p. 9)

Given the enduring nature of these questions and the debates surrounding them, what is to be gained by considering teacher knowledge and teacher learning from a situative perspective? Can this perspective help us think about teaching and teacher learning more productively? We believe it can – that the language and conceptual tools of social, situated and distributed cognition provide powerful lenses for examining teaching, teacher learning and the practices of teacher education (both preserve and inservice) in new ways.

For example, these ideas about cognition have helped us, in our own work, to see more clearly the strengths and limitations of various practices and settings for teacher learning. But this clarity comes only when we look closely at these concepts and their nuances. By starting with the assumption that all knowledge is situated in contexts, we were able to provide support for the general argument that teachers' learning should be grounded in some aspect of their teaching practice. Only by pushing beyond this general idea, however, to examine more closely the question of where to situate teachers' learning, were we able to identify specific advantages and limitations of the various contexts within which teachers' learning might be meaningfully situated: their own classrooms, group settings where participants' teaching is the focus of discussion, and settings emphasising teachers' learning of subject matter. Similarly, ideas about the social and distributed nature of cognition help us think in new ways about the role of technological tools in creating new types of discourse communities for teachers, including unresolved issues regarding the guidance and support needed to ensure that conversations within these communities are educationally meaningful and worthwhile.

References

Ball, D. L. (1994) 'Developing mathematics reform: what don't we know about teacher learning – but would make good working hypotheses?', paper presented at Conference on Teacher Enhancement in Mathematics K-6, Arlington, VA.

Becker, H. J. (1993) 'Instructional computer use: findings from a national survey of school and teacher practices', *The Computing Teacher*, **20**(1), 6–7.

Borko, H., Mayfield, V., Marion, S., Flexer, R. and Cumbo, K. (1997) 'Teachers' developing ideas and practices about mathematics performance assessment: successes, stumbling blocks, and implications for professional development', *Teaching and Teacher Education*, **13**, 259–78.

Brown, A., Ash, D., Rutherford, M., Nakagawa, K., Gordon, A. and Campione, J. G. (1993) 'Distributed expertise in the classroom', in Salomon, G. (ed.), *Distributed Cognitions: Psychological and Educational Considerations*, Cambridge: Cambridge University Press, 188–228.

Brown, J. S., Collins, A. and Duguid, P. (1989) 'Situated cognition and the culture of learning', *Educational Researcher*, **18**(1), 32–42.

Carpenter, T. P., Fennema, E., Peterson, P. L., Chiang, C. and Loef, M. (1989) 'Using knowledge of children's mathematical thinking in classroom teaching: an experimental study', *American Educational Research Journal*, **26**, 499–532.

Cobb, P. (1994) 'Where is the mind? Constructivist and sociocultural perspectives on mathematical development', *Educational Researcher*, **23**(7), 13–19.

Cobb, P. and Bowers, J. W. (1999) 'Cognitive and situated learning perspectives in theory and practice', *Educational Researcher*, **28**(2), 4–15.

Cohen, D. K. (1989) 'Teaching practice: Plus ça change . . .', in Jackson, P. W. (ed.), *Contributing to Educational Change: Perspectives on Research and Practice*, Berkeley: McCutchan, 27–84.

Cuban, L. (1986) *Teachers and Machines: The Classroom use of Technology Since 1920*, New York: Teachers College Press.

Dewey, J. (1896) 'The reflex arc concept in psychology', *Psychological Review*, **3**, 356–70.

DiMarco, V. and Muscella, D. (1995) 'Talking about science: the case of an electronic conversation', paper presented at the Computer Supported Collaborative Learning '95 conference, Indianapolis, IN.

Doyle, W. (1990) 'Case methods in teacher education', *Teacher Education Quarterly*, **17**(1), 7–15.

Driver, R., Asoko, H., Leach, J., Mortimer, E. and Scott, P. (1994) 'Constructing scientific knowledge in the classroom', *Educational Researcher*, **23**(7), 5–12.

Feltovich, P. J., Spiro, R. J. and Coulson, R. L. (1997) 'Issues of expert flexibility in contexts characterized by complexity and change', in Feltovich, P. J., Ford, K. M. and Hoffman, R. R. (eds), *Expertise in Context: Human and Machine*, Cambridge, MA: AAAI/MIT Press, 125–46.

Fennema, E., Carpenter, T. P., Franke, M. L., Levi, L., Jacobs, V. R. and Empson, S. B. (1996) 'A longitudinal study of learning to use children's thinking in mathematics instruction', *Journal for Research in Mathematics Education*, **27**, 403–34.

Fish, S. (1980) *Is There a Text in this Class? The Authority of Interpretive Communities*, Cambridge, MA: Harvard University Press.

Franke, M. L., Carpenter, T., Fennema, E., Ansell, E. and Behrend, J. (1998) 'Understanding teachers' self-sustaining, generative change in the context of professional development', *Teaching and Teacher Education*, **14**, 67–80.

Goldenberg, C. and Gallimore, R. (1991) 'Changing teaching takes more than a one-shot workshop', *Educational Leadership*, **49**(3), 69–72.

Greeno, J. G. (1997) 'On claims that answer the wrong questions', *Educational Researcher*, **26**(1), 5–17.

Greeno, J. G., Collins, A. M. and Resnick, L. B. (1996) 'Cognition and learning', in Berliner, D. and Calfee, R. (eds), *Handbook of Educational Psychology*, New York: Macmillan, 15–46.

Greeno, J. G. and the Middle School Through Applications Project Group (1998) 'The situativity of knowing, learning, and research', *American Psychologist*, **53**, 5–26.

Hutchins, E. (1990) 'The technology of team navigation', in Galegher, J., Kraut, R. E. and Egido, C. (eds), *Intellectual Teamwork: Social and Technological Foundations of Cooperative Work*, Hillsdale, NJ: Erlbaum, 191–220.

Hutchins, E. (1991) 'The social organization of distributed cognition', in Resnick, L. B., Levine, J. M. and Teasley, S. D. (eds), *Perspectives on Socially Shared Cognition*, Washington, DC: American Psychological Association, 283–307.

Labaree, D. F. (1998) 'Educational researchers: living with a lesser form of knowledge', *Educational Researcher*, **27**(8), 4–12.

Lampert, M. (1990) 'When the problem is not the question and the solution is not the answer: mathematical knowing and teaching', *American Educational Research Journal*, **27**, 29–63.

Lampert, M. and Ball, D. L. (1998) *Teaching, Multimedia, and Mathematics: Investigations of Real Practice*, New York: Teachers College Press.

Lave, J. (1988) *Cognition in Practice: Mind, Mathematics and Culture in Everyday Life*, Cambridge: Cambridge University Press.

Lave, J. and Wenger, E. (1991) *Situated Learning: Legitimate Peripheral Participation*, Cambridge: Cambridge University Press.

Leinhardt, G. (1990) 'Capturing craft knowledge in teaching', *Educational Researcher*, **19**(2), 18–25.

Marx, R. W., Blumenfeld, P. C., Krajcik, J. S. and Soloway, E. (1998) 'New technologies for teacher professional development', *Teaching and Teacher Education*, **14**, 33–52.

Means, B. (ed.) (1994) *Technology and Education Reform: The Reality Behind the Promise*, San Francisco: Jossey-Bass.

McLaughlin, M. and Talbert, J. E. (1993) *Contexts that Matter for Teaching and Learning: Strategic Opportunities for Meeting the Nation's Educational Goals*, Stanford, CA: Center for Research on the Context of Secondary School Teaching, Stanford University.

McMahon, T. A. (1996) 'From isolation to interaction? Computer-mediated communications and teacher professional development', unpublished doctoral dissertation, Indiana University

Merseth, K. K. (1996) 'Cases and case methods in teacher education', in Sikula, J. (ed.), *Handbook of Research on Teacher Education* (2nd edn), New York: Macmillan, 722–44.

Merseth, K. K. and Lacey, C. A. (1993) 'Weaving stronger fabric: the pedagogical promise of hypermedia and case methods in teacher education', *Teaching and Teacher Education*, **9**, 283–99.

Michaels, S. and O'Connor, M. C. (1990) 'Literacy as reasoning within multiple discourses: implications for policy and educational reform', paper presented at the Council of Chief State School Officers 1990 Summer Institute: 'Restructuring Learning', Literacies Institute, Educational development Center, Newton, MA.

Office of Technology Assessment (1995) *Teachers and Technology: Making the Connection*, Washington, DC: Author.

Pea, R. (1993) 'Practice of distributed intelligence and designs for education', in Salomon, G. (ed.), *Distributed Cognitions: Psychological and Educational Considerations*, New York: Cambridge University Press, 47–87.

Peck, K. L. and Dorricot, D. (1994) 'Why we use technology?', *Educational Leadership*, **51**(7), 11–14.

Putnam, R. T. and Borko, H. (1997) 'Teacher learning: implications of new views of cognition', in Biddle, B. J., Good, T. L. and Goodson, I. F. (eds), *International Handbook of Teachers & Teaching* (Vol. II), Dordrecht: Kluwer, 1223–96.

Resnick, L. B. (1987) 'Learning in school and out', *Educational Researcher*, **16**(9), 13–20.

Resnick, L. B. (1988), 'Treating mathematics as an ill-structured discipline', in Charles, R. I. and Silver, E. A. (eds), *Research Agenda for Mathematics Education: Vol. 3. The Teaching and Assessing of Mathematical Problem Solving*, Hillsdale, NJ: Erlbaum, 32–60.

Resnick, L. B. (1991) 'Shared cognition: thinking as social practice', in Resnick, L. B., Levine, J. M. and Teasley, S. D. (eds), *Perspectives on Socially Shared Cognition*, Washington, DC: American Psychological Association, 1–20.

Richardson, V. (1992) 'The agenda-setting dilemma in a constructivist staff development process', *Teaching & Teacher Education*, **8**, 287–300.

Richardson, V. and Anders, P. (1994) 'The study of teacher change', in Richardson, V. (ed.), *A Theory of Teacher Change and the Practice of Staff Development: A Case in Reading Instruction*, New York: Teachers College Press, 159–80.

Ruopp, R., Gal, S., Drayton, B. and Pfister, M. (eds) (1993) *LabNet: Toward a Community of Practice*, Hillsdale, NJ: Erlbaum.

Salomon, G. (ed.) (1993a) *Distributed Cognitions: Psychological and Educational Considerations*, Cambridge: Cambridge University Press.

Salomon, G. (1993b) 'On the nature of pedagogic computer tools: the case of the Writing Partner', in Lajoie, S. P. and Derry, S. J. (eds), *Computers as Cognitive Tools*, Hillsdale, NJ; Erlbaum, 179–96.

Sarason, S. (1990) *The Predictable Failure of Educational Reform: Can We Change Course Before it's too Late?*, San Francisco: Jossey-Bass.

Saunders, W., Goldenberg, C. and Hamann, J. (1992) 'Instructional conversations beget instructional conversations', *Teaching & Teacher Education*, **8**, 199–218.

Schifter, D. and Fosnot, C. T. (1993) *Reconstructing Mathematics Education: Stories of Teachers Meeting the Challenges of Reform*, New York: Teachers College Press.

Schoenfeld, A. H. (1992) 'Learning to think mathematically: problem solving, metacognition, and sense making in mathematics', in Grouws, D. (ed.), *Handbook for research on mathematics teaching and learning*, New York: Macmillan, 334–70.

Shepard, L. A., Flexer, R. J., Hiebert, E. H., Marion, S. F., Mayfield, V. and Weston, T. J. (1996) 'Effects of introducing classroom performance assessments on student learning', *Educational Measurement: Issues and Practice*, **15**(3), 7–18.

Shuell, T. J. (1986) 'Cognitive conceptions of learning', *Review of Educational Research*, **56**, 411–36.

Shulman, L. S. (1983) 'Autonomy and obligation: the remote control of teaching', in Shulman, L. S. and Sykes, G. (eds), *Handbook of Teaching and Policy*, New York: Longman, 484–504.

Shulman, L. S. (1986) 'Paradigms and research programs in the study of teaching: a contemporary perspective', in Wittrock, M. C. (ed.), *Handbook of Research on Teaching*, New York: Macmillan, 3–36.

Simon, M. A. and Schifter, D. (1991) 'Towards a constructivist perspective: an intervention study of mathematics teacher development', *Educational Studies in Mathematics*, **22**, 309–31.

Soltis, J. F. (1981) 'Education and the concept of knowledge', in Soltis, J. F. (ed.), *Philosophy and Education*, Chicago: National Society for the Study of Education, 95–113.

Spiro, R. J., Coulson, R. L., Feltovich, P. J. and Anderson, D. K. (1988) 'Cognitive flexibility theory: advanced knowledge acquisition in ill-structured domains', in *Tenth Annual Conference of the Cognitive Science Society*, Hillsdale, NJ: Erlbaum, 375–83.

Sykes, G. and Bird, T. (1992) 'Teacher education and the case idea', *Review of Research in Education*, **18**, 457–521.

Thomas, G., Wineburg, S., Grossman, P., Myhre, O. and Woolworth, S. (1998) 'In the company of colleagues: an interim report on the development of a community of teacher learners', *Teaching and Teacher Education*, **14**, 21–32.

Vygotsky, L. S. (1962) *Thought and Language* (Eugenia Hanfmann and Gertrude Vakar, ed. & trans.), Cambridge, MA: MIT Press. (Original work published in Russian in 1934.)

Watts, G. D. and Castle, S. (1992) 'Electronic networking and the construction of professional knowledge', *Phi Delta Kappan*, **73**, 684–9.

Wineburg, S. and Grossman, P. (1998) 'Creating a community of learners among high school teachers', *Phi Delta Kappan*, **79**, 350–3.

Chapter 3

Getting to scale with good educational practice

Richard F. Elmore

This is an edited version of a paper appearing in *Harvard Educational Review*, **66**, 1. Copyright © by the President and fellows of Harvard College.

The problem of scale in educational reform

Why do good ideas about teaching and learning have so little impact on US educational practice? This question, I argue, raises a central problem of US education: a significant body of circumstantial evidence points to a deep, systemic incapacity of US schools, and the practitioners who work in them, to develop, incorporate and extend new ideas about teaching and learning in anything but a small fraction of schools and classrooms. This incapacity, I argue, is rooted primarily in the incentive structures in which teachers and administrators work. Therefore, solving the problem of scale means substantially changing these incentive structures.

Changing the core: students, teachers and knowledge

The problem of scale in educational innovation can be briefly stated as follows: innovations that require large changes in the core of educational practice seldom penetrate more than a small fraction of US schools and classrooms, and seldom last for very long when they do. By 'the core of educational practice', I mean how teachers understand the nature of knowledge and the student's role in learning, and how these ideas about knowledge and learning are manifested in teaching and classwork. The 'core' also includes structural arrangements of schools, such as the physical layout of classrooms, student grouping practices, teachers' responsibilities for groups of students, and relations among teachers in their work with students as well as processes for assessing student learning and communicating it to students, teachers, parents, administrators and other interested parties.

One can think of schools as generally representing a standard set of solutions to these problems of how to manage the core. Most teachers tend to think of knowledge as discrete bits of information about a particular subject and of student learning as the acquisition of this information through processes of repetition, memorisation, and regular testing of recall (e.g. Cohen, 1988). The teacher, who is generally the centre of attention in the classroom, initiates most of the talk and orchestrates most of the interaction in the classroom around brief factual questions, if there is any discussion at all.

Hence, the teacher is the main source of information, defined as discrete facts, and this information is what qualifies as knowledge. Often students are grouped by age, and again within age groups, according to their perceived capabilities to acquire information. The latter is generally accomplished either through within-class ability groups or, at higher grade levels, through 'tracks', or clusters of courses for students whom teachers judge to have similar abilities. Individual teachers are typically responsible for one group of students for a fixed period of time. Seldom working in groups to decide what a given group of students should know or how that knowledge should be taught, teachers are typically solo practitioners operating in a structure that feeds them students and expectations about what students should be taught. Students' work is typically assessed by asking them to repeat information that has been conveyed by the teacher in the classroom, usually in the form of worksheets or tests that involve discrete, factual, right-or-wrong answers (Elmore, 1995).

At any given time, there are some schools and classrooms that deliberately violate these core patterns. For example, students may initiate a large share of the classroom talk, either in small groups or in teacher-led discussions, often in the context of some problem they are expected to solve. Teachers may ask broad, open-ended questions designed to elicit what students are thinking and how they are thinking, rather than to assess whether they have acquired discrete bits of information. Students' work might involve oral or written responses to complex, open-ended questions or problems for which they are expected to provide explanations that reflect not only their acquisition of information, but also their judgements about what kinds of information are most important or appropriate. Students may be grouped flexibly according to the teacher's judgement about the most appropriate array of strengths and weaknesses for a particular task or subject matter. Teachers may share responsibility for larger groups of students across different ages and ability levels and may work co-operatively to design classroom activities that challenge students working at different levels. In other words, students' learning may be assessed using a broad array of tasks, problems, mediums of expression and formats.

In characterising these divergences from traditional educational practice, I have deliberately avoided using the jargon of contemporary educational reform – 'teaching for understanding', 'whole language', 'authentic assessment', etc. I have done this because I do not want to confuse the problems associated with the implementation of particular innovations with the more general, systemic problem of what happens to practices, by whatever name, that violate or challenge the basic conventions of the core of schooling. The names of these practices change, and the intellectual traditions associated with particular versions of the practices ebb and flow. But, the fundamental problem remains: attempts to change the stable patterns of the core of schooling, in the fundamental ways described above, are usually unsuccessful on anything more than a small scale. It is on this problem that I will focus.

Much of what passes for 'change' in US schooling is not really about changing the core, as defined above. Innovations often embody vague intentions of changing the core through modifications that are weakly related, or not related at all, to the core. US secondary schools, for example, are constantly changing the way they arrange the schedule that students are expected to follow – lengthening or shortening class periods, distributing content in different ways across periods and days, increasing and decreasing class size for certain periods of the day, etc. These changes are often justified as a way to provide space in the day for teachers to do a kind of teaching they would not otherwise be able to do, or to develop a different kind of relationship with students around knowledge.

However, the changes are often not explicitly connected to fundamental changes in the way knowledge is constructed, nor to the division of responsibility between teacher and student, the way students and teachers interact with each other around knowledge, or any of a variety of other stable conditions in the core. Hence, changes in scheduling seldom translate into changes in the fundamental conditions of teaching and learning for students and teachers. Schools, then, might be 'changing' all the time – adopting this or that new structure or schedule or textbook series or tracking system – and never change in any fundamental way what teachers and students actually do when they are together in classrooms. I am not interested, except in passing, in changes that are unrelated to the core of schooling, as I have defined it above. My focus is on that narrower class of changes that directly challenge the fundamental relationships among student, teacher and knowledge.

In some instances, such as the high-performance schools described by Linda Darling-Hammond (1995), a whole school will adopt a dramatically different form of organisation, typically by starting from scratch rather than changing an existing school, and that form of organisation will connect with teaching practices that are dramatically different from those traditionally associated with the core of schooling. At any given time there may be several such model schools, or exemplars of good practice, but as a proportion of the total number of schools, they are always a small fraction. In other words, it is possible to alter organisation and practice in schools dramatically, but it has thus far never been possible to do it on a large scale.

The closer an innovation gets to the core of schooling, the less likely it is that it will influence teaching and learning on a large scale. The corollary of this proposition, of course, is that innovations that are distant from the core will be more readily adopted on a large scale. I will later develop some theoretical propositions about why this might be the case.

The problem of scale is a 'nested' problem. That is, it exists in similar forms at different levels of the system. New practices may spring up in isolated classrooms or in clusters of classrooms within a given school, yet never move to most classrooms within that school. Likewise, whole schools may be created from scratch that embody very different forms of practice, but these schools remain a small proportion of all schools within a given district or state. And finally, some local school systems may be more successful than others at spawning classrooms and schools that embody new practices, but these local systems remain a small fraction of the total number in a state.

The problem of scale is not a problem of the general resistance or failure of schools to change. Most schools are, in fact, constantly changing – adopting new curricula, tests and grouping practices, changing schedules, creating new mechanisms for participation in decision making, adding or subtracting teaching and administrative roles, and a myriad of other modifications. Within this vortex of change, however, basic conceptions of knowledge, of the teacher's and the student's role in constructing knowledge, and of the role of classroom- and school-level structures in enabling student learning remain relatively static.

Nor is the problem of scale a failure of research or of systematic knowledge of what to do. At any given time, there is an abundance of ideas about how to change funda-mental relationships in the core of schooling, some growing out of research and demonstration projects, some growing directly out of teaching practice. Many of these ideas are empirically tested and many are based on relatively coherent theories of student learning. We might wish that these ideas were closer to the language and thought processes of practitioners and that they were packaged and delivered better, but there are more ideas circulating about how to change the core processes of schooling than there are schools and classrooms willing to engage them. There are always arguments among researchers and practitioners about which are the most promising ideas and conflicting evidence about their effects, but the supply of ideas is there. The problem, then, lies not in the supply of new ideas, but in the demand for them. That is, the primary problem of scale is understanding the conditions under which people working in schools seek new knowledge and actively use it to change the fundamental processes of schooling.

Why is the problem of scale important to educational reform?

Two central ideas of the present period of US educational reform raise fundamental, recurring problems of US education. One idea is that teaching and learning in US schools and classrooms is, in its most common form, emotionally flat and intellectually undemanding and unengaging; this idea is captured by that famous, controversial line from *A Nation at Risk*: 'a rising tide of mediocrity' (National Commission on Excellence in Education, 1983). This is a perennial critique of US education, dating back to the first systematic surveys of educational practice in the early twentieth century and confirmed by contemporary evidence. One recent survey characterised typical classroom practice this way:

> No matter what the observational perspective, the same picture emerges. The two activities involving the most students were being lectured to and working on written assignments . . . Students were working alone most of the time, whether individually or in groups. That is, the student listened as one member of a class being lectured, or the student worked individually on a seat assignment . . . In effect, then, the modal classroom configurations which we observed looked like this: the teacher explaining or lecturing to the total class or a single student,

occasionally asking questions requiring factual answers; the teacher, when not lecturing, observing or monitoring students working individually at their desks; students listening or appearing to listen to the teacher and occasionally responding to the teacher's questions; students working individually at their desks on reading or writing assignments; and all with little emotion, from inter-personal warmth to expressions of hostility.

(Goodlad, 1984, p. 230)

Every school can point to its energetic, engaged and effective teachers; many students can recall at least one teacher who inspired in them an engagement in learning and a love of knowledge. We regularly honour and deify these pedagogical geniuses. But these exceptions prove the rule. For the most part, we regard inspired and demanding teaching as an individual trait, much like hair colour or shoe size, rather than as a professional norm. As long as we consider engaging teaching to be an individual trait, rather than a norm that might apply to any teacher, we feel no obligation to ask the broader systemic question of why more evidence of engaging teaching does not exist. The answer to this question is obvious for those who subscribe to the individual trait theory of effective teaching: few teachers are pre-disposed to teach in interesting ways. Alternatively, other explanations for the prevalence of dull, flat, unengaging teaching might be that we fail to select and reward teachers based on their capacity to teach in engaging ways, or that organisational conditions do not promote and sustain good teaching when it occurs.

The other central idea in the present period of reform is captured by the slogan, 'all students can learn'. What reformers seem to mean by this idea is that 'all' students – or most students – are capable of mastering challenging academic content at high levels of understanding, and the fact that many do not is more a testimonial to how they are taught than to whether they are suited for serious academic work. In other words, the slogan is meant to be a charge to schools to make challenging learning available to a much broader segment of students than they have in the past. The touchstone for this critique is consistent evidence over the last two decades or so that US students do reasonably well on lower level tests of achievement and cognitive skill, but relatively poorly on tests that require complex reasoning, inference, judgement, and transfer of knowledge from one type of problem to another (National Center for Education Statistics, 1993).

It is hard to imagine a solution to this problem of the distribution of learning among students that does not entail a solution to the first problem of increasing the frequency of engaging teaching. Clearly, getting more students to learn at higher levels has to entail some change in both the way students are taught and the proportion of teachers who are teaching in ways that cause students to master higher level skills and knowledge. It is possible, of course, that some piece of the problem of the distribution of learning can be solved by simply getting more teachers to teach more demanding academic content, even in boring and unengaging ways, to a broader population of students. But, at some level, it seems implausible that large proportions of students presently disengaged from learning academic content at high levels of understanding will suddenly become more engaged if traditional teaching practices in the modal US classroom remain the norm. Some students overcome the deadening effect of unengaging teaching through extraordinary ability, motivation, or family pressure. Other students, however, require extraordinary teaching to achieve extraordinary results. The problem of scale, then, can be seen in the context of the current reform debate as a need to change the core of schooling in ways that result in most students receiving engaging instruction in challenging academic content.

This view of educational reform, which focuses on changing fundamental conditions affecting the relationship of student, teacher and knowledge, might be criticised as being either too narrow or too broad. My point in focusing the analysis wholly on the core of schooling is not to suggest that teaching and learning can be changed in isolation from an understanding of the contextual factors that influence children's lives. Nor is it to suggest that the object of reform should be to substitute one kind of uniformity of teaching practice for another. Rather, my point is that most educational reforms never reach, much less influence, long-standing patterns of teaching practice, and are therefore largely pointless if their intention is to improve student learning. I am interested in what is required before teaching practice can plausibly be expected to shift from its modal patterns towards more engaging and ambitious practices. These practices might be quite diverse. They might involve creative adaptations and responses to the backgrounds, interests and preferences of students and their families. And they might be wedded in interesting ways to solutions to the multitude of problems that children face outside of school. But the fundamental problem I am interested in is why, when schools seem to be constantly changing, teaching practice changes so little and on so small a scale.

The evidence

The central claims of my argument, then, are that the core of schooling – defined as the standard solutions to the problem of how knowledge is defined, how teachers relate to students around knowledge, how teachers relate to other teachers in the course of their daily work, how students are grouped for purposes of instruction, how content is allocated to time and how students' work is assessed – changes very little, except in a small proportion of schools and classrooms where the changes do not persist for very long. The changes that do tend to 'stick' in schools are those that are most distant from the core.

The progressive period

To evaluate these claims, one would want to look at examples where reformers had ideas that challenged the core of schooling and where these ideas had time to percolate through the system and influence practice. One such example is the progressive period, perhaps the longest and most intense period of educational reform and ferment in the history of the country, running from roughly the early teens into the 1940s. What is most interesting about the progressive period, as compared with other periods of educational reform, is that its aims included explicit attempts to change pedagogy, coupled with a relatively strong intellectual and practical base. Noted intellectuals – John Dewey, in particular – developed ideas about how schools might be different, and these ideas found their way into classrooms and schools. The progressive period had a wide agenda, but one priority was an explicit attempt to change the core of schooling from a teacher-centred, face-centred, recitation-based pedagogy to a pedagogy based on an understanding of children's thought processes and their capacities to learn and use ideas in the context of real-life problems.

In a nutshell, the progressive period produced an enormous amount of innovation, much of it in the core conditions of schooling. This innovation occurred in two broad forms. One was the creation of single schools that exemplified progressive pedagogical practices. The other was an attempt to implement progressive pedagogical practices on a large scale in public school systems. In discussing these two trends, I draw upon Lawrence Cremin's *The Transformation of the American School* (1961), which provides a detailed review of progressive education.

The single schools spawned by the progressive movement represented an astonishing range of pedagogical ideas and institutional forms, spread over the better part of four decades. In their seminal review of pedagogical reform in 1915, *Schools of To-Morrow*, John and Evelyn Dewey documented schools ranging from the Francis Parker School in Chicago to Caroline Pratt's Play School in New York, both exemplars of a single founder's vision. While these schools varied enormously in the particulars of their curricula, activities, grade and grouping structures, and teaching practices, they shared a common aim of breaking the lock of teacher-centred instruction and generating high levels of student engagement through student-initiated inquiry and group activities. Furthermore, these schools drew on a common wellspring of social criticism and prescription, exemplified in John Dewey's lecture, *The School and Society* (1899). According to Cremin, *The School and Society* focused school reform on shifting the centre of gravity in education 'back to the child. His natural impulses to conversation, to inquiry, to construction, and to expression were . . . seen as natural resources . . . of the educative process' (1961, pp. 118–19). Also included in this vision was the notion that school would be 'recalled from isolation to the center of the struggle for a better life' (p. 119).

This dialectic between intellect and practice continued into the 1920s and 1930s, through the publication of several books: William Heard Kilpatrick's *Foundations of Method* (1925), an elaboration of Dewey's thinking about the connection between school and society; Harold Rugg and Ann Schumaker's *The Child-Centred School* (1928), another interpretive survey of pedagogical practice like Dewey's *Schools of To-Morrow*; and Kilpatrick's *The Educational Frontier* (1933), a restatement of progressive theory and philosophy written by a committee of the National Society of College Teachers of Education (Cremin, 1961, pp. 216–29). Individual reformers and major social educational institutions, such as Teachers College and the University of Chicago, designed and developed schools that exemplified the key tenets of progressive thinking.

One example illustrates the power of this connection between ideas and institutions. In 1915, Abraham Flexner, the father of modern medical education, announced his intention to develop a model school that would do for general education what the Johns Hopkins Medical School had done for medical education. He wrote an essay called 'A modern school' (1917), a blueprint for reform describing a school that embodied major changes in curriculum and teaching. It was designed to serve as a laboratory for the scientific study of educational problems. In 1917, Teachers College, in collaboration with Flexner and the General Board of Education, opened the Lincoln School, which became a model and a gathering place for progressive reformers, a major source of new curriculum materials and the intellectual birthplace of many reformers over the next two decades. The school survived until 1948, when it was disbanded in a dispute between its parents' association and the Teachers College administration (Cremin, 1961, pp. 280–91).

The second form of innovation in the progressive period, large-scale reforms of public school systems, drew on the same intellectual base as the founding of individual schools. A notable early example was the Gary, Indiana, school district. The Gary superintendent in 1907 was William Wirt, a former student of John Dewey at the University of Chicago. Wirt initiated the 'Gary Plan', which became the leading exemplar of progressive practice on a large scale in the early progressive period. The key elements of the Gary Plan were 'vastly extended educational opportunity' in the form of playgrounds, libraries, laboratories, machine shops and the like; a 'platoon system' of grouping whereby groups of children moved *en masse* between classrooms and common areas, allowing for economies in facilities; a 'community' system of school organisation in which skilled tradespeople from the community played a role in teaching students; and a heavily project-focused curriculum (Cremin, 1961, pp. 153–60).

In 1919, Winnetka, Illinois, hired Carleton Washburn of the San Francisco State Normal School as its superintendent. Washburn launched a reform agenda based on the idea of individually paced instruction, where the 'common essentials' in the curriculum were divided into 'parcels', through which each student advanced, with the guidance of teachers, at his or her own pace. As students mastered each parcel, they were examined and moved on to the next. This individualised work was combined with 'self-expressive' work in which students were encouraged to develop ideas and projects on their own, as well as group projects in which students worked on issues related to the community life of the school. Over the next decade, the Winnetka plan was imitated by as many as 247 other school districts, but with a crucial modification. Most districts found the practice of tailoring the curriculum to individual students far too complex for their tastes, so they organised students into groups to which they applied the idea of differential progress. In this way, a progressive reform focused on individualised learning led to the development of what is now called tracking (Cremin, 1961, pp. 295–8).

A number of cities, including Denver and Washington, DC, undertook massive curriculum reform projects in the late 1920s and early 1930s. These efforts were extraordinarily sophisticated, even by today's relatively rarefied standards. Typically, teachers were enlisted to meet in curriculum revision committees during regular school hours, and outside experts were enlisted to work with teachers in reformulating the curriculum and in developing new teaching practices. In Denver, Superintendent Jesse Newlon convinced his school board to appropriate $35,500 for this process. Denver became a centre for teacher-initiated and -developed curriculum, resulting in the development of a monograph series of course syllabi that attained a wide national circulation. The resulting curriculum changes were sustained in Denver over roughly two decades, when they were abandoned in the face of growing opposition to progressive pedagogy (Cremin, 1961, pp. 299–302; Cuban, 1984, pp. 67–83). In Washington, DC, Superintendent Frank Ballou led a pared-down version of the Denver curriculum revision model: teacher committees chaired by administrators met after school, without the support of outside specialists. Despite these constraints, the process reached large numbers of teachers in both Black and White schools in the city's segregated system (Cuban, 1984, pp. 83–93).

Larry Cuban concluded in *How Teachers Taught: Constancy and Change in American Classrooms, 1890–1980*, his study of large-scale reforms of curriculum and pedagogy in the late-progressive period, that progressive practices, defined as movement away from teacher-centred and towards student-centred pedagogy, 'seldom appeared in more than one-fourth of the classrooms in any district that systematically tried to install these varied elements' (Cuban, 1984, p. 135). Even in settings where teachers made a conscious effort to incorporate progressive practices, the result was more often than not a hybrid of traditional and progressive, in which the major elements of the traditional core of instruction were largely undisturbed:

> The dominant pattern of instruction, allowing for substantial spread of these hybrid progressive practices, remained teacher centered. Elementary and secondary teachers persisted in teaching from the front of the room, deciding what was to be learned, in what manner, and under what conditions. The primary means of grouping for instruction was the entire class. The major daily classroom activities continued with a teacher telling, explaining, and questioning students while the students listened, answered, read, and wrote. Seatwork or supervised study was an extension of these activities.
>
> (Cuban, 1984, p. 137)

The fate of the progressive movement has been well documented. As the language of progressivism began to permeate educational talk, if not practice, the movement began to lose its intellectual edge and to drift into a series of empty clichés, the most extreme of which was life adjustment education. Opposition to progressivism, which had been building through the 1920s, came to a crescendo in the 1940s. The movement was increasingly portrayed by a sceptical public and press in terms of its most extreme manifestations – watered-down content, a focus on children's psychological adjustment at the expense of learning and a preoccupation with self-expression rather than learning. Abraham Flexner, looking back on his experiences as a moderate progressive, observed that 'there is something queer about the genus "educator"; the loftiest are not immune. I think the cause must lie in their isolation from the rough and tumble contacts with all manner of men. They lose their sense of reality' (Cremin, 1961, p. 160).

The particular structure that educational reform took in the progressive period, though, is deeply rooted in American institutions and persists to this day. First, contrary to much received wisdom, intellectuals found ways to express their ideas about how education could be different in the form of real schools with structures and practices that were radically different from existing schools. There was a direct and vital connection between ideas and practice, a connection that persists up to the present, though in a much diluted form. But this connection took the institutional form of single schools, each an isolated island of practice, connected by a loosely defined intellectual agenda that made few demands for conformity, and each a particular, previous and exotic specimen of a larger genus. So the most vital and direct connections between ideas and practice were deliberately institutionalised as separate, independent entities, incapable of and uninterested in forming replicates of themselves or of pursuing a broader institutional reform agenda. A few exceptions, like the Lincoln School, were deliberately designed to influence educational practice on a larger scale, but the exact means by which that was to happen were quite vague. For the most part, progressive reformers believed that good ideas would travel, of their own volition, into US classrooms and schools.

Second, where public systems did attempt to change pedagogical practice on a large scale, often using techniques that would be considered sophisticated by today's standards, they succeeded in changing practice in only a small fraction of classrooms, and then not necessarily in a sustained way over time. Sometimes, as in the case of Washburn's strategy of individualising instruction in Winnetka, as the reforms moved from one district to another they became sinister caricatures of the original. The district-level reforms produced impressive tangible products, mostly in the form of new curriculum materials that would circulate within and outside the originating districts. The connection to classroom practice, however, was weak. Larry Cuban likens this kind of reform to a hurricane at sea – 'storm-tossed waves on the ocean surface, turbulent water a fathom down, and calm on the ocean floor' (Cuban, 1984, p. 237).

Third, the very successes of progressive reformers became their biggest liabilities as the inevitable political opposition formed. Rather than persist in Dewey's original agenda of influencing public discourse about the nature of education and its relation to society through open public discussion, debate and inquiry, the more militant progressives became increasingly like true believers in a particular version of the faith and increasingly isolated from public scrutiny and discourse. In this way, the developers of progressive pedagogy became increasingly isolated from the public mainstream and increasingly vulnerable to attack from traditionalists.

The pattern that emerges from the progressive period, then, is one where the intellectual and practical energies of serious reformers tended to turn inward, towards the creation of exemplary settings – classrooms or schools – that embodied their best ideas of practice, producing an impressive and attractive array of isolated examples of what practice *could* look like. At the same time, those actors with an interest in what would now be called systemic change focused on developing the tangible, visible and material products of reform – plans, processes, curricula, materials – and focused much less, if at all, on the less tangible problem of what might cause a teacher to teach in new ways, if the materials and support were available to do so. These two forces produced the central dilemma of educational reform: we can produce many examples of how educational practice could look different, but we can produce few, if any, examples of large numbers of teachers engaging in these practices in large-scale institutions designed to deliver education to most children.

Large-scale curriculum development projects

Another, more recent body of evidence on these points comes from large-scale curriculum reforms of the 1950s and 1960s in the United States, which were funded by the National Science Foundation (NSF). In their fundamental structure, these reforms were quite similar to the progressive reforms, although much more tightly focused on content. The central idea of these curriculum reforms was that learning in school should resemble, much more than it usually does, the actual processes by which human beings come to understand their environment, culture and social settings. That is, if students are studying mathematics, science, or social science, they should actually engage in activities similar to those of serious practitioners of these disciplines and, in the process, discover not only the knowledge of the subject, but also the thought processes and methods of inquiry by which that knowledge is constructed. This view suggested that construction of new curriculum for schools should proceed by bringing the best researchers in the various subjects together with school teachers, and using the expertise of both groups to devise new conceptions of content and new strategies for teaching it. The earliest of these projects was the Physical Sciences Study Committee's (PSSC) high school physics curriculum, begun in 1956. Another of these was the Biological Sciences Curriculum Study (BSCS), begun in 1958. A third was *Man: A Course of Study* (MACOS), an ambitious social science curriculum development project, which began in 1959, but only received its first substantial funding from the Ford Foundation in 1962 and NSF support for teacher training in 1969 (Dow, 1991; Elmore, 1993; Grobman, 1969; Marsh, 1964). These were among the largest and most ambitious of the curriculum reform projects, but by no means the only ones.

From the beginning, these curriculum reformers were clear that they aimed to change the core of US schooling, and their aspirations were not fundamentally different from the early progressives. They envisioned teachers becoming coaches and co-investigators with students into the basic phenomena of the physical, biological and social sciences. Students' work was to focus heavily on experimentation, inquiry and study of original sources. The notion of the textbook as the repository of conventional knowledge was to be discarded, and in its place teachers were to use carefully developed course materials and experimental apparatus that were keyed to the big ideas in the areas under study. The object of study was not the assimilation of facts, but learning the methods and concepts of scientific inquiry by doing science in the same way that practitioners of science would do it.

The curriculum development projects grew out of the initiatives of university professors operating from the belief that they could improve the quality of incoming university students by improving the secondary school curriculum. Hence, university professors tended to dominate the curriculum development process, often to the detriment of relations with the teachers and school administrators who were expected to adopt the curricula once they were developed and tested in sample sites. The projects succeeded to varying degrees in engaging actual teachers in the development process, as opposed to simply having teachers field-test lessons that had already been developed.

Teachers were engaged in one way or another at the developmental stage in all projects, but were not always co-developers. In PSSC, a few teachers judged to be talented enough to engage the MIT professors involved in the project were part of the development process; the main involvement of teachers came at the field-testing stage, but their feedback proved to be too voluminous to be accommodated systematically in the final product (Marsh, 1964). In MACOS, one school in the Boston area was a summer test site, and teachers were engaged in the curriculum project relatively early in the process of development. Later versions of the curriculum were extensively tested and marketed in school throughout the country (Dow, 1991).

By far the most ambitious and systematic involvement of teachers as co-developers was in BSCS. BSCS was designed to produce three distinct versions of a secondary biology curriculum (biochemical, ecological and cellular), so that schools and teachers could have a choice of which approach to use. The development process was organised into three distinct teams, each composed of equal numbers of university professors and high school biology teachers. Lessons or units were developed by a pair composed of one professor and one secondary teacher, and each of these units was reviewed and critiqued by another team composed of equal partners. After the curriculum was developed, the teachers who participated in development were drafted to run study groups of teachers using the curriculum units during the school year, and the results of these study groups were fed back into the development process. Interestingly, once the curriculum was developed, NSF abandoned funding for the teacher study groups. NSF's rationale was that the teachers had accomplished their development task, but this cut-off effectively eliminated the teacher study groups, potentially the most powerful device for changing teaching practice (Elmore, 1993; Grobman, 1969).

Evaluations of the NSF-sponsored curriculum development projects generally conclude that their effects were broad but shallow. Hundreds of thousands of teachers and curriculum directors were trained in summer institutes. Tens of thousands of curriculum units were disseminated. Millions of students were exposed to at least some product or by-product of the various projects. In a few schools and school systems, teachers and administrators made concerted efforts to transform curriculum and teaching in accord with the new ideas, but in most instances the results looked like what Cuban (1984) found in his study of progressive teaching practices: a weak, diluted, hybrid form emerged in some settings in which new curricula were shoehorned into old practices, and, in most secondary classrooms, the curricula had no impact on teaching and learning at all. While the curriculum development projects produced valuable materials that are still a resource to many teachers and shaped people's conceptions of the possibilities of secondary science curriculum, their tangible impact on the core of US schooling has been negligible (Elmore, 1993; Stake and Easely, 1978).

Most academic critics agree that the curriculum development projects embodied a naive, discredited and badly conceived model of how to influence teaching practice. The model, if there was one, was that 'good' curriculum and teaching practice were self-explanatory and self-implementing. Once teachers and school administrators recognised the clearly superior ideas embodied in the new curricula, they would simply switch from traditional textbooks to the new materials and change long-standing practices in order to improve their teaching and the chances of their students succeeding in school.

What this model overlooked, however, was the complex process by which local curricular decisions get made, the entrenched and institutionalised political and commercial relationships that support existing textbook-driven curricula, the weak incentives operating on teachers to change their practices in their daily work routines and the extraordinary costs of making large-scale, long-standing changes of a fundamental kind in how knowledge is constructed in classrooms. In the few instances where the advocates for the curriculum development projects appeared to be on the verge of discovering a way to change practice on a large scale – as in the BSCS teacher study groups, for example – they failed to discern the significance of what they were doing because they saw themselves as developers of new ideas about teaching and not as institution-changing actors.

The structural pattern that emerges from the large-scale curriculum development projects is strikingly similar to that of the progressive period. First, the ideas were powerful and engaging, and they found their way into tangible materials and into practice in a few settings. In this sense, the projects were a remarkable achievement in the social organisation of knowledge, pulling the country's most sophisticated thinkers into the orbit of public education and putting them to work on the problem of what students should know and be able to do. Second, the curriculum developers proved to be inept and naive in their grasp of the individual and institutional issues of change associated with their reforms. They assumed that a 'good' product would travel into US classrooms on the basis of its merit, without regard to the complex institutional and individual factors that might constrain its ability to do so. Third, their biggest successes were, in a sense, also their biggest failures. Those few teachers who became accomplished teachers of PSSC physics, BSCS biology, or MACOS approaches to social studies only seemed to confirm what most educators think about talent in the classroom. A few have it, but most do not. A few have the extraordinary energy, commitment, and native ability required to change their practice in some fundamental way; most others do not. The existence of exemplars, without some way of capitalising on their talents, only reinforces the notion that ambitious teaching is an individual trait, not a professional expectation.

The role of incentives

Nested within this broad framework of institutional and political issues is a more specific problem of incentives that reforms need to address in order to get at the problem of scale. Institutional structures influence the behaviour of individuals in part through incentives. The institution and its political context help set the values and rewards that individuals respond to within their daily work life. But individual values are also important. As David Cohen (1995) cogently argues in his discussion of rewards for teacher performance, incentives mobilise individual values; that is, individual values determine to some degree what the institution can elicit with incentives. For example, if teachers or students do not value student academic performance, do not see the relationship between academic performance and personal objectives, or do not believe it is possible to change student performance, then it is hard to use incentives to motivate them to action that would improve performance.

Thus, individual acts like the practice of teaching in complex institutional settings emanate both from the incentives that operate on the individual and from the individual's willingness to recognise and respond to these incentives as legitimate. Individual actions are also a product of the knowledge and the competence that the individual possesses. As Michael Fullan has argued, schools routinely undertake reforms for which they have neither the institutional nor the individual competence, and they resolve this problem by trivialising the reforms, changing the language they use and modifying superficial structures around the practice, but without changing the practice itself (Fullan, 1982; Fullan and Miles, 1992). Individuals are embedded in institutional structures that provide them with incentives to act in certain ways, and they respond to these incentives by testing them against their values and their competence.

One way of thinking about the aforementioned evidence is that it demonstrates a massive failure of schools to harness their institutional incentives to the improvement of practice. I think this failure is rooted not only in the design of the institutions, but also in a deep cultural norm about teaching that I referred to earlier: that successful teaching is an individual trait rather than a set of learned professional competencies acquired over the course of a career.

Both the progressive reformers and the curriculum reforms of the 1950s and 1960s focused on connecting powerful ideas to practice, developing exemplars of good practice and attracting true believers. These efforts largely failed, often in very interesting and instructive ways, to translate their ideas into broad-scale changes in practice. A very large incentive problem is buried in this strategy: reform strategies of this kind rely on the intrinsic motivation of individuals with particular values and competencies – and a particular orientation towards the outside world – to develop and implement reforms in schools.

Without some fundamental change in the incentive structure under which schools and teachers operate, we will continue more or less indefinitely to repeat the experience of the progressives and the curriculum reformers. Like our predecessors, we will design reforms that appeal to the intrinsic values and competencies of a relatively small proportion of the teaching force. We will gather these teachers together in ways that cut them off from contact and connection with those who find ambitious teaching intimidating and unfeasible. We will demonstrate that powerful ideas can be harnessed to changes in practice in a small fraction of settings, but continue to fail in moving those practices beyond the group of teachers who are intrinsically motivated and competent to engage in them.

Working on the problem of scale

What might be done to change this self-reinforcing incentive structure? Probably the first step is to acknowledge that social problems of this complexity are not amenable to quick, comprehensive, rational solutions. Fundamental changes in patterns of incentives occur not by engaging in ambitious, discontinuous reforms, but rather by pushing hard in a few strategic places in the system of relations surrounding the problem, and then carefully observing the results. My recommendations will be of this sort.

Furthermore, it seems important to continue to do what has yielded success in the past and to continue to do it with increasing sophistication. I have argued that the most successful part of the progressive and curriculum reform strategies was the creation of powerful connections between big ideas with large social implications and the micro-world of teaching practice. The progressives succeeded in creating versions of educational reform that both exemplified progressive ideals and embodied concrete changes in the core of schooling. Likewise, the curriculum reformers succeeded in harnessing the talent of the scientific elite to the challenge of secondary school curriculum and teaching.

This connection between the big ideas and the fine grain of practice in the core of schooling is a fundamental precondition for any change in practice. Capacity to make these connections waxes and wanes, and probably depends too heavily on the idiosyncrasies of particular individuals with a particular scientific or ideological axe to grind. One could imagine doing a much better job of institutionalising the connection between big ideas and teaching practice. Examples might include routine major national curriculum reviews composed of groups with equal numbers of school teachers and university researchers, or a national curriculum renewal agenda that targeted particular parts of teaching and curriculum for renewal on a regular cycle. The more basic point, however, is that preserving the connection between big ideas and teaching practice, embodied in earlier reform strategies, is an essential element in tackling the problem of scale.

With these ideas as context, I offer four main proposals for how to begin to tackle the problem of scale. Each grows out of an earlier line of analysis in this article, and each embodies an argument about how incentives should be realigned to tackle the problem of scale.

I Develop strong external normative structures for practice

The key flaw in earlier attempts at large-scale reform was to rely almost exclusively on the intrinsic commitment of talented and highly motivated teachers to carry the burden of reform. Coupled with strong cultural norms about good teaching being an individual trait, this strategy virtually guarantees that good practice will stay with those who learn and will not travel to those who are less predisposed to learn. One promising approach, then, is to create strong professional and social normative structures for good teaching practice that are external to individual teachers and their immediate working environment, and to provide a basis for evaluating how many teachers are approximating good practice at what level of competence.

I use the concept of external normative structures, rather than a term like standards, because I think these structures should be diverse and need to be constructed on different bases of authority in order to be useful in influencing teaching practice.

Why is the existence of external norms important? Because it institutionalises the idea that professionals are responsible for looking outward at challenging conceptions of practice, in addition to looking inward at their values and competencies. Good teaching becomes a matter for public debate and disagreement, for serious reflection and discourse, for positive and negative feedback about one's own practices. Over time, as this predisposition to look outward becomes more routinised and ingrained, trait theories of teaching competence should diminish. Teachers would begin increasingly to think of themselves as operating in a web of professional relations that influence their daily decisions, rather than as solo practitioners inventing practice out of their personalities, prior experiences and assessments of their own strengths and weaknesses. Without external normative structures, teachers have no incentive to think of their practice as anything other than a bundle of traits. The existence of strong external norms also has the effect of legitimating the proportion of teachers in any system who draw their ideas about teaching from a professional community, and who compare themselves against a standard external to their school or community. External norms give visibility and status to those who exemplify them.

2 Develop organisational structures that intensify and focus, rather than dissipate and scatter, intrinsic motivation to engage in challenging practice

The good news about existing reform strategies is that they tend to galvanise commitment among the already motivated by concentrating them in small groups of true believers who reinforce each other. The bad news is that these small groups of self-selected reformers apparently seldom influence their peers. This conclusion suggests that structures should, at a minimum, create diversity among the energetic, already committed reformers and the sceptical and timid. But it also suggests that the unit of work in an organisation that wants to change its teaching practice should be small enough so that members can exercise real influence over each others' practice. Certain types of structures are more likely than others to intensify and focus norms of good practice: organisations in which face-to-face relationships dominate impersonal, bureaucratic ones; organisations in which people routinely interact around common problems of practice; and organisations that focus on the results of their work for students, rather than on the working conditions of professionals. These features can be incorporated into organisations, as well as into the composition of their memberships.

3 Create intentional processes for reproduction of successes

One of the major lessons from past large-scale reforms is their astounding naiveté about how to get their successes to move from one setting to another. The progressives seemed to think that a few good exemplars and a few energetic superintendents pursuing system-wide strategies of reform would ignite a conflagration that would consume all of US education. If any social movement had the possibility of doing that, it was the progressive movement, since it had, at least initially, a high degree of focus, a steady supply of serious intellectual capital and an infrastructure of committed reformers. But it did not succeed at influencing more than a small fraction of schools and classrooms. The curriculum reformers thought that good curriculum models would create their own demand, an astoundingly naive idea in retrospect, give what we know about the limits within which teachers work, the complex webs of institutional and political relationships that surround curriculum decisions and the weak incentives for teachers to pay attention to external ideas about teaching practice.

I suggest five theories that might serve as the basis for experimentation with processes designed to get exemplary practices to scale.

Incremental growth

The usual way of thinking about increases in scale in social systems is incremental growth. For example, according to the incremental growth theory, the proportion of teachers teaching in a particular way would increase by some modest constant each year, until the proportion approached 100 per cent. This model implies a fixed capacity for training a given number of teachers per year in an organisation.

The problems with this model are not difficult to identify. The idea that new practice 'takes' after a teacher has been trained is highly suspect. The notion that a fixed number of teachers could be trained to teach in a given way by circulating them through a training experience seems implausible, although it is probably the way most training programmes are designed. Teaching practice is unlikely to change as a result of exposure to training, unless that training also brings with it some kind of external normative structure, a network of social relationships that personalise that structure, and supports interaction around problems of practice. The incremental model, if it is to work, needs a different kind of specification, which I will call the cumulative model.

Cumulative growth

The cumulative growth model suggests that 'getting to scale' is a slower, less linear process than that described by the incremental model. It involves not only creating interventions that expose teachers to new practices, but also monitoring the effects of these interventions on teaching practice. When necessary, processes may be created to compensate for the weaknesses of initial effects. Cumulative growth not only adds an increment of practitioners who are exposed to a new practice each year, but also involves a backlog of practitioners from previous years who may or may not have responded to past training. This problem requires a more complex solution than simply continuing to provide exposure to new practice at a given rate. It might require, for example, the creation of professional networks to support the practice of teachers who are in the process of changing their practice, or connecting the more advanced with the less advanced through some sort of mentoring scheme.

Discontinuous growth

Another possibility is a sharply increasing, or discontinuous, growth model. This could occur through a process like a chain letter, in which an initial group of teachers learned a new kind of practice, and each member of that group worked with another group, and so on: the rate of growth might go, for example from $\times$, to $10\times$, to $100\times$, to $1000\times$, etc.

This discontinuous growth model shares the same problem with the incremental growth model, but on a larger scale. As the number of teachers exposed to new practices increases, so too does the backlog of teachers for whom the initial intervention was inadequate, eventually reaching the point at which this accumulation of teachers overwhelms the system. It also seems likely that the discontinuous growth model would create serious quality control problems. As growth accelerates, it becomes more and more difficult to distinguish between teachers who are accomplished practitioners of new ways of teaching, and those who are accomplished at making it appear as though they have mastered new ways of teaching.

In all the examples of growth models so far, teachers operate in a system of relationships that provides training and support, but not as members of organisations called schools. In addition to these three models that construct training and support around teachers, two additional models treat teachers as practitioners working in schools.

Unbalanced growth

One of these models is the unbalanced growth model. This extends and modifies the standard model of innovation in education: collecting true believers in a few settings. Whereas the standard model socially isolates true believers from everyone else, virtually guaranteeing that new practices do not spread, versions of the unbalanced growth model correct for these deficiencies. A version of unbalanced growth might involve concentrating a critical mass of high-performing teachers in a few schools, with an explicit charge to develop each other's capacities to teach in new ways. The growth of new practice would be 'unbalanced' initially because some schools would be deliberately constructed to bring like-minded practitioners together to develop their skills. Such schools might be called 'pioneer' schools or 'leading edge' schools to communicate that they are designed to serve as places where new practices are developed, nurtured and taught to an ever-increasing number of practitioners. Over time, these schools would be deliberately staffed with larger proportions of less accomplished practitioners and teachers not yet introduced to new models of practice. The competencies developed in the high-performing organisations would then socialise new teachers into the norms of good practice.

The main problem with this model is that it goes against the grain of existing personnel practices in most school systems. Teaching assignments are typically made through collectively bargained seniority and/or principal entrepreneurship, rather than on the basis of a systematic interest in using schools as places to socialise teachers to new practice. Younger teachers are typically assigned to schools with the largest proportions of difficult-to-teach children, and spend their careers working their way into more desirable assignments. Principals who understand and have mastered the assignment system often use it to gather teachers with whom they prefer to work. In order for the unbalanced growth model to work, a school system would have to devise some deliberate strategy for placing teachers in settings where they would be most likely to develop new skills. Teachers, likewise, would have to be willing to work in settings where they could learn to develop their practice as part of their professional responsibility.

Cell division or reproduction

The other model of growth that treats teachers as practitioners working in schools is the cell division, or reproduction, model. This model works from the analogy of reproductive biology. Rather than trying to change teaching practice by influencing the flow of teachers through schools, as in the unbalanced growth model, the cell division model involves systematically increasing the number and proportion of schools characterised by distinctive pedagogical practices.

The cell division model works by first creating a number of settings in which exemplary practitioners are concentrated and allowed to develop new approaches to teaching practice. Then, on a more or less predictable schedule, a number of these practitioners are asked to form another school, using the 'genetic material' of their own knowledge and understanding to recruit a new cadre of teachers whom they educate to a new set of expectations about practice. Over time, several such schools would surface with strong communities of teachers invested in particular approaches to teaching.

These alternative models of growth each embody an explicit practical theory of how to propagate or reproduce practice. They also have a transparent logic that can be understood and adapted by others for use in other settings. More such theories, and more documented examples of how they work in use, should help in understanding how to get to scale with good educational practice.

4 Creative structures that promote learning of new practices and incentive systems that support them

Reformers typically make very heroic and unrealistic assumptions about what ordinary human beings can do, and they generalise these assumptions to a wide population of teachers. Cremin (1961) made the following observation about progressive education:

> From the beginning progressivism cast the teacher is an almost impossible role: [she] was to be an artist of consummate skill, properly knowledgeable in [her] field, meticulously trained in the science of pedagogy, and thoroughly imbued with a burning zeal for social improvement. It need hardly be said that here as elsewhere . . . the gap between the real and the ideal was appalling.
>
> (p. 168)

Likewise, the curriculum reformers appeared to assume that teachers, given the existence of clearly superior content, would simply use the new curricula and learn what was needed in order to teach differently. Missing from this view is an explicit model of how teachers engage in intentional learning about new ways to teach. According to Fullan and Miles (1992), 'change involves learning and . . . all change involves coming to understand and to be good at something new' (p. 749). While knowledge is not deep on this subject, the following seem plausible: teachers are more likely to learn from direct observation of practice and trial and error in their own classrooms than they are from abstract descriptions of new teaching; changing teaching practice even for committed teachers, takes a long time, and several cycles of trial and error; teachers have to feel that there is some compelling reason for them to practise differently, with the best direct evidence being that students learn better; and teachers need feedback from sources they trust about whether students are actually learning what they are taught.

These conditions accompany the learning of any new, complicated practice. Yet, reform efforts seldom, if ever, incorporate these conditions. Teachers are often tossed headlong into discussion groups to work out the classroom logistics of implementing a new curriculum. They are encouraged to develop model lessons as a group activity and then sent back to their classrooms to implement them as solo practitioners.

Teachers are seldom asked to judge if this new curriculum translates well into concrete actions in the classroom, nor are they often asked to participate as co-designers of the ideas in the first place. The feedback teachers receive on the effects of their practice usually comes in the form of generalised test scores that have no relationship to the specific objectives of the new practice. In other words, the conditions under which teachers are asked to engage in new practices bear no relationship whatsoever to the conditions required for learning how to implement complex and new practices with success. Why would anyone want to change their practice under such conditions.

A basic prerequisite for tackling the problem of scale, then, is to insist that reforms that purport to change practice embody an explicit theory about how human beings learn to do things differently. Presently, there are few, if any, well-developed theories that meet this requirement, although I have sketched out a few above. Furthermore, these theories have to make sense at the individual and at the organisational level. That is, if you ask teachers to change the way they deal with students and to relate to their colleagues differently, the incentives that operate at the organisational level have to reinforce and promote those behaviours. Encouragement and support, access to special knowledge, time to focus on the requirements of the new task, time to observe others doing it – all suggest ways in which the environment of incentives in the organisation comes to reflect the requirements of learning.

References

Cohen, D. (1988) 'Teaching practice: plus que ça change . . .', in Jackson, P. (ed.), *Contribution to Educational Change: Perspectives on Research and Practice*, Berkeley, CA: McCutcheon.

Cohen, D. (1995) 'Rewarding teachers for student performance', in Fuhrman, S. and O'Day, J. (eds), *Rewards and Reforms: Creating Educational Incentives that Work*, San Francisco: Jossey-Bass.

Cremin, L. (1961) *The Transformation of the American School*, New York: Knopf.

Cuban, L. (1984) *How Teachers Taught: Constancy and Change in American Classrooms, 1890–1980*, New York: Longman.

Cuban, L. (1990) 'Reforming again, again, and again', *Educational Researcher*, **19**(1), 3–13.

Darling-Hammond, L. (1995) 'Restructuring schools for high performance', in Fuhrman, S. and O'Day, J. (eds), *Restructuring Schools for High Performance*, San Francisco: Jossey-Bass.

Dewey, J. (1899) *The School and Society*, Chicago: University of Chicago Press.

Dewey, J. and Dewey, E. (1915) *Schools of To-Morrow*, New York: E. P. Dutton.

Dow, P. (1991) *Schoolhouse Politics: Lessons from the Sputnik Era*, Cambridge, MA: Harvard University Press.

Elmore, R. (1993) 'The Development and Implementation of Large-Scale Curriculum Reforms', paper prepared for the American Association for the Advancement of Science, Cambridge, MA: Harvard Graduate School for Education, Center for Policy Research in Education.

Elmore, R. (1995) 'Teaching, learning, and school organization: principles of practice and the regularities of schooling', *Educational Administration Quarterly*, **31**, 355–74.

Flexner, A. (1917) 'A modern school', in *Publications of the General Education Board* (Occasional papers, No. 3), New York: General Education Board.

Fullan, M. (1982) *The Meaning of Education Change*, New York: Teachers College Press.

Fullan, M. and Miles, M. (1992) 'Getting reform right: what works and what doesn't', *Phi Delta Kappan*, **73**, 744–52.

Goodlad, J. (1984) *A Place Called School*, New York: McGraw-Hill.

Grobman, A. (1969) *The Changing Classroom: The Role of the Biological Sciences Curriculum Study*, New York: Doubleday.

Kilpatrick, W. H. (1925) *Foundations of Method: Informal Talks on Teaching by William Heard Kilpatrick*, New York: Macmillan.

Kilpatrick, W. H. (1933) *The Educational Frontier*, New York: Century Company.

Marsh, P. (1964) 'The Physical Sciences study committee: a case history of nationwide curriculum development, 1956–1961', unpublished doctoral dissertation, Harvard University Graduate School of Education, Cambridge, MA.

National Center for Education Statistics (1993) *NAEP 1992 Mathematics Report Card for the Nation and the States: Data from the National and Trial State Assessments*, Washington, DC: US Department of Education.

National Commission on Excellence in Education (1983) *A Nation at Risk: The Imperative for Educational Reform*, Washington, DC: US Department of Education.

Powell, A., Farrar, E. and Cohen, D. (1985) *The Shopping Mall High School*, Boston: Houghton Mifflin.

Rugg, H. A. and Schumaker, A. (1928) *The Child-Centered School*, Chicago: World Book.

Stake, R. and Easely, J. (1978) 'Case studies in science education', in *The Case Reports*, Vol. 1 & 2, Washington, DC: US Government Printing Office.

Models of leading professional development

Chapter 4

School leadership: some key ideas

Brian Fidler

This is an edited version of an article previously published in *School Leadership & Management*, **17**, 1, 1997.

Introduction

The intention of this article is to highlight some key ideas on leadership from the literature on organisations and educational literature. In particular, curricular or instructional leadership will be reviewed. This is being done for two reasons. First, to help practitioners and others to increase their range of conceptualisations and theoretical insights into leadership in order to aid their understanding of school leadership and their ability to formulate plans for action. Second, to encourage researchers to use theoretical models in their studies of practice and to increase the interaction between theoretical formulations of leadership and empirical investigation. Hallinger and Heck (1996) in an article reassessing the principal's role in school effectiveness, based on research over a recent 15-year period, noted, with approval, the greater number of studies in this period that had taken a theoretical approach to leadership compared to earlier periods. They considered that this trend held great promise for future understanding.

   This recapitulation of existing ideas has inevitably been highly selective and makes no claim to include a complete review of all the literature. It concentrates on theoretical literature rather than empirical findings. It does not seek to preclude the formulation of new theory, but rather suggests that any new perspective needs to take account of the complexities that current formulations of leadership have uncovered. New theories should aim to aid understanding rather than simply be prescriptive. New prescriptions of what heads of school should be doing that highlight particular features of their work and ignore others are unlikely to offer much progress in the longer term. The aim of this article is to present a number of theoretical perspectives for analysis and understanding.

   Having clarified the aim of this article, the way is clear for the substantive task of clarifying the notion of leadership and presenting some formulations of key concepts. Leadership has been recognised as vitally important for schools by politicians, inspectors, researchers, and by practitioners. However, the function that will be identified as leadership has not been consistently referred to as such by authors. There has been a good deal of similarity between leadership and aspects of management in the British literature and administration or management in the North American literature. This indicates that leadership is not easy to encapsulate and differentiate from management. Whilst some authors still use the words interchangeably, over the last few years there has been a trend in the educational and organisational literature to identify particular facets of the management process as leadership.

Periodically the concept of leadership seems to be rediscovered, often at times of crisis. At the present time there is renewed interest on both sides of the Atlantic and in other parts of the world. This is a time when the challenges for school leaders are more demanding than ever – quality improvements, social fragmentation, diverse expectations and all at a time of resource scarcity. This article is an attempt to bring together what I consider to be enduring ideas from previous attempts to conceptualise leadership. This is to redress what seems to be a popular tendency to use the term only in the sense of charismatic or heroic leadership. It is contended here that most leadership is not of this kind. Thus, although it may be disappointing, the study of leadership involves some worthwhile but more prosaic ideas.

The article begins by examining the concept of leadership and differentiating it from management and administration. This leads on to five perspectives on leadership. The first is that appropriate leadership needs to take account of circumstances or, in other words, be situational. The second perspective is of four frames or lenses through which to view leadership. Each is related to one of four alternative ways of viewing organisations – structural, human relations, political and symbolic. The third perspective recognises that the leadership of professionally staffed organisations has some special features and suggests two components – chief executive and leading professional. The fourth draws attention to the moral component of leading schools and the fifth considers curriculum leadership in some detail.

The search for leadership

Often the need for leadership is signalled by its absence. There seems to be three types of reaction to particular examples of leadership – approbation, neutrality and dislike. Except in the case where a particularly challenging situation for an organisation has been surmounted to everyone's satisfaction, approbation is rare. Neutrality and dislike may signal a leadership problem, but not necessarily so. More often a vague feeling that the organisation or part of it is out of control and everyone is powerless to do anything about it is an indication of a leadership vacuum. As Bennis (1989) suggests, leadership is rather like beauty: it is hard to define but individuals can recognise it when they see it.

Many authors have attempted to define leadership, but, like many complex concepts, simple definitions obscure as much as they reveal. Two key features of leadership are:

- a sense of purpose and confidence is engendered in followers;
- followers are influenced towards goal achievement.

As this formulation makes clear, the effects of leadership are apparent in the feelings and actions of followers and in task achievement. This is somewhat at odds with the common identification of leadership with a person. As Murphy (1988) has pointed out, associating leadership with a person rather than an interaction between a leader and followers has led research findings to sideline the influence of followers on leaders and of the context. Studies of leaders out of context do not provide many insights into leadership.

Early studies of leadership concentrated on a search for personal characteristics that leaders possessed. The search yielded little of value. Immegart (1988), after reviewing extensive reviews of research findings on leadership, concluded that the traits of intelligence, dominance, self-confidence and high energy/activity level were most often associated with successful leadership. But, beyond this group, the findings were inconsistent.

Nevertheless, there is a sense in which leadership is more personal than, say, management. Whilst the influence of managers is supported by the structural attributes of organisations, it is personal action that is at the core of leadership. On the other hand, one of the recurring themes of this article is the presumption that leadership should be contingent. What is appropriate leadership at a particular point in time depends on: the context and its pre-history; the nature of followers; the particular issues involves; in addition to the predispositions of the leader. Thus, although a leader may have a preferred leadership style, this may need to be varied according to circumstances.

The reference to context draws attention to a connection between leadership and organisations. Organisations need leadership. However, as Ogawa and Bossert (1995) argue, this is more than a requirement for a few people at the top of the organisation. They argue that leadership should be associated with roles throughout an organis-ation, although the needs of leadership will change depending on the position in the organisation. They also argue that outcomes of leadership should be viewed more broadly than goal attainment.

The relationship of leadership and management

Similar frameworks have been used to examine both leadership and management. The two dimensions of consideration (concern for people) and initiating structure (concern for results) have been used to identify two independent components of the role. Similarly, the sources of power and influence used by leaders and managers share a common framework:

- power based on organisational position;
- power based on expertise;
- power based on personal characteristics or behaviour.

Figure 4.1 **Proactive and reactive elements of leadership and administration**

The close way in which leadership and aspects of management have been treated in the literature is an indication of their intimate connection. As Schon (1984) observed, managers should be leaders, but not all leaders need be in management positions. This indicates a close relationship between the two tasks. Both leadership and management of organisations are essential for their successful operation and there is a great deal of overlap, particularly in respect of motivating people and giving a sense of purpose to the organisation.

An identifiable trend over the last few years has been to identify leadership with the more formative and proactive aspects of the direction of an organisation's affairs. In this way leadership is associated with such activities as problem solving (Leithwood and Steinbach, 1995), formulating and communicating a strategy based on a vision of a better future (Fidler *et al.*, 1996) and inspiring followers to strive towards it. Management is assigned to a more supportive role. This support involves planning and systematic procedures to ensure that activities resulting from leadership activities actually happen. Procedures for maintaining the steady-state are consigned to the area of administration. Diagrammatically this may be illustrated as shown in Figure 4.1.

This formulation can be helpful in demonstrating the need to consider the future and take an organisation forward in a way that engenders the support of all who work there. It also indicates the need for systematic procedures to be planned and put in place to ensure that developments take place and problems are solved. Clearly these two activities are complementary and have to be synchronised.

> Organizations which are overmanaged but underled eventually lose any sense of spirit or purpose. Poorly managed organizations with strong charismatic leaders may soar temporarily only to crash shortly thereafter. The challenges of modern organizations require the objective perspective of the manager as well as the brilliant flashes of vision and commitment that wise leadership provides.
> (Bolman and Deal, 1991, pp. xiii–xiv)

In terms of personal flair and individualism this formulation implies that leadership is likely to be high in these aspects and the more routine and systematic work of management is likely to be more mundane. This may be only a matter of degree. Active leadership is likely to be concerned with exceptional situations where new activities and new ways of working are being contemplated. In this case every situation will demand a unique outcome even if there are common features. However, whilst management may be seen as a more systematic set of procedures, these too will have to be tailored to the situation. And, there will be less active phases of leadership where continuing to give meaning to the work of followers and to stimulate the efforts of followers will be important.

Perspectives on leadership

Five perspectives on leadership are included here:

1   situational leadership;
2   four frames of leadership;
3   leading professional and chief executive;
4   moral leadership;
5   curricular leadership.

This is in the belief that no one theory nor any one approach can subsume the complexities of leadership and, indeed, that a search for such an all-encompassing theory may be illusory. It is, therefore, a matter of choosing one or more conceptualisations of leadership that appear appropriate in order to understand a particular situation and, using these, to formulate actions. The choice of conceptualisation will depend on the situation and on the purpose for which understanding is being sought.

The effectiveness of leadership needs some discussion. The word effectiveness may suggest objectivity, but any assessment of effectiveness will involve varying degrees of subjectivity depending on who assesses and how. There are two distinct but related approaches. Assessment can be made on the basis of the effectiveness of the process or of the outcomes, i.e.

• the actions of leaders;
• the results of the actions of leaders.

Where leaders are carrying out necessary but unpopular tasks to achieve desirable ends there may be very different assessments resulting from these two approaches. In addition to these differences, there may also be differences depending on who makes any judgement and on the basis on which it is made. Some bases for judging leadership behaviour in school are by reference to:

• personal subjective attitudes;
• general moral and philosophical principles;
• theoretical leadership prescriptions.

The first assessment is a very personal one from those who are directly influenced by leadership. A number of research studies ask followers to rate leadership effectiveness in this way. Such raters have to weigh in their ratings such disparate factors as: the accomplishments of the leader; the appropriateness of the leader's style of operating; their personal likes and dislikes of the leader and his or her actions. The case of unpopular actions by a leader carrying out an unpleasant task but bringing it to a successful conclusion illustrates the ambiguities of such an approach assessing leadership.

The second form of assessment asks for a judgement of the actions of the leader based upon moral and philosophical principles. If this were not to be a personal value judgement, the principles on which the assessment was to be made would need to be specified and agreed. The third assessment is based on the extent to which specified theoretical leadership prescriptions have been followed.

Assessment of outcomes also presents difficulties. First, in the choice of outcomes and, second, in the assessment of the leader's part in the attainment of outcomes. The leader is likely to have played a major part in the formulation of intended school outcomes. In so far as these are not wholly shared by all assessors there will be differences in value judgements about the desirability of different outcomes. Whilst an assessment of the leader's part in attaining specified school outcomes may eliminate some difference due to different value positions, it is also problematic. This is because of the complexity of school outcomes and their unclear relationship to individual process measures. There may be difficulties in identifying a direct leadership influence on outcomes. Instead, effectiveness as judged by the effect of leadership on intermediate variables connected to school outcomes, such as staff attitudes, may be all that is feasible.

A further complication raised by Brass (1960) is that of the timescale for the judgement of results. He argued that leadership should be judged in the longer term, since short-term effects may have been accomplished to the detriment of longer term ones. He therefore suggested calling short-term effects 'successful' leadership to distinguish it from longer term effectiveness.

Situational leadership

Much of the early writing on leadership was concerned with prescription and, implicitly, with 'one best way' type approaches. This was generally done without explicitly recognising the inherent inflexibility of practice that was being suggested for a diverse range of situations. One major breakthrough in conceptualisations of leadership has been the recognition that a contingent or situational approach is necessary. What is appropriate and likely to work well will depend on a number of factors. One important factor will be the context in which leadership is to operate. Hersey and Blanchard (1988) describe situational approaches as being in the 'mainstream of leadership thought'.

Early approaches to the two factor theory of management styles – concern for people and relationships, and concern for task and outcomes – asserted that there was one best style (Blake and Mouton, 1964). Other writers went on to propose conditions for effectiveness. Other key variables in choosing an effective leadership style have been proposed, for example:

- leader's preferred style of leadership;
- maturity of followers;
- expectations of followers;
- nature of the task to be undertaken

(see Hersey and Blanchard, 1988; Yukl, 1989 for a discussion). Thus situational or contingency theories of management and leadership were proposed. The appropriate leadership style depended on the context. As always, theoretical constructs walk the tightrope between, on the one hand, trying to take every factor into account and being more accurate, but at the expense of becoming increasingly complex or, on the other hand, trying to oversimplify in the interests of comprehensibility, but failing to capture important aspects of the situation.

Bolman and Deal's four frames

In a similar vein to the present article, Bolman and Deal (1991) have attempted to widen the range of formulations of leadership, from which leaders may choose to illuminate their practice

> The basic aim . . . is to expand and enrich the ideas and styles that leaders and managers apply to problems and dilemmas. Too often they bring too few ideas to the challenges that they face. They live in psychic prisons because they cannot look at old problems in a new light and attack old challenges with different and more powerful tools – they cannot *reframe*.
>
> (p. 4)

From a study of leaders of large commercial organisations they have suggested a framework with four approaches to leadership:

- structural;
- human relations;
- political;
- symbolic.

They recognise that appropriate leadership needs to be situational, but they also recognise that individual leaders will have a preferred, if not dominant, style that reflects their own personality. Each style has advantages and disadvantages. They identify successful combinations where a particular style of a chief executive is complemented by a different style from another senior manager in the organisation. The result of analysing the leader's style and comparing this with the needs of the organisation at that particular time may throw up additional leadership requirements for the organisation to be successful.

The structural framework is largely focused on a rational view of management. Leadership concentrates on goals and uses rational analysis and formal mechanisms operating through a hierarchy of control and a well-designed organisational structure. Planning involves effectiveness and efficiency. The human relations framework, on the other hand, concentrates on the behavioural aspects of management and harnessing the motivation and commitment of employees. Individuals are delegated substantial tasks and allowed the freedom to perform them in their own ways by taking initiative. Much management training has emphasised these human relations skills.

The political framework recognises that individuals both within and without the organisation have their own private agendas of interests. Thus there will be seats of power that may lead to conflicts if skilful political arts of forming coalitions, bargaining and negotiation are not used (Hoyle, 1986; Ball, 1987). The political leader acts as advocate and builds coalitions.

The symbolic framework is also referred to as visionary leadership and Burns (1978) also used the term transformational leadership for a similar activity. Each of these terms helps to sketch the facets of this this framework. Transformational leadership is contrasted with steady-state or transactional leadership. Transactional leadership is concerned with carrying out routine tasks rather than taking on new challenges (this would be called management or administration in the formulation offered in this article). Visionary leadership is concerned with providing followers with insights into the nature of new challenges and what is to be achieved. The symbolic leader is a creator of possibilities (Bolman and Heller, 1995). This is more than merely concerned with immediate tasks and represents a distant improved future. It provides followers with a rationale for their work. The vision of the future may be drawn up collaboratively, but the leader has the task of articulating this in a compelling way. Finally, symbolism gives meaning to the task and provides a way of demonstrating the new approach and inspiring and giving confidence to organisation members.

Leading professional and chief executive

Situational leadership has been drawn from general ideas on the leadership of organisations and is relevant to many kinds of organisations. However, schools have some special features that may have implications for leadership at both theoretical and practical levels:

- diffuse, value-based and, to some extent, self-selected outcomes;
- means and ends are both important;
- the organisation has a moral purpose;
- the core workforce is professional.

Whilst there is a certain role and function that the head of any organisation needs to discharge, including directing the core processes of the organisation and integrating functions such as staffing, finance and external relations, there may be additional requirements of a leader in a professionally staffed organisation and there may be still further requirements of a leader of a school (Morgan *et al.*, 1983). A leader needs to act as chief executive in a managerial capacity and as a leader in the symbolic and political senses. In addition, the leader of a professionally staffed organisation also needs to be the leading professional or at least a leading professional (Hughes, 1985). He or she must espouse professional values and possess appropriate professional knowledge and judgement. If the headteacher is to lead and influence classroom practice, this has implications for the quality and recency of the pedagogic and curricular knowledge which he or she needs.

In England and Wales delegation of financial and other management activities to school level together with a greater responsibility for school success has encouraged headteachers to take on the perspective of a chief executive. Research by Jenkins (1997) shows that, after a little reluctance, they have accommodated to this task. However, since the advent of school inspections in 1993 by professional educators under a framework devised by the Office for Standards in Education (OFSTED), which has a clear focus on classroom processes, there has been a refocusing of headteachers' attention on professional issues.

Moral leadership

Organisational culture is not only a reflection of 'how we do things around here' but also the more value-laden 'how we think it right to do things here'. There has recently been increasing attention to the ethical principles of management. Whilst this applies to all organisations, there are some features that are specific to schools. Schools are likely to have either an implicit or an explicit requirement to contribute to the moral education of the young. Thus school leaders should be moral leaders (Sergiovanni, 1991). This raises questions about whether leaders should have certain moral qualities and whether their personal actions should have particular moral require- ments. There are further questions concerned with whether the education of children needs to be organised in a moral way in order to develop adults with a moral sense. Finally, does the management of a moral institution have to be conducted in a specially moral way in view of the moral education (of children) within them?

Duignan and Macpherson (1992), in their theory of educative leadership, ascribe a 'realm of ideas' to judgements about what is of value and what is significant in the education of children. They see this as a third component, in addition to manage- ment and leadership, which is required of an educational leader. Within this realm of ideas some writers attach importance to the moral qualities of the leader and the moral processes that go on in schools.

Some argue the need for coherence in these matters and therefore argue for a democratic form of school management in view of the need to educate children for a democratic society (Bottery, 1992). Others argue that a school's purpose is educational no matter whether this is applied to children or to staff. Thus staff should also be learning in a school, with the implication that this learning should also be moral learning.

Curricular leadership

The concept of a leading professional implies that the headteacher has an impact on the professional work of the school, including the teaching and learning that goes on in classrooms. If this is to be more than rhetoric, then interesting questions concern the mechanisms by which this might take place.

Instructional leadership. In the USA this issue has been taken up under the title 'instructional leadership'. This can be considered from two points of view – the tasks to be achieved (or functional approach) and the means by which these tasks are achieved (or process approach).

Functional approach. Krug (1992), writing in a USA context, identifies five components of instructional leadership:

1   defining mission;
2   managing curriculum and instruction;
3   supervising teaching;
4   monitoring student progress;
5   promoting instructional climate.

   1 *Defining mission.* The mission includes both the ends of schooling and the means of educating. These need to be communicated to staff and pupils. The inference is that the principal does this, although he or she could use participative means to decide on both of these.
   2 *Managing curriculum and teaching.* Managing curriculum and teaching has two components. First, there is the organisation of curriculum and teaching (Bossert *et al.*, 1982). This involves co-ordination of the work of teachers and the making of school-level decisions about, for example, pupil grouping and time allocations for subjects. Second, leaders need to provide information that teachers need to plan their classes and also stimulate curriculum development. Thus leaders need up-to-date knowledge of curriculum research and theoretical developments.
   3 *Supervising teaching.* In the USA, principals have a role in the summative evaluation of teaching, but, it is argued, there needs to be a more formative element focusing on development rather than evaluation. This would involve working with each teacher.
   4 *Monitoring student progress.* Student progress is the reason for the whole activity and so the principal's role is to understand student assessment and to check on progress 'in ways that help teachers and students improve and help parents understand where and why improvement is needed' (Krug, 1992, p. 433).
   5 *Promoting positive teaching climate.* Experienced principals recognise that 'their real primary objective is to motivate people by creating conditions under which people want to do what needs to be done' (Krug, 1992, p. 433) and protecting them from external interference. By affecting the school-level climate and culture,

the expectation is that the classroom-level climate and culture may also be influenced.

Whilst further work can be done in elaborating these features, this obscures a sense of coherence for the whole undertaking. From work with a small number of principals, Krug (1992) found that the way in which school leaders construed the events was more important than each individual activity in terms of overall effectiveness.

Process approach. The five categories above give a functional view of the components of curriculum leadership, but give little insight into how they may be accomplished. A number of writers have offered suggestions. Firestone and Wilson (1985) identified three means of linking the behaviour of the principal to classroom processes:

- bureaucratic and structural linkages;
- direct interpersonal linkages;
- cultural linkages.

Bossert *et al.* (1982) drew attention to the importance of political mechanisms for negotiating and bargaining among different power bases in a school. Whilst these conceptualisations of the means by which curriculum leadership may be accomplished are not the same as the Bolman and Deal formulation of leadership in non-educational organisations, they do show a remarkable similarity.

1 *Bureaucratic and structural linkages.* The structural mechanisms for linking principal behaviour to classroom teaching (Leitner, 1994) include the following: policies, rules and procedures; plans and schedules; vertical information systems; supervision and evaluation. These include clarifying in general terms what has to be done, planning how it should be done, devising information systems to monitor what is being done and, finally, evaluating outcomes and processes.

2 *Direct interpersonal linkages.* These include working with and influencing individual teachers' classroom practice. This may be in association with classroom observation or more general one-to-one interaction.

3 *Cultural linkages.* Cultural linkages involve shared meanings and assumptions (Fidler, 1997). These assumptions are very powerful as a means of influencing actions because they are implicit and rarely questioned at the conscious level. Firestone and Wilson (1985) identify three cultural mechanisms: stories, icons and rituals. From a more general perspective, Schein (1992) has identified a range of primary and secondary embedding mechanisms. Many leadership actions may have a symbolic value in terms of indicating organisational priorities. Thus, what leaders pay attention to matters a great deal. There needs to be consonance between what are declared as priorities and what are seen to command time and resources. The importance of symbolic actions as a means of influencing the organisational culture should not be underestimated.

Firestone and Wilson (1985) point out that the effective schools research has rather tended to highlight individual principal behaviour and the effects of direct supervision of teachers and under-emphasised the more indirect structural and cultural linkages. They suggest that bureaucratic and cultural influences should reinforce each other.

References

Ball, S. J. (1987) *Micro-Politics of the School: Towards a Theory of School Organization*, London: Methuen.

Bennis, W. G. (1989) *On Becoming a Leader*, Reading, MA: Addison-Wesley.

Blake, R. R. and Mouton, J. S. (1964) *The Managerial Grid*, Houston, TX: Gulf Publishing.

Bolman, L. G. and Deal, T. E. (1991) *Reforming Organizations: Artistry, Choice and Leadership*, San Francisco: Jossey-Bass.

Bolman, L. G. and Heller, R. (1995) 'Research on school leadership: the state of the art', in Bacharach, S. B. and Mundell, B. (eds), *Images of Schools*, Thousand Oaks, CA: Corwin Press.

Bossert, S. T., Dwyer, D. C., Rowan, B. and Lee, G. V. (1982) 'The instructional management role of the principal', *Educational Administration Quarterly*, **18**(3), 34–64.

Bottery, M. (1992) *The Ethics of Educational Management*, London: Cassell.

Brass, B. M. (1960) *Leadership, Psychology and Organizational Behavior*, New York: Harper & Brothers.

Burns, J. M. (1978) *Leadership*, New York: Harper & Row.

Duignan, P. A. and Macpherson, R. J. S. (1992) 'A practical theory of educative leadership', in Duignan, P. A. and Macpherson, R. J. S. (eds), *Educative Leadership: A Practical Theory for New Administrators and Managers*, London: Falmer.

Fidler, B. (1997) 'Addressing the tensions: culture and values', in Fidler, B., Russell, S. and Simkin, T. (eds), *Choices for Self-Managing Schools: Autonomy and Accountability*, London: Paul Chapman.

Fidler, B., Edwards, M., Evans, B., Mann, P. and Thomas, P. (1996) *Strategic Planning for School Improvement*, London: Pitman.

Firestone, W. A. and Wilson, B. L. (1985) 'Using bureaucratic and cultural linkages to improve instruction: the principal's contribution', *Educational Administration Quarterly*, **21**(2), 7–30.

Hallinger, P. and Heck, R. H. (1996) 'Reassessing the principal's role in school effectiveness: a review of empirical research, 1980–1995', *Educational Administration Quarterly*, **32**, 5–44.

Hersey, P. and Blanchard, K. (1988) *Management of Organizational Behavior: Utilizing Human Resources* (5th edn), Englewood Cliffs, NJ: Prentice-Hall.

Hoyle, E. (1986) *The Politics of School Management*, London: Hodder & Stoughton.

Hughes, M. (1985) 'Leadership in professionally staffed organisations', in Hughes, M., Ribbins, P. and Thomas, H. (eds), *Managing Education: The System and the Institution*, London: Cassell.

Immegart, G. L. (1988) 'Leadership and leader behavior', in Boyan, N. J. (ed.), *Handbook of Research on Educational Administration*, New York: Longman, 259–77.

Jenkins, H. O. (1997) 'Leadership: a model of cultural change', in Fidler, B., Russell, S. and Simkins T. (eds), *Choices for Self-Managing Schools: Autonomy and Accountability*, London: Paul Chapman.

Krug, S. E. (1992) 'Instructional leadership: a constructivist perspective', *Educational Administration Quarterly*, **28**(3), 430–43.

Leithwood, K. and Steinbach, R. (1995) *Expert Problem Solving: Evidence from School and District Leaders*, New York: SUNY.

Leitner, D. (1994) 'Do principals affect student outcomes: an organizational perspective', *School Effectiveness and School Improvement*, **5**, 219–38.

Morgan, C., Hall, V. and McKay, H. (1983) *The Selection of Secondary School Headteachers*, Milton Keynes: Open University Press.

Murphy, J. (1988) 'Methodological, measurement, and conceptual problems in the study of instructional leadership', *Educational Evaluation and Policy Analysis*, **10**(2), 117–39.

Ogawa, R. T. and Bossert, S. T. (1995) 'Leadership as an organizational quality', *Educational Administration Quarterly*, **31**(2), 224–43.

Schein, E. H. (1992) *Organizational Culture and Leadership* (2nd edn), San Francisco: Jossey-Bass.

Schon, D. A. (1984) 'Leadership as a reflection-in-action', in Sergiovanni, T. J. and Corbally, J. E. (eds), *Leadership and Organizational Culture: New Perspectives on Administrative Theory and Practice*, Urbana, IL: University of Illinois Press.

Sergiovanni, T. J. (1991) *The Principalship: A Reflective Practice Perspective* (2nd edn), Needham Heights, MA: Allyn & Bacon.

Yukl, G. A. (1989) *Leadership in Organizations* (2nd edn), Englewood Cliffs, NJ: Prentice-Hall.

Chapter 5

Leadership for learning: re-engineering 'mind sets'

John West-Burnham

This is an edited version of an article previously published in *School Leadership & Management*, 17, 2, 1997.

The purpose of this article is to explore the extent to which the language that is used in talking about leadership in schools is compatible with the notion that learning is the core purpose of schools. The semantics of leadership are fundamental to the creation of meaning and so to perceptions, expectations and behaviour. For Sergiovanni (1992) this

> has to do with the mindscapes, or theories of practice, that leaders develop over time, and with their ability, in the light of these theories, to reflect on the situations they face.
>
> (p. 7)

He quotes Diana Lam:

> I believe leadership is an attitude which informs behaviour rather than a set of discrete skills or qualities, whether innate or acquired.
>
> (p. 1)

Attitudes and 'theories of practice' are constructs derived from a prevailing culture and expressed, reinforced and elaborated into practice through language. The vocabulary, definitions and metaphors of leadership will be powerful forces in formulating attitudes, expressed, as they are, through the symbolism of schools, the content of training and development activities and the discourse that is employed in all the events that inform the culture of a school.

If schools are to respond to the fundamental changes that are taking place in social and economic terms, then it is necessary to re-conceptualise leadership. In British society in particular much of the formulation of the concept of leadership is essentially nineteenth century in origin. People in Britain are subjects, not citizens, and this has a profound impact on how the language of leadership has developed and the way in which associated behaviour is accepted. In essence, leadership is expressed in terms of individuality, hierarchy and essentially masculine language.

This has produced a culture of formal accountability, control and dependency. However much this is mitigated by personal characteristics, the fact remains that most schools are essentially archaic in organisational terms, resembling classic bureaucracies that, by definition, lack flexibility, adaptability and the potential to be transformed. If a school, or any organisation, is to be capable of transforming itself, then it has to be led by people who are capable of personal transformation. If schools are to re-engineer themselves, then one of the starting points has to be re-engineering the perceptions of leadership.

One of the most powerful determinants of the mindscape or attitude of leadership is experience. The experience of leadership in many schools is expressed through a number of key concepts; for example, *Head*teacher, *Senior Management* team, *Line* management, *Head* of department, etc. Although the practice can and does vary, the underlying mindscape is one of hierarchy, control and linearity. Somewhat paradoxically, this language is combined with that of professionalism. Saul (1992) characterises the situation thus:

> The myth of salvation through efficient management is now so strong that no one pays much attention to the premise upon which the new elites are being educated.

> Efficiency. Professionalism. A belief in 'right' answers, which can only be produced by professionals.

One of the results of this has been a tendency to express leadership as 'super-management'; leaders are more competent at a wider range of tasks. Thus the model of headship is one of omnicompetence: the skilled classroom practitioner plus curriculum leader, plus technical expert, plus all the manifestations associated with being the figurehead. It is no wonder that so many headteachers seek early retirement or suffer a range of work-related illnesses. The job as historically constituted is almost impossible.

An implication of this view is the formulation of the role of the teacher and the status of the curriculum. Both in terms of content and delivery, the National Curriculum is predicated as a control culture based on the right answers. This is manifested in the often significant confusions between the functions of teaching and learning; the inference, for example, that there is a logical correlation between the two and that efficiency in the former will necessarily lead to the latter taking place. The consequence of a hierarchically based mindset for leadership has a number of implications for the implementation of learning in schools: automatic, cohort-related, chronological progression; time-constrained compartmentalisation; assessment based on 'right' answers; emphasis on the recording of information.

What emerges is a picture of uniformity, dependence and an implicit definition of learning that is generic and essentially passive. Of course, this is a stereotype and caricature, but the absence of appropriate definitions of leadership and learning, at the very least, allows the possibility of elements of what has been described to be found in schools. However, even if the reality is much softer than implied, there are still serious doubts that the underlying culture described is an appropriate one for the changing context in which schools will have to operate.

Schools are moving into an era that has the potential to challenge every existing premise on which current notions of leadership and learning are posited. Four key trends can be identified.

First, as the self-managing school movement reaches maturity, notably in England and Wales, the level of significance attached to institutional leadership and management will increase. This is a direct function of prevailing models of accountability, which are both personal to the headteacher in terms of legal and contractual issues and specific to the institution in terms of inspections, league tables, etc. Schools are increasingly vulnerable in that the historic support mechanisms and limited public exposure have been replaced by direct answerability. The quality of decision making at school level is becoming increasingly important as mistakes and failures are visited directly on the institutions and its members. Errors or omissions in planning, budgeting, staff deployment, etc. have direct, immediate and specific consequences.

Second, and directly related to the first point, is the increasing emphasis being placed on performance at institutional and personal levels. The need to demonstrate value added, value for money, year-on-year improvement, target achievement, etc. has fundamentally altered the view of the school as one stage in a lifelong process where outcomes may not be manifested for many years. The growing importance being attached to results, usually in a quantitative form, calls into question the view of learning as an iterative process.

Third, these first two trends are taking place in the context of exponential social, economic and technological change. Caldwell and Davies have explored the implications of these trends in more detail elsewhere in this volume; the issue for schools is the extent to which they can legitimise the way in which they function in the context of rapid environmental change. It may be that the current formulations of leadership and learning are correct and appropriate, but if education is a function of society and society is changing, then the a priori conditions on which schooling is based at the very least has to be visited and re-affirmed. There is the possibility that schools will become increasingly dysfunctional because they are working to mindscapes which owe more to nineteenth-century maps of Africa (vast tracts of land labelled 'unexplored' and then turned into colonies with straight line boundaries totally ignoring local realities) than to the latest satellite images.

Fourth, and perhaps most significantly, is the growing awareness that the world is not linear, but is rather complex and chaotic. Most prevailing orthodoxies in management and learning assume a linear and controllable universe,

> But chaos theory has proved these assumptions false. The world is far more sensitive than we had ever thought. We may harbour the hope that we will regain predictability as soon as we can learn how to account for all variables, but in

fact no level of detail can ever satisfy the desire. Iteration creates powerful and unpredictable effects in non-linear systems. In complex ways that no model will ever capture, the system feeds back on itself, enfolding all that has happened, magnifying slight variances, encoding it in the system's memory – and prohibiting prediction, ever.

(Wheatley, 1992, p. 127)

Almost every teacher will recognise what Wheatley is describing – it is the dynamics of the classroom and staffroom, meetings and lessons, interviews and plans. Most importantly, Wheatley is describing the learning process, where each child in the class is a variable and each child is made up of a complex range of variables that determine how they might learn. Equally, every school leader spends most of his or her time managing unpredictability – yet this is rarely reflected in role descriptions, the deployment of time, organisational structures, etc. One of the reasons why schools can be such demanding places to work in (for children and adults) is that people have to live in a state of permanent tension between the superficial simplicity of management and the deep complexity of learning and leading.

If schools are not to become asynchronous, then the way that a school is led has to become a macrocosm of the learning process: in design terminology, form has to follow function. The language that is used to talk about leadership has to be changed to reflect the world in which leaders can lead and learners can learn. This is an incredibly complex task, but it is one that we regularly engage in; joining the staff of a new school, a club or even getting married involve developing (or re-aligning) our vocabularies that determine our understanding of the way we are to function, to be together. As Sergiovanni (1996) puts it:

> The heart and soul of school culture is what people believe, the assumptions they make about how schools work, and what they consider to be true and real. These factors in turn provide a *theory of acceptability* that lets people know how they should behave . . . Efforts to change school cultures inevitably involve changing theories of schooling and school life.
>
> (p. 3)

Theories are mental constructs and as such are the products of our choice of formulations to describe the reality we wish to create. Much of our social understanding is created by ostensive definitions – relating a name to an object or process. The terms leadership and learning continue to be applied to processes that are no longer valid or appropriate. The process of creating meaning is described by St Augustine in the *Confessions* (quoted by Wittgenstein, 1968)

> Thus, as I heard words repeatedly used in their proper places in various sentences, I gradually learnt to understand what objects they signified; and after I had trained my mouth to these signs, I used them to express my own desires.
>
> (p. 3)

The rest of this article is concerned with identifying which words should be used, what are the 'proper places' and how everyone in the school can be helped to express their own desires. In the context of (a) the changing world that has already been described and (b) the need for leadership to be reformulated to make it logically consistent with the learning process, the following concepts are proposed:

- intellectualism;
- artistry;
- spirituality;
- moral confidence;
- subsidiarity;
- emotional intelligence.

There are two important points to be made about this list. First, there is a danger with any list that a hierarchy of significance will be imposed on it. This is not intended, indeed, the important thing is to see the six elements as inter-dependent and contributing to a holistic view of the nature of leadership. Second, these are all elusive concepts, subject to a variety of interpretations and applications.

A helpful metaphor is provided by Valerie Stewart (1990) in *The David Solution*

> When Michelangelo looked at the block of marble he was to carve, he looked beyond the outside and saw the shape of the statue he was to create. He could see the real beauty hidden within the waste.
>
> (p. 1)

The process of personal growth, development and change has to start with a visualisation of how we want to be. David was a unique personal creation that can be understood by all who see it. A parallel metaphor for the school might be the building of a cathedral. The patron's vision had to be interpreted by the architect whose drawings had in turn to be interpreted by a wide variety of skilled workers. The minutae of specific tasks were held together and made meaningful by an overarching vision that had to be understood, interpreted and translated into actions. In both cases, David and the cathedral, the vision had to be made meaningful through specific intent 'you just chip away the bits that don't look like David' (p. IX); each mullion, gargoyle and piece of stained glass had to be put in place.

If the primary purpose of educational leadership is to facilitate learning, then what follows is an attempt to describe the appropriate components − even the most spectacular flying buttress is eventually rooted in the foundations and secured to the main body of the building. There is a danger in describing the six elements separately − they might be interpreted as being discontinuous, whereas the argument here is that they are inter-related elements of a holistic model.

Intellectualism

One of the most depressing outcomes of the self-managing schools movement coupled with the introduction of a national curriculum and its associated testing regimes is the increasing emphasis on school leadership and management as a technical skill. Increasing levels of definition, specification and imposed goal setting have served to diminish the creative and critical components of leading and managing. Prescription of the right answers and associated models of accountability may have contributed to the creation of an accepting and conformist culture. Giroux (1988) argues for teachers as 'transformative intellectuals' because

> The category of intellectual is helpful in a number of ways. First, it provides a theoretical basis for examining teacher work as a form of intellectual labour, as opposed to defining it in purely instrumental or technical forms. Second, it clarifies the kinds of ideological and practical conditions necessary for teachers to function as intellectuals. Third, it helps to make clear the role teachers play in producing and legitimating various political, economic and social interests through the pedagogies they utilise. By viewing teachers as intellectuals, we can illuminate the important idea that all human activity involves some form of thinking.
>
> (p. 125)

The assertion of the role of teacher as intellectual is essential if the educative and transformational role of schooling is to be refined and strengthened. At no point in the development of educational practice – whether at national policy level or decisions about learning strategies in schools and classrooms – are there uncontentious decisions. The process of being an educator is the process of making decisions, of choosing and interpreting the outcomes in ideological and practical terms. Policies may be prescribed at a variety of levels, but the implementation of those policies involves 'forms of knowledge, language practices, social relations and values that are particular selections and exclusions from a wider culture' (p. 126). Decisions as to modes of practice involve the conscious legitimisation of specific options; that legitimisation has to be an intellectual process if it is not to be reductionist, bureaucratic and a denial of the social purposes of education as opposed to training.

A further dimension to the concept of the 'teacher-as-intellectual' is that it is very difficult to see how the notion of the 'reflective practitioner' can be developed except in the context of an intellectual perspective. Reflective practice implies the ability to conceptualise, analyse, establish causal relationships, draw conclusions, etc. These qualities are at the heart of effective pedagogic practice, just as they are central to the learning process and therefore have to be axiomatic to any notion of leadership.

Said (1996) argues that one of the greatest barriers to the true functioning of the intellectual is the 'attitude' of professionalism:

thinking of your work as an intellectual as something you do for a living, between the hours of nine and five with one eye on the clock, and another cocked at what is considered to be proper professional behaviour – not rocking the boat, not straying outside the accepted paradigms or limits, making yourself marketable and above all presentable, hence uncontroversial and unpolitical and 'objective'.

(p. 74)

He goes on (pp. 76–83) to identify four characteristics that mark out the true intellectual:

- love for, and unquenchable interest in, the larger picture;
- making connections;
- refusing to specialise;
- caring for ideas and values.

Said argues that the most appropriate counter to the imperatives of specialisation, expertise, power and authority is that

The intellectual today ought to be an amateur, someone who considers that to be a thinking and concerned member of a society one is entitled to raise moral issues at the heart of even the most technical and professionalised activity.

(p. 82)

For leaders in schools Said's four points offer a powerful parallel between the qualities of leadership and the overarching educative purpose of the school. If leaders function as intellectuals, then they are more likely to create a culture in which others are able to function in the same way, even though this might be extremely uncomfortable at times. However, given the moral nature and social significance of the educational process, the development of a critical and creative perspective as an essential component of leadership seems axiomatic.

Artistry

Stewart's (1990) metaphor of Michaelangelo's David provides a helpful model of the distinctions to be drawn between aspects of leadership and management. What makes the statue so distinctive is the artistry that transforms the physical material into a powerful image. Management can only function within the context of the vision of the completed work. Equally, the traditional management skills are unable to cope with the complexity of the creative process, they are the tools to facilitate it. Schemes of work, school timetables, etc. are literally pointless if they are not set within the context of a vision of the school as a learning community.

The leader as artist is thus a central notion to the process of realisation – translating ideals into concrete outcomes. Leaders need three qualities that are found in artists –

vision, creativity and the ability to communicate. Much has been written on the centrality of vision to quality, school improvement and school effectiveness. However, it is unlikely that any school can have a vision *per se*, it has to be a school understanding that is initially individually articulated.

The process that leads to the articulation of the vision is a complex one. In discussing the origins of the creative process (Gardner) 1993 argues

> At first accepting the common language or symbol system of the domain, each creator finds soon enough that it proves inadequate in one or more respects . . .

> . . . because the creative individual is dissatisfied with an ad hoc solution or because the particular problem can only be solved by a fundamental reorientation.
>
> (p. 33)

Given the context that schools are increasingly having to function in and the complexity of creating a learning organisation, it is essential that leaders are capable of the 'fundamental reorientation': conceptualising a new paradigm. This process is well known in the arts and sciences – Michaelangelo, Beethoven, Darwin, Einstein, etc. Similar qualities may well be appropriate to respond to the changing demands on schools. Reference to the intellectual giants of Western culture may be intimidating, each is unique (and male) and there are 25,000 schools in Britain! However, it is possible to argue for artistry and creativity to be given higher significance in our understanding of what constitutes the elements of leadership. According to Henry (1991)

> Change is occurring too fast for quantitative extrapolation, rather we will have to re-open the part of us that 'knows' in some other way; the sure judge with the courage to risk, the imagination to challenge, the sensitivity to know when to act and whom to involve.
>
> (p. XI)

For Henry creativity is

> a thinking process associated with imagination, insight, invention, innovation, ingenuity, intuition, inspiration and illumination.
>
> (p. 3)

What is highly significant about this listing is that it has much in common with what happens when people learn – the creative process is one of understanding a new phenomenon and this applies equally to student, teacher and headteacher. However, if the latter is managing rather than leading, the outcomes are more likely to be replication, reiteration, reinforcement and resignation.

There is an obvious tension between the creative individual and the needs of any organisation – the need for some stability in order to support innovation. Kao (1996) uses a musical analogy, jazz improvisation, to examine the potential conflict:

> A well-managed enterprise can't survive without some sheet music. It allows the management of complexity, without which the modern symphony orchestra . , would degenerate into cacophony. Most large-scale human interactions require their specific blue-prints, rituals, road maps, scripts, whatever, but they also require improvisation.

A detailed examination of the process of creativity is outside the remit of this discussion. The essential points to make are its centrality to appropriate models of leadership for learning and re-engineering and the fact that it can be developed in individuals.

> The real reason why we have done so very little about creativity is very simple. We have not understood it at all. We have not understood the process of ideation. We have not understood creativity because it is impossible to do so in terms of the passive information universe . . . No matter how hard we try in the wrong universe, we shall not understand creativity.
>
> (de Bono, 1991, p. 218)

If we are in the 'wrong universe' with regard to creativity, then the chances are that we are inhabiting the wrong universe with regard to leadership and learning. A very high warp factor may be needed to bring about the paradigm shift required.

The final element of artistry is the ability to communicate the new insight or vision. This assumes a sophisticated level of competence in order to bridge the gap between vision and understanding. The first performance of Stravinsky's *Rite of Spring* produced a riot in the audience. Stravinsky's vision was not understood and so not accepted. Many innovators have experienced a similar response – although riots in staff meetings are mercifully rare. Any product of a creative process will challenge existing norms and force new ways of thinking. In an educational context the issue of effective communication cannot depend on the passage of time to gain acceptance. The leader as artist has to educate her or his audience, to help them learn and understand and in this respect is no different to the effective teacher.

Spirituality

One of the limitations of competence approaches to management is that they miss the holistic view of the 'person'. Any discussion of the qualities of leadership has to address what is usually described as the 'spiritual', although this is an unsatisfactory word as it is not proposed to advocate a metaphysical or transcendental component *per se*. What is important is the recognition that many leaders possess what might be called 'higher order' perspectives. These may well be, and often are, represented by a specific religious affiliation. However, these perspectives may come from a range of sources – Covey (1992) refers to them as principles and characterises them thus:

> Principles are deep, fundamental truths, classic truths, generic common denominators. They are tightly interwoven threads running with exactness, consistency, beauty, and strength through the fabric of life.
>
> . . we can be secure in the knowledge that principles are bigger than people or circumstances, and that thousands of years of history have seen them triumph, time and time again.
>
> (p. 122)

Such principles are necessary for self-understanding, they are the means by which the individual is able to contextualise herself or himself in a chaotic, complex and often bizarrely contradictory world. A personal 'world view' is the basis of self-awareness, interpretation and an essential prerequisite to the process of reflection that is the key to personal learning and so to growth through transformation.

Most educational leaders will experience failure, disappointment, frustration, rejection and hostility at some time during their professional lives. The lack of a set of fundamental principles makes such reverses almost impossible to bear and may actually give rise to acute dysfunction. When faced with personal rejection we can either seek to reaffirm the principles by which we work or become reactive, pragmatic and expedient. As Gardner (1995) puts it

> The creator must in some sense embody his story, although he need not be saintly. . . . The individual who does not embody her messages will eventually be found out, even as the inarticulate individual who leads the exemplary life may eventually come to be appreciated.
>
> (p. 293)

Terry (1993) affirms this emphasis

> Faith in authenticity must undergird our actions. To be faithful, we must believe that any authentic act, no matter how small or seemingly insignificant is upheld by the universe as worthy and honourable. Leadership is spiritually grounded.
>
> (p. 274)

In terms of leadership development this area has often been seen as too 'personal' or too elusive to be regarded as a significant factor. Yet this is not a matter of seeking to establish religious faith (although a significant number of schools do require that information), but rather 'what do you believe in?' and 'how do you translate your beliefs into action?'.

This implies a degree of sophistication in being able to articulate a belief system and use it as a benchmark in a variety of personal and professional contexts. Given the sensitivity of personal beliefs systems this is an obvious area for development through reflection-in-action and mentoring.

Moral confidence

This quality is clearly closely related to spirituality in that a moral code is often the most overt manifestation of any personal belief system. However, because of its significance in the context of school leadership, it requires specific discussion.

The term 'moral confidence' is used to stress the importance attached to the capacity to act in a way that is consistent with an ethical system and is consistent over time. This requires confidence in terms of acceptance and understanding of the ethical system and the ability to interpret it in a wide range of situations. Schools are highly complex communities – there are no value-free decisions where the learning of young people is involved. Equally, schools are understood through the actions of individuals – what in the Total Quality movement are known as 'moments of truth', actions that are the direct and immediate reflection of a moral code. As Etzioni (1995) expresses it, schools

> provide experiences that tend to have deep educational effects, either positive or negative. Thus the first step towards enhancing the moral educational role of schools is to *increase the awareness and analysis of the school as a set of experiences.*
>
> (p. 104)

Two issues emerge from this assertion. First, the role of leaders in creating the 'awareness and analysis', i.e. a morally competent community. Second, the importance of leaders being able to validate their own actions in explicit moral terms. Sergiovanni (1996) reinforces this when he tells of the need

> to accept as part of our role responsibilities the necessity to practice leadership as a form of pedagogy. Aristotle would suggest that nothing could be more natural for schools since he defined pedagogy as a *good*; as a virtue.
>
> (p. 96)

'Leadership as pedagogy' (or practise what you preach) captures the essence of leadership for transformed schools. At a time of social and moral uncertainty the need for leaders to exemplify not so much a specific code but rather the existence and understanding of a personal ethical framework and the ability to translate it into validated and justified outcomes would seem to be essential. If the school *qua* organisation is going through turbulent times, then its moral purpose needs to be clear so that it can be debated, understood and applied. There are numerous issues in schools (child protection, equity, health and safety, access, etc.) that do not permit ambiguity in terms of practice.

The morally confident teacher is someone who can:

- demonstrate causal consistency between principle and practice;
- apply principles to new situations;

- create shared understanding and a common vocabulary;
- explain and justify decisions in moral terms;
- sustain principles over time;
- reinterpret and restate principles as necessary.

These attributes might appear to be a 'counsel of perfection' and they are undoubtedly demanding. However, they relate very closely to the concept of the leader as intellectual discussed above. In essence, moral confidence is the product of a learning process that makes direct use of higher order cognitive skills. The process of becoming and developing as a leader is the process of learning to think and of learning to learn.

Subsidiarity

It is impossible to dance if every joint is locked rigid, it is impossible to have a conversation if those involved only talk in monologues, it is impossible to lead if control is seen as the necessary condition. One of the problems with hierarchies is that they are manifested through increasing accountability, which appears to require increasing capacity to control. At a time of complexity, chaos and rapid change, leadership through control will inevitably produce brittle organisations and brittle people.

The relationship between leadership, hierarchy, power and control is endemic to British organisations. If nothing else, it is reflected in the symbols of status – in schools it is manifested in time and space. This apparently endemic view has been powerfully challenged by Charles Handy (1989), who quoted a papal encyclical:

> It is injustice, a grave evil and a disturbance of the right order for a large and higher organisation to abrogate to itself functions which can be performed efficiently by smaller and lower bodies.
>
> (p. 100)

This statement is a fundamental and profound challenge to the semantics of leadership in education and in particular the mindscapes that inform the behaviour of headteachers and principals. Subsidiarity confronts the status of headship, the validity of hierarchy and the notion of delegation as the basis of effective leadership. Control and delegation, and the cultural manifestations of seniority, are inappropriate models for organisations that have to change rapidly and that are primarily concerned with learning. Central to the concept of subsidiarity is the notion of trust – willingly *surrendering* power rather than delegating it and structuring organisations to institutionalise and reinforce trust. As Fukuyama (1995) puts it

> If people who have to work together in an enterprise trust one another because they are all operating to a common set of ethical norms, doing business costs less. Such a society will be better able to innovate organisationally, since

the high degree of trust will permit a wide variety of social relationships to emerge . . .

By contrast, people who do not trust one another will end up co-operating only under a system of formal rules and regulations, which have to be negotiated, agreed to, litigated and enforced, sometimes by coercive means.

(p. 27)

The purpose of leadership in the context of a culture of subsidiarity, or what Handy calls a federal organisation, is not to manage but rather to enable, facilitate, interpret, create meaning and to develop through trust.

Emotional intelligence

Emotional intelligence is a problematic concept – to many it is an oxymoron. Goleman (1996) has argued persuasively for the importance of emotional intelligence as a balance, if not an antidote, to the implicit supremacy of cognitive intelligence in the language that is used about individual and organisational life.

The concept is introduced in this context because schools are places in which emotions play a highly significant role. Relationships between student and student, teacher and student, teacher and teacher, parent and teacher, senior manager and teacher, etc. are often expressed in emotional terms. For institutions so founded on cognition and rationality, most people's experience of schools is in fact in terms of fear, joy, apprehension, worry, love, hate, grief, jealousy and resentment.

The process of transformation that, we are arguing, schools will have to go through is likely to increase the range and intensity of emotions. It therefore seems appropriate to argue for an understanding of the place of emotions in the repertoire of qualities desirable in a leader. Goleman (1996) quotes Gardner

Many people with IQ's of 160 work for people with IQ's of 100, if the former have poor intrapersonal intelligence and the latter a high one. And in the day-to-day world no intelligence is more important than interpersonal.

(p. 42)

Goleman (p. 43) argues that emotional intelligence is made up of five main domains:

1   knowing one's emotions;
2   managing emotions;
3   motivating oneself;
4   recognising emotions in others;
5   handling relationships.

Developing capability in each of these domains is an intimidating prospect, but as Goleman argues

The underlying basis for our level of ability is, no doubt, neural, but as we will see, the brain is remarkably plastic, constantly learning. Lapses in emotional skills can be remedied.

(p. 44)

The development of emotional intelligence in leaders is perhaps the most complex of all the qualities raised in this article, but

Imagine the benefits for work of being skilled in the basic emotional competencies – being attuned to the feeling of those we deal with, being able to handle disagreements so they do not escalate, having the ability to get into flow states while doing our work. Leadership is not domination, but the act of persuading people to work towards a common goal.

(p. 149)

Conclusion

This article has set out some of the possible variables in developing a new vocabulary for leadership in schools, so influencing the prevailing mindscapes and thus behaviour. If schools are to change in order to respond to a changing world, then a disjointed incremental approach is not appropriate, if for no other reason than the toll it takes. The response to profound externally imposed change (such as the 1988 Education Reform Act in England and Wales) has usually been based on piecemeal approaches derived from professional commitment, e.g. 'working harder'. This is reflected in the level of demand for early retirement, levels of stress-related illness, etc. Profound and fundamental changes in what has to be done have to be replicated in an equally significant shift in how it is done – and this has to start with the conceptualisation of leadership.

There is, of course, a need for the technical managerial components of leadership to be addressed through appropriate training. However, that training has to be contextualised, set within a mindscape that is responsive to a complex and chaotic world, schools that are focused on learning, individuals that are capable of personal transformation and growth and so able to lead schools for the twenty-first century rather than the nineteenth century.

References

Covey, S. (1992) *Seven Habits of Highly Effective People*, London: Simon & Schuster.
de Bono, E. (1991) *I Am Right, You Are Wrong*, London: Penguin Books.
Etzioni, A. (1995) *The Spirit of Community*, London: Fontana.
Fukuyama, F. (1995) *Trust: The Social Virtues and the Creation of Prosperity*, London: Hamish Hamilton.
Gardner, H. (1993) *Creating Minds*, New York: Basic Books.
Gardner, H. (1995) *Leading Minds*, New York: Basic Books.

Giroux, H. A. (1988) *Teachers as Intellectuals*, New York: Bergin & Garvey.

Goleman, D. (1996) *Emotional Intelligence*, London: Bloomsbury.

Handy, C. (1989) *The Age of Uncertainty*, London: Business Books.

Henry, J. (1991) *Creative Management*, London: Sage.

Kao, J. (1996) *Jamming: The Art and Discipline of Business Creativity*, London: Harper Collins.

Said, E. W. (1996) *Representations of the Intellectual*, New York: Vintage Books.

Saul, J. R. (1992) *Voltaire's Bastards*, New York: Vintage Books.

Sergiovanni, T. J. (1992) *Moral Leadership: Getting to the Heart of School Improvement*, San Francisco: Jossey Bass.

Sergiovanni, T. J. (1996) *Leadership for the School House*, San Francisco: Jossey Bass.

Stewart, V. (1990) *The David Solution*, Aldershot: Gower.

Terry, R. W. (1993) *Authentic Leadership: Courage in Action*, San Francisco: Jossey Bass.

Wheatley, M. J. (1992) *Leadership and the New Science*, San Francisco: Bennett-Koehler.

Wittgenstein, L. (1968) *Philosophical Investigations*, Oxford: Basil Blackwell.

Chapter 6

Leadership of school subject areas: tensions and dimensions of managing in the middle

Hugh Busher and Alma Harris

This is an edited version of an article previously published in *School Leadership & Management*, **19**, 3, 1999.

Introduction

Research evidence concerning school improvement underlines the importance of focusing change efforts at different levels within the organisation (Fullan, 1992; Hopkins *et al.*, 1994; Hopkins *et al.*, 1997). The largest study of differential school effectiveness in the UK highlighted the importance of differences between departments in explaining differences in school performance (Sammons *et al.*, 1997). It provided evidence that both schools and departments are differentially effective with pupils of different abilities and of different social and ethnic backgrounds. Furthermore, the study suggested a need to re-conceptualise school leadership more broadly to include leadership at middle management level. However, as Glover *et al.* (1998) have argued most recently, the distinction between middle and senior management remains blurred and leadership functions are still not adequately delineated, or defined. Yet, in view of the overwhelming evidence of the influence of departmental performance upon school performance, such clarity concerning leadership at middle management level would seem imperative.

Leadership: tensions and dimensions of managing in the middle

One of the fundamental tenets of school effectiveness and school improvement research concerns the powerful impact of leadership. Research findings from diverse countries and school contexts draw similar conclusions (e.g. van Velzen *et al.*, 1985; Ainscow *et al.*, 1994; Hopkins *et al.*, 1994; Stoll and Fink, 1996). Essentially, schools that are effective and have the capacity to improve are led by headteachers who make a significant and measurable contribution to the effectiveness of their staff. Whatever else is disputed about this complex area of activity, the centrality of leadership in the achievement of school effectiveness and school improvement remains unequivocal.

This broadening of interest in, and understanding of, the leadership role parallels the pattern of development of leadership theory generally. There has been an increasing emphasis within school development upon the links between leadership and the culture of the organisation. This has led to a move away from the notion of leadership as a series of transactions within a given cultural context towards a view of leadership as transformational, having the potential to alter the cultural context in which people work. This transformational leadership perspective, as Duignan and Macpherson (1992) explain, focuses on the moral values and value-laden activities of a leader and how these are disclosed to other colleagues. Blase and Anderson (1995) argue that leaders acting in this mode try to use power with, or through, other people rather than exercising control over them. Implicit in this view is also a notion of shared or devolved leadership activity where leadership activity is not chiefly the preserve of the headteacher.

UK research suggests that subject leaders can make a difference to departmental performance in much the same way as headteachers contribute to overall school performance (Sammons *et al.*, 1996; Harris *et al.*, 1996a and b; Harris, 1998). This departmental sphere of influence has been termed the 'realm of knowledge' because of the importance of the subject boundary (Siskin, 1994). Furthermore, it has been suggested that at the department level there is a major potential and possibility to influence whole school development. Huberman (1990, p. 5) states:

> From the artisan's logic, I would rather look to the department as the unit of collaborative planning and execution [since] in a secondary school this is where people have concrete things to tell one another and where the contexts of instruction actually overlap.

In hierarchical terms the head of department is a middle manager. He or she is not part of the senior management team, responsible for the overall strategic development of a school, but someone responsible for the operational work of others, namely classroom teachers. Site supervisors and senior office administrators might, along with heads of academic and pastoral departments in secondary schools, also be classed as middle managers, being operationally responsible for overseeing and developing the work of their colleagues.

In schools these organisational hierarchical distinctions are not neatly delineated. Many staff will be involved in a complex switching of roles and lines of accountability between different aspects of their work. For example, most teachers will be responsible to both academic and pastoral heads of department for different aspects of their work. The demands of these two arenas may conflict. Heads of academic departments will also be classroom teachers in their own or other subject areas. Heads of pastoral departments and senior staff will work in subject areas and be accountable for this aspect of their work to academic heads of department.

Within this complex matrix of leadership and accountability, heads of department are increasingly acknowledge to be key figures. Early research into the role of heads of department (Bailey, 1973; Busher, 1988; Earley and Fletcher-Campbell, 1989) was concerned mainly with the responsibilities and time pressures upon heads of department. Most recently, attention has turned towards their leadership role and the relationship between departmental leadership and the differential performance of departments (Bennett, 1995; Harris *et al.*, 1995; Turner, 1996; Sammons *et al.*, 1997; Harris, 1998).

This raises a number of important issues about the leadership role of subject leaders in schools and how they deal with the tensions between different functions of their role. Drawing upon the work of Glover *et al.* (1998) it is possible to identify four dimensions of the head of department's work. The first dimension concerns the way in which heads of department translate the perspectives and policies of senior staff into the practices of individual classrooms. This bridging or brokering function, although only perceived by the Teacher Training Agency (TTA, 1998) and the Office for Standards in Education (OFSTED) as one of the functions of subject leaders, remains a central responsibility. It implies a transactional leadership role, wherein heads of department make use of power – usually 'power over' others (Blase and Anderson, 1995) – to attempt to secure working agreements with departmental colleagues about how to achieve school and departmental goals and practices. Part of this role is the managing and allocating of resources.

A second dimension focuses on how heads of department encourage a group of staff to cohere and develop a group identity. The area, or areas, of subject knowledge that the department shares usually defines the boundaries of the group. An important role for the head of department, therefore, is to foster collegiality within the group by shaping and establishing a shared vision. This necessarily implies a leadership style that empowers others and that involves subject leaders using 'power with' or 'power through' other people to generate collaborative departmental cultures (Blase and Anderson, 1995). This style of leadership is people-oriented and requires a leadership approach that helps other people to transform their feelings, attitudes and beliefs. Transformational leaders not only manage structure but they also purposefully impact upon the culture in order to change it. Hence an important dimension of the head of department's work is to shape and manage departmental culture.

A third dimension concerns improving staff and student performance. At one level this implies a transactional leadership role for the head of department in monitoring the attainment of school goals and meeting particular prescribed levels of curriculum performance. On the other hand, as Glover *et al.* (1998) note, it suggests an important mentoring, or supervisory leadership role in supporting colleagues' development and the development of pupils academically and socially. It also draws on the expert knowledge of heads of department and that of their referent power as sources of power to bring about improvement in practice (French and Raven, 1968).

The final dimension of a head of department's work is a liaison or representative role. This requires them to be in touch with a variety of actors and sources of information in the external environment of the school and to negotiate, where necessary, on behalf of the other members of the department (Busher, 1988, 1992). One aspect of this dimension is in helping departmental colleagues keep in touch with others in their subject area and with the views and needs of colleagues in other school departments. Part of this dimension of the role, then, is representing the views of departmental colleagues to senior staff and other middle managers within the school (Busher, 1992).

These four dimensions of the head of department's leadership role create both complementary and potentially competing demands. They reflect the complexity of a management role within the middle of a hierarchy and reveal the tensions facing leaders in a middle management position. However, for individual heads of department this role is made even more challenging because of the wide variation in departmental structure and cultures. The very fact that departments vary in size, configuration, status, resource power and staff expertise makes the job of each head of department contextually different from that experienced by other heads of department either within the same school, or in other schools. Consequently, to explore fully the tensions and dimensions within this role, we must consider how different departmental cultures affect potential leadership performance.

In analysing departmental cultures so as to understand the problems involved in managing different types of departments, there seem to be four main parameters. The first relates to the structural organisational configuration of a department, i.e. size, membership, institutional location and subject affiliation. The second relates to the degree of social cohesion and collegiality within a department. Writers such as Hargreaves (1995) and Hopkins *et al.* (1994) have demonstrated how the dimensions of 'social cohesion' and 'social control' can delineate different types of school culture. Consequently, these dimensions are used as tools for exploring the social relationships and processes within a department. The third parameter focuses on the status or esteem in which a department is held. It concerns those socio-political forces that shape the relationship of a department to its wider organisational contexts both within and outside a school. The fourth parameter that invisibly permeates all these other three is that of power: in terms of what constitutes power in social situations (French and Raven, 1968; Foucault (in Ball, 1990); Siskin, 1994), the power imbalance between leaders and followers (Hofstede, 1991) and the strategies through which leaders and followers exercise power (Busher, 1992; Blase and Anderson, 1995), be it formal authority or informal influence.

Departmental structure: implications for leadership

The realm of academic departments in secondary schools presents a considerable range of organisational differentiation. Departments in secondary schools range from multidisciplinary departments such as design and technology departments, or science departments with many staff in them, to departments staffed by one or two people or even one person (the subject leader) and several part-time staff (e.g. a music department or history department). Furthermore, some larger departments may well have several subject leaders, each with a particular subject specialism, responsible for creating an inspiring vision in their area that fits within the overall vision of a faculty area. In such academic departments (e.g. a humanities, or science department), the head of faculty may supervise the work of a specialist subject area and also have responsibility for co-ordinating the work of the other subject leaders in the area (Kemp and Nathan, 1989; Blease and Busher, in press). This suggests that not only do heads of department face competing leadership demands but that they also have widely differing arenas in which to exercise their power.

In secondary schools different departmental structures can be easily defined by size, configuration, staff-membership and subject expertise. Using these defining features, we can identify five departmental types. The first two, and largest, contain many staff and possess generous resources. The first type is the 'federal' department, such as science faculties, or humanities departments. These are likely to contain and support the teaching of several subject areas. Yet these subject areas may work closely together because their subjects and pedagogies are perceived as cognate and their cultures are substantially homogeneous.

On the other hand some large multi-subject departments can be seen as primarily an administrative convenience, as in the case, perhaps, of some design and technology departments. These might be described as 'confederate' departments. Here, subject areas are allied together but share little in common. Confederate cultures are likely to be heterogeneous, with individual subject areas creating their own identities that may be in conflict.

A third type of large-scale department is the 'unitary' department, defined by a single subject area, e.g. English or mathematics. Only one area of subject knowledge would be taught within the unitary department, and this is likely to have a strong influence on its culture (Siskin, 1994).

Smaller than unitary departments, 'impacted' departments also teach only a single-subject area. These have very few staff, some of whom are part-time and/or teach other subjects too. They are likely only to have a few rooms in which to teach, and may have relatively small budgets. Although this type of department can be free-standing within a school's organisational structure – including departments such as music, history and geography – it can also be part of a larger federal department – a biology department in a science faculty, for example.

The fifth type of departmental structure can be termed 'diffuse'. For example, information technology may have no identifiable base in a school and may be taught by a wide variety of staff under the guidance of a school co-ordinator. It may be very difficult for the subject leader to create a sense of subject identity under these conditions. Consequently co-ordination may fall into a largely technical, instrumental process with the subject leader creating materials for the other staff to use. Such informal administrative processes are likely to be supplemented by infrequent team meetings focusing on predominantly instrumental matters.

These different departmental structures inevitably affect the leadership approaches of a head of department. The extent to which cognate subjects within a federal department actually work together in various strategic and operational ways will depend on the quality of leadership both of the whole faculty and of the semi-autonomous subject areas within it. Other factors likely to affect this process are the demands made upon it by school senior staff and the external environment. The historical development of the department and the formal and informal distribution of power and authority within it will also affect how it works. An implication, however, in the notion of a federal department is that the 'centre', held by the department or faculty leader, is sufficiently powerful organisationally to ensure that in key decisions, such as processes of change or resource allocation, the members of the department will work as a unit.

In confederate departments, however, the 'centre' is not sufficiently powerful to ensure the members of the department work together on key decisions. Consequently, leadership is likely to involve a great deal of micropolitical activity between the allied subject areas. Formal meetings might well be relatively formalised processes of statements of position by leaders of the subject areas, with the real negotiations taking place informally outside the meetings. The management of joint resources, including staff development, is likely to be a tense process, with each subject area making its own arrangements as far as possible.

In unitary departments, leadership is likely to display less obviously some of the more central characteristics of micropolitical activity found in the first two types of departments described. On the other hand, it will still include complementary formal and informal processes of interacting with and co-ordinating the work of staff and pupils. The more effective of these departments are likely to display a well-developed homogeneous culture.

In the smaller impacted departments, many of the dimensions of leadership may be constrained into a network of informal processes. There may be too few staff, or they may have other duties in other departments, to make formal processes worthwhile except as a gesture to the administrative demands of the school. Although the norms and procedures of the department are likely to be strongly upheld by the few full-time staff, they are likely to be held progressively more weakly by those with lesser organisational commitment to it. Leaders of such departments are likely to find themselves in weak positions when negotiating with senior staff.

As departmental structures vary in size, configuration and resource base, so they also differ in the cultural norms and values they establish. As departmental structures are enacted and create formal and publicly accepted rules, so cultures create informal and often implicit rules. Both represent forms of constraint upon the individual, and as such represent statements of power relationships between members of the organisation. However, just as structures are susceptible to both direct and organic change, so cultures are not fixed either. The possibility of creating a new set of norms to replace those of the existing culture is one potential form of departmental and whole school change.

Social cohesion and departments: implications for leadership

It has been consistently argued that unravelling the culture of a department will cast light on how teachers and support staff understand notions of collegiality and collaborative leadership (Ribbins, 1992; Busher and Saran, 1995; Sammons *et al.*, 1997). Schein (1990, p. 5) suggests that 'the only thing of real importance that leaders do is to create and manage culture', and Siskin (1994) makes a similar claim for departmental leaders. In this respect, heads of department have points of reference and influence that, in some sense, transcend many of the formal structures within the school. Consequently, their leadership style is fundamentally important in shaping the direction and cohesiveness of subject departments. Siskin maintains that 'collaborative', 'administrative', 'dictatorial' and 'non-leader' styles of leadership can be related to department cultures identified using the dimensions of 'inclusion' and 'commitment'. These dimensions can be used to identify different departmental cultures. Hence, it is important to explore the dynamic between departmental structure, culture and leadership style.

Subject departments are not just smaller pieces of the same school social environment, or bureaucratic labels, as Bennett (1995) points out. They are separate worlds, with their own

> ethnocentric way of looking at things. They are sites where distinct groups of people come together and together share in and reinforce the distinctive agreements on perspectives, rules and norms which make up subject cultures and communities.
>
> (Siskin, 1994, p. 81)

Departmental cultures, then, represent the enacted views, values and beliefs of teachers and support staff about what it means to teach students in particular subject areas within particular institutional contexts. These are moral relationships (Hodgkinson, 1991) rather than instrumental ones that exist both between the people in, for example, a subject department, and between them and their surrounding institutional and socio-political contexts. Such cultures will be represented through a variety of cultural artefacts (Samier, 1997), including rituals, ceremonies, language and other agreed educational practices that people undertake (Beare *et al.*, 1989).

A defining feature of departmental culture in secondary schools has been shown to be the nature and discourse of the academic subject knowledge (Siskin, 1994), which provides the focus of identity to a department. This is not merely the structure of school curriculum content, texts and tests, but also includes the values, methodologies of study and foci of work. These elements of its epistemology play a fundamental part in shaping teachers' individual approaches to teaching and learning and, hence, the departmental culture.

The development of this subject-oriented culture is of key importance in the creation of staff identities. To a teacher it is frequently the subject department, rather than the school, that is seen as the central and immediate unit of organisation (Little, 1995). Thus, subject departments often represent the primary point of reference or professional home for most teachers (Siskin and Little, 1995), especially those who perceive themselves as subject specialists (Bennett, 1995, p. 52). This process is helped by the subject department often being the most common organisational unit for organising secondary school teaching. Therefore, subject departments exhibit very powerful social relations functions in schools, as Goodson (1996) pointed out. Where teachers spend time together and work together, this can, positively, lead to the development of friendship groups. Conversely, subject departments can become sites of inter-personal rivalry. Where this conflict cannot be diffused through the trust between colleagues (Blase and Anderson, 1995; Stoll and Fink, 1996) it is likely to degenerate into confrontation or continuous friction. Thus the informal and formal relationships between teachers can create disparate working cultures between and within schools and departments. In the case of the least effective departments, research has indicated how dysfunctional staff relationships within a department can negatively affect departmental culture and performance (Harris, 1997, 1998).

The views on subject knowledge and pedagogy held by their heads of department are, then, of major concern to subject staff. Further, how well middle managers act as transformational leaders and exercise inter-personal skills will affect the extent to which they build a genuine collaborative culture (Blase, 1995). Stoll and Fink (1996) cite this as indicative of healthy departments and schools that are likely to bring about improvement in practice.

Subject departments have an administrative function (Goodson, 1996) in the functional organisation of secondary schools. They provide the structures and channels for managing the teaching and learning of students and staff. In doing so they tend to serve as arenas for communication between staff in distant parts of a school. In both these aspects, a department is likely to be judged by its members and its observers for the effectiveness of its processes. Where these processes are effective, the head of department as manager of these formal communications is in an influential position to shape the professional interactions and perceptions of staff. Control of these communication channels can also contribute to the strength and bargaining power of department heads in their claims for increased resources (Busher, 1992). Heads of department who know how to make contact and bargain with colleagues through an array of micropolitical processes are in a stronger position to implement or defend the policies of their departments than are those who do not. Subject departments therefore play important mediating roles between the demands of a subject area on staff and the demands of the school on them.

Local and national socio-political environments also have a major influence on the culture of schools and departments (Earley, 1998) and on members' leadership styles of heads. Glatter (1997) makes the point that researchers into the management of school organisations tend to overlook the importance and influence of external environment on internal school processes. Simkins et al. (1992) and Wallace (1993) point out the impact that the introduction of local management for schools in England and Wales has had on the internal workings of schools. Hargreaves (1994) debates how the roles of teachers are changing as a consequence of the changes in the socio-political contexts of their work.

Grace (1995) suggests that, in part, the relationships that formally appointed school leaders at any level develop with their teacher colleagues depends on how they view and respond to changes in the national socio-political environment. Hence, the culture of a department will be affected by how its leader mediates legal and curriculum changes facing schools from agencies in the national or local environment. Influencing leaders' actions and interpretations will be not only their subject expertise, but also their educational, social and political values.

A particular external influence on heads of department in secondary schools in England and Wales in the mid-to-late 1990s is that of the Office for Standards in Education (OFSTED). Through its inspection process, this agency sets a series of demands about how subject departments should be run in order to deliver what it considers to be quality teaching and learning. Heads of department, under the guidance of more senior staff, have to interpret and implement these demands. This external influence has reinforced hierarchical processes and strengthened imbalances of power between leaders and followers amongst staff at whatever level in a school. Successful heads of department are expected to have a clear awareness of what the OFSTED process expects of themselves and their colleagues and to be able to advise departmental colleagues on how to implement the required processes effectively. How heads of department act in these circumstances is likely to have a considerable impact on the culture of a department.

It is increasingly stated that effective management requires staff at all levels to be involved in decision making and policy formation. As Peters (1988, p. 23) remarked, writing within a business context, in a fully developed organisation, the front line person should be capable of being involved in strategy making. Heads of department are very much in the front line, but their degree of involvement in strategic matters or organisation decision making is likely to vary according to the nature of the organisation, the management approach of senior staff and the culture of the organisation.

References

Ainscow, M., Hopkins, D., Southworth, G. and West, M. (1994) *Creating the Conditions for School Improvement*, London: David Fulton Publishers.

Bailey, P. (1973) 'The functions of heads of departments in comprehensive schools', *Journal of Educational Administration and History*, **1**, 52–8.

Ball, S. (1990) *Foucault and Education: Discipline and Knowledge*, London: Routledge.

Beare, H., Caldwell, B. and Millikan, E. (1989) *Creating an Excellent School*, London: Routledge.

Bennett, N. (1995) *Managing Professional Teachers: Middle Management in Primary and Secondary Schools*, London: Paul Chapman.

Blase, J. (1995) 'The micropolitical orientation of facilitative school principals and its effects on teachers' senses of empowerment', paper presented at the *American Educational Research Association (AERA) Conference*, San Francisco, April.

Blase, J. and Anderson, G. L. (1995) *The Micropolitics of Educational Leadership: From Control to Empowerment*, London: Cassell.

Blease, J. and Busher, H. (1999) 'The role and management of laboratory technicians in secondary school science departments', *School Science Review*, **80**(293).

Busher, H. (1988) 'Reducing role overload for a head of department: a rationale for fostering staff development', *School Organisation*, **8**(1), 99–108.

Busher, H. (1992) 'The politics of working in secondary school: some teacher perspectives on their schools as organisations', unpublished PhD thesis, Leeds: University of Leeds, School of Education.

Busher, H. and Saran, R. (1995) 'Managing staff professionally', in Busher, H. and Saran, R. (eds), *Managing Teachers as Professionals in Schools*, London: Kogan Page.

Duignan, P. A. and Macpherson, R. J. S. (1992) *Educative Leadership: A Practical Theory for New Administrators and Managers*, London: Falmer Press.

Earley, P. (ed.) (1998) *School Improvement after Inspection? School and LEA Responses*, London: Paul Chapman.

Earley, P. and Fletcher-Campbell, F. (1989) *The Time to Manage?* Windsor: NFER/Nelson.

French, J. and Raven, B. (1968) 'The bases of social power', in Cartwright D. and Zander, A. (eds), *Group Dynamics, Research and Theory*, London: Tavistock Press.

Fullan, M. (1992) *The New Meaning of Educational Change*, London: Cassell.

Grace, G. (1995) *School Leadership: Beyond Education Management, an Essay in Policy Scholarship*, London: Falmer Press.

Glatter, R. (1997) 'Context and capability in educational management', *Educational Management and Administration*, **25**(2), 181–95.

Glover, D. C., Gleeson, D., Gough, G. and Johnson, M. (1998) 'The meaning of management: the development needs of middle managers in secondary schools', *Educational Management and Administration*, **26**(3), 279–92.

Goodson, I. (1996) *Studying School Subjects*, London: Falmer Press.

Hargreaves, A. (1994) *Changing Teachers Changing Times: Teachers' Work and Culture in the Post-Modern Age*, London: Cassell.

Hargreaves, D. (1995) 'School culture, school effectiveness and school improvement', *International Journal of School Effectiveness and School Improvement*, **6**(1).

Harris, A., Jamieson, I. M. and Russ, J. (1995) 'A study of "effective" departments in secondary schools', *School Organisation*, **15**, 283–99.

Harris, A., Jamieson, I. M. and Russ, J. (1996a) 'What makes an effective department?', *Management in Education*, **10**, 7–9.

Harris, A., Jamieson, I. M. and Russ, J. (1996b) 'How to be effective: what marks out departments where pupils achieve most', *Times Educational Supplement*, School Management Update, 10 November.

Harris, A. (1997) 'Differential departmental culture and strategies for change', paper presented at the *BERA Conference*, York, September.

Harris, A. (1998) 'Improving the effective department: strategies for growth and development', *Education Management and Administration*, **26**(3), 269–78.

Hodgkinson, C. (1991) *Educational Leadership: The Moral Art*, Albany: State University of New York Press.

Hofstede, G. (1991) *Cultures and Organisations*, New York: Harper Collins.

Hopkins, D., Ainscow, M. and West, M. (1994) *School Improvement in an Era of Change*, London: Cassell.

Hopkins, D., West, M., Ainscow, M., Harris, A. and Beresford, J. (1997) *Creating the Conditions for Classroom Improvement*, London: David Fulton.

Huberman, M. (1990) 'The model of the independent artisan in teachers' professional relations', paper presented at *AERA Conference*, Boston.

Kemp, R. and Nathan, M. (1989) *Middle Management in Schools: A Survival Guide*, Oxford: Blackwell.

Little, J. (1995) 'Subject affiliations in high schools that restructure', in Siskin, L. and

Little, J. (eds), *The Subject Department: Continuities and Critiques*, New York: Teachers College Press.

Peters, T. (1988) *Thriving on Chaos: A Handbook for Management Revolution*, London: Macmillan.

Ribbins, P. (1992) 'What professionalism means to teachers', paper presented at *British Educational Management and Administration Society (BEMAS) Fourth Research Conference*, Nottingham, 6–8 April.

Samier, E. (1997) 'Administrative ritual and ceremony: social aesthetics, myth and language use in the rituals of everyday organisational life', *Educational Management and Administration*, **25**(4), 417–36.

Sammons, P., Thomas, S. and Mortimore, P. (1996) 'Promoting school and departmental effectiveness', *Management in Education*, **10**, 22–4.

Sammons, P., Thomas, S. and Mortimore, P. (1997) *Forging Links: Effective Schools and Effective Departments*, London: Paul Chapman.

Schein, E. (1990) *Organisational Culture and Leadership: A Dynamic Views*, San Francisco: Jossey Bass.

Simkins, T., Ellison, L. and Garret V. (eds) (1992) *Implementing Educational Reform: The Early Lessons*, Harlow: Longman.

Siskin, L. S. (1994) *Realms of Knowledge: Academic Departments in Secondary Schools*, London: Falmer Press.

Siskin, L. S. and Little, J. (1995) *The Subject Department: Continuities and Critiques*, New York: Teachers College Press.

Stoll, L. and Fink, D. (1996) *Changing our Schools*, Buckingham: Open University Press.

Teacher Training Agency (1998) *Standards for Subject Leaders*, London: Teacher Training Agency.

Turner, C. K. (1996) 'The roles and tasks of a subject head of department in secondary schools in England and Wales: a neglected area of research?', *School Organisation*, **16**(2), 203–18.

van Vezlen, W., Miles, M., Elkholm, M., Hameyer, U. and Robin, D. (1985) *Making School Improvement Work*, Leuven, Belgium.

Wallace, G. (ed.) (1993) *Local Management: Central Control: Schools in the Market Place*, Bournemouth: Hyde Publications.

Skills and processes in the leadership of professional development

Chapter 7

Mentoring in professional development: the English and Welsh experience

John Butcher

Commissioned for this volume (2000).

Introduction

> Mentoring is a key professional development activity. Current practice varies and teachers have found benefits from mentor relationships with other teachers . . . We have found that in many cases the relationship offers the mentor as much opportunity to develop as the person being mentored. We should like schools to extend this excellent practice.
>
> (DfEE, 2000, p. 15)

The concept of mentoring is highly relevant to all teachers, lecturers and related practitioners engaged in leading professional development. In England and Wales, there is a great reservoir of experience in using mentoring to support the pre-service training of teachers. Many of the skills employed by mentors are generic, and transferable to all aspects of professional development. An interesting challenge is the extent to which the pre-service experience can be translated to the context in which professional development takes place.

This article will explore a generic conceptualisation of mentoring and suggest circumstances in which mentoring skills can be used in the leadership of professional development. These will include the mentoring of newly qualified teachers (NQTs) during induction, those new to middle manager roles, newly appointed leaders and those leading the implementation of new curriculum policies.

Mentoring in education can be characterised in a variety of ways. One view of mentoring sees it as a framework of positive support by skilled and experienced practitioners to other practitioners who need to acquire complex new skills. This apprenticeship model is based on the mentor as 'interpreter' or guide (Maynard and Furlong, 1995), providing access to the craft of the classroom by collaborative teaching, modelling, observation and discussion.

Another view is linked to the competence-based system of pre-service training in

England and Wales. A mentor who systematically and actively helps a student teacher reach a threshold in a set of pre-defined professional competences is perceived as an instructor, trainer or coach.

A third view of mentoring recognises that growth in teaching is a process over time. A mentor focuses on learning rather than teaching, and engages in co-enquiry to encourage reflection on teaching as a process. This reflective model incorporates a more critical element in the mentoring process to move teachers from novice through to expert status (Berliner, 1994). Such a conceptualisation of mentoring utilises open-minded challenge to confront beliefs and values, as well as support. Inevitably, elements from all three interpretations come together in the processes underpinning mentoring in professional development.

In England and Wales, policy directives to implement a more school-focused framework for pre-service training have strengthened the role of mentors in pre-service teacher education. Over the last decade, a series of policy initiatives (DES, 1992; DFE, 1993; DfEE, 1997, 1998) have prompted school-based staff to a more active, assessment driven mentoring role. Mentors have been required to do much more than supervise a student placement. They have been responsible for formative and summative assessment, managing a coherent training programme, providing support and acting as a professional role model.

Judging by the number and range of books and journal articles published, and conference papers presented, mentoring has become a well established component in the support of intending teachers during school-based training in England and Wales. However, discussion of mentor skills in this pre-service phase has not been fully extended to the domain of subsequent professional development.

Mentoring has the potential to play a pivotal part in making teaching a 'learning profession' (DfEE, 2000), in the context of a 'learning community' (Elliott and Calderhead, 1995) supporting a dynamic process of change. The leader of professional development in education can take responsibility for this professional learning by using mentor skills at all stages of professional development.

One discussion of mentoring (Blandford, 2000) has attempted to separate a vocational role, in which goals are clarified, standards are established and networking encouraged, from an interpersonal role in which strategies like sharing, role modelling and counselling are employed.

However, mentoring is dynamic and changes over time as relationships and needs mature. It is elusive, not predetermined, and depends on the characteristics of a particular relationship. It is complex, but widely applicable, allowing a generic concept to be gradually refined. Clarity about the differing context-dependent mentor roles and relationships is vital. The more extensive the definition and application of the role, the richer the relationship is likely to be.

Mentoring is a multi-faceted concept (Bush et al., 1996): at one level providing personal support, at the other more rigorous professional development leading to enhanced competence. Organisational performance depends critically not just on the selection, but also on the development and motivation of staff. In this context mentoring becomes integrated into professional life, and opportunities to enlarge and enhance the range of skills used can be incorporated into institutional practice.

> Mentoring is a continuous staff development activity which, once a system is in place, happens during normal school life.
>
> (Blandford, 2000)

Generic mentoring skills

Mentoring skills are exercised in context. The professional development of education practitioners is more likely to be successful if the skills are exercised by many staff across a range of settings. A constant professional dialogue has the potential to elicit development needs, even if the mentoring is not formally codified. If educational institutions emphasise the processes underpinning mentoring skills, rather than a role attached to any individual mentor, this is likely to bridge the gap between ideal prescriptions of mentoring behaviours and descriptive realities of what mentors actually do (Burgess and Butcher, 1999).

Many of the skills necessary for effective mentoring practised by many teachers in pre-service school experience do appear to transfer to the domain of professional development. These skills include classroom observation, the conducting of review meetings and target setting. Effective mentors create realistic frameworks for support and know how to exploit contextual factors. They demonstrate the processes of:

- listening and counselling;
- motivating;
- support;
- consultation;
- drawing out;
- target setting;
- renewing and reflecting;
- sharing;
- problem solving;
- developing a common approach.

One conceptual framework that has attracted much attention in mentoring in education is Kolb's model of professional learning (Kolb, 1984). This experiential approach describes the systematic and purposeful development of the whole person. In essence this is about a mentor affirming, inspiring and challenging to bring about changes. For the mentor, the skills are related to making connections and facilitating experimentation. For the mentee, learning enables specific targets to be reached.

Generic mentoring skills may prompt greater reflection on classroom methodology (Shaw, 1995). This provides a 'value-added' benefit when an institution develops mentoring as a central element in professional development. Mentoring can enhance other areas of the professional role and improve work with pupils and students, not

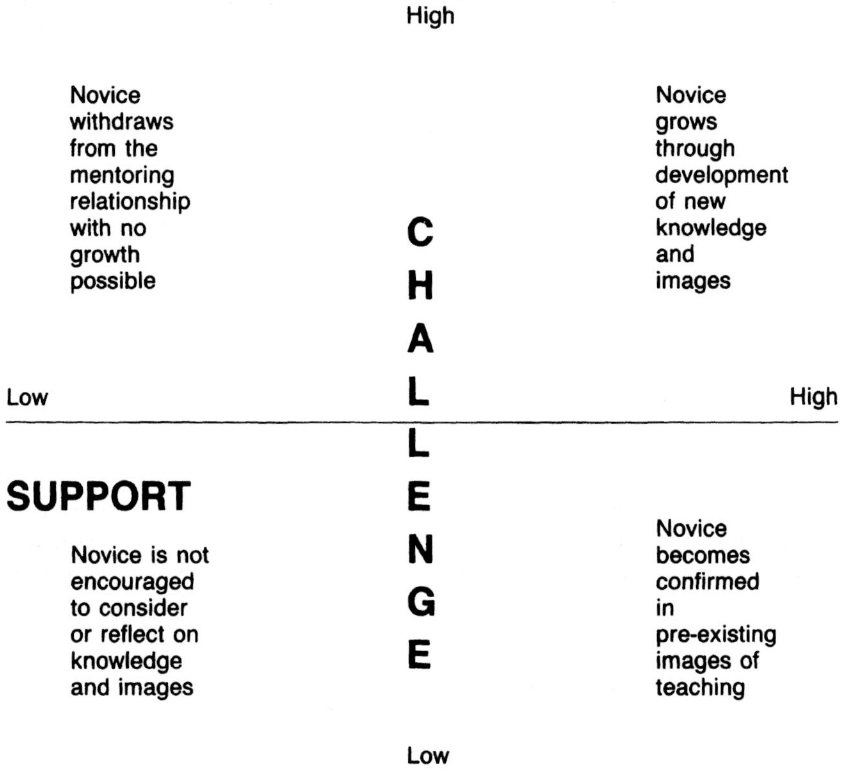

High

Novice withdraws from the mentoring relationship with no growth possible		Novice grows through development of new knowledge and images

C
H
A

Low   L   High

L

SUPPORT   E

Novice is not encouraged to consider or reflect on knowledge and images

N

G

E

Novice becomes confirmed in pre-existing images of teaching

Low

Figure 7.1 Elliot and Calderhead's two-dimensional model of mentoring relationships. (Source: Kerry and Shelton (1995))

least by enhanced self-esteem and self-image and greater understanding of learners' needs.

The vital component necessary to ensure that mentoring skills can be exercised is compatibility: the quality of the match between mentor and mentee. There are three factors that impact on the opportunities available to mentors to utilise and develop the necessary skills:

1   The importance of time, to enable both parties to meet. Often, senior teachers have the requisite experience, but because they carry many roles, lack the time to prioritise mentoring.

2   The match, the interpersonal relationship between professionals. Its centrality lies in 'attending', that is the mentor's openness to listening and feeding back with complete commitment and confidentiality.

3   Relative status: an emphasis on hierarchy can inhibit effective mentoring. Role
     status may be a barrier to an admission of professional needs over anything other
     than the short term.

Reflection on developing professional skills is important in all contexts. Is the
priority for the mentor to listen (counsel) or intervene (coach)? Whichever approach
is taken (or more likely approaches), trust, confidentiality, discretion and rapport
are vital attributes. Mentoring can provide a sense of being professionally at ease in
a context of professional integrity and credibility, but such strategies need grafting
on to a notion of professional support that advances both knowledge and practice.
For this, challenge (rigour) is necessary as well as support (Elliott and Calderhead,
1995).

Mentoring skills in pre-service education and training

There are specific attributes that can be associated with mentoring at the pre-service
phase. Students on placement in schools are generally perceived as *learners*, needing a
planned learning programme. Their curriculum is managed and implemented
in schools by a mentor and is often delivered collaboratively. This contrasts, for
example, with newly qualified teachers undergoing induction and more experienced
teachers newly in post are perceived as *teachers* for whom learning is incidental.
Mentor roles in professional development are then often conceptualised as more
informal 'buddying' with less attention to individual need and less attention to any
planned programme (Figure 7.2 in McIntyre and Hagger, 1996).

   The pre-service mentor can empathise by remembering what it was like to be a
trainee, as well as possessing a sound knowledge of educational and curricular
development. They have a clear training role, which has to balance with the primacy
of prioritising the needs of pupils. Their support is concentrated in four particular
areas:

1   Targeting pupil/student learning at the planning stage (and mediating
     co-mentor involvement).
2   Linking theory and practice during teaching observation. This can commence
     with collaborative teaching, and move into an agreed focus on a solo lesson.
3   Evaluation of lesson strategies. Constructive feedback challenges the uncritical
     repetition of 'success' and the neglect of innovatory experiments.
4   Networking, which ensures the pastoral and extra curricula dimensions of a
     teacher's role are not ignored. Socialisation into the culture of the institution is
     important.

A trainee is entitled to a stimulating and supportive start to a career, and mentoring
can play a crucial role in establishing a student's commitment to teaching as a
profession. School leaders have a crucial role in ensuring mentors are trained, possess

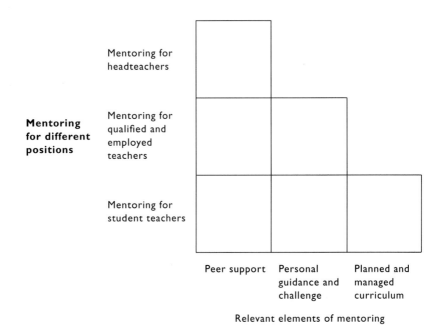

Figure 7.2 Conceptions of mentoring for people in different positions.
(Source: McIntyre and Hagger (1996))

a guaranteed reduction in teaching time and even have some salary enhancement. If a school-wide support, advice and evaluation is integrated into the programme, real, lasting professional development is likely to occur.

Mentoring and the induction of newly qualified teachers

Legislation in England and Wales (DfEE, 1999) has relatively recently introduced the role of 'Induction Tutor'. The process of induction at the start of a career recognises the transition from student to professional. The regular, formally structured mentor meetings, recognisable in the best pre-service practice, can offer an effective induction model for the future. Under the induction arrangements, the induction tutor's tasks are recognisable from the formal mentor role in initial training. These include responsibility for formative and summative assessment, with regular observations focusing on objectives for development. Written records are required from such observations to inform these formative and summative assessments, building into a professional Review of Progress every half-term. The requirement for systematic observation includes ensuring:

NQT has continued to meet the Standards for the Award of QTS consistently as well as confirming the NQT:

> takes responsibility for their own professional development, setting objectives for improvements, and taking action to keep up-to-date with research and developments in pedagogy and in the subject they teach.

(DfEE, 1999)

This role also involves the management of any necessary arrangements for the NQT's support programme that makes effective use of the time released by a reduced teaching load. More and more NQTs are carrying over their understanding of the mentor role into the induction phase. However, the mentor/induction tutor role remains at this stage under-conceptualised, with no reference to the place of active guidance and challenge. The need to differentiate provision for individuals may necessitate a blurring of the formality implicit in the mentor relationship with the notion of a 'professional friend'.

Mentoring new heads and principals

Until the Headteacher Mentoring Scheme (1992–3), mentoring for school head-teachers in the UK was a substitute for training rather than part of it. NPQH (National Professional Qualification for Headship), LPSH (The Leadership Programme for Serving Heads) and HEADLAMP (for newly appointed heads) have since formalised the relationship.

The process of mentoring can identify distinctive staff development needs for heads and aspiring heads. Experienced heads are used to interpret aspects of the role for new appointees. Mentoring is aimed at reducing professional isolation and providing support and feedback on performance. This form of mentoring is predominantly at the level of personal relationships, a novice supported by a more experienced peer in coming to terms with a new role.

Peer support has been the dominant mentoring approach for heads. Evidence has been provided (Blandford, 2000) of a novice–expert relationship from some mentees, and limited socialisation into the role. The mentor has been perceived as a catalyst or sounding board allowing constructive analysis in a structured, sanctioned, professional relationship. The potential loneliness of individual heads and principals, and the increasing range of skills required to exercise their role, makes peer mentoring a vital component of an effective training network.

Mentoring for new curriculum models

In England and Wales a variety of new curriculum initiatives have been introduced in recent years. A more formal approach to incorporate mentor support could have been of value in a number of instances.

An example is General National Vocational Qualifications (GNVQs), which were introduced into schools in England and Wales in the mid-1990s and required teachers and learners to work in new ways in a new and complex curriculum area.

A fully incorporated model of mentoring could have made the experience of GNVQ more successful for individual teachers and made for a more effective learning experience for pupils (Butcher, 1998). Schools opting for GNVQs for the first time faced the inadequacies and cost of *ad hoc* arrangements for assessor/verifier awards as statutory staff training for teachers. This in-service model of training was a key issue at the heart of the implementation problem. One view of the role of GNVQ internal verifiers was:

> To provide support and guidance to the teachers in their role as assessors.
>
> (OFSTED, 1996)

For GNVQ to succeed in schools, teachers appointed as internal assessors and verifiers needed a commitment to continuing professional development. But if trained verifiers had been explicitly encouraged to take on a GNVQ mentor role with less confident colleagues, many of the difficulties faced by staff struggling to cope with new complexities would have been avoided.

Leaders of professional development are in a position to be proactive in the face of new curriculum demands. Mentoring programmes can overcome the stresses of implementing new curriculum models.

Mentoring and appraisal

Mentor skills and strategies are closely linked to appraisal (Earley, 1995). The appraisal process identifies strengths and weaknesses and also identifies needs. A mentor harmonises institutional and individual needs in a pattern of holistic professional development (Kelly *et al.*, 1995). Appraisers can be mentors, using coaching to enhance changes in practice. So a mentor becomes a change agent, mediating appraisal targets in the context of shared criteria for effective practice. An appraisal cycle incorporates professional learning through review and reflection, modelling and disseminating good practice.

The mentoring institution

Those leading the professional development of teachers and lecturers can make use of mentoring as an in-house support for professional learning if mentoring has been embedded. Where teaching staff are working together, and professional development is to be institution-based, mentoring and the functions associated with it can provide benefits for staff and their pupils/students. The mentoring relationship itself will require an induction period, in which the processes are embedded in a framework for further development. This points to the necessity for a continuing evaluative loop of quality assurance, which, if shared with all staff, is likely to enhance understanding of mentoring within the institution.

Institutions can behave as explicit learning communities, and recognise the significance of an adult learning milieu: not the least aspect of which is a place for a distinctive and comprehensive language of practice (Elliott and Calderhead, 1995) with which to discuss professional development needs and classroom understandings.

The involvement of external partnership staff, from advisory services or universities, for example, may be important in inculcating a mentoring culture to underpin professional development.

The mentoring institution will be characterised by:

1   leadership in the area of professional development from the head or principal.
2   challenge and debate accepted as a way to prompt professional learning in a spirit of cognitive dissonance through open debate amongst all professionals.
3   encouragement given to all staff to engage in meaningful professional development. Mentor involvement thus needs to be critical rather than merely conforming.

An institution-wide approach to mentoring can ensure all staff and governors are aware that what is in place is important. Volunteer mentors, led by a senior colleague who offers a coherent training programme (perhaps using HE accreditation) are in a good position to have an impact on professional learning. These may be expert practitioners with empathetic interpersonal skills, keen to work with positive mentee learners.

Educational organisations can be transformed through mentors harnessing the fruits of professional development. Staff stress can be limited with sympathetic mentor support. Mentors themselves can gain reappraisal of their own practice from the new ideas of a mentee. Discussion of pedagogy by a mentor with a mentee can reinvigorate professional interests. Improved career prospects, sometimes enhanced by accreditation, can be significant. The mentoring institution, in which active professional development is led in the context of an integrated policy that includes pre-service and induction points to an interesting model for professional development in the future.

Recent developments in mentoring have introduced a new professional role to teachers, offering real job satisfaction (Kerry and Shelton Mayes, 1995). Mentoring has the potential to take a pivotal role in staff development, across the career continuum running from pre-service, through induction into appraisal and advanced professional development. Mentoring can be a strong component underpinning all stages of professional learning.

Conclusion

Significant changes have occurred over the last decade in the expectation teachers and lecturers have of their own professional development. These are to some extent a result of a changed institutional and external environment (Elliott and Calderhead,

1995). The link between professional learning and a discourse that articulates that learning is an important area for mentors to exploit.

For this to be successful, mentoring itself must be reframed in relation to a firm understanding of how teachers themselves learn. Hence a successionist view of mentoring offers an important way of supporting teachers at different stages of their professional development.

References

Berliner, D. C. (1994) 'Teacher expertise', in Moon, B. and Shelton Mayes, A. (eds), *Teaching and Learning in Secondary Schools*, London: Routledge.

Blandford, S. (2000) *Managing Professional Development in Schools*, London: Routledge.

Burgess, H. and Butcher, J. (1999) 'To challenge or not to challenge: the mentor's dilemma', *Mentoring and Tutoring*, **6**(3).

Bush, T. *et al.* (1996) 'Mentoring and continuing professional development', in McIntyre, D. and Hagger, H. (eds), *Mentors in Schools*, London: David Fulton.

Butcher, J. (1998) 'The conundrum of GNVQs: a case study of the training needs of school-based GNVQ teachers', *Journal of Vocational Education and Training*, **50**(4).

DES (1992) *Circular 9/92: Initial Teacher Training (Secondary Phase)*, London: DES.

DFE (1993) *Circular 14/93: The Initial Training of Primary School Teachers*, London: DFE.

DfEE (1997) *Circular 10/97: Requirements for Courses of Initial Teacher Training*, London: DfEE.

DfEE (1998) *Circular 4/98 Teaching: High Status, High Standards*, London: DfEE.

DfEE (1999) *Circular 5/99: The Induction Period for Newly Qualified Teachers*, London: DfEE.

DfEE (2000) *Professional Development*, London: DfEE.

Earley, P. (1995) 'Initiation rights: beginning teachers' professional development and the objectives of induction training', in Kerry, T. and Shelton Mayes, A. (eds), *Issues in Mentoring*, London: Routledge.

Elliott, B. and Calderhead, J. (1995) 'Mentoring for teacher development: possibilities and caveats', in Kerry, T. and Shelton Mayes, A., ibid.

Kelly, M. *et al.* (1995) 'Mentoring as a staff development activity', in Kerry, T. and Shelton Mayes, A., ibid.

Kerry, T. and Shelton Mayes, A. (eds) (1995) *Issues in Mentoring*, London: Routledge.

Kolb, D. (1984) *Experiential Learning: Experience as the Source of Learning and Development*, Eaglewood Cliffs, NJ: Prentice Hall.

Maynard, T. and Furlong, J. (1995) 'Learning to teach and models of mentoring', in Kerry, T. and Shelton Mayes, A., op cit.

McIntyre, D. and Hagger, H. (eds) (1996) *Mentors in Schools*, London: David Fulton.

OFSTED (1996) *Assessment of GNVQs in Schools 1995/6*, London: HMSO.

Shaw, R. (1995) 'Mentoring', in Kerry, T. and Shelton Mayes, A., op cit.

Chapter 8

Teachers supporting teachers through peer coaching

Jeanne Swafford

This is an edited version of an article previously published in *Support for Learning*, **13**, 2, May 1998.

Teaching is more demanding today than ever before. The diversity of the student population presents new challenges for teachers. Children come to school from varied cultural and socioeconomic backgrounds and bring different kinds of experiences with them. Because of high mobility, children in a single classroom may come from several countries and speak a number of languages, which may be different from the language used for instruction. In addition, laws that mandate inclusion of children with special needs into regular classroom settings mean that all teachers must become more cognisant of effective instructional methods for exceptional children and work together to support student learning.

Many teachers recognise that the skills they developed in the past are no longer sufficient to meet their students' diverse needs. They see a need for change and seek opportunities to develop their knowledge and repertoire of effective instructional practices. Teachers often seek out professional development opportunities on their own and attempt to apply new knowledge and teaching strategies without the help of others. More times than not, teachers are unable to successfully implement new ideas. One reason for this is that the methods may be very different from those that teachers have used in the past. Another reason is that teachers have no support from others as they attempt to grow in their knowledge and change their practices. Gallimore and Tharp (1990) propose that the isolation of teachers is at the heart of this problem. Teachers typically have limited opportunities to work with others who can support them as they learn new ways of teaching.

In the United States today, many school personnel are changing this situation. They are designing staff development programmes that involve setting goals collectively and then developing in-service training that supports those goals. Rather than approaching staff development from a traditional perspective in which teachers attend workshops or training institutes that present new information but result in little change (Showers *et al.*, 1987; Costa and Garmston, 1994), they develop staff development programmes in which peer support in the form of 'coaching' is an essential component. Peer coaching involves teachers supporting teachers as they apply and reflect on new ways of teaching that will better meet the diverse needs of students.

The concept of coaching as it relates to teaching was introduced by Joyce and Showers (1982). After reviewing research about how individuals best learn new skills, they investigated the usefulness of peer coaching for helping teachers to develop expertise with new teaching techniques and to sustain their use. What they found was that peer coaching did, in fact, make a difference. A meta-analysis of studies that examined the outcomes of staff development programmes revealed that peer coaching was more powerful in terms of transfer of training than all the other training components (e.g. information, theory, demonstration, practice and feedback) combined (Gingiss, 1993; Showers *et al.*, 1987).

What counts as peer coaching has evolved over the years. An article by Showers (1996) describes coaching as entire faculties collaborating to determine students' most pressing needs, to design teacher training to meet students' needs and to assess the impact of instruction. Robbins (1995) defines peer coaching as 'a confidential process through which two or more professional colleagues work together to reflect upon current practices; expand, refine, and build new skills; share ideas; conduct action research; teach one another; or problem solve within the workplace' (p. 206).

Peer coaching may include out-of-class activities and in-class activities (Robbins, 1995; Showers, 1996). Out-of-class activities include co-planning, study groups, problem solving and curriculum development. In-class forms of coaching typically involve teachers observing one another's teaching. Pre-observation conferences set the stage for observations and the teacher requesting assistance describes the desired focus of the observation. Post-observation conferences provide opportunities for the teacher and coach to discuss, analyse and reflect on classroom instruction.

In-class coaching may take different forms depending on the purposes and goals for coaching. *Technical coaching* involves the transfer of teaching methods, introduced in workshops, to the classroom (Hargreaves and Dawe, 1990; Joyce and Showers, 1982). *Expert coaching* utilises specially trained teachers with expertise using particular methods. They observe, support and provide feedback to other teachers (Ackland, 1991). *Reciprocal coaching* involves teachers who observe and coach each other so that instruction may be improved (Ackland, 1991). *Reflective coaching* (Nolan, 1991) and *cognitive coaching* (Garmston, *et al.*, 1993; Costa and Garmston, 1994) involve engaging teachers in on-going dialogue about their classroom practices and exploring their meanings.

The form of coaching that will be most beneficial depends on the needs of particular teachers. As their needs change, the form of coaching also changes (Glickman *et al.*, 1995). For example, when first learning an unfamiliar instructional strategy, teachers typically request technical or expert coaching with procedural aspects of a strategy. Modelling and feedback from a more experienced peer is especially useful at this point. As teachers become more proficient using a particular strategy, they may wish to reflect on and refine their skills and examine the effects on student learning. Reciprocal or cognitive coaching is especially beneficial when teachers are at this point. Rarely will coaching focus on one form of coaching to the exclusion of others. Learning and implementing new instructional strategies requires not only technical expertise but also the ability to decide when to use particular strategies and how to modify them so they optimise learning.

Peer coaching has been utilised in a variety of settings, but the goal is always the same: to improve instruction for all children. For example, peer coaching has been used to enhance early literacy instruction for children who are at risk of failing (Swafford *et al.*, 1997). Others have used peer coaching to promote more effective science and math instruction in secondary schools Ponticell *et al.*, 1995). Gordon *et al.* (1995) describe how peer coaching helped teachers learn and refine teaching strategies such as co-operative learning. Galbraith and Anstrom (1995) discuss how peer coaching between classroom teachers and bilingual teachers can provide better instruction for linguistically and culturally diverse students. Other researchers describe how special education teachers and regular classroom teachers work together in peer coaching teams to facilitate inclusion of students with special needs into regular classrooms (Kohler *et al.*, 1995; Kovic, 1996).

Early literacy instruction

In a qualitative study my colleagues and I conducted (Swafford *et al.*, 1997), we examined teachers' and coaches' perspectives on the efficacy of peer coaching during the first year of implementation of an early literacy instruction framework, developed at the Ohio State University. This framework is designed to engage students in a variety of literacy experiences through carefully planned instruction that is responsive to their needs. The framework includes both reading and writing components such as read alouds, shared reading and writing, guided reading and writing, independent reading and writing, and interactive writing (Pinnell and McCarrier, 1994). Special attention is given to examining letters and words, to extending literature through the use of themes and to documenting student progress. Effective implementation of the framework involves not only technical expertise but also requires that teachers use their theoretical knowledge of the reading and writing processes and their knowledge of children's literacy strengths to inform instruction. When the framework is implemented skilfully, reflectively and responsively, instruction meets the needs of students with diverse needs and experiences.

Two teacher–coaches and eighteen kindergarten, first and second grade teachers from six schools participated in the study. Five of the schools are minority schools with high student mobility rates and a large percentage of students who receive free or reduced lunch. Teachers were involved in a number of staff development activities throughout the year. Before school started, teachers and coaches attended a week-long training session that introduced the components of the early literacy framework. Throughout the year, they met weekly in a graduate course. During the class sessions they engaged in a number of activities such as discussions of the theoretical and research bases for the framework, watched demonstrations and viewed videotapes of exemplary early literacy teaching. During the year, teachers also had the opportunity to visit each other's classrooms and the kindergarten classroom taught by the coaches.

They were also involved in peer coaching activities. One of the peer coaches met with teachers at least once a month to assist them as they implemented the framework. They observed in teachers' classrooms, videotaped the lessons and met with teachers in post-observation conferences. Teachers also engaged in self-reflection about the videotaped lessons. The forms of peer coaching varied depending on teachers' needs, as suggested by Glickman *et al.* (1995).

To determine the efficacy of peer coaching, we collected data throughout the year from teacher and coach interviews, audiotaped post-observation conferences and three sets of teacher self-reflection papers. The data were analysed using inductive data analysis procedures (Bogdan and Biklen, 1982).

We found that the overriding theme that linked the data was the benefits of peer coaching. One benefit of peer coaching that permeated the data was that it provided teachers with the support they needed when implementing new instructional practices. Coaches provided three kinds of support for teachers: procedural (technical), affective (emotional) and reflective. When teachers first began to implement a particular component of the literacy framework, they needed *procedural support* most often. To provide that support, coaches answered questions, highlighted teachers' strengths, suggested alternative practices, emphasised important teaching points and facilitated problem solving. Coaches also assisted teachers as they selected materials for instruction and suggested classroom management and organisational strategies.

The coaches also provided *affective* or *emotional support* for the teachers. They reassured teachers when they had doubts about the effectiveness of their teaching and confirmed what teachers knew about the framework and its implementation, their teaching strengths and areas in which they could improve. The affective support encouraged teachers to take risks in the classroom and not to give up when they experienced difficulty implementing the different components of the framework.

The peer coaches also provided *reflective support* for the teachers. Coaches scaffolded conversations in post-observation conferences so they moved beyond discussions of procedures to clarifying issues, verbalising teaching objectives and reflecting on teachers' strengths and their choices of materials, questioning strategies and classroom organisational structure. The discussions also led teachers to think about future lessons and changes they would make.

A second benefit of peer coaching was that teacher change was facilitated. Teachers changed in terms of (a) procedural (or technical) expertise, (b) their feelings about the effectiveness of classroom instruction and (c) their reflections about teaching and learning. As we expected, teachers became more adept at implementing the different components of the framework and more able to integrate the components effectively as the year progressed. Their confidence grew about their understandings of the literacy framework and how well they applied their understandings in the classroom. Teachers who, at the beginning of the year, were hesitant to attempt to implement the components of the framework in their classrooms, confidently and expertly shared their expertise with others at the end of the year. Teachers also became more reflective about their practice. Discussions in post-observation conferences became more reflective rather than technical. Teachers began to verbalise their realisation that implementation of the framework was not a technique that could be learned and then repeated in a routine fashion. Rather, their instruction would change as the students grew and as the teachers' own knowledge of teaching and learning developed. Teachers began to internalise the notion of reflective practice.

A third benefit of peer coaching was that it provided different lenses through which teachers could view their instruction. Teachers viewed lessons through the eyes of an experienced peer coach and from an observer's perspective by means of a videotape. Both 'lenses' provided opportunities for teachers to revisit a lesson and engage in assisted reflection and self-reflection.

Our data analysis also revealed particular characteristics of coaching that the teachers found beneficial. First, post-observation conferences are most effective when they occur soon after the observation. Second, conferencing with a more experienced peer is important because the coach can relate to the concerns teachers experience and help them solve problems. Third, frequent visits (at least twice a month) were preferred by the majority of teachers. Fourth, observations should begin early in the school year to provide teachers with guidance as they begin applying new methods and to help build confidence about using those methods.

To summarise, the results of our study provide insights into the benefits of peer coaching from teachers' and coaches' perspectives. In essence, the role of the coach is to be a resource for the teachers in terms of procedural and affective concerns, as well as in terms of providing scaffolding so that teachers can move from implementing techniques to becoming reflective practitioners.

Special education

Peer coaching has also been found to benefit special education teachers and regular classroom teachers as inclusion programmes are implemented in schools. Kovic (1996) studied the effectiveness of peer coaching for enhancing teachers' skills and monitoring and responding to teachers' needs as children with Down's syndrome were integrated into a second grade classroom. During the second year of the inclusion project, seven teachers (classroom teacher, special education teacher, speech pathologist, occupational therapist, physical therapist, teaching assistant and peer coach) worked together to provide appropriate instruction for the students. Based on the teachers' comments about the successes and challenges of the first year of implementation, Kovic focused her coaching efforts on seven areas that she thought were crucial for the success of the inclusion programme: collaboration, flexibility, creativity, communication, leadership and initiative, self-concept and common goals.

Based on the results of her work with the teachers, Kovic recommends that coaches should provide procedural and affective support to teachers through frequent teacher–coach meetings, team meetings, classroom observations and informal conversations. Objective feedback during post-observation conferences is important for facilitating professional dialogue among the teachers and helping them reflect on their practice. Assisting teachers as they work towards thinking flexibly and creatively about modifications of materials, curriculum plans, time management and use of personnel is another important job of a coach. Encouraging teachers to take the initiative to identify and solve their own problems rather than relying on the coach is also important. When a number of teachers are working together, the coach also assists in clarifying their roles and responsibilities and identifying the solving problems related to communication. The coach should intervene when problems develop among team members so that positive relationships are fostered. Because teachers may have different styles, concerns and levels of expertise, the coach can help meet each teacher's particular needs in individual conferences and informal conversations, which helps build confidence and promote positive self concepts. By meeting with teams, the coach can encourage teachers to work together and focus on their common goal of providing appropriate instruction for all children in the classroom.

In summary, for inclusion programmes to be successful, teachers need to work together to plan and deliver instruction. New ways of teaching need to be shared and new ways of communicating with team members need to be fostered. Support by a peer coach can help teachers work as a team to decide how best to meet all students' needs in the most appropriate ways.

Recommendations

Designing effective staff development programmes that support teacher development and promote instructional change is challenging. Although peer coaching is a very important component of staff development programmes, it is not sufficient by itself. Several researchers (Beninghof, 1996; Glickman et al., 1995; Kovic, 1996; Swafford et al., 1997) recommend multidimensional approaches to staff development. Because teachers have differing interests and needs, they may seek different kinds of information and assistance as they work towards implementing educational innovations. Beninghof (1996) suggests that teachers should be provided with a spectrum of staff development activities, from activities that promote basic awareness of an innovation to activities that promote collaboration and reflection, including peer coaching.

There are several 'musts' that practitioners and researchers recommend when considering the use of peer coaching in staff development programmes. First, Showers (1996) and Hargreaves and Dawe (1990) stress the importance of paying attention to the social organisation of the school when implementing peer coaching. Both administrators and teachers must be committed to facilitating peer coaching (Cox et al., 1991) and recognise that everyone on the staff is working together towards a common goal – to improve the quality of instruction for all students (Kovic, 1996; Pellicer and Anderson, 1995). Moreover, administrators must provide verbal and tangible support for the programme (Garmston et al., 1993; Gingiss, 1993; Gordon et al., 1995; Pellicer and Anderson, 1995) and teachers must actively participate in designing peer coaching programmes (Desrochers and Klein, 1990; Robbins, 1995). Involvement in peer coaching must be voluntary (Desrochers and Klein, 1990; Hargreaves and Dawe, 1990; Robbins, 1995), and teachers should select their peer coaching partners and determine the focus of peer coaching observations and conferences (Gordon *et al.*, 1995; Nolan, 1991; Ponticell *et al.*, 1995). For peer coaching to be successful, training to promote effective observation and conferencing skills is also essential (Chase and Wolfe, 1989; Cox *et al.*, 1991; Garmston *et al.*, 1993). In addition, time must be provided, preferably during the school day, for teachers to observe each other's teaching, to reflect together after observations and to engage in other collaborative activities (Gingiss, 1993; Gordon *et al.*, 1995, Kohler, 1995). Peer coaching must be non-evaluative (Garmston *et al.*, 1993; Gingiss, 1993; Koballa *et al.*, 1992) and non-judgemental (Pellicer and Anderson, 1995). Above all, for peer coaching to be successful, an atmosphere of trust, respect, collegiality and confidentiality must be fostered to provide a safe atmosphere in which teachers are willing to take risks as they learn new ways of teaching (Chase and Wolfe, 1989; Cox *et al.*, 1991; Kohler, 1995).

Conclusion

Teachers' continuing professional development is essential to meet the ever-changing needs of students in today's schools. However, traditional types of staff development are not sufficient to ensure that new ways of teaching will become the norm in classrooms. Not only do teachers need time to practise new instructional practices in the context of their classrooms, but they also need support from their peers. Tharp and Gallimore (1988) stress the importance of building a collaborative environment in schools in which teachers provide each other with assistance as they work together towards common goals and seek to improve and change instruction. Peer coaching provides teachers with the opportunities 'to investigate and explore instructional alternatives, reflect on their effectiveness, make adjustments when necessary, and then investigate and explore again . . . Peer coaching can help build a professional culture that supports teachers who are knowledgeable and responsive to all students, regardless of their needs' (Kovic, 1996, p. 30).

References

Ackland, R. (1991) 'A review of the peer coaching literature', *Journal of Staff Development*, **12**(1), 22–7.

Beninghof, A. M. (1996) 'Using a spectrum of staff development activities to support inclusion', *Journal of Staff Development*, **17**(3), 12–15.

Bogdan, R. C. and Biklen, S. K. (1982) *Qualitative Research in Education: An Introduction to Theory and Methods*, Boston: Allyn and Bacon.

Chase, A. and Wolfe, P. (1989) 'Off to a good start in peer coaching'. *Education Leadership*, **46**(3), 37

Costa, A. L. and Garmston, R. J. (1994) *Cognitive Coaching: A Foundation for Renaissance Schools*, Norwood, MA: Christopher-Gordon Publishers.

Cox, C. L., Gabry, M. M. and Johnson, L. (1991) 'Peer coaching: a process for developing professionalism, achieving instructional excellence, and improving student learning', *Thresholds in Education*, **17**(4), 23–6.

Desrochers, C. and Klein, S. R. (1990) 'Teacher-directed peer coaching as a follow-up to staff development', *Journal of Staff Development*, **11**(2), 6–10.

Galbraith, P. and Anstrom, K. (1995) 'Peer coaching: an effective staff development model for educators of linguistically and culturally diverse students', *Directions in Language and Education*, **1**(3), 1–8 (ERIC Document Reproduction Service No. ED 394 300).

Gallimore, R. and Tharp, R. (1990) 'Teaching mind in society: teaching, schooling and literate discourse', in Moll, L. C. (ed.), *Vygotsky and Education; Instructional Implications and Applications of Sociohistorical Psychology*, Cambridge: Cambridge University Press.

Garmston, R. J., Linder, C. and Whitaker, J. (1993) 'Reflections on cognitive coaching', *Educational Leadership*, **51**(2), 57–61.

Gingiss, P. L. (1993) 'Peer coaching: building collegial support for using innovative health programs', *Journal of School Health*, **63**(2), 79–85.

Glickman, C. D., Gordon, S. P. and Ross-Gordon, J. M. (1995) *Supervision of Instruction: A Developmental Approach* (3rd edn), Boston: Allyn and Bacon.

Gordon, S. P., Nolan, J. F. and Forlenza, V. A. (1995) 'Peer coaching: a cross-site comparison', *Journal of Personnel Evaluation in Education*, **9**, 69–91.

Hargreaves, A. and Dawe, R. (1990) 'Paths of professional development: contrived collegiality, collaborative culture, and the case of peer coaching', *Teaching and Teacher Education*, **6**, 227–41.

Joyce, B. and Showers, B. (1982) 'The coaching of teaching', *Educational Leadership*, **40**(1), 4–10.

Koballa, T. R., Eidson, S. D., Finco-Kent, D., Grimes, S., Kight, C. R. and Sambs, H. (1992) 'Peer coaching: capitalizing on constructive criticism', *Science Teacher*, **59**(6), 42–5.

Kohler, F. W. (1995) 'Designing a comprehensive and sustainable innovation by blending two different approaches to school reform', *Education and Treatment of Children*, **16**(4), 382–400.

Kohler, F. W., McCullough, K. M. and Buchan, K. A. (1995) 'Using peer coaching to enhance preschool teachers' development and refinement of classroom activities', *Early Education and Development*, **6**, 215–39.

Kovic, S. (1996) 'Peer coaching to facilitate inclusion: A job-embedded staff development model', *Journal of Staff Development*, **17**(1), 28–31.

Nolan, J. F. (1991) 'The effects of a reflective coaching project for veteran teachers', *Journal of Curriculum and Supervision*, **7**, 62–76.

Pellicer, L. O. and Anderson, L. W. (1995) *A Handbook for Teacher Leaders*, Thousand Oaks, CA: Corwin Press.

Pinnell, G. S. and McCarrier, A. (1994) 'Interactive writing: a transition tool for assisting children in learning to read and write', in Hiebert, E. B. and Taylor, B. M. (eds), *Getting Reading Right from the Start: Effective Early Literacy Interventions*, Boston, MA: Allyn and Bacon.

Ponticell, J., Olson, G. E. and Charlier, P. S. (1995) 'Project MASTER: peer coaching and collaboration as catalysts for professional growth in urban high schools', in O'Hair, M. J. and Odell, S. J. (eds), *Educating Teachers for Leadership and Change*, Thousand Oaks, CA; Corwin Press.

Robbins, P. (1995) 'Peer coaching: quality through collaborative work', in Block, J., Everson, S. F. and Guskey, T. R. (eds), *School Improvement Programs: A Handbook for Educational Leaders*, New York: Scholastic.

Showers, B. (1996) 'The evolution of peer coaching', *Educational Leadership*, **53**(6), 12–16.

Showers, B., Joyce, B. and Bennett, B. (1987) 'Synthesis of research on staff development: a framework for future study and a state-of-the-art analysis', *Educational Leadership*, **45**(3), 77–87.

Swafford, J., Maltsberger, A., Button, K. and Furgerson, P. (1997) 'Peer coaching for facilitating effective literacy instruction', in Kinzer, C. K., Hinchman, K. A. and Leu, D. J., *Inquiries in Literacy Theory and Practice*, Chicago: National Reading Conference.

Tharp, R. G. and Gallimore, R. (1988) *Rousing Minds to Life: Teaching, Learning, and Schooling in Social Context*, Cambridge: Cambridge University Press.

Chapter 9

A new approach to teaching and learning in journal club

Khalid S. Khan and Harry Gee

This is an edited version of an article previously published in
Medical Teacher, **21**, 3, 1999.

Introduction

Medical practice is changing, and the change requires use of the medical literature more effectively. This paradigm shift is based on the explicit and judicious use of current evidence in making decisions about the clinical care of patients (Sackett *et al.*, 1996). The successful implementation of this new philosophy requires integration of clinical expertise with high-quality research evidence. Medical trainees need to learn specific skills in searching literature, appraising it and incorporating it into clinical practice (Rosenberg and Donald, 1995). These skills are generally not taught formally. Traditional training strategy puts high value on authority based on content and clinical expertise (Chalmers, 1983). It leaves physicians dependent on 'experts' for sorting out clinical problems (Light, 1979). They do not gain skills to evaluate evidence independently and thus they are unable to assess critically the opinions being offered by experts (Evidence-based Medicine Working Group, 1992).

The need to change medical curricula to equip physicians with the capacity to acquire, appraise and apply new knowledge and to adapt to changing circumstances has been well recognised (General Medical Council, 1993), and medical curricula are gradually changing to bring education in line with this philosophy. Journal club meetings provide a forum for keeping abreast of new knowledge. Although the earliest reference to a journal club dates back over a century (Lizner, 1987), in recent years it has become a part and parcel of formal postgraduate medical education (Sidorov, 1995; Alguire, 1998). This trend has been driven largely by an explicit requirement that training programmes should have regular journal clubs to teach literature appraisal and to improve reading habits (Daonini-Lenhoff, 1997). However, learning activities in journal club have generally remained unstructured, diminishing the educational value of the journal club.

The recent trends in medical education are rooted in the realisation that the aim of teaching is to facilitate learning. In particular, educational programmes should inculcate deep learning. This is because in contrast with surface learning, which circles around memorising and reproducing (and forgetting soon after examinations), the deep approach helps trainees make sense out of the subject-matter (Brown and Atkins, 1988; Gibbs, 1992). The deep approach is fostered when the process of learning builds on activation of trainees' existing knowledge; construction of new knowledge over and above what exists; and refinement of the newly acquired knowledge. To achieve this objective in the journal club a clinical context is required that motivates trainees to take an active role and to interact with others in the learning process (Gibbs, 1992). In this chapter, we describe what is wrong with the teaching and learning strategy of the traditional journal club and we propose some ways of changing the teaching strategy to make it compatible with the goal of fostering deep and lifelong learning.

Traditional journal clubs

An analysis of a traditional journal club meeting shows that the trainee is left to select and appraise the articles with little or no structure and often no clear purpose. The trainee picks up articles at random without a systematic literature search and evaluates them without any guidelines or method of appraisal. Untrained in medical research, most trainees do not appraise the quality of the studies, which is an important omission, as a large proportion of published medical literature is known to be of poor quality (Haynes, 1993). The presentation consists of a summary of the article, the authors' results and conclusions. Without critical appraisal the journal club session becomes an exercise for presentation skills. The presenters often end up being criticised by the mentors for not appropriately selecting or appraising the articles. Mentors' comments are generally based on personal experience and opinion, which is usually methodologically unsound. Other junior members of the journal club who attend do not gain any scientific knowledge about literature appraisal and hardly feel enthused to take the role of a presenter in subsequent journal club sessions.

The traditional journal club described above does not facilitate the deep learning process. There is no prior delineation of learning objectives and there is a lack of context. The articles appraised are generally not relevant to trainees' current clinical practice as they are chosen at random. The motivational context is absent as the journal club is not driven by the need to know something about patient problems. As the trainee's existing knowledge or experience is not brought to bear in the process, the opportunity to build on existing concepts is lost. Although the trainee is active in the process of preparation for journal club, the learning activity is unplanned and it does not draw on a structured critical appraisal. The level of mentor assistance in this process is variable so that the trainee is often left to prepare without guidance. The journal club presentation itself provides an opportunity for interaction with others but the learning environment is threatening and anxiety provoking. Following the presentation, the article and the associated information are not reflected upon, seldom processed or refined for utilisation in clinical practice and quickly forgotten. Sadly the opportunity of learning-for-understanding is lost (see Figure 9.1).

To address these problems, postgraduate training programmes have started to

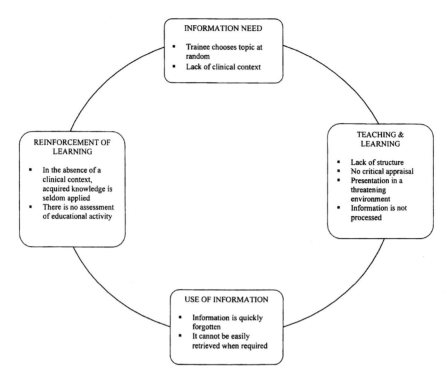

Figure 9.1 Traditional journal club

define the role of the journal club in terms of objectives and learning outcomes. The most common objectives of the journal club have been to teach critical appraisal of the medical literature, to keep up to date with the literature, to teach research design and to have an impact on clinical practice (Alguire, 1998). Many journal clubs have attempted to incorporate the recent trends of teaching to facilitate learning in their format, for example by adoption of approaches based on active learner participation (Inui, 1981) and problem-based learning (Joorabchi, 1984). However, the efforts to improve the educational value of journal clubs in terms of trainees' learning outcomes have been limited (Sidorov, 1995; Alguire, 1998) and controlled trials assessing the value of journal clubs for teaching critical appraisal skills have shown only moderate educational improvements (Norman and Shannon, 1998). This is likely to be due to the limited use of approaches to foster deep learning.

The way of the future

The teaching and learning methods that promote deep learning can be applied in journal club. We have organised a journal club module based on a guided discovery approach, which puts the learning process in the context of clinical problem solving. The journal club is structured with careful selection of learning experiences to enhance deep learning of literature appraisal skills.

The learning outcomes of the journal club are clearly delineated and include acquisition of skills for problem defining, searching, evaluating and applying medical literature (Table 9.1) (Khan *et al.*, 1999). It is crucial that literature appraisal skills are taught in the context of patient problems that the learner is currently confronting. This also provides a motivational context while demonstrating that literature appraisal is central and pragmatic, not an academic or tangential aspect of optimal patient care. The trainees are asked to identify a current patient care problem that they consider important but for which they do not feel certain about its best management (possibly in the light of conflicting expert opinion). In other words, they bring out issues that they feel are worth the effort of exploring the medical literature to address their uncertainty. These clinical problems are discussed in a small group where they are converted into focused, answerable questions by defining the population, intervention and outcome (Rosenberg and Donald, 1995). In light of the evidence that journal clubs independent of faculty are more successful, we have arranged for the problem formulation process to be led by trainees themselves (Sidorov, 1995).

The next step after identifying the clinical problem is search of the literature to identify relevant articles. Facilities for computerised literature search of electronic biographic databases are provided in our postgraduate education resource centre. Usually, a systematic online computerised literature search based on the clinical question is conducted during the journal club session using projection of the video display unit. These searches are conducted using key words representing the population, intervention and outcome of interest and often the search is limited by an evidence-based medicine search filter for therapy, diagnosis, prognosis or aetiology (Haynes *et al.*, 1994). Often questions are also searched using the Cochrane Library, an up-to-date electronic database of meta-analyses of randomised trials. After going through the citation list the journal club members collectively decide on an article/articles that are potentially relevant. These articles are retrieved from our library or ordered through the interlibrary loan system. Our initial experience with searching concurs with previous evidence that searching electronic databases in a clinical setting is feasible with brief training and it is believed to be associated with improvement in patient care (Haynes *et al.*, 1990).

After acquiring the identified article the trainee appraises it independently at his or her own pace. The appraisal is based on structured guidelines because this approach enhances the value of journal clubs (Burstein *et al.*, 1996). The structured appraisal is facilitated by use of a reading resource and computer software that employs few simple criteria for methodological rigour. The software also performs the calculations of clinically meaningful measures of effect and allows the appraisal to be stored in an electronic retrievable form (Badenoch *et al.*, 1998). In the process of appraisal the trainee applies the methodological guidelines for critical appraisal provided in the reading resource to the selected article during independent learning. The use of

Table 9.1 The journal club module

Module title
Journal Club

Site
Education Resource Centre, Birmingham Women's Hospital

Timetabling
Weekly lunchtime meetings lasting 1 hour every Monday except on public holidays

Aim
To familiarise journal club members with the use of evidence from medical literature in guiding clinical decision-making

Objectives
To prepare journal club members to identify, appraise and present in turn published articles concerning aetiology, diagnosis, prognosis and therapy of patient problems seen in day-to-day clinical practice

Learning outcomes
At the end of each journal club session, the presenter, given a clinical question about aetiology, diagnosis, prognosis and therapy should be comfortable with:

- framing clinical questions in an answerable form
- conducting a simple search for an electronic bibliographic database to identify relevant articles
- critical appraisal of the article for validity, significance of results and clinical applicability
- recording the above information in an electronic form using computer software

Reading/learning resource
Before the journal club presentation, the presenter will receive a relevant methodological paper on aetiology, diagnosis, prognosis or therapy. Using the guidelines in these papers the presenter will appraise articles from the medical literature to inform clinical decision making regarding a current clinical problem. Computer software will be provided in the Education Resource Centre Resource Room for performing simple calculations and for making an electronic record of the critically appraised topic

Learning/teaching methods
For each journal club presentation, the teaching and learning strategy would involve:

- deciding how to respond to a clinical scenario (small-group discussion)
- understanding the methodological guidelines for critical appraisal (independent learning, one-to-one tutoring and peer tutoring)
- appraisal of research paper using the methodological guidelines (independent learning, one-to-one tutoring and peer tutoring)
- deciding how to respond to the findings of research article (small-group discussion)

Contact time
1 hour (one-to-one tutoring)
1 hour (peer tutoring, small-group discussion and feedback during journal club session)

Student-directed learning
1–2 hours (independent learning)

Assessment
- Peer assessment of learning objectives and feedback at the end of journal club session
- Self-assessment
- The critical appraisal of articles forms part of trainees' progress record in their personal development file

the software is facilitated by exploring the critical appraisal package independently or by assistance of a peer trainee who is familiar with the software. Then, prior to the journal club presentation, the trainee has a one-to-one tutorial with a mentor who helps clarify any difficult methodological concepts and calculations, an approach that has been associated with success of journal clubs (Sidorov, 1995). The trainee and the mentor together refine the electronic appraisal, decide on the format of the journal club presentation and produce instructional materials.

In this manner the trainee presents in the journal club with as much prior preparation as possible, which helps increase his or her confidence and reduce his or her anxiety. The journal club is used by the presenter as an opportunity to learn by peer tutoring, an approach that leads to learning-for-understanding as trainees have to be able to provide an explanation to others. The mentor's role in the journal club presentation is simply to aid in the peer-tutoring process and to help the presenter deal with difficult members of the audience. At the end of the presentation the presenter gets feedback and has a chance for reflection. The appraisal is modified in light of the discussion in the journal club meeting. A final version of the appraisal with the trainee identified as the appraiser is stored electronically on our hospital's computer network. The appraised topics can be retrieved from this electronic bank for use in clinical service areas. The electronic aspect of the journal club provides an incentive for the trainees to disseminate their work to other trainers and trainees who could not attend the journal club. The information abstracted from the appraisal of the article in this manner can be applied to resolve patient management problems, which reinforces the impact of problem-solving skills learnt during preparation for the journal club. Finally, because assessment is a major determinant of learning (Swanson *et al.*, 1995), the trainee's performance in the journal club is used as part of his or her formative assessment. A paper copy of the appraisal becomes part of the trainee's personal development file.

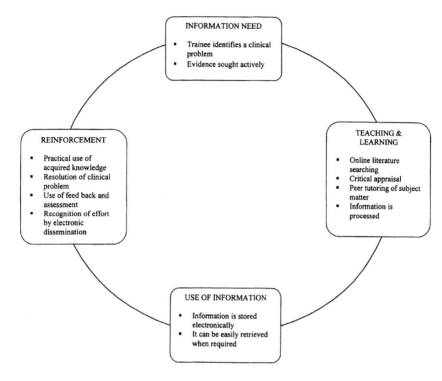

Figure 9.2 New journal club

Conclusion

Aware of the limitations of traditional approaches to teaching and learning in journal clubs, we have adopted a new approach to inculcate deep learning of problem-solving skills (see Figure 9.2). These skills are essential in building physicians' capacity to adapt to changing circumstances.

References

Alguire, P. C. (1998) 'A review of journal clubs in postgraduate medical education', *Journal of General Internal Medicine,* **13**, 347–53.

Badenoch, D., Sackett, D. and Straus, S. (1998) *Catmaker 98,* Oxford: NHS R&D Centre for Evidence Based Medicine.

Brown, G. and Atkins, M. (1988) 'Studies of student learning', in Brown, G. and Atkins, M. (eds), *Effective Teaching in Higher Education,* London: Routledge, 150–8.

Burstein, J. L., Hollander, J. E. and Barlas, D. (1996) 'Enhancing the value of journal club: use of a structured review instrument', *American Journal of Emergency Medicine,* **14**, 561–3.

Chalmers, I. (1983) 'Scientific inquiry and authoritarianism in perinatal care and education', *Birth*, **10**, 151–64.

Daonini-Lenhoff, F. (1997) 'Program requirements for residency education in internal medicine', in Daonini-Lenhoff, F. (ed.), *Graduate Medical Education Directory 1997–98*, Chicago, IL: American Medical Association, 87.

Evidence-Based Medicine Working Group (1992) 'Evidence-based medicine. A new approach to teaching the practice of medicine', *Journal of the American Medical Association*, **268**, 2420–5.

General Medical Council (1993) *Tomorrow's Doctors, Recommendations on Undergraduate Medical Education*, London: General Medical Council.

Gibbs, G. (1992) 'The nature of quality of learning', in Gibbs, G. (ed.), *Improving the Quality of Student Learning*, Bristol: Technical and Educational Services, 1–11.

Haynes, R. B. (1993) 'Where is the meat in clinical journals?', *American College of Physicians Journal Club*, **119**, A22–3.

Haynes, R. B., McKibbon, K. A., Walker, C. J., Ryan, N., Fitzgerald, D. and Ramsden, M. E. (1990) 'Online access to medline in clinical settings: a study of use and usefulness', *Annals of Internal Medicine*, **112**, 78–84.

Haynes, R. B., Wilczynski, N., McKibbon, K. A., Walker, C. J. and Sinclair, J. C. (1994) 'Developing optimal search strategies for detecting clinically sound studies in MEDLINE', *Journal of the American Medical Information Association*, **1**(6), 447–58.

Inui, T. S. (1981) 'Critical reading seminars for medical residents. A report of a teaching technique', *Medical Care*, **19**, 122–4.

Joorabchi, B. (1984) 'A problem-based journal club', *Journal of Medical Education*, **59**, 755–7.

Khan, K. S., Dwarakanath, L. S., Pakkal, M., Brace, V. and Awonuga, A. (1999), 'Postgraduate journal club as a means of promoting evidence-based obstetrics and gynaecology', *Journal of Obstetrics and Gynaecology*, **19**(3), 231–4.

Light, D. W. (1979) 'Uncertainty and control in professional training', *Journal of Health and Social Behaviour*, **20**, 310–32.

Lizner, D. W. (1987) 'The journal club and medical education: over one hundred years of unrecorded history', *Postgraduate Medical Journal*, **63**, 475–8.

Norman, G. R. and Shannon, S. I. (1998) 'Effectiveness of instruction in critical appraisal skills: a critical appraisal', *Canadian Medical Association Journal*, **158**, 177–81.

Rosenberg, W. and Donald, A. (1995) 'Evidence-based medicine: an approach to clinical problem solving', *British Medical Journal*, **310**, 1122–6.

Sackett, D. L., Richardson, W. S., Rosenberg, W. M. C. and Haynes, R. B. (1996) *Evidence-based Medicine: How to Practise and Teach Evidence-based Medicine*, London: Churchill-Livingstone.

Sidorov, J. (1995) 'How are internal medicine residency journal clubs organized, and what makes them successful?', *Archives of Internal Medicine*, **155**, 1193–7.

Swanson, D. B., Norman, G. R. and Linn, R. L. (1995) 'Performance based assessment: lessons from the health professions', *Educational Research*, B24, 5–11.

Chapter 10

Teachers' work groups as professional development: what do the teachers learn?

Araceli Estebaranz, Pilar Mingorance and Carlos Marcelo

This is an edited version of an article previously published in *Teachers and Teaching: Theory and Practice*, 5, 2, 1999.

Professional development in Spain

In the past 20 years, teacher professional development in Spain has undergone profound changes: from an on-going training centred on the university, using centralised, content-based training models, to more decentralised, more independent models managed by the teachers themselves. From their birth, 'Permanent Seminars' have helped to develop a more democratic and more grass roots professional development of teachers. The concern of successive socialist governments of Andalusia in on-going teacher training has been to offer teachers a variety of training modalities. The result is short courses (workshops) together with innovation projects and school-based training. Why have such modalities appeared in Andalusia? The answer lies in the setting in motion of a left-wing policy aimed at enabling teachers to manage their whole training independently: a policy to give innovating teachers their head in setting up teams for renovation in teaching. This policy has been well received by the teaching staff, especially the more innovative.

In Andalusia, the term 'self-training programme' is applied to the various training modalities that are aimed at the development of teachers under their own initiative and responsibility. It is intended to create work groups of teachers (who might or might not belong to the same school), able to diagnose a teaching problem, whether curricular or administrative, and develop a project to solve it. This project is assumed to give cohesion to the group of teachers, giving them room to learn about what they want and are motivated by.

The permanent seminars are a prime self-training modality financed by the Board of Education and Science of the Junta de Andalucía. Permanent seminars have a long tradition in Andalusia. They were one of the main measures adopted in 1983 by the Junta de Andalucía (the Regional Government) when it became responsible for educational policy. A policy to give support to teachers, who want to change their practice, by setting up teams for innovation and teaching. What are they and how are they organised? Their members are teachers – a minimum of four, and a maximum of ten. These teachers may belong to the same school or not; they may belong to the same educational level or not – it depends completely on them. They decide who will form part of the seminar.

A feature of the permanent seminars is that to be recognised and to receive public funds, they must present a work project. This project has to consider specific problems and situations of everyday practice of the teachers taking part in the seminar. In this article, we analyse some topics identified during our research.

The permanent seminars should incorporate training activities, such as work in groups or individually. There are no strict rules as to when the members should meet, nor how often, except for an established minimum of 20 hours a year for the study and development of the chosen topic. Through this meeting and study, the teachers direct their own training. The co-ordination and working of the permanent seminars is completely the responsibility of the teaching staff, and so is broadly democratic. The permanent seminars may receive outside advice when the teachers think it necessary. Such advice is generally given by advisors belonging to Andalusian Teacher Centres. However, a common complaint of teachers is that the level of advice is low due to the small number of advisors available.

What is the role of the university in the working of the permanent seminars? In principle, none. The on-going training of the teaching staff in Andalusia is organised by the teacher centres. These are run by teachers of infants, primary, or secondary education, and include, as mentioned before, a number of training advisors, who are also teachers. University teachers can also act as advisors on any appropriate topic, at the request of a permanent seminar.

In 1992, the 'Andalusian Plan of Permanent Training for Teachers' was set up. This was an attempt to establish a general framework of action and co-ordination in the training of teaching staff. The permanent seminar is meant to be a self-development activity: 'a continuing system of group self-education and reflection in teams of teachers'. It must have the following characteristics:

- Team work for communication and the sharing of experiences in educational tasks.
- The activity carried out in the seminar emerges from the group as a whole. The functioning of the seminar comes from particular situations linked to the reality of the classroom.

Permanent seminars are a mode of work in the group/team as a continuing system of self-development and reflection in the practice of teaching. They are a form of study, analysis and reflection on a topic chosen by the teachers themselves to acquire a deeper knowledge of that topic. They are a necessary connection between the acquiring of new knowledge, and the analysis and interchange of experiences. They are a meeting point between teachers with different training backgrounds, in which the reflection and the interchange of experiences takes precedence over practice.

Research

This article presents a study on the permanent seminars in Andalusia, from the point of view of their internal conditions of learning and development. It is a *descriptive* work on the internal characteristics indicated by the teachers themselves, their intended goals, their topics of common interest and the individual and collaborative learning strategies they use. Our fundamental questions are: What learning can we expect of teachers working in permanent seminars? What achievements can be considered relevant? What are the implications for the programmes of professional development of teachers?

We consider permanent seminars an essential instrument for the professional development of teachers, for innovation and for the improvement of the school; and we attempt to identify the characteristics and the work system of the teachers necessary for success in training activities. In a previous study on the Projects of Innovation, carried out in the academic year 1994–95, we showed that the first step in carrying out projects of innovation is determined by the permanent seminars (Marcelo *et al.*, 1996).

Techniques of data collection: the questionnaire

The data for the study were obtained using a group questionnaire, intended to be answered by all or a large majority of the teachers taking part in each seminar. It consisted of 34 items, including both multiple-choice and open responses, based on the six dimensions shown in Figure 10.1.

First, there are *descriptive* data: the title of the seminar, variables describing the members (number, level, curricular areas), and the meeting place, etc. Secondly, the *administrative* characteristics defining it and control by the authority, including contributions of economic or other type of support. Thirdly, the different aspects of *group work: experience, topic chosen*, how the idea arose, how the members work (description of a normal session), and tasks carried out. Fourthly, the *interpersonal relationships* established or maintained between group members, between the group and the management team of the school, and with other colleagues; at the same time, how co-ordination was achieved and what problems were encountered. Fifthly, information on the *planning of the seminar*, including the aims, the most-frequent activities, the resources, and the internal evaluation of the group. The sixth and last dimension refers to the *learning of the teachers*, explored as three aspects: teaching, organisation and the group work itself.

The sample

The Consejería de Educación of the Junta de Andalucía supplied us with a list of all the seminars approved for the year 1995–96: there were 2000. We did not make a selection from the sample, but approached the co-ordinators of all the permanent seminars, inviting them to take part in the study and sent them the group question-

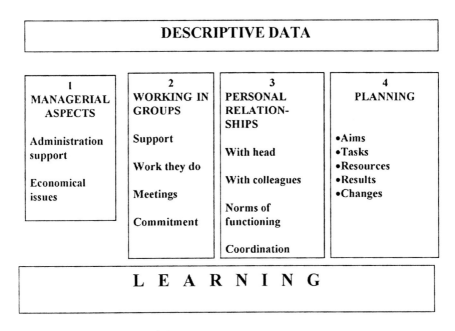

DESCRIPTIVE DATA

1 MANAGERIAL ASPECTS	2 WORKING IN GROUPS	3 PERSONAL RELATION-SHIPS	4 PLANNING
Administration support	Support	With head	•Aims
			•Tasks
	Work they do	With colleagues	•Resources
Economical issues			•Results
	Meetings	Norms of	•Changes
		functioning	
	Commitment		
		Coordination	

L E A R N I N G

Figure 10.1 Dimensions of the questionnaires

naire. We studied the work of all the permanent seminars that returned a response: 616 permanent seminars (30.8% of the population), which included 4840 teachers. In Andalusia at that time there were about 80,000 teachers (preschool, primary and secondary), so more or less 6% participate in a permanent seminar.

In these permanent seminars, the number of members ranged between four and ten (the minimum and maximum respectively established by the Education Authority, except in exceptional cases, when a seminar of up to 14 teachers can be approved). Most of the seminars had six, seven or eight members.

The teachers of a permanent seminar might belong to the same school or to various. It is interesting that the total number of schools included in the sample of teachers was 1658. Most were from public schools (87.3%), with the rest from private schools.

Continuing with the descriptive data of the sample, we think it is important to indicate that with regard to *educational level,* the highest percentage was for those seminars carried out at primary level, followed by infants and primary simultaneously. The number of seminars including teachers at secondary level was also high (Figure 10.2).

The questionnaire was sent out to the co-ordinator of the permanent seminar, with the request that the response was made at a meeting. This was done in 59% of cases. In 30.7%, the response was made by the co-ordinator.

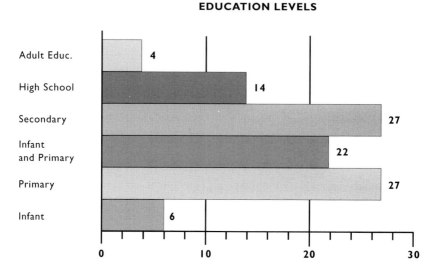

Figure 10.2 Educational level of the sample

Results

We present the results of our work as the following topics: *aims* – what are the intentions of the teachers making up a permanent seminar?; the *group* – what are the seminars, and how do they work?; and *learning* – what do the participating teachers learn?

Who takes part and why?

Of the teachers taking part in a permanent seminar, 42.4% belong to the same school, 12% to two schools, 9% to three, 10% to four and 5.5% to five. Moreover, when the teachers belong to different schools, 52% of these schools are in the same town or city. Meetings are generally held in one of the schools to which the teachers belong, although it is not uncommon that they are in other places, such as a teacher's house. The meetings last between 1 and 3 hours, and their frequency varies: 53% of the seminars meet each fortnight, while 23% meet weekly.

When we asked the teachers 'How did the idea of creating a permanent seminar come up?', most (52%) replied 'from shared needs of the group', or because of an 'attempt to solve a problem' (40%).

The permanent seminars operate in an open-ended way, and their composition varies throughout the training process. Of those that replied to the questionnaire, 62% had been in operation for more than one year, while 35% were newly set up. Some 18% had been working for two years, 12% three years, 8% four years, another

8% five years and 4% six years. At the same time, 57% of the seminars said the number of their members had changed. The main cause of leaving the seminar was a change of school (35.9%). The percentage for personal conflicts was very low (4.2%).

Aims

What are the intentions of the teachers who make up a permanent seminar? Table 10.1 shows the results of the analysis of qualitative content, established in classes, subclasses and specific codes referring to the aims included in each, as generated by the data. It also shows the frequency with which these aims appear.

As can be seen, the aims are grouped around the three basic components of education: the pupils, the teachers and the curriculum.

Aims regarding the pupils

Pupils are considered by teachers as subjects who learn and who could learn more and better. The first subclass emerging from the data is *learning*. What is the learning that concerns or interests teachers? First, there is *culture*, to help the pupils discover the Andalusian culture and to become cultured citizens who know, value and 'renew' the real form and expression of their historical, artistic, linguistic and literary heritage. Another important learning technique, although at a considerably lower level, is *thought: 'learning to think'*, or to develop cognitive and metacognitive skills: as a medium inducing pupils to become more active and self-dependent in their learning; to *learn to be* (personal learning), and to integrate other areas of learning, such as habits of health, clarification of values, the acquisition of sexual identity, and the development of self-concept and self-esteem; to *learn to live together and to co-operate*, respecting plurality (social learning); and, finally, to *learn to do* (technological learning), above all to use the new technologies. At a third level of importance is *ecological learning* – interest in the respect for and care of the environment.

All these aims are included in the educational reform, so that permanent seminars contribute to its implementation. At the same time, we think it significant that three of the seven topics proposed by the authority for study in the self-training projects are precisely 'Andalusian culture', 'Transverse cores of the curriculum' and 'New technologies of Information and Communication'. In only a few cases do teachers propose to reduce educational failure by improving the educational quality.

Aims regarding teachers

Permanent seminars are a means of learning for teachers, promoting their professional development, and are so considered by them. The first subclass that emerges is what we have called *research/training*, from the teachers' own terminology: 'to convert the Seminar into a research community where we can share our classroom experiences, and, through them, dialogue' (S.P.003, 2749–51). The most precise aims refer to

Table 10.1 Classes of aims and their frequency in the permanent seminars

Class/Code and meaning	Frequency
Aims regarding pupils	
Learning	
ACU – Cultural learning	103
AIN – Intellectual learning	60
APE – Personal learning	59
ASO – Social learning	57
ATE – Technological learning	55
AEC – Ecological learning	26
Reduction of educational failure	
MCE – Improvement of educational quality	16
Aims regarding teachers	
Research and training	
IEX – Interchange of experiences	86
ACO – Updating of knowledge	81
DRC – Discussion and critical reflection	77
RMT – A methodological revolution	54
RPE – Constant review of teaching–learning processes	32
MPD – Improvement in teaching practice	27
MRS – Improvement in social relationships between sectors of the community	14
Adaptation to the reform	
ALS – Adoption and application of the LOGSE	59
Co-ordination	
CAE – Co-ordination between the various educational agencies	28
FPP – Facilitation of parent participation	19
Motivation	
IPP – Interest the rest of the teaching staff in the project	21
MCA – Stimulate the staff and motivate the pupils	18
Aims regarding the curriculum	
Planning	
SOC – Team work to sequence aims and content	77
PLA – Draw up and review plans and programmes	42
DMI – Develop an interdisciplinary methodology	42
Experimentation	
REM – Establish and experiment with curricular materials	179
NTA – Bring new technologies into service of the curricular areas	56
EAP – Experimentation in the classroom and evaluation of the project	53
ICM – Curricular integration and motivation	31

professional growth: the *interchange of experiences*, the *updating of scientific knowledge*, and *discussion and critical reflection*. In the second place are those learning techniques that have an impact on teaching, such as *changes in methods*, the *review of teaching–learning processes*, and the *improvement of teaching practice*. Lastly, there is the desire to *improve relationships between all the sectors of the community*, by learning to collaborate in groups.

Other aims proposed by the teachers regarding their professional development are *to know* and to assimilate the educational vision in the LOGSE (Ley de Ordenación General del Sistema Educativo; or Statute for the General Organization of the Education System), which was passed in 1990, but is still in the implementation phase; to *co-ordinate with other educational agencies and with parents*; and to *promote the interest of other teachers and stimulate both staff and pupils* of the school.

Aims regarding the curriculum

Curricular innovation is a fundamental pillar of educational reform in Spain, and teachers are also interested in promoting and contributing to changes in the curriculum. Two subclasses of aims emerge: *planning and experimentation*. With regard to **planning**, it must be said that to understand the curriculum as a responsibility of teachers and school is in itself an important change; above all, the teachers consider that the curriculum is a joint responsibility requiring collaboration, co-ordination and constant reviewing to make it coherent and continuous. Three fundamental aims are proposed: team work to *sequence aims and content, to prepare and review plans and programmes*, and to *develop an interdisciplinary methodology*. The implementation of a new curriculum means **experimentation**, which in the case of the permanent seminars refers to *new curricular materials*, prepared or not by the teachers, to *new technologies*, and to testing the ideas learned in the group. Teachers also begin to experiment with an *overall, integral curriculum*, to help *motivate* the pupils.

Description of the permanent seminars

What are they and how do they work?

The permanent seminars that we have studied are a meeting point between teachers with different training backgrounds. Their prime aspect is the interchange of experiences and reflection on practice. Their nature coincides with what Fullan and Hargreaves (1992) consider as elemental in the collaborative attitude and work of teachers:

- They *arise* spontaneously, emerging from the teachers as a social group.
- The individuals taking part are *volunteers* in collaborative work, which they see as an asset deriving from their experience, inclination or non-coercive persuasion; they work together with enthusiasm and with results.
- *Orientated towards development*. Teachers work together primarily to carry out their own ideas, or those in which they have a commitment although supported from outside, within a single space and time. permanent seminars are unpredictable in that the collaborative attitude is incompatible with the scholastic system in which curriculum and evaluation are centralised.

It is important that the idea of forming a work group among teachers arises from *shared needs* of the participants. These needs are, in most cases, very similar, although it is not easy to distinguish which is the foremost: the teachers' responses indicate that the needs can be satisfied by the interchange of experiences, the establishment of links between the various curricular areas and ability to prepare curricular materials, or by the solving of the problems that crop up, such as motivation and improvement in school practices, the improvement of co-existence, and unification of criteria of action, such as evaluation. One element uniting teachers is the topic of study and reflection chosen, which is selected by the group depending on a common interest. Some 27% of the permanent seminars refer to curricular planning in general, and the other 73% have selected one area of the curriculum, or particular aspects of certain areas.

The activity to which most time is devoted is, by a long chalk, the preparation of materials for classroom use with the pupils. This takes up some 65% of seminar time, followed by analysis of the practical problems found, and the discussion and analysis of lectures and documents by the members of the seminar.

The permanent seminars devote their meetings mainly to preparing curricular materials for classroom use and to analysing, discussing and reflecting on the problems found in practice. Other options such as dissertations or demonstrations by experts, classroom observations or meetings with other teachers not belonging to the seminar are of low priority.

In the questionnaire completed by the teachers, we asked about the working of the group: participation, task assignment, degree of completing tasks, etc. We found that the seminars usually have a permanent co-ordinator (74%) and in only 12% was co-ordination rotated. The tasks to be carried out by seminar members were assigned voluntarily, and depending on the level of knowledge and specialisation of each one, although in 23.5% of the seminars, all the teachers carried out the same tasks. In 74% of cases, the teachers claimed that the degree to which the commitments are carried out is high, while for 23.4%, it is average. The permanent seminars operate as work groups, but ones in which personal relationships count.

Learning of the teachers

Hopkins and others (1994) indicate that teaching and learning are the prime focus of effort for school improvement. The key element in professional development is that of the work group, because that is where teachers get understanding of new practices, see demonstrations of teaching strategies that they can acquire and have the opportunity to practise. In addition, they can themselves transfer these skills to the school and to the classroom. One item of the questionnaire asked the teachers to say, in their own words, what they had learned and how they had improved as a result of taking part in the permanent seminar. We made a qualitative analysis of their responses, grouping the open replies into categories.

The field where the learning of the teachers is most felt is in the *classroom and in the concrete day-to-day work* of the school. This means it is important that the

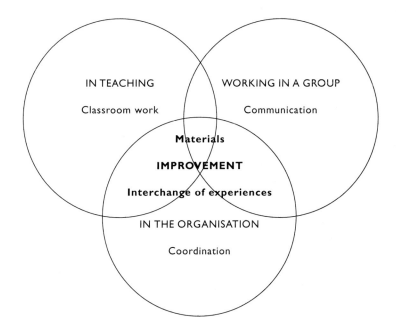

Figure 10.3 Dimensions and teachers' learning

learning is significant; for adults this means connection and recognition of ideas. Significant learning is essentially creative.

Figure 10.3 shows the three great fields of learning of teachers: learning about questions of classroom teaching, about working in group as professional requirement and about organisational learning.

To illustrate these results we have selected the most representative sentences written by the teachers in the open-ended questions of the questionnaire. One of the most important parts of the teachers' learning is classroom work and all that is related with it – basically, changes in the way of giving classes: 'we have been able to improve or change in some cases the way of giving our class', 'more-detailed methods', 'organising our class and tasks', 'a more encouraging method, which has helped for all the rest'.

What has changed in the way of giving classes? The explanations given are varied – we will use the teachers' own words to describe the changes, and attempt to show what they mean. This is a method *based on play*, that is, the use of play as a teaching resource; it is *dynamic, active, participative, creative, attractive* and *novel* for the pupil. all the members of the group reflect on and interchange their experiences of working in the classroom, trying to find new resources among themselves, to resolve the problems cropping up and to learn from them. New methods enable an approach to new contents, or at least allow them to be dealt with in a different way; their

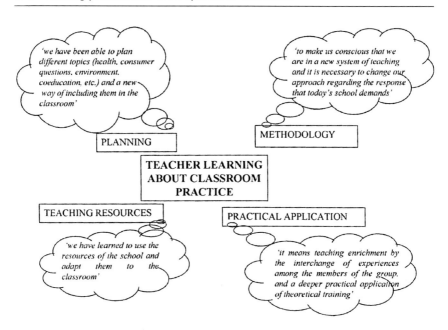

Figure 10.4 Teacher learning about classroom practice

intention is 'to make us conscious that we are in a new system of teaching and it is necessary to change our approach regarding the response that today's school demands'. The teachers are concerned about topics such as the environment, drug prevention, music, ceramics (a typical Andalusian art form), reading. In summary: they have adopted 'an open attitude towards innovation', which is an important aspect of learning for classroom work.

What most interests teachers is, obviously, the daily teaching–learning process, but there is also some interest in getting new knowledge and concepts, providing an innovative understanding of *the philosophy in the reform: work on curricular projects both at school level* and within a particular curricular area. In addition, there is a need to learn how to make the recommended curricular adaptations possible, by both *better planning of the teaching units and greater adaptation to the needs of the pupil* (Figure 10.4).

This need extends to other aspects, such as the preparation of materials, the capacity to lead a class to different levels, and adaptation of the curriculum in the different schools to which the teachers of the seminar belong; in summary, *teaching and curricular planning* for adaptation to the needs of pupils – a new field for innovation, with a wider view on special educational needs, implying greater thrust from teachers in their classroom delivery; and giving teachers the chance to gain confidence regarding innovations, which they understand 'as a new attitude in front of a new class, like a challenge'. They also gain information about specific topics, and about the culture of the pupils. Planning is a professional situation in which the teachers indicate what they have learned by working together. This means the preparation and programming of new, all-encompassing subjects, the preparation of work guides for use in the classroom, and an open attitude towards innovation: 'we have been able to plan different topics (health, consumer questions, environment, coeducation, etc.) and a new way of including them in the classroom, together – the educational community'. This situation has given the teachers an opportunity to share teaching experiences and to become better informed about what is happening in the schools. At the same time, it has provided a practical opportunity for improved analysis in the classroom, based on observation and experimentation: 'we have learned to define and identify the behaviour of our pupils clearly, to act consistently and automatically in difficult situations, and to break up classroom isolation'.

With regard to *teaching resources*, the seminar has a double function: it promotes the preparation of new materials, 'to have more materials for studying the environment and to count on the support of experience', and, at the same time, it is an occasion for getting to know and attempting to use new materials, above all those connected with the *New Technologies* 'improvement in mastering the computer, in particular word processors and databases for educational aims'. Teachers also recognise that via the seminar they have a greater stimulus to use more resources in general: 'we have learned to use the resources of the school and adapt them to the classroom'. *Evaluation* is a source of learning for teachers, but to a lesser degree; few groups referred to the topic; the greatest interest was the search for unified criteria in formative evaluation, which could, in turn, help in the evaluation of learning processes.

Practical application of what they learn is another concern of teachers in their training. They need to have a clear idea of the effectiveness of their learning; in this sense, they feel motivated for group work because 'it means teaching enrichment by the interchange of experiences among the members of the group, and a deeper practical application of theoretical training'.

The learning of teachers via the group

Practically all learning phenomena are the result of direct experience, though they may derive vicariously from observing the behaviour of others and the consequences of such behaviour. *Learning by observation* enables the individual to generate and regulate patterns of behaviour, and thus has a great effect in the practice of teaching. Teachers, during group work, are immersed in networks of professional relationships. The opinions and behaviour of those enjoying the same professional status have a great effect in the dissemination of the practices adopted by certain members of the group.

What have the teachers taking part in the permanent seminars achieved?

Almost all learning is the result of direct experience, although it may be vicarious, by observation of the behaviour of others and of the consequences that such behaviour produces. The ability to learn from observation allows the individual to generate and regulate patterns of behaviour, and thus has a great impact on the practice of teaching. In this regard, the teachers are quite clear about the learning acquired. Above all, they emphasise *positive personal relationships*, which, however, have to be worked at: 'our relationships inside the group are very good; at first, there were quite a lot of problems which we overcame with time; there is friction from time to time, disagreements and differences, but we get over it', in addition, they think it important 'to know how to take criticism from colleagues and how to pick up the pieces when topics are begun badly', because it is a great opportunity to increase knowledge and improve practice. All the groups mentioned the need 'to be tolerant and respect the ideas of others, even when the members of the group have very different inclinations'. In most cases, the results are favourable: 'we have enjoyed a great friendliness and have learned from each other'. 'Interpersonal relationships have been cemented, ideas have been proposed and worked on in common'.

Learning requires *processes of deliberation* as an essential part of the projects carried out in common, in which, according to the teachers, 'we have learned to consent on certain topics'. The teachers also feel the need of *joint reflection*; group work provides, above all, 'many occasions for reflection', because 'what is important is to reflect together, to find the co-operation and support of colleagues'. By communication, deliberation and reflection they are able *to learn together* what is done by others: 'we have been able to go inside each classroom and see how each teacher deals with conflicts, and what solutions are proposed', 'we have been shown different ways of resolving problems, and the possibility of proposing solutions at group rather than individual level'. Nevertheless, there are difficulties arising from the diversity of the members of the group: 'the more-hardworking and intelligent, whatever their age, should not be held back by the rest of the group'. However, they recognise that professional improvement requires this interchange and joint reflection: 'the group is also supportive; we have to solve the problems ourselves, with everybody contributing'. The evaluation of the group, as a learning situation, is very positive: 'group work really is possible', and develops 'the capacity to learn, above all, from the experience of other teachers'. The result is the *interchange of experiences* with the 'improvement in attitude towards teamwork and the interchange of experiences', 'the best thing has been the experience of working with teachers of other areas with the same aims' (Figure 10.5).

In summary, we transcribe what one group of teachers said: 'we have achieved good interpersonal relationships, and at the same time the creation of the seminar has allowed us to reflect on topics that concern us all, to analyse them, and to look for solutions. We think it is very important to know the opinions and experiences of each and every one of the colleagues making up the group, to be able, if necessary, to change or improve our educational practice, and to intervene actively in the playground to improve it and transform it, with the aim that should always be uppermost in our mind: to put the children into contact with the open spaces and different materials that form the building of knowledge, starting from their own activity in continuous interchange and interaction with the environment. We have learned together by reflection, interchanging ideas and experiences'.

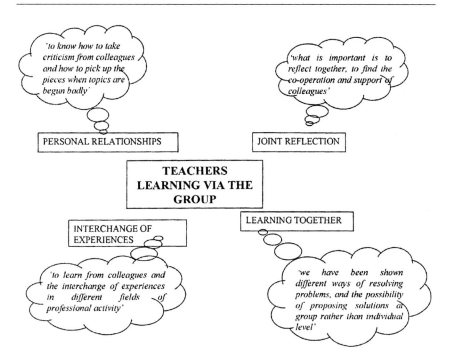

Figure 10.5 Teachers learning via the group

The learning of teachers: the organisational aspect (Figure 10.6)

Item 32 of the questionnaire asked about the impact the development of the permanent seminars had on educational centres. One specific aspect was that of organisation: what did innovation mean for the organisation of the school? The frequency of response indicates that this is not a topic greatly concerning the groups; moreover, they consider that a change affecting the school as a whole causes problems – because of a difference of interests, or from involvement in common tasks, or from leadership and advisors: 'from the organisational point of view, it is difficult to learn when the interests of each one are so different: salary weightings and similar distractions'; 'from the organisational point of view, if outside help is not available, it's always the same ones who take the brunt'; 'the organisational aspect is perhaps where we have advanced least due to the lack of training and advice that we needed but lacked'. However, the replies do indicate which topics were of most concern. One is *co-ordination* among colleagues: 'a good opportunity to co-ordinate work rationally, to have it ready at the correct moment'; 'the permanent seminars are necessary for improving co-ordination among teachers and tutors' and 'there is much co-ordination

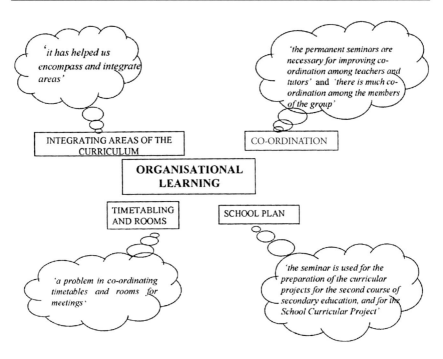

Figure 10.6 Organisational learning

among the members of the group' by 'the sharing out of tasks, and through their co-ordination, we communicate and prepare work strategies'.

Another aspect is the preparation of the *school plan*, an educational project in common that is the main work of some groups: 'we are preparing the S.P.'; 'the seminar is used for the preparation of the curricular projects for the second course of secondary education, and for the School Curricular Project'. In such cases, co-ordination is seen to be necessary between the different courses, among the teachers, and between the department of orientation and the tutors. An oft-repeated reference is that of *integrating the different areas of the curriculum*. This means *co-ordination of the different areas* regarding curricular content and the search for interdisciplinary features, and in the use of resources: 'it has helped us encompass and integrate areas'; 'we have gone deeper into co-ordination and integration of the different subject areas'; 'our intention was always that this activity was inter-disciplinary, although we did find certain problems'; 'it has helped us encompass and integrate areas'. An organisational topic that cannot be left out is that of *timetabling and rooms*, although it appears very rarely, and is always related with some problem concerning the group: 'a problem in co-ordinating timetables and rooms for meetings'.

Conclusions

Comparison of the goals of self-development proposed by the permanent seminars with the learning acquired by the teachers reveals a great coherence and coincidence. If the present study has shown anything, it is that the *work group* is an ideal situation for professional development. Teachers find in it a way to improve their ideas and practices, and to achieve a greater sense and satisfaction in their professional life. However, they also find the curriculum as a source for organising a coherent and valuable whole, being founded on an *attitude of collaboration* that orientates the school in carrying out a *Common Educational Project*.

What does this experience show us that could be useful in programmes of professional development? We believe that the study demonstrates certain conditions that the programmes should include:

School-based learning group

Learning in the workplace is being considered a new approach to teacher development. This means that individuals or groups acquire, interpret, re-organise, assimilate or change information, skills and feelings jointly. In this new paradigm, the learning design emphasises critical reflection. However, learning within the workplace involves reflection, because reflection of evaluation of what has been done, becomes part of the way in which individuals do something in a particular place.

Teachers' learning should be from their own experience and from direct contact with the problems. Gil Rodríguez and Garcia Saiz (1993) note that in informal groups, the factors necessary for agreement among members are (apart from physical closeness) common personal needs, interests and experience in work, and established relationships, as we have found in this study.

Constructing from experience and developing group skills

Since professional knowledge is based on practice and observing the experiences of others, there have to be opportunities not only for mutual observation, but also for creating situations in which individuals and groups can think about the processes and content of their learning. At the same time, group learning should be the object of reflection, focusing discussion on how the experiences of the members can have an impact on their work through increased participation and collaboration in classroom activity.

Creating a climate of support gives sense to the professional community of the members, their collaboration and their professional dialogue, not only when dealing with groups formally constituted to participate in training projects of the Education Authority, as in this case, but also with more informal groups seeking school improvement. Groups cannot be 'grafted onto' existing structures, but must be real cells of a new kind of organisation.

References

Fullan, M. and Hargreaves, A. (1992) *What's Worth Fighting for in Your School? Working Together for Improvement*, Buckingham: Open University.

Gil Rodríguez, F. and Garcia Saiz, M. (1993) *Grupos en las Organizaciones*, Madrid: Eudema.

Hopkins, D., Ainscow, M. and West, M. (1994) *School Improvement in an Era of Change*, London: Cassell.

Marcello, C. *et al.* (1996) 'Educational innovations as staff development: an evaluative approach', *British Journal of In-Service Education*, **22**(2), 185–201.

Chapter 11

Teams

John West-Burnham

This is an edited version of a chapter previously published in *Managing Quality in Schools*, Harlow: Longman, 1992.

Introduction

A team is a quality group. Almost all organisations, and schools in particular, create teams as the major vehicle for organising work. However, there is a substantial gap between labelling a group a team and creating an effective work team that is able to function in a total quality environment. Too often teams are established and expected to operate simply by virtue of having delegated tasks – little consideration is given to the way in which the team actually functions. Designing and developing teams is rarely seen as a priority in schools. They are created by virtue of knowledge, experience and status, not by the ability of the individuals to work collaboratively. The purpose of this article is to examine:

- the significance of teams;
- the characteristics of effective teams;
- team building;
- team development.

The significance of teams

Effective teams have come to be seen as one of the crucial characteristics of quality organisations and, equally significantly, one of the most powerful catalysts in an organisation for implementing change. As Katzenbach and Smith (1993) explain:

> In any situation requiring the real time combination of multiple skills, experience and judgements, a team inevitably gets better results than a collection of individuals . . . teams are more flexible . . . teams are more productive than groups . . . Teams and performance are an unbeatable combination.
>
> (p. 15)

However much emphasis on team work has become commonplace of management writing, schools do seem to be remarkably unwilling or unable to convert themselves into team-based organisations This may be attributed to three related factors. First, the organisational structures and career patterns of education are profoundly hierarchical. Second, the concept of professional autonomy has led to, and consistently reinforces the notion of, individual working and personal accountability. Third, the actual organisation of many schools means that teachers are geographically isolated for much of their working day. (What percentage of your week is spent working away from other adults?) This culture of individualism is at the heart of many of the dysfunctional aspects of school life and even when teachers do come together their capacity to work as a team, rather than as a group, is inevitably constrained. Senge (1990) describes this phenomenon as the unaligned team with individuals with varying levels of power heading in different directions:

> The fundamental characteristic of the relatively unaligned team is wasted energy. Individuals may work extraordinarily hard, but their efforts do not efficiently translate to team effort. By contrast when a team becomes more aligned, a commonality of direction emerges and individuals' energies harmonise. There is less wasted energy.
>
> (p. 234)

Senge contrasts the coherent and focused light of a laser with the diffuse and incoherent light of a light bulb in which a substantial proportion of the energy is dissipated as heat, or hot air – a well known phenomenon in ineffective groups.

A further significant attribute of a team-based approach is related to organisational growth and development. Organisations cannot learn, only individuals can, and they then articulate and share their learning in order to create a common understanding. In most circumstances we learn better in teams. Taylor and McKenzie (1997) demonstrate how an approach to team learning for students has had an impact on teachers' behaviour:

> Teacher collegiality is increased; they discuss problems that arise, deal with issues that are of importance to them and provide support for each other. This model steps beyond the token gesture at collegiality, largely anecdotal, to be a more sophisticated and useful form of professionals treating each other with respect and developing meaningful, practical solutions to the challenges that are faced by the team.
>
> (p. 153)

More importantly perhaps is the fact that the way teachers work together is a model for the way students work together:

> These students have the opportunity to experience success, through working co-operatively and sharing their unique knowledge with others in a structured

situation. Co-operative social behaviour is taught and developed. . . . They also understand that a team approach to problem-solving or assignment work is often more welcome . . . as there is a richness in the quality and quantity of ideas.

(p. 154)

Much of our learning takes place through articulation, explanation, questioning, modelling and responding to others. These processes are much more likely to be effective if they take place in a socially sophisticated environment, i.e. a team. Simple sociometrics will indicate that we are unable to relate effectively with all the members of the organisation to which we belong. An optimum number appears to be between four and twelve, depending on the task. Organisations therefore need to be seen as the sum of their teams, just as teams are the sum of their members, but with the potential to be greater than the sum. Organisational learning and thus growth and improvement are only likely if individuals are learning in aligned teams.

A final manifestation of the significance of teams is to be found in what might be termed personal integrity and potential. Although many of the greatest break-throughs in art and science are highly and uniquely personal, most of us live in response to others, we create meaning and develop social understanding through our patterns of social relationships. Teams, therefore, may be a highly significant component in personal realisation. Covey (1989) argues this point as follows:

The person who is truly effective has the humility and reverence to recognise his own perceptual limitations and to appreciate the rich resources available through interactions with the hearts and minds of other human beings. That person values the differences because those differences add to his knowledge, to his understanding of reality. When we're left to our own experiences we constantly suffer from shortage of data.

(p. 277)

Teams do make a difference – there are abundant analogies to be drawn from sporting activities but they can all be summarised by considering the relationship between sporting expertise and skill, leadership and team success. Technical skill does not guarantee success, the expert practitioner is not necessarily the best captain, and assembling the most talented individuals does not always create a winning team. Just as expertise with the cricket bat is not necessarily indicative of leadership skills, so expertise in the classroom is no guarantee of the ability to collaborate with colleagues. There can be a real tension between the autonomy (and isolation) of the classroom and the need to work in a team. This view is reflected in the work of Murgatroyd (1985) and Torrington *et al.* (1989); synthesising their views produces an analysis of the problematic nature of teams in schools.

1   School 'teams' place great emphasis on the tasks (agendas) of managing and little emphasis on the processes (networks). 'Getting the job done' is seen as more

significant than how the job is done. However, the lack of concern with process can often be to the detriment of task achievement.

2   'Teams' in schools lack a 'bias for action' – they spend too much time debating issues and principles (over which they may have little or no control) and too little time solving problems, formulating solutions and developing a commitment to action. Groups debate – teams act.

3   Poorly managed 'teams' in schools are reactive – responding to events rather than anticipating them and often seeking solace in routine chores rather than driving the vision and becoming anticipatory. This leads to work becoming a chore and ritualistic.

4   'Teams' are often not concerned with their own social needs. They spend insufficient time recognising, reinforcing and celebrating each other. Equally they will not devote time to planning and reviewing their work nor will they seek to develop their skills as a team or the potential of individuals to become effective team members.

The working of these 'immature' teams will often be characterised by very formal social exchanges (e.g. the use of titles rather than first names); the use of quasi-parliamentary procedures (e.g. 'On a point of information, headmistress, may I enquire through the chair . . . ?'); the reading of documents to the team and the active pursuit of red herrings (e.g. debating the influence of social hierarchies of nineteenth-century England when planning the seating arrangement for prize giving).

At best teams are a compromise between individual perceptions, needs and values and organisational imperatives. The tension between the individual and the organisation can never be truly reconciled but teams offer the best hope of respecting individual integrity and the demands of the organisation. More positively, teams offer the basis for enhancing the individual while allowing the school to function.

The characteristics of effective teams

A synthesis of the research of McGregor (1960), Likert (1961) and Blake and Mouton (1964) produces the 'map' of effective team functioning, shown in Figure 11.1.

The strength and creative potential of teams is derived from the application of each of these characteristics, but more importantly from the critical mass achieved when they are linked and synergy is achieved. At that point the 'whole' is considerably greater than the sum of the parts. Each characteristic is complex and demanding in its own right and needs to be explored in some detail.

Explicit and shared values

It is worth stressing that no team can operate effectively unless it is working in a context where the values are clear and agreed and translated into a mission. Equally it is important that the personal values of team members are public and understood.

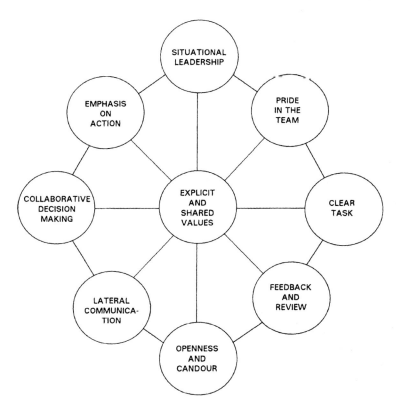

Figure 11.1 The components of effective team work.
(Source: West-Burnham (1992))

Each person knows the values everyone else brings to the team so they are not being continually debated (see 'forming' and 'storming' in Table 11.2).

Situational leadership

Effective teams require leadership that displays all the characteristics explored previously. However, in the context of team working a new dimension is necessary: the willingness and ability of the designated leader to defer, to stand back and to allow other team members to assume control according to the needs of the situation. This implies a detailed understanding of the knowledge and capabilities of each team member and the 'grace' to pass on authority. For example, a deputy headteacher may have highly sophisticated decision-making and interpersonal skills and so is the best person to chair management meetings. A relatively junior member of staff may be the most knowledgeable about flexible learning – she should be allowed to lead and is entitled to the wholehearted support of the team. In this way the team is effective and a team member is empowered.

Pride in the team

This implies commitment and involvement and is manifested in high morale and loyalty. Team members believe in themselves, in each other and in the team as a whole and this is expressed frequently both internally and externally. There is a self-fulfilling belief: 'We are good and we can deliver quality'. Departments in schools that are doing well and feel good about themselves quickly transmit this. There is even the possibility of displays of enthusiasm.

Clear task

Without a clear task, effective team work is impossible. Teams that are set intangible goals, unclear outcomes and lack information, resources and a timescale are unlikely to be motivated; in fact they are more likely to plod and amble rather than spring. For a team to sprint it requires:

- specific outcomes;
- performance indicators;
- realistic targets;
- information and resources;
- nurture and reinforcement;
- a timescale.

Sprint teams have their eyes clearly on the tape, know exactly how far they have to travel and explode into action. Too often in schools, teams are sent on country rambles when they need to be racing. To alter the sporting metaphor somewhat, teams do not win by debating if the goal posts are moving – they win by scoring goals.

Feedback and review

Effective teams are very self-conscious; they devote time to getting feedback from their clients and from each other. Team review is a permanent feature of every activity. This is not introspection for its own sake but rather review as part of a learning process. The review of task completion and team processes provides the basis for change through learning. Sophisticated teams will abandon the task to explore what is happening in process teams – to identify and reinforce success and to tackle problems until they are solved. The team that does not invest in itself is unlikely to add value to its way of working.

Openness and candour

All issues are open to discussion, there are no 'hidden agendas' and every member of the team feels able to offer suggestions, ideas, comments, information, praise and criticism. Relationships are comfortable and relaxed and the climate is supportive;

'Yes, and . . .' is used rather than 'Yes, but . . .'. Criticism is frank and direct and aimed at the problem not the person. Further, it is not negative but is used to remove an obstacle. Team members express their feelings as well as their opinions on the task; the effective team cultivates the ability to talk easily about emotional and personal responses.

Lateral communication

Effective teams are also characterised by lateral communication; team members are able to communicate with each other without reference to the team leader or other members of the team. Complex networks are formed and nourished by the team – they are not seen as a threat but rather as potential enrichment. Equally, sub-sets within the team are open and report back. This process in itself develops skills and reinforces relationships to the benefit of the team as a whole.

Collaborative decision making

Effective teams make the best decisions – the decision is the 'best fit' and will be fully implemented by team members. Quality decisions emerge from the full utilisation of the knowledge and skills of the team members, which means that the decision will have been made in the minimum time but to maximum effect. Collaborative decision making avoids voting, alternative viewpoints are worked through and disagreements resolved. Crucially the team is enhanced socially by the decision-making process.

Emphasis on action

Teams make things happen – their decisions are expressed in terms of action. Each team member knows what has to be done, by whom and when. Effective teams do not write minutes of their meetings – they issue agreed actions.

Effective teams expect to accomplish the impossible. Miracles may take a little longer. Teams balance task and process – what the job is and how it is done (see Figure 11.2). Position A represents an ideal, the optimum to be worked for where the task is achieved effectively and there are high-level personal relationships. Quality is delivered in terms of product and process. Any other position on the grid compromises one or both. High concern for tasks with little regard for process denies the social significance of work; high concern for process at the expense of task removes the point of the team's existence. The design, recruitment and development of the team will have a significant impact on its outcomes in terms of both task and process.

Team building

Effective teams do not happen by chance; they have to be created deliberately and managed systematically. Given the significance of the outcomes of educational

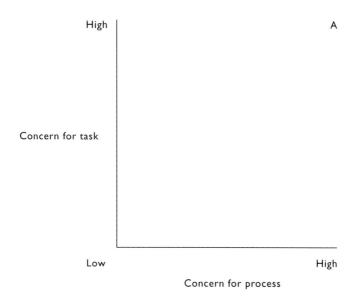

Figure 11.2 Task and process. (Source: after Blake and Mouton (1978))

decision making and the pressures on the time of teachers and managers in schools, the importance of creating effective teams cannot be overstated. Teams in schools are rarely created with principles of team building in mind. Team membership is often a low-order selection factor if it is an issue at all. Induction is likely to be in terms of administrative procedures if it takes place.

It may be appropriate to distinguish between structural and ad hoc teams in schools. Structural teams will include the senior management team, academic and pastoral units and groups set up to manage specific issues such as the curriculum, budget or staff development. Ad hoc groups are set up to manage specific issues, e.g. cross-curricular initiatives, implementation of a particular reform or event. In both cases the capability of teachers to work as leader or member of a team will not be an issue. Membership will be on the basis of experience, status or volunteering. Significance might be attached to consultation; rarely will the capabilities of the person as a team member be a factor. This might help to explain the frustration often experienced by so-called team members in schools – the frustration arises because they cannot function as members of teams. Table 11.1 provides a starting point for analysing team effectiveness.

A score in excess of 35 indicates that the rest of this chapter is probably redundant; 25–35 indicates there will probably be something of interest to you; 9–24 I just hope this chapter can meet your needs. Once you have completed this analysis get other members of your team to complete it independently. Then use a team meeting to discuss your perceptions by displaying the scores on a flip chart or OHP and

Table 11.1 Team effectiveness analysis

Complete this analysis thinking of a team of which you are currently a member. Score each section according to how you perceive the applicability of each set of statements

1	Values and purpose are not discussed	1	2	3	4	5	We share and implement common values
2	Leadership is restricted to one or two people	1	2	3	4	5	Leadership is shared according to need
3	Team membership is a chore and a bore	1	2	3	4	5	There is genuine pride in team membership
4	Objectives are not shared or understood	1	2	3	4	5	We are committed to our objectives
5	We never talk about how we are doing	1	2	3	4	5	We systematically review our performance
6	Communication is restricted, cautious	1	2	3	4	5	Communication is open, robust, honest
7	The team leader dominates	1	2	3	4	5	Our abilities are fully utilised, we are trusted
8	Decisions are taken by voting or by the leader	1	2	3	4	5	We all share and support decisions
9	Action is unclear or absent	1	2	3	4	5	We all know who does what by when

(Source: West-Burnham (1992))

analysing the significance of any discrepancies in perceptions. If your score is below 20–25, it will probably be very difficult to get this review on the agenda.

Another means of analysing the maturity of the team is to consider its level of development. Tuckman (1985) suggests that teams go through a series of clear stages in the move to effectiveness, as illustrated in Table 11.2.

The central principle in team building is to minimise the time spent forming and storming, to make norming as powerful as possible and to devote the maximum amount of time to performing. It is not possible to 'short circuit' the process, i.e. avoid forming and storming, but with deliberate team management the negative aspects can be minimised. Analysis of the way in which some teams work suggests that they never get beyond the first two stages, all their time being spent in debating the task and sorting out personal relationships. Eventually they have to accept an imposed decision and are unable to produce acceptable conclusions in the time available. There are a number of possible explanations for this.

1   The task itself is impossible – it has not been properly defined or is beyond the resources of the team, i.e. it is inappropriate.

Table 11.2 Stages in team maturity

Task	Stage	Process
Clarification of outcomes sought, roles uncertain	Forming	Anxiety, uncertainty, domination, ambiguity
Value and feasibility of task questioned, principles and methods debated	Storming	Conflict between group's resistance to leader, individual initiatives, opinions polarised
Planning starts, working standards laid down, roles clear	Norming	Working procedures established, communication of feelings, mutual support, sense of team identity
Solutions to problems emerge, more output in less time, quality of outcomes improves, decisions are translated into action	Performing	High levels of trust and interdependence, roles are flexible, individuals and team relaxed and confident

(Source: West-Burnham (1992))

2   The team has not been designed to accomplish the task, i.e. the wrong people have been nominated or allowed to volunteer.
3   The team lacks the skills to work together.

The first problem can be resolved only by appropriate delegation, the second issue is dealt with below and the third in the next section, team development.

If teams are to move rapidly from forming to performing, then the capabilities of team members to work in a team have to play an important role in team design and recruitment. Some of the most important work in this respect has been done by Belbin (1981). Belbin analysed the performance of management teams and found that there was not always a correlation between a team's ability to perform and the intellectual qualities and experience of its members. In fact, the so-called 'alpha' teams – the brightest and best – were often out-performed by apparently random groupings. In analysing the reasons for this Belbin concluded that the behaviour of individuals in teams may be a more significant factor than either ability or experience. Teams are social entities and their performance will be determined by social interactions and these, according to Belbin, can be identified and analysed.

Belbin (1993) postulates nine team roles as outlined in Table 11.3.

Table 11.3 Belbin's team roles

Role	Contribution	Allowable weakness
Plant	Creative, imaginative, unorthodox Solves difficult problems	Ignores details Too preoccupied to communicate effectively
Resource investigator	Extrovert, enthusiastic communicative Explores opportunities	Over-optimistic Loses interest once initial enthusiasm has passed
Co-ordinator	Mature, confident, a good chairperson Clarifies goals, promotes decision making, delegates well	Can be seen as manipulative Delegates personal work
Shaper	Challenging, dynamic, thrives on pressure Has the drive and courage to overcome obstacles	Can provoke others Hurts people's feelings
Monitor/ evaluator	Sober, strategic and discerning Sees all options Judges accurately	Lacks drive and ability to inspire others Overly critical
Team worker	Co-operative, mild, perceptive and diplomatic Listens, builds, averts friction, calms the waters	Indecisive in crunch situations Can be easily influenced
Implementer	Disciplined, reliable, conservative and efficient Turns ideas into practical actions	Somewhat inflexible Slow to respond to new possibilities
Completer	Painstaking, conscientious, anxious Searches out errors and omissions Delivers on time	Inclined to worry unduly Reluctant to delegate Can be a nitpicker
Specialist	Single-minded, self-starting, dedicated Provides knowledge and skills in rare supply	Contributes on only a narrow front Dwells on technicalities Overlooks the 'big picture'

(Source: West-Burnham (1992))

Belbin's team roles

A person's team characteristics are identifies on the basis of completing a diagnostic inventory. This will usually identify one or two roles that score significantly higher than others, i.e. the dominant types of behaviour. Other types will receive very low scores and are probably not available. The interpretation of individual results needs to bear a number of points in mind:

- there are no right or wrong or 'good or bad' types – all are valid and appropriate.
- the balance of the scoring will probably indicate a range of possible team behaviours;
- the scoring will reflect the types in a given context at a certain time – both factors are variable and scoring can change;
- the secondary type can often be developed.

Although the Belbin inventory provides the basis for useful personal insights and self-appraisal it is even more powerful if used by a whole team as the basis for analysis of the team's working patterns. This can be a useful exercise at the forming stage. Consider a team that is made up of three shapers, one chair and a company worker. It is more than likely that the storming stage will reach hurricane proportions as the majority of the team will be striving to be dominant and the company worker will have a negative experience. If status is added into the equation, then the chances are that the team's inability to function will lead to decisions being made outside the team and imposed.

The converse example is also problematic – a team that is composed of company and team workers with perhaps a resource investigator is just as likely to fail to achieve its task. A further issue for schools is that, on the basis of observation, many teams in schools lack monitor evaluators and completer finishers. This has significant implications for teams being able to complete tasks on time and according to specification.

The effective team, the quality team, is one that balances team roles so that task completion and the process issues are balanced. There can be no prescription for the ideal or optimum team but there do seem to be some guidelines.

- there should be one chair or one shaper, not both;
- according to the size of the team there should be a balance of team and company workers;
- other types should be included according to the nature of the task.

The senior management team of a highly regarded secondary school has the following make-up:

Post	Primary role	Secondary role
Head	Resource investigator	Chair
Deputy (Curriculum)	Implementer	Shaper
Deputy (Pastoral)	Chair	Team worker
Senior teacher (Admin)	Completer	Implementer
Senior teacher (TVEI)	Team worker	Resource investigator

More by luck than planning the school is led by a team that has a range of complementary roles with secondary roles that allow for flexibility according to circumstances. Research in one primary school revealed that the head was a shaper/team worker and all her staff were company/team workers. Harmony reigned but the burden on the head was enormous. A working party on appraisal in one particular secondary school failed perhaps because the designated chair was a company worker, the other members of the group were either shapers or innovators and there was no completer or monitor evaluator.

Belbin's work is problematic – the inventory was not designed for use in the education sector, his types derive from a study of small groups on management courses and the scientific validity of his research has yet to be fully tested. However, his work has met with a high degree of acceptance and it does provide the starting point for detailed and systematic analysis. In the context of team building the Belbin inventory can help by:

- providing data for the analysis of team working and so facilitating discussion;
- indicating possible causes of failure and potential remedies;
- acting as a dispassionate means of discussing individual behaviour;
- identifying the composition of a team and so informing team development needs;
- helping with recruitment of team members when other appropriate factors have been taken into account;
- diagnosing individual development needs;
- identifying factors in team success, so allowing them to be replicated.

Team building is too complex to be left to serendipity. There are undoubtedly many already successful teams – but perhaps they could be better. Time is too precious to accept unsatisfactory teams as inevitable, team membership being a crucial determinant of an individual's perception of work.

Belbin demonstrates that teams that are successful:

> develop well informed self-insight and took appropriate action in managing their style of operation.
>
> (p. 50)

Such action:

> needed to be triggered off by an awareness of the collective self-image and a desire to manage what was there effectively. A coherent self-image emerged therefore, not only as an advantage for the progression of individuals, but for the team itself.
>
> (ibid.)

Team development

Effective teams result from empowered individuals learning to collaborate so that individual knowledge, skills and qualities are deployed to maximum effect. The group

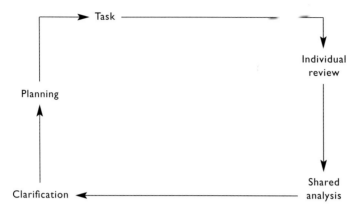

Figure 11.3 How teams learn. (Source: West-Burnham (1990))

is one of the most powerful learning vehicles so the effective team has the potential to heighten the learning of its members if its standard operating procedures are perceived as learning opportunities. This involves an understanding of:

- how teams learn;
- what they need to learn;
- what techniques are appropriate.

Teams learn by relating experience to analysis and by changing their behaviour in the future (see Figure 11.3).

Having completed a task, individual members of the team review their own behaviour, that of their colleagues and of the team as a whole, in terms of both task achievement and team processes. These individual perceptions are then shared and a consensus view of the team's performance emerges: problems are identified, reasons for failure established and the factors involved in success celebrated and reinforced. This allows the team to clarify, to understand its behaviour and so to agree how to approach the next task, what behaviour to stress and what to minimise so as to improve its performance. Three vital functions are taking place in this process.

1   The team is learning from direct, real experience – the most powerful learning agent.
2   The team is looking to improve its performance continuously.
3   The learning process is part of the work process – there is no artificial divide in terms of significance or loss of work time.

Two changes in team management are necessary to create a learning team. First, time has to be built into the team's activities to allow for planning and review; in essence

Listening	Collaborating decision making
Questioning	Problem solving
Giving feedback	Conflict resolution
Summarising	Time management
Proposing ideas	Stress management
Building on suggestions	Managing meetings
Being open about feelings	Public speaking
Assertiveness	Written communication

Figure 11.4 Skills for effective team work. (Source: West-Burnham (1992))

this means that review becomes an agenda item. Second, this review needs to be detailed and systematic ensuring that every team member feels able to contribute fully. This implies a range of skills that need to be developed.

The components of effective teams identified in Figure 11.1 provide the context from which team training needs can be identified. In many ways the list corresponds to any portfolio of management development activities. The crucial difference is that the training is for the team as an entity and not in piecemeal form for the individuals in it. Too many team development courses are attended by individuals representing the team – this inevitably compromises the impact and integrity of the training. The team that trains together develops together.

The skills appropriate to effective team working are set out in Figure 11.4. This list might appear somewhat intimidating unless it is recognised that:

- teams will not work effectively without them ('If you think training's expensive, try ignorance');
- they are generic skills and will transfer into a wide variety of situations, notably the classroom.

The methods that are appropriate to the development of these skills are widely understood but not always applied.

1 The team must train and learn together.
2 It is often easier to start the process away from the work place.
3 Consultants/facilitators can drive the process and help keep the focus.
4 Non-threatening activities, the notorious management games, are often the best way to start.
5 Outdoor team development can be very powerful, instructive and fun.

6 The training should be designed by team members on the basis of perceived need.

7 The training should focus on the issues of implementation.

8 The initial event should be seen as the start of the learning process, not the process itself.

9 Team activities subsequent to the training should make constant reference to the lessons learnt.

10 The skills and expertise of team members must be used as a permanent resource.

Team training and development activities are rather like circling the earth in a space shuttle. The angle of re-entry is crucial – too steep (or enthusiastic) and the team is burnt up in the rich atmosphere of colleagues' cynicism; too shallow and the team bounces off the atmosphere, doomed to circle the real world and become management consultants. Training works if it is manifested in behaviour – there is no other justification for it.

Summary

- A team is a quality group and quality programmes depend on effective team work.
- Teams in schools are often teams in name only.
- Effective teams display nine key characteristics.
- Clear values, pride and appropriate leadership are requisites to effective team working.
- Teams cannot operate without a clear task, regular feedback and review, and openness and candour.
- Team processes involve lateral communication, collaborative decision making and outcomes in terms of action.
- Effective teams balance task and process.
- Team building requires awareness of the stages of team development and the factors influencing individual behaviour.
- Team development involves seeing learning as a crucial component of team activity.
- Teamwork requires a range of generic skills.

References

Belbin, M. (1993) *Team Roles at Work*, Butterworth-Heinemann.
Belbin, R. M. (1981) *Management Teams: Why they Succeed or Fail*, Heinemann.
Blake, R. R. and Mouton, J. S. (1964) *The Managerial Grid*, Gulf Publishing Co.
Blake, R. R. and Mouton, J. S. (1978) *The New Managerial Grid*, Gulf Publishing Co.
Covey, S. (1989) *Seven Habits of Highly Effective People*, Simon and Schuster.
Davies, B., Ellison, L., Osborne, A. and West-Burnham, J. (1990) *Education Management for the 1990s*, Longman Group UK.

Katzenbach, J. and Smith, D. (1993) *The Wisdom of Teams*, Harvard Business School Press.

Likert, R. (1961) *New Patterns of Management*, McGraw-Hill.

McGregor, D. (1960) *The Human Side of Enterprise*, McGraw-Hill.

Murgatroyd, S. (1985) 'Management teams and the promotion of staff well being', *School Organisation*, **6**(1).

Senge, P. M. (1990) *The Fifth Discipline*, Doubleday.

Taylor, S. and McKenzie, I. (1997) 'The team solution', in Davies, B. and West-Burnham, J. (1997) *Reengineering and Total Quality in Schools*, Pitman.

Torrington, D., Weightman, J. and Johns, K. (1989) *Effective Management: People and Organisation*, Prentice Hall International.

Torrington, D., Weightman, J. and Johns, K. (1989) *The Reality of School Management*, Basil Blackwell.

Tuckman, B. W. (1985) 'Development sequence in small groups', *Psychological Bulletin*, **63**.

West-Burnham, J. (1990) 'Human resource management', in Davies, B. et al. (op cit.).

West-Burnham, J. (1992) *Managing Quality in Schools*, Longman.

Chapter 12

The role of school managers in monitoring and evaluating the work of a school: inspectors' judgements and schools' responses

Sheila Russell

This is an edited version of an article previously published in *School Organisation*, **16**, 3, October 1996.

Introduction

Since 1993 systems of regular formal external inspections of schools under national and statutory frameworks have been introduced in England and Wales, managed by the Offices for Standards in Education (known as OFSTED in England). At the same time OFSTED has emphasised the value of schools developing for themselves some formal processes for evaluating their success and effectiveness. It is recognised that the two systems of internal and external evaluation have not yet been brought together in a coherent and systematic way (MacBeath *et al.*, 1996) and that there are methodological differences in the two approaches (Moon, 1995). In attempting to integrate the systems with the aim of providing support for improvement, it is important to examine the differences between what schools understand by monitoring and evaluation and what inspectors expect to find. This article draws on the written material in OFSTED reports and school action plans to begin some contribution to that exploration.

Background

Earlier research (Metcalfe and Russell, 1996; Russell, 1996) into the effects of school inspection on teachers' working lives has identified a strong pressure on senior and middle managers in secondary schools to become more involved in monitoring the work of their colleagues in the classroom. This expectation was set out clearly in the Chief Inspector's Annual Report (OFSTED, 1995a): 'the monitoring and evaluation of the curriculum, the quality of teaching, and standards of pupils' work by head-teachers were, however, weak in many schools' (para. 77), and was further reinforced in the following year's summary:

> Around half the schools need to pay more systematic and formal attention to observing how curriculum and pedagogic initiatives affect pupil learning.

At present, the tendency in many schools is to rely on impressionistic judgements. Monitoring to see that agreed procedures are being used and evaluation to discover their effects on the performance of pupils are poorly developed.

(OFSTED, 1996, para. 228)

One headteacher, writing in 1995, suggested that his colleagues were a little wary of taking on the recommendations of OFSTED inspectors on these issues:

You cannot help but salute these new OFSTED inspectors. In their first year of existence they have discovered the educational equivalent of turning lead into gold. To listen to them for any length of time it becomes blindingly obvious why so many of our schools are under-performing. Headteachers are just not up to scratch when it comes to monitoring and evaluation . . . Many of us would welcome it with open arms if we could be shown the value of all the time and effort that would be involved.

(Mooney, 1995)

The Teacher Training Agency (1995) has added yet a further dimension to the emphasis on monitoring and evaluation by defining professional development for middle managers in secondary schools as a national priority, stating that: 'good leadership and management at subject level is essential if the quality of teaching and learning is to be systematically and effectively monitored, evaluated and improved. Many heads of department need support and training, particularly in this aspect of their team leader role'.

A national, collective and practical understanding of 'monitoring' and 'evaluation', and their value in schools, has continued to develop since the start of OFSTED inspections in 1993. The judgements of inspectors have had some influence on what managers have begun to expect of themselves and of others. A variety of interpretations of the processes and their purposes has led, however, to different applications in schools, OFSTED inspectors are clearly instructed (OFSTED, 1995b) that inspection issues should relate directly to the improvement of teaching and learning and that there should be a strong emphasis on the teaching process in forming their judgements. Despite this, there is a danger that innovations in school monitoring and evaluation brought about as a result of inspection recommendations may become detached from their prime purpose of school improvement.

Mooney's scepticism, cited above, calls for consideration as part of the contextual-isation of this study. Is the capacity to monitor and evaluate indeed a characteristic of effective schools, and in what way? In their summary of key characteristics of effective schools, Sammons *et al.* (1995) highlight monitoring progress as an important feature of effective schools, but qualify this by noting that 'these procedures may be formal or informal, but either way they contribute to a focus on teaching and learning'. They quote the work of Murphy (1990), whose studies of effective leaders in the USA showed that they practise a range of monitoring procedures, feed back their interpretation of these to teachers and integrate these procedures with evaluation and goal setting.

Nevertheless, it is hard to find a strong research basis for the belief that effective leadership and effective schools depend on specific formal processes of individual and institutional review. Ethnographic studies, such as those of Little (1982) and Rosenholtz (1989), identify the importance of a climate where teachers engage in frequent talk about teaching practice and build up a shared language. In successful schools they may be observed teaching and provided with critical evaluations of their work. Darling-Hammond (1990) makes a useful distinction between bureaucratic evaluation and professional evaluation. professional evaluation is akin to that engaged in by a learning organisation, which, in Leithwood and Aitkin's (1995) definition, involves continuous development by a group of people of more effective and efficient ways of accomplishing a purpose, the value of which is also continually under review. Yet it is possible, even likely, that a school's reaction to a bureaucratic process such as external inspection will be the adoption of further internal bureaucratic procedures. Without a more critical examination of the nature of the evaluation that is being recommended or adopted, it may be that schools will not benefit from the advice they are being given.

The research study methods

The objectives of this study, undertaken in the academic year 1995–96, were to explore what evidence had led OFSTED inspectors to attach a priority to monitoring and evaluation of classroom practice as a key issue for a school and to investigate how the schools themselves had interpreted the recommendations made. Accordingly, a selection was made of schools where the linked issues of monitoring and evaluation and classroom practice had been highlighted in inspection reports and, for those schools, a classification was made of the kinds of weaknesses perceived by inspectors. Information was obtained from action plans about the changes schools proposed to make in response and analysed to characterise the range of school responses. This study of documents provides a framework for the second stage of the research (to be undertaken in the summer term 1996), when the progress of three schools will be investigated through a case study approach, with the aim of exploring how the intentions were translated into changed practice.

In order to sample a wide range of schools, 100 inspection reports were read (all those inspected in the north and east of England in the spring term 1995). This sample was 16% of the secondary schools inspected in that academic year and included schools from 23 metropolitan districts and 13 shire counties. Of the 100 schools, 79 were local education (LEA) maintained schools, 13 were voluntary schools and 8 grant-maintained schools. There was a slightly higher percentage of LEA schools than in the full group inspected nationally in that year.

From these 100 schools, 22 reports met the criterion of recommending action on an issue, or issues, that referred to introducing monitoring and evaluation linked to the improvement of teaching quality and to the responsibilities of subject managers.

A further 18 schools had issues about monitoring and evaluation, but less clearly linked to improving classroom practice. The first stage of the study was an analysis of the 22 reports, and the action plans that had been produced by these schools, in response to the requirement of the legislation governing OFSTED inspection. Where relevant, comparison was made with findings made available by OFSTED from the aggregated data for all secondary schools inspected in 1994–95, in the Statistical Digest of data held in the OFSTED Educational Information System (EIS). Although inspectors pass on their judgements about teaching quality, leadership and management to OFSTED in the form of grades on a 7-point scale, these grades are not made public for individual schools and confidentiality is maintained by OFSTED. In this research, therefore, interpretations of each school's strengths and weaknesses were derived from the written judgements of inspectors, which mirrors the experience of those in schools, who, despite some oral feedback, have to manage the governors' response mainly on the basis of what they understand from what is written down.

The schools

Background data about the schools are set out in Table 12.1, where the schools are listed with code letters (column 1) in order of a proxy measure of social disadvantage, the percentage of pupils eligible for free school meals (column 2). The type and size of school are shown in column 3 of Table 12.1. Information from the inspectors' reports about examination success, in terms of the percentage of pupils obtaining five grades A*–C in 1994, is shown in the table as column 4. Most reports quantify the proportion of lessons observed in the course of the inspection that were judged to be very good or good and these figures, where available, are shown in column 5. Column 6 shows the percentage of lessons observed that were deemed to be at least satisfactory.

There appeared to be nothing distinctive in terms of standards, social context, type of school or quality of teaching that differentiated the group of 22 schools from the national sample – broadly, those that emerged as research schools were representative of the secondary schools inspected in 1994–95. The standards achieved at GCSE in the research schools are distributed evenly about the national average and there is no indication that those with poor examination results were more likely than the more successful schools to be advised to undertake further monitoring. The standards of teaching quality range widely and the average for the 19 schools for which figures were available is close to the national average.

Issues and evidence

Inspectors are advised that, in a well written report, 'key issues will arise from the main findings, be specific to the school, central to its development, and improvements and set clear and achievable targets at which to aim' (OFSTED, 1994). There has, however, been some criticism because 'some of the key issues for action to be addressed in preparing an action plan for school improvement are thought to lack

Table 12.1 Contextual information about schools in sample

School	% Free school meals	Type and size	% Gaining A*–C at GCSE (1994)	% Lessons graded 1–2	% Lessons graded 1–3
A	5	11–18 Grammar, county, medium	100	75	96
B	6	11–16 Comp., county, small	40	73	93
C	6.7	11–16 Comp., county, small	49.2	35	77
D	7.4	11–18 Comp., VA, large	61	48	88
E	7.6	11–18 Comp., GM, large	47	53	82
F	7.77	11–16 Comp., county, medium	36.5	33	
G	11.5	11–16 Comp., VA, large	48.2	39	83
H	11.8	11–16 Comp., county, medium	39.3	50	85
I	12.6	11–18 Comp., county, large	42.2		80
J	13.3	11–16 Comp., county, medium	32	40	80
K	14.1	11–16 Comp., county, medium	57	33	80
L	16.2	11–16 Comp., GM, medium	37	34	75
M	25	13–19 Comp., county, medium	31.5	45	87
N	28.7	13–18 Comp., county, medium	13.2		
O	30	11–16 Comp., county, medium	29.7	22	77
P	30.1	11–18 Comp., county, medium	28.6	50	92
Q	32	11–18 Comp., county, medium	21	45	83
R	37	11–18 girls Comp., county, large	26	43	85
S	37.4	11–16 Comp., county, medium	24.8	20	73
T	39	11–18 Comp., county, medium	15.9	37	77
U	44	11–16 Comp., county, medium	10.7		
V	63	11–16 Comp., county, medium	23.4	25	62

clarity and precision' (OFSTED, 1995c). In the study described in this article it was found that some inspectors were very precise in linking their recommendation about monitoring to teaching, as in 'ensure that strategies for monitoring are effective in extending good classroom practice' (school A), but that sometimes the wording was more general and open to interpretation, as in 'review the functions and responsibilities of the senior management team and heads of faculty, and develop their roles in monitoring, reviewing and evaluating the work of the school' (school H).

Schools and researchers may question the objectivity of the conclusion that a school will benefit from further monitoring. The criterion that leads to this judgement is set out in the *Framework* (OFSTED, 1995b): 'management is to be judged in terms of the extent to which the school has an effective procedure for the evaluation of its work'. This is one of eight criteria used to evaluate leadership and management. The others are listed here in Table 12.2, which shows the average grades (from scores of 1–7, where 1 is excellent) for the national sample of secondary schools inspected in 1994–95. The rating for the effectiveness of reviewing the school's work is one of the poorest scores (indicated by a higher numerical grade) nationally for all the criteria on which schools are judged (only four others have an average of more than four, the median score). One conclusion to be drawn is that inspectors judge that

Table 12.2 Mean OFSTED inspection grades for secondary schools inspected in 1994/95 (*n* = 687)

The routine administration and organisation are very effective	2.18
Internal and external communications promote effective operations	2.52
The ethos and direction of the school promote high standards and quality very well	2.8
Working relationships to achieve common goals are very effective	2.66
The leadership of the school promotes quality of learning and standards of achievement	2.68
Planning is carried out effectively and achievable priorities and targets are set	3.49
The implementation of plans and policies is very effective	3.64
Reviewing of the school's work is very effective	4.14

most schools will benefit from an improvement to their review procedures and this interpretation is consistent with the lack of a unifying distinguishing feature for the group of research schools in this study.

Inspectors are guided in what to look for by the *Framework*, which, in the version in use in 1995 (OFSTED, 1993), suggested that positive features would be:

- the implementation of plans is monitored;
- firm arrangements for periodic reviews exist;
- performance indicators (or success criteria) are used and comparative information sought;
- lessons learned are fed back to staff and governors.

Guidance to inspectors means that they will hold this model in mind, but they are further instructed only to recommend management changes when these are seen to be a necessary step to improvement and they are advised that they should not seek to impose a particular management style on a school. In looking at inspectors' recommendations it therefore seemed crucial to determine to what extent they were clearly phrased in relation to an improvement of teaching and a raising of standards. It was found that the evidence supporting the priority given to the monitoring and evaluation issue can be grouped under three broad headings.

The first category is unacceptable variability of, or weakness in, teaching. For example, school G was advised to 'develop strategies to share best practice in teaching more widely' because 'unsatisfactory teaching was seen in some lessons in most subjects but most frequently in mathematics, geography, history and design technology'. School K was recommended to 'review teaching and learning styles to ensure that all pupils develop the full repertoire of learning skills' because 'the present quality of the teaching in the school could be further enhanced by a greater focus on the learning needs of pupils. There is a need to extend the range of teaching strategies'. And school S was required to 'implement effective procedures for monitoring and developing the quality of teaching' and 'develop the range of teaching used so as to promote pupils learning' because 'there are variations in the quality of teaching within many subject areas. Teaching is generally sound or better but when it has shortcomings the quality of learning is affected. Strategies for monitoring teaching in the classroom are not effective'.

The second category is where weaknesses are described as a lack of clarity in the definition of the head of department role or a lack of acceptance of their role by middle managers. School C, for instance, is instructed to 'improve the management of the school through clearer policies, better development planning, improved subject and aspect co-ordination and thorough monitoring of the work of the school; and work with the staff to ensure greater pace in lessons and more challenging, open-ended opportunities for pupils, especially the more able' because:

> The headteacher and the governors have a clear long term view of where the school should be heading. This focuses on the need to promote effective learning, high standards and the spiritual, moral, social and cultural development of the pupils. The school is moderately successful in achieving these aims. There is however a lack of ownership by the whole staff and subject co-ordinators do not link their own aims closely enough with those of the school.

The report on school C states that clear direction is compromised by a few staff who fail to understand the role they should play in running and developing the school.

For school L the issue is phrased in general managerial terms: 'plan to improve the cost-effectiveness of the system, with priority on management training at senior and middle management, quality assurance functions and improvement of the management information base available for decision-making', while evidence to be found in the report is more specific about the nature of the weakness:

> The senior staff have worked together for many years and know each other's strengths. They tend not to challenge each other or to step into each other's areas of work. This results in a patchy use of talent, and does not encourage a self-evaluative ethos. The roles and responsibilities of senior management are not evenly distributed and have not benefited from review.

In the third category inspectors perceive a weakness in quality assurance arrangements, according to an OFSTED model of an effective process. School G is informed that:

> Informal systems for monitoring, reviewing and evaluating the work of the school are effective in some areas, as for example in science and modern foreign languages. Elsewhere monitoring is generally supportive and in line with the caring ethos of the school, but it lacks sufficient rigour to drive development and ensure consistency of policy in practice, as for example in the assessment of pupils, in arrangements for staff development and appraisal and in the co-ordination of special educational needs provision. Informal systems, even

where responsibilities are clearly understood, lack rigour of accountability to senior management. The school should develop formal systems and procedures for monitoring, reviewing and evaluating its work.

School J is expected to: 'improve the implementation of existing plans and policies by better monitoring and evaluation (e.g. the policies on assessment, recording and reporting, the personal development of pupils, special educational needs, equal opportunity, staff development, homework, the library)'. In this instance the evidence of need is given very precisely in the report:

> There are two middle management groups which relate to the senior management team through the appropriate deputy head in the case of the pastoral group and through the whole team in the case of the team leaders group. Both groups meet regularly and effectively. Neither group has terms of reference; contribution to policy is assumed but is not explicit. Consideration should now be given to formalising the roles of senior management, the middle management groups and middle management generally with respect to policy generation, monitoring and evaluation.

Although inspectors do use criteria, their judgement on these matters seems subjective and often based on a view of management that is divorced from outcomes. The same criticism might be made of inspectors' judgements of teaching, but is mitigated by the fact that the teaching process is itself closer to the outcomes. There is less secure knowledge about the effects of management. Moreover, it is doubtful that either poor teaching or poor management can miraculously be changed for the better by the application of a prescribed set of techniques, but this is sometimes the message that schools receive.

Schools' responses

Even when the issue and the evidence are precise and linked to teaching and learning, the school may apparently not understand the recommendation. School Q, for instance, was told by the inspectors that

> Not enough has as yet been done to develop ways to monitor the quality of classroom experience, and to check on the systematic operation of policies, such as the positive behaviour programme, as they are implemented in the classroom. The development of effective ways of undertaking this evaluation is a matter of priority for the school.

Its action response was to plan to use in-service training (INSET) time to review the inspection, to review the successes and areas of concern, to review its department plans and to evaluate the first year of its planning cycle. The action plan described hoped for outcomes as 'full staff participation in planning role; the production of an updated school development plan; and procedures operating as indicated'. This is an example of a school where, despite the clarity of the report, the culture of the school has enabled it to avoid explicitly addressing the issue of classroom practice.

In reading school action plans there are limitations to what can fairly be deduced about the school itself and the likelihood of successful action. Sometimes it is hard to see why a strategy has been chosen, for instance when the hoped for outcomes are not stated in the plan or are merely a list of the tasks to be completed. For other schools it is hard to tell what is going to be done, when the tasks themselves are imprecise. A clear report does not necessarily lead to an effective action plan. As one might expect, some other forces are at work, and these may be the culture of the school, the informal relationship with the inspection team, the staff and school attitude to external inspection or the perceived urgency of the recommended issue. At this interim stage of the research project the objective is to seek to understand the intentions behind the school action plans and to conjecture what it is the school thought the inspectors wanted them to do.

Of the 22 schools, 10 wrote action plans where either the issue was avoided or was addressed superficially, a finding that replicates that of Gray and Wilcox (1995). Of the other 12, some were less precise at the stage of submission because of a stated intention to involve others more fully in the subsequent action and often indicated a relatively leisurely approach to this collaboration, as in school U's response: 'consult with middle management post holders to assist in identifying the best possible processes to ensure effective implementation of this key issue'. For this school internal monitoring of progress on the plan was described as 'ongoing monitoring', with no dates given. Typical of an apparently superficial response was school N, whose action comprised 'discussion and negotiation of revised management structure' with a performance indicator of 'clear identification of individual responsibilities'. School M's action plan, submitted more than a year after the inspection took place, despite reminders from OFSTED, took a fairly relaxed line in its objectives: 'the school needs to consider what performance indicators are appropriate other than exams and assessments to evaluate success in teaching and learning more systematically. INSET is hard to come by on this matter, but senior staff and heads of departments in particular will need to consider it'.

The more precise plans included those that adopted a bureaucratic model, with a strong hierarchical flavour, as for instance that of school T, which stated:

> Curriculum and pastoral managers will be required to initiate, develop and implement action plans which will be monitored and overseen by the senior management team.
> Middle managers will be given a brief to review their department's effective-ness and report to the senior management team. the criteria for assessing the effectiveness of departments will be determined by senior management team and closely monitored.

Another school (S) has a plan that is also clear in its expectations, but allows for more variation in practice between departments and presents individual department action plans attached to its main submission to OFSTED. The main plan states 'A practical and effective strategy of classroom observation will be implemented and a proforma will be devised, trialled and evaluated'. Success is defined by 'classroom observation of teaching is implemented'. The departments each set out how they interpret this, with very varied practice emerging across departments. The mathematics department, for instance, involves all members of department in peer observation, focusing on aspects 'we are trying to improve', while the English department opts for annual classroom visits by the head of department or senior managers.

A further small group of three schools have plans that are precise and clear, yet indicate that a collaborative approach to action will be pursued. Extracts from the data about these schools (E, O and V) are shown in Tables 12.3–12.5, where the key issues, inspectors' evidence and school response are shown side by side. In each case the action plan demonstrates an understanding that an implementation of the inspectors' recommendation should affect the quality of teaching.

Conclusion

It was found that inspectors' choice of a recommendation to increase the use of monitoring and evaluation is not strongly determined by the nature of other findings, such as those on standards, quality of teaching or management. It is likely that this is because formal monitoring is a relatively new process for all schools and that it is believed to be a 'good thing', so, rather like cod-liver oil, can be offered to the ailing and the healthy indiscriminately. The inspectors' decision that a school needs to adopt further quality assurance processes may derive from evidence of unacceptable variation in teaching quality or unacceptable variation in departmental management or it may be that the model of quality assurance the school uses is not convincing to inspectors. Schools' responses to these judgements vary. It appears that some schools struggle with a wish to make a collaborative response to what is essentially a bureaucratic demand; some respond with a vague insouciance, others adopt a top-down precise plan, others manage to convey that they will blend firmness and clarity with consultation and collaboration.

Cody (1989) writes that: 'conformity to institutional norms may ensure that minimal levels of performance are maintained and managerial competence can improve efficiency, but educational excellence derives from personal initiative and personal autonomy'. There seems to be little hope that genuine improvement will come about when inspectors have merely passed on a bureaucratic demand. Murphy (1991) notes the capacity of education to deflect improvement efforts and to respond to change in a ritualistic fashion. Although further monitoring and evaluation may be one of the keys to improvement and to a greater focus on teaching and learning by school managers, it may still be diverted into old channels of behaviour.

In the OFSTED process a school will hear the key issues and will then seek out the

Table 12.3 Issues, evidence and planned action: School E

Key issue	Evidence	Action
• Achieve greater consistency of practice within departments by improving middle management's means of monitoring practice and evaluating procedures • Develop more rigorous practices to ensure accountability by extending the link role of the senior management team with departments and by undertaking more systematic evaluation of the extent to which school policies are implemented	The management style is one of delegation and many staff respond positively to this. However, there is a need to develop more rigorous strategies of monitoring, collection of evidence and evaluation to ensure that what began as good initiatives actually work consistently across the whole school. A good start has been made with the analysis of the examination results. This systematic analysis of results and evaluation of progress could be extended to other aspects of school life, in particular the marking and assessment of pupils' work	• Consideration of whole school internal evaluation focusing on certain issues • Nature and role of curriculum management meeting to change to include more discussion of classroom practice and assessment • Senior staff to spend more time on liaison with departments and observing classroom practice • Appraisal to encourage the setting of targets to do with classroom practice and to encourage classroom observation across departments • Senior member of staff given responsibility for developing questioning skills, oracy and reading across the curriculum

Table 12.4 Issues, evidence and planned action: School O

Key issue	Evidence	Action
• Senior management should evaluate the effectiveness of policies with particular reference to classroom practice and assessment arrangements	The quality of middle management is variable. Not all directors of faculty and heads of departments have come to terms with their changing roles and lines of communication below senior management are not always effective	• Senior staff will observe all teachers in their curriculum link teams at least once, to look specifically at the pace of lessons, and discuss in detail department planning targets and resourcing with HODs • Each member of staff will have had the opportunity to team teach or observe the teaching of another member of staff

Table 12.5 Issues, evidence and planned action: School V

Key issue	Evidence	Action
• Put in place a programme to review teaching styles and approaches in order to provide (i) a wider range of teaching techniques (ii) more appropriate materials and content to enrich learning, especially for the more able (iii) improved motivation and behaviour of pupils • Review management structures and delegate more responsibilities to middle managers, providing them with the training to meet this challenge	Teachers' command of their subjects is variable, with a range of responses to presentation of the National Curriculum programmes of study. The range of teaching methods employed is not as wide as the circumstances demand, with the result that pace and challenge are often limited, especially for the most able, for whom too few opportunities are created for research, independent thinking and broad reading	• HODs to draw up lesson observation schedule • SMT to draw up list of criteria in addition • Each member of staff to have been observed teaching on at least one occasion by HOD with written feedback in relation to criteria • SMT to monitor teaching in subject areas and feedback to HOD • HODs to have opportunities to share good practice through the meetings structure

written evidence in the report or in the notes of feedback. Although inspectors may have clearly linked the main findings and the key issues, it is nevertheless not easy for schools to pick up the spirit of a recommendation. Teaching staff in the school undergo a process of having to digest all the information at one time, rather than, as the inspectors did, gradually distilling the key issues from the evidence. There are parallels with effective teaching – even if a teacher knows the right answer to an A-level mathematics problem, it is of no use for her merely to tell the students, who in the end have to work it out for themselves and make their own sense of it. Issues from school self-evaluation, in contrast to those raised in inspection, may perhaps arise more naturally from the findings and there may be a continuous process of growth in understanding of the conditions in the school. Action may be planned as a natural process drawing on this understanding. External inspection is, however, argued to be necessary because there is some legitimate doubt that these natural processes will bring about improvement, without the force added by an external requirement. The question remains – can an effective system of self-review be forced onto a school?

For some schools the OFSTED process has concentrated the minds of managers on the question Mooney (1995) raised and may yet provide the evidence of the worth of internal evaluation he asked for. On the other hand, an unproductive, bureaucratic, managerial leadership style may be fostered by the legislative approach of OFSTED, and particularly the official timescale of 40 days for producing action plans. There is, nevertheless, positive evidence from this analysis of inspectors' reports and school action plans that a minority of schools are endeavouring to implement the action suggested by the OFSTED issue in a way that involves individuals and fosters collaboration, in a way that Smyth (1989) describes as educative and that Russ (1995) identifies as characteristic of an improving school. Where this optimal outcome does not take place the hindrance comes from lack of understanding or acceptance of the inspectors' evidence, disagreement over relative priority or urgency and possibly from the dysfunctional nature of the culture of the school already identified in the report.

References

Cody, J. (1989) 'Educational leadership as reflective action', in Smyth, J. (ed.), *Critical Perspectives on Educational Leadership*, London: Falmer.

Darling-Hammond, L. (1990) 'Teacher professionalism: why and how', in Lieberman, A. (ed.), *Schools as Collaborative Cultures: Creating the Future Now*, Basingstoke: Falmer.

Gray, J. and Wilcox, B. (1995) 'In the aftermath of inspection: the nature and fate of inspection report recommendations', *Research Papers in Education*, **10**, 1–18.

Leithwood, K. and Aitken, R. (1995) *Making Schools Smarter: A System for Monitoring School and District Progress*, Newbury Park, CA: Corwin.

Little, J. (1982) 'Norms of collegiality and experimentation: workplace conditions of school success', *American Educational Research Journal*, **19**, 325–40.

MacBeath, J., Boyd, B., Rand, J. and Bell, S. (1996) *Schools Speak for Themselves*, London: National Union of Teachers.

Metcalfe, C. and Russell, S. (1996) 'School inspection and the process of change', paper presented at the *British Educational Management and Administration Society Research Conference*, Cambridge.

Moon, B. (1995) 'Judgement and evidence: redefining professionality in a new era of school accountability', in Brighouse, T. and Moon, B. (eds), *School Inspection*, London: Pitman.

Mooney, T. (1995) 'Paying attention to ME', *Education*, 28 April, 10.

Murphy, J. (1990) 'Principal instructional leadership', in Thuston, P. and Lotto, L. (eds), *Recent Advances in Educational Administration*, Greenwich, CT: JAI Press.

Murphy, J. (1991) *Restructuring Schools*, London: Cassell.

OFSTED (1993) *The Handbook for the Inspection of Schools*, London: HMSO.

OFSTED (1994) *Good Practice in Inspection*, London: OFSTED.

OFSTED (1995a) *Annual Report of Her Majesty's Chief Inspector of Schools, Part 1, Standards and Quality in Education 1993/4*, London: HMSO.

OFSTED (1995b) *The Framework for the Inspection of Schools*, London: HMSO.

OFSTED (1995c) *Inspection Quality 1994/5*, London: OFSTED.

OFSTED (1996) *Annual Report of Her Majesty's Chief Inspector of Schools, Standards and Quality in Education 1994/5*, London: HMSO.

Rosenholtz, S. (1989) *Teachers' Workplace: The Social Organisation of Schools*, New York: Teachers' College Press.

Russ, J. (1995) 'Collaborative management and school improvement: research findings from "improving schools" in England', *International Studies in Educational Administration*, **23**, 3–9.

Russell, S. (1996) 'Schools' experience of inspection', in Earley, P., Fidler, B. and Ouston, J. (eds), *Inspection: The Early Experiences*, London: David Fulton.

Sammons, P., Hillman, J. and Mortimore, P. (1995) *Key Characteristics of Effective Schools: A Review of School Effectiveness Research*, London: OFSTED.

Smyth, J. (1989) 'A "Pedagogical" and "Educative" View of Leadership', in Smyth, J. (ed.), *Critical Perspectives on Educational Leadership*, London: Falmer.

Teacher Training Agency (1995) *Initial Advice to the Secretary of State on the Continuing Professional Development of Teachers*, London: TTA.

Chapter 13

Evaluation: Who needs it?
Who cares?

Marvin C. Alkin

This is an edited version of an article previously published in
Studies in Educational Evaluation, 1, 3, 1975.

Evaluation: Who needs it? Who cares? Surely, we are all aware of and convinced of the value of evaluation. Yet, how often have we encountered situations when a study is completed by an evaluator amidst the claims of his colleagues that he has indeed performed one of the finest evaluation endeavours to date – the research design, statistical methods and quality of data were beyond reproof. Despite the evaluation community's hopeful expectations, the 'technically perfect' evaluation apparently had absolutely no effect on the programme's decision-makers or upon the decisions made. No one apparently needed it, no one apparently cared.

To understand why it is even of concern whether the evaluation is ultimately utilised in decision-making one must recognise the distinction between 'evaluation' and 'research'. The author has for some years felt that it was important to recognise the distinction between studies designed primarily to add to the body of knowledge (research) and those designed primarily to provide information for decision-making (evaluation) (Alkin, 1973). Thus, while the comment 'even if the results of a study were not utilized, its redeeming feature is its intrinsic value and its contribution to the corpus of knowledge' is appropriate as a statement for a study designed primarily as research, it is *not* appropriate for an evaluation study. In short, in an evaluation it is important if someone 'needs' the evaluation and someone 'cares'. As Weiss (1972) has aptly stated, 'The basic rationale for evaluation is that it provides information for action. Its primary justification is that it contributes to the rationalization of decision-making.'

Utilisation of evaluation findings

In the example just presented, what might have caused this breach between evaluator and decision-maker – a technically 'perfect' evaluation with no impact on subsequent decisions? Further, how can an evaluation be considered to be of highest quality by evaluators and yet be of no use to decision-makers? What factors limit the potential utilisation of evaluation information in decision-making?

For purposes of categorising those things that perhaps determine the extent to which evaluation findings will be utilised, I will consider four sets of factors in this paper. They are:

1　the decision-maker/decision process;
2　the programme and social context;
3　the nature of the evaluator;
4　the evaluation process/evaluation report.

Decision-maker/decision process

The first question of all is who is the decision-maker? For whom is the evaluation report? One of the major factors impeding the utilisation of the evaluation findings is the improper initial recognition of who makes what decisions. One of the major distinguishing characteristics of an evaluation in contradistinction to a research report is an initial concern for identifying the decision-maker or decision audience that is intended as the prime recipient of the evaluation report. If a study is completed with *no* particular decision-maker or decision audience initially identified as its recipient, it is possible for the study to provide valuable new information about the nature of an entity, but it is not likely to lead to related decisions. Alternatively, it may be possible for a single-study to attempt to meet the information needs of many decision-makers or decision audiences, but in all likelihood no one will be served well in such a situation.

Even when a decision-maker has been identified, it is important to recognise that each individual has his own value system and that the extent to which evaluation findings become utilised will be a function of philosophical orientation, political ambition, personality make-up and who knows what else. The nature of decision-making and the characteristics of decision-makers that provide indication of the likelihood of utilising evaluation information have been explored by a number of researchers and theoreticians including Carlson (1965), Wirt and Kirst (1972), Braybrooke and Lindblom (1963) and Johnson (1970). Moreover, Weiss (1972) has pointed out the necessity of early identification of potential users of the evaluation information as well as the selection of appropriate issues of concern.

Sieber (1972) has added an interesting insight to an understanding of decision-maker practitioners. He derives three strategies of planned educational change with each strategy based upon the image of the practitioner: as a rational man, as a co-operator, or as a powerless functionary. Each of these images, no doubt, necessitates a different evaluation strategy.

This comment leads us to a second factor to be considered: 'What is the decision purpose?' At the outset of a commissioned evaluation, there is usually a purpose in the mind of those who commissioned the study. Sometimes there are even possible decisions that will occur based upon the information to be presented by the evaluation report. While intentions can be modified, the surest predictor of likely utilisation is still an intended utilisation at the outset of the project. In instances where there is a lack of decision purpose, where decision-makers contracting for evaluation reports do not have in mind an intended usage of that report and a decision purpose, then it is not likely that evaluation relevant to decision-making will take place, nor that utilisation will occur.

Sometimes there is no intention that a real decision will take place; the evaluation has been contracted with a different purpose in mind: either no decision is intended or the decision intended has been predetermined prior to the initiation of the evaluation project. Let us consider within this category four different types of situations:

1   window dressing;
2   legal requirements;
3   public relations;
4   professional prestige.

In the first instance, evaluations are sometimes commissioned purely for purposes of *window dressing*, or *post hoc* justification of decisions that have already been made. In some instances the future decision is already positive and the evaluation is intended, in the words of Suchman (1967), as either eye-wash ('an attempt to justify a weak or bad program by deliberately selecting . . . those aspects that "look good" '), or whitewash ('an attempt to cover up program failure or errors by avoiding any objective appraisal'). Sometimes, according to Suchman, the evaluation is intended as an attempt to torpedo ('provide a rationale for doing away with the program regardless of its effectiveness'). This is relatively easy to do since no programme is perfect and, if one is so intentioned, areas of programme deficiency can be noted in almost any evaluation report.

Sometimes, evaluations are commissioned simply to maintain compliance with *legal requirements* by another agency. For the programme director, continuance of his programme is the primary goal and consequently he may fear that a negative evaluation or an evaluation that points out any deficiencies will result in a reduction of funds or even a total curtailment of the programme. Thus, the evaluation is not looked at by him with a sympathetic and eager-for-information posture. In such instances, where the evaluator is hired by the programme director and not by the external agency, the intention is usually to do the utmost to assure that the evaluation is solely a pro forma exercise designed only to meet legal requirements.

Often an evaluation is commissioned simply as a *public relations* gesture where the intend may be to demonstrate the objectivity of project personnel by the mere fact that they have commissioned an evaluation. What is important in the eyes of the decision-maker is the *commissioning* of the evaluation and not the potential results that may emerge. In fact, given their preference, most decision-makers who commission evaluations with such intentions in mind would far prefer (after the initial publicity has taken place) that the evaluator float away and never again be seen by mortals. Enough frivolity, let me proceed.

The final category of evaluation report commissioning in which no decision is intended, I have referred to as *professional prestige*. Occasionally, administrators view themselves as 'men on the move' and all decisions and actions taken are seen as serving this master objective. Thus, to build a reputation as an innovator, it is necessary to have commissioned at least one evaluation to demonstrate one's own recognition and awareness of this new innovative procedure. If the results of the evaluation demonstrate the success of the 'innovative' programme that the administrator has started, all is well and good: otherwise, it is enough simply to have commissioned an 'innovative' evaluation whose results are unlikely to see the light of day.

As a final comment in this section on decision-makers and decision processes, let us assume that the best of all possible worlds exists and that a real decision is likely at the conclusion of the evaluation report. In that instance, it is imperative that the evaluator be aware of the kind of decision that is intended.

Dexter (1966) has noted that while it may be unwise for the evaluator to state explicitly the client's ulterior motives for commissioning the evaluation, the evaluator none the less should attempt to determine whether such motives exist. Only then is the evaluator able to determine whether to take the assignment and, if so, to understand his or her potential difficulties. There is a great deal of communications research offering potential transfer value to evaluation-utilisation research. One such study that provides amplification for the above point was performed by Greenwald (1965) who examined the effects of prior commitment on behaviour change after a persuasive communication. Among subjects who had a strong prior commitment against a position favoured by the persuasive communication, Greenwald found that while the communication significantly modified the attitude, it did not modify behaviour. One would have to wonder about the results of a similar study extended to an educational evaluation situation.

Programme and social context

The characteristics of the programme and the nature of the contextual setting in which it rests are 'apparently' important factors in determining the potential utilisation of evaluation studies in decision-making. I have said 'apparently' because it is almost a truism among researchers to consider these variables as being important, yet the research evidence at this point cannot be considered as particularly well organised. It is my belief that the nature of the programme and the characteristics of the programme staff are essential elements in the set of interactions that will determine the potential utilisation of evaluation data. In my current research studies on the utilisation of evaluation findings, I have been considering factors such as the organisational constraints, the formal and informal structure of the organisation and the nature of competing groups within the organisation.

Outside the organisation itself, I believe that the political alignments of the various external interest groups are a decisive determiner of utilisation/non-utilisation. The importance of the characteristics of the community (socio-economic status, other demographic traits) that the programme serves were investigated in an earlier study (Alkin *et al.*, 1974).

Patton *et al.* (1975) listed five sets of characteristics of organisations that they felt might influence utilisation of evaluation report findings. These were:

1   The constraints of decision-making in national bureaucratic organisations.
2   New and innovative agencies vs. older, established agencies.
3   Communication patterns in organisations.
4   Level in the organisation where evaluation is done.
5   The degree of politicisation of the organisation.

The extent to which these and other programme and social context variables affect the utilisation of evaluation findings in decision-making is not yet clear. Ferman (1969) has noted that 'the influence of the social context is important and shapes some of the considerations of logical inquiry . . . These conflicting networks of self-interest and values are important data to be considered in any evaluation . . . the same considerations often influence the utilization of the findings of an evaluation.' In an excellent article dealing with problems involved in the utilisation of information, Deats (1974) concluded that information transmission and utilisation occur within the context of a social system involving social interactions and perceptions that significantly influence utilisation. While these and a great number of other contentions point to the importance of social context in the content of evaluation information, there is a paucity of research data.

Nature of the evaluator

Who is so naïve among us as not to recognise that who we are as evaluators, our past reputation, our organisational affiliation, and – oh yes – our personality traits, have a great impact upon the extent to which someone 'needs', 'cares', or utilises the evaluation report that we produce? Bernstein and Freeman (1975) and Alkin *et al.* (1974) have investigated evaluator characteristics in relationship to quality of evaluation report and ultimate utilisation of those findings in decision-making. Bernstein and Freeman reached some conclusions on the most important charac-teristics of evaluators *vis-à-vis* organisational affiliation and academic background, but their study was limited primarily to the consideration of evaluation quality (under a limited definition of quality) rather than a consideration of utilisation findings. Alkin *et al.* (1974) explored a group of variables that they called the evaluation context. Included in this group was the distinction between internal and external evaluator. The results pointed out the necessity for more careful definition of what constitutes internal and external evaluation.

Patton *et al.* (1975) noted that perhaps the most important utilisation factor is the personal human factor of an interested and committed evaluator (especially when accompanied by an interested and committed decision-maker).

Where the personal human factor emerges, where some individual takes direct, personal responsibility for getting the information to the right people, evaluations have an impact. Where the personal factor is absent, there is a marked absence of impact. Utilization is not simply determined by some configuration of abstract factors; it is determined in large part by real, live, caring human beings.

Archibald (1970) confirmed the importance of the reputation and legitimacy of the evaluator as an important factor in the potential utilisation of evaluation findings. Ashburn (1973) would apparently agree, citing the perceived nature of the individuals involved in the evaluation system as one cause of the credibility gap regarding evaluation.

Evaluation process/evaluation report

The nature and characteristics of the evaluation report including the process engaged in during the course of the evaluation are important elements related to the ultimate utilisation of evaluation findings. For purposes of discussing this issue, I have conceived six subheadings for discussion, as follows:

1   Attention to appropriate goals.
2   Technical credibility.
3   Report comprehensibility.
4   Report timeliness.
5   Scope of recommendations.
6   Evaluator relationships.

Attention to appropriate goals

In part, the issue of attending to appropriate goals has been considered in a previous section under the heading of decision-maker/decision process. It is, however, such an overarching question that it must be considered as well in the discussion of the characteristics of the evaluation process. After all, in looking at the evaluation report, what could be more basic than the question of the congruity of the goals and objectives measured and examined by the evaluator with those considered to be of interest by decision-makers and decision audiences. Far too many studies are conducted dealing with issues splendidly isolated from the educational policy issues at hand. The lack of appropriateness of goals used within an evaluation is, undoubtedly, a more important reason for the lack of utilisation of evaluation results than any other characteristic of evaluation reports.

I have discussed in another source (Alkin, 1975) the nature of the process that evaluators must undertake in order to clarify who will be making what kinds of decisions within the decision structure as well as to clarify the extent to which other agencies will be receiving, and intending to utilise for decision-making, the evaluation information presented in the report. It is important to seek clarification and agreement from all parties involved, prior to the collection of any data, that the goals being employed in the evaluation are those that are considered relevant for the programme at hand. There is substantial agreement on this point. Bend (1970) attributes many evaluation difficulties to initial misunderstanding of and lack of agreement upon the 'objectives, activities, and outputs of the evaluative research project'. Bosco (1971) has an interesting article geared to administrators in which he has as his purpose instructing administrators on how to manage educational evaluation so as to maximise their usefulness. One major piece of advice provided to administrators is that they must take care to ensure that the information collected is relevant to the decisions they must make, with particular attention to those factors that will really make a difference when the decision is made. Perhaps Bosco is correct, and the key to greater utilisation is more instructions to administrators on the potential uses of evaluation.

Technical credibility

Technical soundness or credibility in the way the evaluation was performed is not the *sine qua non* of evaluation utilisation (evaluation reports that are by no means technically well done have in many instances been pointed to as the basis for decisions that have been made). On the other hand, lack of attainment of technical credibility provides the first, easy and instinctive means for the dismissal of the conclusions of an evaluation report when a decision-maker wishes to forgo making decisions logically related to those conclusions. That is, failure to attend to technical soundness in an evaluation report provides decision-makers with the most basic of reasons for dismissal of the report. Even the least technically sophisticated of decision-makers (who could not normally distinguish a multiple R from a 't' test) suddenly emerge as technical wizards able to find methodological flaws in evaluation results not to their liking. An alternative tactic is for decision-makers to obtain someone (another consultant?) who can and will willingly (in part to build their own professional prestige) find those flaws. Apparently, one of the best conscientious defences against non-utilisation of evaluation findings is a technical sound, methodologically credible study.[1]

One of the areas of threat to the credibility of evaluation findings is a set of factors that in large part are beyond the control of the evaluator. I refer here to what I will call 'programme controlled factors'. There are ways in which programmes operate and function that severely inhibit the nature of the evaluation that can be conducted. For example, one must be concerned that the programme be initially established in a way that would even make an evaluation possible. There are instances where the policy established by decision-makers with respect to the nature of the programme – who will be in it, the assignment/non-assignment of teachers – virtually assures that a technically credible design cannot be attained. In these instances, there is great like-lihood that the evaluation is doomed at the start. Flanagan (1970) has asserted that administrators must use comprehensive, rigorous procedures in making the decision to try out an innovation. Advanced planning is the key to successful implementation and ultimately to successful evaluation.

In addition to the way in which a programme is conceived and initially organised, the way in which it is operated may also destroy the technical credibility of the evaluation. Where the programme is implemented unevenly across classes or schools, and perhaps even with variations in the procedures utilised by programme personnel, doubts may again be raised about the credibility of the evaluation based, not upon the deficiencies of the evaluator, but upon programme operational problems beyond his or her control. Sometimes, also, reliance on programme staff for assistance in the collection of routine data, the administering of instruments, or even providing time to be personally interviewed may all provide sources of potential breakdown in the data collection that are partially beyond the responsibility of the evaluators.

There are other factors related to technical credibility that are more dependent upon the particular skills and knowledge of the evaluator. Obviously, the evaluator's ingenuity in devising an appropriate design is of vital importance. Despite the clear distinction between research and evaluation, the use of experimental designs is highly desirable in order to provide for the strongest possible inferences related to the measurable outcomes of programmes. But failing this, the evaluator must select the strongest design possible given the situation.

Another area of potential technical deficiency of evaluation is the quality of the data collected. In part, data quality can be improved in terms of its potential utilisability to decision-makers by the evaluator engaging in the process of initially simulating the possible findings of the study. I have engaged in this process with decision-makers by providing simulated findings based upon data sources being proposed in order to determine from decision-makers at the outset of the process (prior to data collection) the adequacy of these sources for the potential decisions that might be made. In essence, this pre-data-collection activity involves considerable interaction between evaluator and decision-maker in which the evaluator attempts to determine the extent to which various data items would be considered convincing evidence for decisions. I firmly believe that one important element related to increasing the utilisation of evaluation information is the reaching of agreement at the onset of a study on the kinds of data that would be considered acceptable if presented at the end of a study.

Of course, there are other issues related to the production of quality data. The question of selecting the appropriate measuring instrument is always an essential element in producing a technically competent study. Issues related to the extent to which the instrument selected measures the desired objective of the programme is a standard measurement question that is dealt with in most, if not all, textbooks. Likewise, the debate about the relative virtue and appropriateness of standardised tests vs. criterion-referenced tests is also a topic that has been dealt with effectively in prior literature (Popham, 1975; Millman, 1974; Harris *et al.*, 1974).

Another descriptive attribute of an evaluation report is the data analysis procedures used. Bernstein and Freeman (1975) paid particular heed to the technical sophistication of the data analysis procedure used by evaluators. I am personally not convinced that technical sophistication *per se* is a prime concern for evaluators (after all, evaluations should not be attempts at mathematical magic or exercises in esoterica).

Report comprehensibility

The evaluation report must be in language understandable to the decision-maker. Since decision-making is, in practice, a very diffuse process, frequently including lay community and other decision audiences, evaluation reports face a severe test. The reports must, on the other hand, be simple enough to be understood by the technically unsophisticated yet rigorous enough to withstand the tests of technical credibility.

This twofold dilemma of both credibility and comprehensibility offers an imposing task for would-be evaluators. How can a report on the one hand be easily understood by non-technical persons yet on the other hand have sufficient technical credibility that it is not easily dismissed as unworthy of utilisation? Sometimes (or do I mean usually?) those engaged in the process solve the dilemma by ignoring the potential utilisation question and simply prepare the evaluation reports in a format appropriate for reading by their academically oriented colleagues. Thus, the evaluator–researcher has at least heightened his or her own reputation with colleagues even if no decision is to come of the evaluation.

Weiss (1972) has made a number of recommendations for improving the effectiveness of evaluation reports:

- presentation (of the report) must be clear and attractive;
- the implications of evaluation findings must be fully considered;
- many audiences require evaluation reporting procedures other than bulky written reports;
- recommendations and other positions taken by the evaluator should not be presented in a lukewarm manner but, rather, advocated forcefully.

I have found it helpful to combine a fully documented report with short readable 'executive summaries' and oral presentations of findings. A typical format that I have been using consists of short executive summaries at the beginning of the evaluation report. (Typically, this section of the report is printed on a different-coloured paper for ease in dealing with it and to ensure that those not interested in a full report treatment do not get 'mixed up' in the full body of the report.) Usually a single page is used for each predetermined decision question, with the summary filling no more than one page and with each question starting a new page. Each page of the executive summary begins with a predetermined statement of the decision question and a short paragraph elaborating the nature of the question. Another paragraph summarises the findings related to that specific question with a reference to the pages of the complete report in which a more extensive treatment of the findings may be found. This assures the reader that the simple statement of findings has been substantiated in a technically credible fashion elsewhere and enables him to examine the full procedure if he wishes. Finally, the last item on the executive summary page is a listing of the recommendations (if any) with reference to the pages in the full report in which they are formulated and justified.

In more comprehensive evaluation reports, I have included a technical appendix that presents detailed analyses, instrumentation, etc., that were felt to be too much for the main body of the report. Thus, the report has sections presenting various degrees of technical complexity depending upon the needs of the particular reader.

I have found this procedure to be helpful in attaining greater utilisation of evaluation findings; although it should be noted that the value of this format and procedure has not been tested empirically. Weiss (1972) would agree that this is an important area worthy of further research. In her list of evaluation procedures identified as particularly important for study, she had discussed 'the effective presentation of findings and dissemination of information'.

Report timeliness

Another important evaluation report attribute related to potential utilisation of evaluation findings is its timeliness. Ammunition received after a battle is over, food provided to a person dead of starvation and evaluation reports received after a decision has been made are of equal worth. They each represent degrees of worthlessness.

An evaluation must provide the information that a decision-maker needs before the decision is made. Despite the obvious, this is most frequently neglected. For example, most evaluation reports are presented to governmental agencies at the conclusion of the school year (naturally, this is so since end-of-year student-achievement data must be included). Unfortunately, this does not correspond well with government budget-making cycles. Most decisions about the funding of programmes for a subsequent year have already been made by the time that evaluation reports are received.

This factor was noted as a possible cause of the lack of utilisation of evaluation findings for federal decision-making related to project funding (Alkin *et al.*, 1974). In essence, the projects had already been funded for the next year prior to receipt of evaluation reports. Thus, there could be little likelihood that evaluation information would be utilised in this important area of decision-making.

On the other hand, in the same study, evaluation information was considered to be of value by local decision-makers, for whom the evaluation reporting was timely. Clearly the timeliness of reports is an important factor in ultimate utilisation for decision-making.

Scope of recommendations

Another characteristic of the evaluation report that has been suggested to us by Patton *et al.* (1975) is the 'scope of recommendations for change'. They suggest that essentially bureaucratic organisations are slow to accept findings that require massive reorganisations of the system and that evaluation findings that in essence present minor modifications are more likely to be adopted in subsequent decisions. With these statements, a caveat must be offered – there are unique decision contexts that would increase rather than decrease the probability that recommendations of major scope would be utilised and accepted in subsequent decisions (e.g. a new administrator who would relish the opportunity of demonstrating the relative prior inefficiency by making major changes).

Evaluator relationships

The worth and ultimate utilisation of evaluation findings and reports can be greatly affected by the personal relationships developed between evaluator and decision-maker. Evaluation involves far more than the presentation of reports (albeit credible and comprehensive reports).

The simple fact is that even the scientific endeavour of performing the evaluation of programmes rests heavily for its success on the relationships built between individuals. To the extent to which school staff, decision-makers and others engaged in the programme that was evaluated came to trust and respect the integrity and honesty of the evaluator, the likelihood of utilisation of findings is increased. Likewise, the absence of basic tensions and/or antagonism between participating parties is also an important element in evaluation success (i.e. utilisation). Rodman and Kolodny (1964) expressed concern about the evaluator/decision-maker relationship and argued that role differences as well as the formal social organisation of the programme are the principal causative factors in the development of a strained relationship between the evaluator and the practitioner decision-maker. Forehand (1970) is so concerned about the nature of the relationship that he has argued that an evaluator/decision-maker dichotomy should not be discussed but rather one must contemplate a unified decision-making process.

As simplistic as these comments about the importance of relations between individuals appear to be, they none the less warrant inclusion. Frequently, we become so involved in the technical and mechanistic aspects of evaluation that the non-scientific human relations questions are ignored – all to the detriment of effective evaluation.

Realistic perceptions of utilisation

The argument goes that: 'evaluation has no impact upon decision-making, so why bother doing it? A simple examination of the evaluation literature finds very few instances where the findings of evaluation were adopted and led to a set of concurrent programme decisions.' The point we must make (and we are reminded of it by Patton *et al.*, 1975) is that judgements of utilisation/non-utilisation cannot be made based upon the extent to which evaluation findings are *totally* accepted and implemented. It is naïve to assume that no information existed prior to the conduct of the specific study that had been commissioned. Rather, evaluation findings must be viewed as an additional source that will hopefully affect the decision in part. Patton *et al.* (1975) noted in their study of the evaluations of 20 health programmes that 'none of the impacts described was of the type where new findings from an evaluation were directly and immediately used in the making of major concrete program decisions. The more typical, in fact, was one where the evaluation findings provided additional pieces of information.' In essence, a more realistic perception of evaluation utilisation rests upon the use of evaluation information as an element in the making of complex decisions.

> The view of evaluation research that emerges in our interviews stands in stark contrast to the image of utilization that is presented as the ideal in the bulk of the evaluation literature, or at least, the impression with which that literature left us. The ideal held forth in the literature we reviewed earlier is one of major impact on concrete decisions. The image that emerges in our interviews is that there are few major, direction-changing decisions in most programming, and that evaluation research is used as one piece of information that feeds into a slow, evolutionary process of program development. Program development is a process of 'muddling through' and evaluation research is part of the muddling.
>
> (Patton *et al.*, 1975)

Who needs it? Who cares?

It is true that decision-makers involved in the process of educational improvement have a need for information. Evaluators provide information in the belief that it will lead to rational (e.g. data-based) decision-making. Although this sounds like an effective relationship, it implies some rather simplistic assumptions on the part of many evaluators. First, the mere presentation of data is not alone likely to improve decision-making. In addition to presenting technically credible evaluation reports related to appropriate goals, it is necessary that evaluators pay heed to appropriate methods of information presentation so that the right person gets the proper information at the proper time and in the proper format. Moreover, the complexities of decision context and social context in which programme decisions are ultimately embedded require that evaluators become more fully aware of these factors. Evaluators will be better prepared to provide the right kind of information if they understand who the decision-makers are, the decisions they make and the constraints upon their decision-making. Also, it is essential that we maintain a proper perspective on the potential role that evaluation might play in making an impact upon decision-making and not become frustrated by attaining minor impacts only. Finally, in considering these factors, perhaps it is important as evaluators that we learn to distinguish those situations in which the context and decision factors are so predetermined that it can be inevitably said that no one needs it and no one cares. Finally, I would urge that evaluators make more judicious selections of where and how to apply their evaluation talents.[2]

Endnotes

1 Of course, the 'best' defence against non-utilisation is performing an evaluation that produces favourable results in line with a decision that someone in authority wanted to make initially.

2 The work upon which this publication is based was performed pursuant to a contract with the National Institute of Education, Department of Health, Education and Welfare. Points of view or opinions stated do not necessarily represent official NIE position or policy.

References

Alkin, M. C. (1973) 'Evaluacion: investigacion o praxis?', *Educacion Hoy*, Colombia, Bogota: Asociacion de Publicaciones Educativas, Ano 111, No. 17.

Alkin, M. C. (1975) 'Framing the decision context', *AERA Cassette Series in Evaluation*, Washington, DC: American Educational Research Association.

Alkin, M. C., Kosecoff, J., Fitzgibbon, C. and Seligman, R. (1974) 'Evaluation and decision-making: the Title VII experience', *CSE Monograph Series in Evaluation No. 4*, Los Angeles Center for the Study of Evaluation, University of California.

Archibald, K. (1970) 'Alternative orientations to social science utilization', *Social Science Information*, **9**(2), 7–34.

Ashburn, A. G. (1973) 'Credibility gaps and the institutionalizing of educational evaluation functions', *Planning and Changing. A Journal for School Administrators*, **4**(1), 18–28.

Bend, E. (1970) 'The impact of the social setting upon evaluative research', *Evaluative Research*, AIR, 109–28.

Bernstein, I. N. and Freeman, H. W. (1975) *Academic and Entrepreneurial Research*, New York: Russell Sage Foundation.

Bosco, J. (1971) 'The role of the administrator in the improvement of evaluation studies', *Education*, **92**(2), 70–4.

Braybrooke, D. and Lindblom, C. E. (1963) *A Strategy of Decision*, New York: The Free Press.

Carlson, R. O. (1965) *Adoption of Educational Innovations*, Eugene: University of Oregon Press.

Deats, T. (1974) 'Moving and using information', *Teachers' College Record*, **75**(3), 383–93.

Dexter, L. A. (1966) 'Impressions about utility and wastefulness in applied social science studies', *American Behavioral Scientist*, **9**(6), 9–10.

Ferman, L. A. (1969) 'Some perspectives on evaluating social welfare programs', *The Annals of the American Academy of Political and Social Science*, no. 385, 143–56.

Flanagan, J. C. (1970) 'Administrative behaviour in implementing educational innovations', *Education*, **90**(3), 213–20.

Forehand, G. A. (1970) 'Curriculum evaluation as decision-making process', *Journal of Research and Development in Education*, **3**(4), 27–37.

Greenwald, A. G. (1965) 'Effects of prior commitment on behaviour change after persuasive communication', *Public Opinion Quarterly*, **29**(4), 595–610.

Harris, C., Alkin, M. C. and Popham, W. J. (eds) (1974) 'Problems in criterion-referenced measurement', *CSE Monograph Series in Evaluation No. 3*, Los Angeles Center for the Study of Evaluation, University of California.

Johnson, G. H. (1970) 'The purpose of evaluation and the role of the evaluator', *Evaluative Research*, AIR.

Millman, J. (1974) 'Criterion-referenced measurement', in *Evaluation in Education: Current Applications*, Berkeley, CA: McCutchan Publishing.

Patton, M. Q., Grimes, P. S., Guthrie, K., Brennan, N. J., French, B. D. and Blyth, D. A. (1975) *In Search of Impact: an Analysis of the Utilization of Federal Health Evaluation Research*, Minneapolis: University of Minnesota Press.

Popham, W. J. (1975) *Educational Evaluation*, New Jersey: Prentice-Hall.

Rodman, H. and Kolodny, R. L. (1964) 'Organizational strains in the researcher–practitioner relationship', *Human Organization*, **23**(2), 171–82.

Sieber, S. D. (1972) 'Images of the practitioner and strategies of educational change', *Sociology of Education*, **45**(4), 362–85.

Suchman, E. A. (1967) *Evaluative Research: Principles in Public Service and Action Programs*, New York: Russell Sage Foundation.

Weiss, C. H. (1972) 'Utilization of evaluation: toward comparative study', in Weiss, C. H. (ed.), *Evaluating Action Programs*, Boston: Allyn & Bacon.

Wirt, F. M. and Kirst, M. W. (1972) *The Political Web of American Schools*, Boston: Little, Brown & Co.

Evidence in the development of professional knowledge

Chapter 14

The teachers' construction of knowledge

Britt-Mari Barth

This is an edited version of a chapter previously published in
S. Maclure and P. Davies (eds), *Learning to Think: Learning to Learn*,
Oxford: Pergamon Press, 1991.

As a researcher and teacher educator, my main concern is how to convey conceptual understanding of the learning process to future teachers so that they can enhance children's higher-order thinking and help them become aware of their own thinking capacities.

There is now general agreement that it is important for learners to construct their own knowledge. No one else can do it for them. But this consensus poses major pedagogical problems: it means that teachers must assist learners in their personal construction of knowledge rather than giving it to them ready made. When one considers how this can best be done many questions arise:

1　What does it mean to construct one's knowledge? How does a symbol come to carry meaning?
2　How can we describe the cognitive processes by which individuals construct their knowledge in a way that permits the teacher:

- to recognise it when it occurs;
- to make it occur by providing adequate learning situations;
- to make the learners themselves aware of what occurs so that they can learn to regulate their own thought processes?

My own research project – motivated by observation of the destructive effect school failure has on children – started out in the early 1970s from these kinds of questions. Observation of children's misconceptions in learning situations at s chool led me to identify three main difficulties, independent of age and subject matter:

1　confusion between the word and the meaning;
2　confusion between relevant and non-relevant factors;
3　inadequate reasoning, since rote learning is inappropriate.

This analysis made me aware of the close relationship between the thought process itself and what one thinks about; the two cannot be separated. Knowledge, then, could not be an accumulation of facts passively received from the outside, but must be more like a complex system of connections actively constructed from within. If the first approach comes closer to the way teachers tend to think of knowledge, it is little wonder that learning problems arise. Piaget was no doubt right when he said that it is not the subject matter that the children do not understand, but the lessons they are given.

At this point in my questioning I discovered *A Study of Thinking* (Bruner *et al.*, 1956). It was a revelation to me. It described perception as information processing, showing what happens when individuals try to make order in their environment, i.e. by which mental strategies they come to consider different things as similar. Bruner insists on the importance of conceptualisation; almost all cognitive activity depends on it.

I started building upon a conceptual framework of psychological theory (enlarged over the years to include recent theories in psychology as well as in other cognitive sciences), as I moved between theory and practice. This background led me to develop 'models' to illustrate these abstract cognitive processes in a concrete form in order to observe them and to gain a deeper understanding of what we actually do when we think and learn.

These models take the form of learning–teaching strategies that are elaborated in such a way as to put the processes concerned into action. Some of the models focus separately on each of these processes (like comparison, for example), others on the integrated process of concept formation. One model examines the structure of knowledge itself. They are all conceived to be used within the school curriculum or for teachers' education.

The difficulty in constructing models that put abstract processes into action lies in the need first to identify these processes. My own observation and understanding of children's conceptions and misconceptions, gained through developing and trying out the models with them, made me choose and explore the following processes as being essential parts of the conceptualisation process:

- discrimination;
- comparison (analogical and analytical);
- inference (inductive and deductive), testing it;
- hypothesis (testing it: considering evidence, detecting inconsistency, arguments).

Even if these processes can be applied in different ways, it seems necessary to start by being aware of the conceptualisation process as a universal form of thought.

The proposed models (in their present form) can be used as teaching methods that enhance conceptual learning. They have been experimented with for this purpose and are presently being used in many classrooms as an alternative to expository methods, still common in France. But their main benefit lies perhaps in using them in order to study the link between action and thought, to understand how pedagogical procedures enhance cognitive procedures. In other words, by offering a live experience of a modelled thought process to learners (at their level, independent of age), they enable learners to return to it, to separate the process from its content, identify the process, understand which factors favour its appearance and which ones hinder it.

In many ways, the difficulties in teacher education are similar to those encountered in school; how to convey complex, abstract knowledge in such a way that the learners integrate it, with transfer. Transfer is the central problem. An individual has to derive a conceptual understanding of abstract knowledge (permitting transfer) from multiple, concrete experiences and then compare them in order to transform his or her initial conceptions. If thinking is the most important area of the curriculum, then thinking is what the learner needs experience in. But thinking cannot occur without a content. In my view, thinking is best developed by an in-depth study of a particular subject (which is not to say that introductory exercises across the curriculum could not be useful). This is why it is essential (through initial teacher education) to provide all teachers with the necessary tools to enable them to develop their students' thinking capacities through the study of their subjects and then, further, to make their students aware of these capacities. Transfer of thinking skills from one area to another does not always happen spontaneously.

My own experience in teacher training has confirmed this conviction: a thorough study of thought processes by teachers develops their capacities of analysis and critical judgement, as well as creative solutions to learning difficulties. I have seen teachers of all levels, well versed in their disciplines, transform their expository methods so as to guide their students to acquire an essential understanding of their subjects. When teachers are capable of recognising and inducing higher-order thinking processes, making students aware of them as they proceed, they no longer need models; they can create their own, knowing for what purpose. The value of a model does not lie in its degree of truth, but rather in its capacity for improving our understanding, and thus our actions. Our improved actions will then further increase our understanding, and that will enable us to create new, more accurate models.

So far I have been discussing the proposed models in a general way. Let me now give some details of how two of them function: first a model to examine knowledge itself and then one to examine the process of concept formation. What difficulties in the learning process do they try to illustrate? What solutions do they suggest? What conditions affecting the learning process do they imply?

The following discussion will be easier to follow with some specific examples in mind. *Knowledge*, a vast general term, is used here to cover specific knowledge, as it appears within any subject in the curriculum. In biology, it could be the study of how the heart functions or what a microbe is. In physics, it could be understanding the difference between solids, liquids and gases or knowing what energy is. In history, it could be the study of different political systems or understanding what characterises a revolution. Knowledge could be a grammatical rule, a mathematical theorem or an economic theory. Knowledge could also be very subjective and personal, like 'beauty' or 'people in whom I have confidence'. In order to visualise the progression of

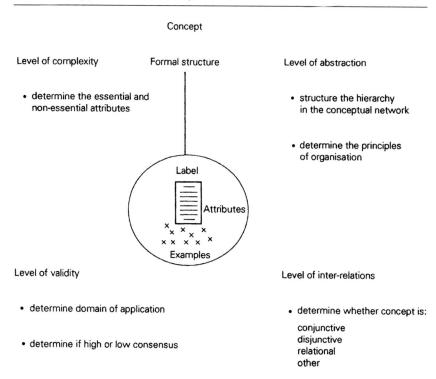

Figure 14.1 The concept as a model to examine the structure of knowledge

examples (or model cases) of some specific piece of knowledge, it may be helpful to keep a visual concept in mind, such as the style of painting called 'Impressionism'.

One obstacle to the learning process is inherent in the nature of knowledge itself: traditionally we treat knowledge as a preconstructed truth and present it as a linear accumulation of facts to our student. This way of proceeding can only work if teachers' and learners' knowledge is similar, which is rarely the case. It then becomes important for teachers to explore the 'school knowledge', not in order to mirror their own expert knowledge but in order to adapt it to the students' novice knowledge. This is why a first model is proposed in order to reflect upon the knowledge to be taught and make it 'accessible' to the learner who is to explore its meaning.

This model, shown in Figure 14.1, is based on the structure of a concept, which can be applied to any knowledge. Knowledge is thus formalised as a complex structure of relationships. This structure is not the same, however, for every individual; the knowledge of the 'expert' is organised in a more complex way than that of the 'novice'. Experts situate the elements in relation to a whole conceptual network they have worked out through their experience. But the novices' organisation is not yet very solid; it often consists of isolated elements that they relate to a few disparate experiences that they cannot yet generalise. Alternatively, they may create a false organisation that is too solid. If the latter is not modified in time, the students will find themselves in trouble later. Hence, the way 'what we know' as organised should be a subject for teachers' reflection, for the way we perceive and conceive new knowledge depends on this organisation. In other words, the organisation of our old knowledge determines the way we integrate new knowledge. It is the gap between the expert's knowledge and the novice's knowledge that makes the exchange difficult. So the problem is how to make them adjust to each other in order to bring out the same meaning.

With this goal in mind, the model of the concept is proposed as a pedagogical tool for examining the teacher–expert's 'knowledgeable knowledge' in terms of the student–novice's construction of knowledge. The model makes it possible to formulate general questions about knowledge.[1]

Other general categories of attributes – for example, purpose, process, cause and effect – can be useful in order to examine and reflect upon knowledge. Most disciplines also have their own specific categories of questions that enhance appropriate thinking skills:

- What is essential for the learner? (level of complexity)
- For what purpose? What transfer? For what fields of application? (level of validity)
- Where is this knowledge situated in a conceptual hierarchy? (level of abstraction)
- What is the relationship between the specific elements? (level of inter-relationship)

In the case of impressionism it could apply as in Figure 14.2.

There is a dual advantage in analysing knowledge in this way. On the one hand, the analysis allows the teacher to examine knowledge and to define it in terms of the person who is then to construct it. Experience shows that teachers have great difficulty in formalising knowledge and in verbalising essential attributes, even if they master them implicitly (which is true for all experts). On the other hand, it allows the learner to discover that it is possible to approach all knowledge in a formal way. This realisation completely transforms the cognitive behaviour of the learner: he or she understands what to look for. This is the first step towards cognitive autonomy, which will then allow the learner knowingly to set up a strategy for constructing meaning.

This first reflection on the structure of knowledge itself already contains a portion of the answer to an essential question that shapes the whole process of learning: the intellectual receptivity of the learner. What can be done to make the learner want to think and be attentive? That requires a considerable cognitive effort. Constructing knowledge in a school setting is not a spontaneous act.

Wishing to be attentive is not always sufficient to make one so, especially if the content is of no particular interest to students. But it is easier to get their attention if they have something specific to do, hence the idea of creating anticipation of a goal through the task itself: a task that is structured, with a beginning and an end, a

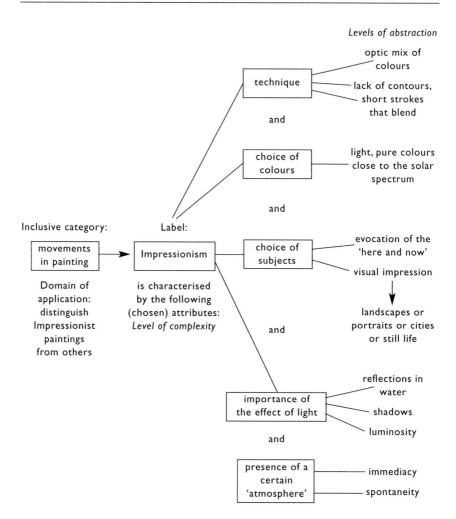

Figure 14.2 The example of Impressionism

task that can be mastered by the student while it presents some sort of intellectual challenge. Thus we create an anticipation of the goal to be attained – without which there is no attention – by proposing a task that is conceived so as to set off a process of conceptualisation. It is important for the students to understand what they have to do, and to be capable of doing it, for them to expect success from the start. Discouragement is the greatest enemy of any intellectual activity.

A well-conceived task can thus stimulate different types of motivation, according to the individual – an interest for the activity itself, an intellectual challenge, the genuine possibility of success, the need for self-esteem – while at the same time it provokes thought and stimulates reasoning. The intellect and the emotions are inseparable. The pedagogical procedure itself must involve the student affectively. It is the teacher's responsibility to accomplish this.

If the choice of the task is important for all these reasons, it is also strictly linked to another factor that conditions learning: the way learners come in contact with the new knowledge. Are they going to listen to a definition? Look at diagrams? Handle objects? The task–procedure proposed to the students in this pedagogical model consists in getting them to construct the concept gradually from the very precise, concrete examples and counter-examples. Knowing what a concept is, they are asked to compare the examples in order to discover what they have in common. All suggestions are written down, then crossed out when no longer relevant.

The function of the examples is to multiply experiences with the knowledge in its concrete form. Abstraction grows out of real experience; if the student has not yet had any experience (consciously, in a specific context), he or she must be supplied with it. Counter-examples, by their contrast, allow the students to be guided towards a finer perception, to make them aware of relevant similarities and differences of concepts within a given field of application. A wise choice of these examples is essential to broaden and transform the initial perception of the learners. They have to be tested with them to see whether they have the desired effect, which is to allow abstraction to be constructed by a continuous alternation between concrete examples (model cases) and formulations of what they have in common.

Impressionism, as defined earlier, could be illustrated by slides representing paintings by typical Impressionist painters, like Renoir, Monet, Pisarro, clearly exhibiting the chosen attributes. Non-essential attributes, also present, like the kind of subjects (landscape, portraits, cities, still life) or the season, would have to be varied in order not to cause confusion. The counter-examples could be, to start with, abstract paintings in strong colours, like Picasso, Kandinsky or Braque, where no common attributes are to be found. If the technique of the Impressionist painters is not well distinguished, a counter-example showing the opposite kind of technique could be shown, such as certain of Matisse's paintings. Observations like 'it looks blurred', or 'there are no lines' could be linked to comparisons of techniques; others, like 'I would prefer to be in that painting', could be linked to comparisons of different atmospheres. 'It's soft' could lead to an observation of colours, as compared to other paintings. To show the natural 'here and now' kind of subjects typical of the Impressionists, counter-examples with a historical or mythical theme, painted in a studio, could be contrasted with 'the impression' a real landscape offers. To show the importance of the effect of natural light, reflections in the water, coloured shadows and general luminosity, could be compared to plain surfaces. To put the perception of subtle distinctions to a test, counter-examples that come very close, like pre-, post- and neoimpressionists could be compared (but only at the end): how are a Turner, a Signac, a Seurat or a van Gogh different? Alike? What conclusions do we draw?

The examples must be sufficient in number and variety for their comparison to involve the student in a real epistemological search. (A prior understanding, by the student, of the structure of the concept–knowledge is the condition for this.) The variety of examples and counter-examples encourages the learner to make multiple comparisons and to put the concept in its conceptual framework. A concept does not exist alone but always in a conceptual framework, and it is important for the student to be able to distinguish subtle differences between similar concepts so as not to confuse them.

The order of the examples is also important. It allows the teacher to make sure that temporary knowledge can settle in before it is upset by the introduction of an example that causes amazement or doubt. Before a learner is able to modify a conception, he or she must be aware of it.

The dialogue that accompanies the confrontation of examples and counter-examples allows the students to clarify and rectify the models they are constructing. This confrontation appears at different levels. First, new knowledge is confronted with the learners' existing knowledge. This is expressed through their verbal observations and thus permits the teacher to find out what their initial perceptions are. Then there is a confrontation between the students' different perceptions, as expressed in their verbal interaction and argumentation. Finally, there is a confrontation between the students and the teacher, generated by the latter's questions, which lead to analysis and critical judgement, as well as to the search for precise formulations.

This dialogue also allows reasoning to be revealed. When the teacher thinks aloud with the learners he or she gives them the actual experience of an abstract process: this experience will then make it possible for them, not to imitate it, but to become aware of it and make it their own. Thus it is the students who are led to think and reason; the teacher's role is to guide this reasoning and help the students go further in the development of their knowledge than they could have done on their own. Verbal formulation is part of the learning process itself: language becomes a tool for thinking that allows experience to be transformed and assimilated.

The cognitive process is thus set in motion by a cognitive procedure (Figure 14.3) conveyed by the instructions for the task and the choice of examples. This choice can create astonishment, questions, hypothetical answers, argumentation. The teacher's role is to help students to perceive links and encourage formulation, verification and reformulation. This mediation allows the learner to establish a connection with the teacher's empirical knowledge and, progressively, to transform it; it limits the separation of empirical knowledge and declarative knowledge, which prevents the transfer from taking place. It stimulates the relating of various mental images to each other, whether they be visual, auditory, or kinesthetic.

Learners build their abstract knowledge from direct confrontation with real examples (chosen for them) of this knowledge, helped by the person who is guiding them, somehow negotiating the meaning with them. The teacher becomes the 'co-constructor' of meaning. The procedure is flexible and may vary but this process of constructing meaning – a close alternation between intuition and analysis, between hypothesis and verification – should always be set in motion by the learner. Individual differences may be taken into consideration within this universal process. The role of the mediator may also be taken by a more experienced peer, but it is

TIME to represent the task

I N S T R U C T I O N S	TIME to perceive, absorb, the new information	perception: distinguish differences
	TIME to compare the new information with what one already knows	comparison: analogical or analytical
	TIME to explain, account for, one's intuitive perceptions (memory support)	first inferences: inductive or deductive
	TIME to explore (the right to errors, crossing out what is no longer relevant	verification

TIME to perceive links, make new   new inferences
       connections, restructure

Beginning of synthesis

A S S E S S M E N T	TIME to compare the new connections with other people's	
	TIME to rectify and reformulate	
	TIME to verify and transform	new verifications
	TIME to make final formulations	generalisation, hypothesis
	TIME to consolidate and memorise	

The *procedure* can be varied: time, task,   The *process* is directed
modes of presentation or of grouping, etc.   (but not necessarily linear)

Figure 14.3 Guiding the process: co-construction

insufficient to put students into a group for interactions to be of high quality. On the other hand, with the rules of the game well defined and understood (which are actually rules for thinking) and with training to act as a member of a group, students profit by learning together.

The assessment of learning is a part of the process and starts at the outset. It is formative, allowing for constant correcting along the way. A mistake has a positive role, for it leads to the analysis and transformation of initial and intermediary conceptions. Counter-examples can function as a set of 'mistakes' that, when well chosen, surprise students and induce them to ask questions, reflecting a genuine interrogation on their part.

Admittedly this approach takes time: this is the prerequisite for reflection, which one tends to overlook. But this time is saved in the long run, for the student learns how to regulate his or her thinking and is thus prepared for cognitive autonomy. This type of evaluation in which students are led to analyse new examples by justifying their conclusions is an efficient way to break them of the habit of always wanting to give the 'right' answer, which defeats real learning. Justification leads to critical judgement, argumentation and self-evaluation. The students participate in the assessment of their learning; once they have understood the essential criteria, present in the model cases, they can easily check themselves: '*If* such and such an element (attribute) is present, *then* I am looking at such and such a phenomenon (concept).' This is hypothetical reasoning, verified during the thinking process and concluded by a generalisation. This active exploration is indispensable for memorisation and transfer. It also lays the foundation for a later realisation of the nature of reasoning itself.

The final evaluation is to be found at three levels: meaning (attributes), symbol (the word), and production of personal examples (transfer). This evaluation makes sure that acquisition has not remained on the level of verbal association (recognition of a few examples in response to a stimulus) but has moved up to the level of *conceptualisation* (ability to generalise, to extend the criteria observed to a whole category).

In this way, a higher level of reflection (induced in the students through the teacher's mediation) allows students to acquire knowledge on the level of conceptualisation; but it is possible for them to go further – consciously mobilising their minds for future learning tasks. To bring about transfer of cognitive processes, the teacher must be able to recognise them. Before practising metacognition with one's pupils, one needs to have a clear idea of what cognition is. One must be able to separate the teaching content from the cognitive processes used to assimilate it, in order to have children think about the process itself. It would be worthwhile to pursue the question of metacognitive teaching, not only in learning situations provided and guided by the teacher, but also when using a good computer program. If the use of the computer is to enhance transfer of thinking skills in the learner, one would need to elicit reflection on why it was good, and what it helped the learner to do.

The teacher's role in this approach is essential and specific: as the mediator between the learner and knowledge, he or she is responsible for putting the students in a position from which to construct knowledge rather than supplying them with ready-made knowledge. The teacher does this by providing an adequate learning task and by modelling higher-order thinking while guiding the students' thinking. Further, by teaching in a metacognitive way, he or she makes it possible for the learners to become aware of, and later integrate the thinking process itself.

My research lies within a Vygotskian and Brunerian theoretical framework. The following quotation from Bruner, interpreting the 'zone of proximal development', as defined by Vygotsky, makes this apparent:

> If the child is enabled to advance by being under the tutelage of an adult or a
> more competent peer, then the tutor or the peer serves the learner as a vicarious

form of consciousness until such a time as the learner is able to master his own action through his own consciousness and control . . . it is then he is able to use it as a tool.

(Bruner, 1985)

With this background, my own work with children and teachers has added a theoretical and operational understanding of the thinking processes and the conditions under which these can be better developed. There is much work needed to gain a deeper knowledge in this field of study. In the meantime we must use the knowledge we already have to create the best conditions for teachers and pupils to succeed in their respective tasks.

Howard Gardner's theories of multiple intelligences (Gardner, 1983) are certainly among those that can permit us to draw further conclusions on how these universal thinking processes can be applied in different ways, depending on how various symbol systems shape them. Today's transdisciplinary research in cognitive sciences should help to give further clues to the eternal philosophical question: how does the mind work?

In the meantime, we have to use the knowledge we possess in order to create the optimum conditions under which teachers and learners can best fulfil their tasks. Helping teachers to acquire a conceptual understanding of what understanding is, as well as to be good thinkers themselves, promises to produce a qualitative change in the way we teach. This change might best come about through a kind of a partnership between researchers and teachers in a common search for how our current knowledge can be applied to the greatest benefit of our schoolchildren.

Endnotes

1 This formal approach to knowledge, as a structure of connections, could be further developed. See Perkins (1986).

References

Barth, B.-M. (1987) *L'apprentissage de l'abstraction, méthodes pour une meilleure réussite de l'école*, Paris: RETZ.

Bruner, J. S. (1985) 'Vygotsky: a historical and conceptual perspective', in Wertsch, J. V. (ed.), *Culture, Communication and Cognition: Vygotskian Perspectives*, Cambridge: Cambridge University Press.

Bruner, J. S., Goodnow, J. J. and Austin, G. A. (1956) *A Study of Thinking*, New York: Wiley.

Gardner, H. (1983) *Frames of Mind: The Theory of Multiple Intelligences*, New York: Basic Books.

Perkins, D. N. (1986) *Knowledge as Design*, Hillsdale, NJ: Erlbaum.

Chapter 15

Teaching as a research-based profession: possibilities and prospects

David H. Hargreaves

Teacher Training Agency Annual Lecture 1996.

Introduction

Teaching is not at present a research-based profession. I have no doubt that if it were, teaching would be more effective and more satisfying. The goal of enhancing effectiveness and satisfaction can be achieved only by a combination of several means, of which an adequate research base is just one. It is in my view a singularly important one that deserves to be given priority. However, I shall argue in this chapter that providing that research base will require a radical change both in the kind of research that is done and in the way in which it is organised. To make my case I shall look inside the profession and the research community to examine what we now do; but I shall also look at another profession to detect what lessons can be learned about creating a genuinely research-based profession.

The £50–60 million we spend annually on educational research is poor value for money in terms of improving the quality of education provided in schools. In fundamental respects the teaching profession has, I believe, been inadequately served by us. It need not be so. If the defects in the way educational research is organised were remedied, research would play a more effective role in advancing the professional quality and standing of teachers. Left to ourselves, we educational researchers will not choose the necessary radical reforms. It needs others, including practising teachers, to give the firm push to get researchers on the move.

My lecture is in three parts: educational research in a comparative professional framework; diagnosing what went wrong; and finally, the way forward.

Part one: educational research in a comparative professional framework

Rarely have teachers looked at other professional fields to examine whether they might learn from their structures and cultures. The comparison I make now is with medicine, and in particular with doctors in hospitals. The medical profession has gained in public prestige concurrently with the growth of its research. The teaching profession has not. We need to investigate why this is so and what can be done to change things.

My own research in schools and hospitals indicates that both education and medicine are profoundly people-centred professions. Neither believes that helping people is merely a matter of a simple technical application but rather a highly skilled process in which a sophisticated judgement matches a professional decision to the unique needs of each client. Yet the two professions see the role of scientific knowledge in informing professional practice in very different ways. The kind of science, and so the kind of research, involved in each profession is very different. The academic infrastructure of medicine is rooted in the natural sciences (anatomy, physiology, pharmacology, etc.). No doctor denies that medical competence requires a grasp of this infrastructure. Doctors draw on this knowledge-base for the technical language of the profession.

There is no agreed knowledge-base for teachers, so they largely lack a shared technical language. It was once hoped that the so-called foundation disciplines of education – psychology, sociology, philosophy and history – would provide this knowledge base and so were given great importance in the curriculum of teacher training, BEd courses especially. Unfortunately, very few successful practising teachers themselves had this knowledge-base or thought it important for practice. It remains true that teachers are able to be effective in their work in almost total ignorance of this infrastructure. After qualification teachers largely abandon these academic influences and the use of social scientific terms within their professional discourse declines: the disciplines of education are seen to consist of 'theory' that is strongly separated from practice. Trainee teachers soon spot the yawning gap between theory and practice and the low value of research as a guide to the solution of practical problems.

In medicine, as in the natural sciences, research has a broadly cumulative character. Research projects seek explicitly to build on earlier research – by confirming or falsifying it, by extending or refining it, by replacing it with better evidence or theory, and so on.

Much educational research is, by contrast, non-cumulative, in part because few researchers seek to create a body of knowledge that is then tested, extended or replaced in some systematic way. A few small-scale investigations of an issue that are never followed up inevitably produce inconclusive and contestable findings of little practical relevance. Replications, which are more necessary in the social than the natural sciences because of the importance of contextual and cultural variations, are astonishingly rare. Moreover, educational researchers, like other social scientists, are often engaged in bitter disputes among themselves about the philosophy and methodology of the social sciences. Given the huge amounts of educational research conducted over the last fifty years or more, there are few areas that have yielded a corpus of research evidence regarded as scientifically sound and as a worthwhile resource to guide professional action – and this is true in areas that might be regarded as fundamental. In many educational areas a line of research ends with a change of fashion, sometimes (and often pretentiously) called a 'paradigm shift', not because the problems in it have been solved. Post-modernists argue that it has been an illusion to imagine that the social sciences could ever be cumulative: social science is just another mode of discourse with no legitimate claim to any special or privileged authority. To concede this is, in my view, to undermine the *raison d'etre* of most of the research that is currently funded. Nor for a minute do I accept the charge that educational research is *in principle* misguided; my argument is that the profession needs educational research but that it must be a very different kind of research if it is to influence practice.

A yet more striking difference between the professions is the identity of the people who actually *do* the research. In medicine, it is possible to draw on the basic sciences that are not in themselves specifically medical – genetics, biochemistry, neuro-physiology – where developments and discoveries are potentially relevant to medical advance. In the same way, educators can draw on other basic sciences – say, cognitive science – where there is potential for educational application.

But there is a very sharp difference in the way the two professions approach *applied* research. Much medical research is not itself basic research (which is left to the basic sciences or medical scientists drawing on such work) but a type of applied research that gathers evidence about what works in what circumstances. It is a search for more accurate means of diagnosing medical problems; better ways of managing the patient; the determination of more effective treatments. The people best placed to do this work are not basic scientists or or a special category of medical researchers, but medical practitioners. A considerable proportion of the articles in popular as well as specialist medical journals comes from practitioners in hospitals and general practice.

A tiny proportion of educational research – that is, funded research, carried out by proper procedures and then made public knowledge through publication – is undertaken by practising teachers: the vast majority of such research is conducted by university-based academics involved in teacher education who do not teach in schools.

In medicine, then, there is little difference between researchers and users: all are practitioners. In education, by contrast, researchers are rarely users and so there are major problems of communication. This shows in the way research is written up and transmitted in the two professions. In medicine there are journals (*The British Medical Journal, The Lancet*) that aim to communicate to the whole profession on general medical issues as well as selected advances within specialities. In education the only regular journal that potentially reaches most teachers is the *Times Educational Supplement* where relatively little space is given to research. There is not a scrap of evidence that teachers complain about their lack of access to the findings of educational research. Educational researchers write mainly for one another in their countless academic journals, which are not to be found in a school staffroom.

It is this gap between researchers and practitioners that betrays the fatal flaw in educational research. For it is the researchers, not the practitioners, who determine the agenda of educational research. If practising doctors, especially those in hospitals, stopped doing research and left it almost entirely to a special breed of people called 'medical researchers' who were mainly university academics without patients, then medical research would go the same way as educational research – a private, esoteric activity, seen as irrelevant by most practitioners. Educational research is caught between two stools, that of the basic social sciences (psychology, sociology) and that of practitioners in schools. Educational researchers have become adept at falling off both stools, achieving neither prestige from the social scientists (e.g. mainstream psychologists) nor gratitude from classroom teachers.

How different it is for doctors! The spread of evidence-based medicine is rooting much medical research firmly in the day-to-day professional practices of doctors. In the past, a surgeon asked why he was treating a patient by means of a particular operation, or why he was using one operating technique rather than another, would often refer back to his training – 'I do it this way because I trained under Sir Lancelot Spratt at St Swithin's.' Today doctors are relying less heavily on the clinical practices in which they were trained and more on an evidence-based approach, in which research into the effects of treatment is used, by both trainers and trainees, as the basis and justification for treatment. In short, some of the most important research in medicine, conducted by practitioners, aims to evaluate the effects of one treatment or one technique rather than another. Is lumpectomy as effective as radical mastectomy as a treatment for breast cancer? Because evidence-based medicine, though fallible, has direct and often immediate relevance to the improvement of their practice and patient benefit, there is a huge incentive for doctors to keep up to date.

Far less medical practice is based on evidence than lay people commonly suppose. Medical treatment is not invariably followed by clinical improvement any more than classroom teaching is invariably followed by student learning. Indeed, when doctors concede that

> a large proportion of treatments, not to say investigations and referrals, are no more than a face-saving disguise for medical impotence[1]

one is tempted to shout a deeply sympathetic 'snap' with an equivalent admission that much teaching, specific lessons and acts of individual attention to students, are no more than a face-saving disguise for pedagogic impotence. 'All day and every day,' says another leading medical expert,

> we are forced to make what we hope are adequate decisions on woefully inadequate evidence. We are not altogether comfortable living in a world of uncertainty, but we have grown accustomed to it.[2]

Does not this sound more like a teacher than a doctor?

The significant difference between the professions, however, is that whereas doctors are demanding and getting more evidence-based research, teachers are not even seeing their severe lack of evidence-based research as a problem in urgent need of remedy.

To become an effective doctor, then, means learning both from one's seniors and from research – and the two are tied because one's seniors are researchers and are familiar with more research than the juniors. Doctors learn to respect and call upon research evidence. In hospitals in particular, doctors will introduce references to research and to scholarly journals within their routine conversations about patients and the diagnosis or treatment of their conditions.

In education there is simply not enough evidence on the effects and effectiveness of what teachers do in classrooms to provide an evidence-based corpus of knowledge. The failure of educational researchers, with a few exceptions, to create a substantial body of knowledge equivalent to evidence-based medicine means that teaching is not – and never will be – a research-based profession unless there is major change in the kind of research that is done in education. Today teachers still have to discover or adopt most of their own professional practices by personal preference, guided by neither the accumulated wisdom of seniors nor by practitioner-relevant research. They see no need to keep abreast of research developments and rightly regard research journals as being directed to fellow academics, not to them. Teachers rely heavily on what they learn from their own experience, private trial and error. For a teacher to cite research in a staffroom conversation about a pupil would almost certainly indicate that he or she was studying for a part-time higher degree in education or rehearsing for an OFSTED visit – and would be regarded by most colleagues as showing off.

In hospital medicine, then, the acquisition of expertise means becoming more effective not just in terms of practical skills, but also by familiarity, with the practice-relevant research. Promotion in hospitals is slow: one remains a junior doctor, working under the supervision of a consultant who 'owns' the patients, until one's late thirties or so. Promotion to the higher echelons of the profession is closely related to the acquisition of knowledge well beyond that required for initial registration, namely the FRCS and equivalent examinations, which are difficult and have a specified content. Consultants are outstanding practitioners and they have to prove it. A consultant in (say) surgery, and even more so a professor of surgery, would be a practising surgeon of outstanding achievement. Advances in medicine are made by leading practitioners who are for this reason deeply respected by juniors – and trusted by their patients.

In education, by stark contrast, we have de-coupled promotion from both practitioner expertise and knowledge of expertise. A headteacher or a professor of education, though perhaps formerly an outstanding practitioner, rarely has regular teaching duties in a school. Teachers get transformed by promotion into managers, administrators or academics and lack the deep respect junior doctors show to their seniors. A higher degree in education may be advantageous to a teacher's promotion, but it is not a necessary condition. A Master's degree is nowadays easily gained, is variable in content, and gives little indication of the knowledge or skills thereby acquired.

Now the purpose of this comparison has been not to suggest we slavishly imitate doctors – though in some ways we could with advantage be more like them – but rather to show that in other professions there is a far more productive relationship between research and professional practice and to suggest that solutions to the problems in educational research may require structural and cultural change. In education, to achieve an end result not unlike that of the medics means taking a different research route.

Part two: diagnosing what went wrong

Something has indeed gone badly wrong. Research is having little impact on the improvement of practice and teachers I talk to do not think they get value for money from the £50–60 million we spend annually on educational research. The research community has yet to face up to the problem. It protects itself and the *status quo* by a series of defences.

Educational research used to be dominated by the linear model, which draws a direct line from basic research (say psychological research on learning) to applied research (on school children learning an aspect of the curriculum) to the dissemination of findings (which then leads to an improvement in professional practice everywhere). It was widely believed that this model would transform schools and produce professional practice that would be research-based. We now know that this model is simplistic and does not work in its classic form: indeed, most researchers say that they no longer believe in it. It was concluded that research has an *indirect* influence on policy and practice,[3] which, whilst true, had the unintended side-effect of deflecting investigation into the reasons for this lack of direct impact and of persuading many researchers that it was not worth trying to achieve direct effects on practice. Rationalising failure to improve practice through research became a self-fulfilling prophecy.

In reality, researchers continue to adhere to some aspects of the linear model, for they define one of the main problems of educational research to be the *dissemination* of research findings to practitioners. Some researchers blame themselves for not disseminating their results; others blame their sponsors for not funding dissemination; and yet others – to my astonishment – blame the teachers for ignoring the research findings and failing to act on them.[4] Seeing the main problem as one of dissemination assumes there is something worthwhile to be disseminated. It also assumes that the process of commissioning research and the research itself is in good shape: apparently all would be well if one could simply improve the dissemination of results.

I think these conclusions by researchers are for the most part off-target. There is no vast body of research that, if only it were disseminated and acted upon by teachers, would yield huge benefits in the quality of teaching and learning. One must ask the essential question: just how much research is there that (i) demonstrates conclusively that if teachers change their practice from x to y there will be a significant and enduring improvement in teaching and learning and (ii) has developed an effective method of convincing teachers of the benefits of, and means to, changing from x to y?

We do not have much powerful evidence about effective professional practice, which indicates that the main problem is not with dissemination but at the other end of the research process: how the research is commissioned and set in train. Almost all the money devoted to educational research is allocated on the basis of peer review, that is, researchers themselves decide which research and researchers are worth funding. Even where the body commissioning the research does not itself consist of researchers, the commissioners almost always rely to a considerable degree on peer review.

Now there is much sense in peer review. Those who, on the basis of knowledge and experience, are experts in a field are in many ways most fitted to make judgements on the quality of a research proposal. In a research field that is successful and healthy, peer review works well. But educational research is not in a healthy state; it is not having adequate influence on the improvement of practice; it is not good value for money. In these circumstances peer review serves to perpetuate a very unsatisfactory *status quo*.

Researchers continue their work on their own self-validating terms; they are accountable to themselves; so there is absolutely no reason why they should change. Educational research lacks the 'pull' of industry that generates the effective application of engineering research and the 'push' of the Health Service and drug companies that ensures the application of medical research. In education the key fault is the lack of involvement of 'users', that is, practitioners and policy-makers, in the peer review or allocation system: it is their exclusion that prevents the re-direction of educational research towards the improvement of practice.

Part three: the way forward

I offer two ways of introducing the necessary pressures and incentives to change educational research so that it improves the practice of teachers in schools. The first concerns how the educational research agenda is set and the process of research managed; and the second concerns research funding.

Changing the research agenda and research process means adopting as an essential prerequisite of improvement, the involvement of user communities, policy-makers and practitioners, in all aspects of the research process, from the creation of strategic research plans, the selection of research priorities and the funding of projects through to the dissemination and implementation of policies and practices arising from or influenced by research findings. It means establishing the machinery for creating *a national strategy for educational research*, including the formulation of short- and long-term priorities, with some mechanism for co-ordinating the work of the various funding agencies to increase knowledge of all parties about what topics are being funded for what reasons and what the outcomes of research are.

A new partnership between researchers and practitioners must be at the heart of any reform. Success here will help to solve so many other problems. Partnerships must (and of course do) exist at the level of the individual research institution and individual research project. All this is to be applauded, as is the pressure the ESRC now puts on researchers to demonstrate consultation with, and involvement of, users as a condition of getting a research grant.

In the field of education much more is needed to change the culture and practices of users or researchers; indeed, there is a danger of researchers playing at user involvement in a rhetorical way because the rules of the 'game' of obtaining funds and doing research have only superficially changed. Practitioners and policy-makers must take an active role in shaping the direction of educational research as a whole, not just in influencing projects in which they happen to be involved; and researchers need to know that users are powerful partners with whom many aspects of research need to be negotiated and to whom in a real sense the research community is in part accountable.

It would be desirable to establish a *National Educational Research Forum*, whose function would be to establish a continuing dialogue between all the stakeholders and to shape the agenda of educational research and its policy implications and applications. The Forum's directors would be formed from a mixture of policy-makers (at national and local levels), practitioners (heads, teachers), representatives from funding bodies (research councils, charities and trusts) and relevant lay persons (governors, parents) as well as researchers themselves. The Forum would be the arena in which all stakeholders could talk to one another in that necessarily broad and open conversation about matters of educational interest in which research 'is just *one* element in the complex mix of experience, conventional wisdom and political accommodation that enters into decision making.[5]

Building on these interchanges, the Forum would, say every four to five years, conduct or commission a review of current achievements, omissions and problems in educational research, leading to a research foresight exercise, involving researcher, user and lay communities, and the establishment thereafter of a national research strategy. Such a strategy would be in broad outline, based on the Forum's conclusions on the most desirable, practicable and applicable research.

The establishment of the Forum and the involvement of users would, I believe, lead to one significant change in the character of research: there would be a dramatic increase in the need for evidence-based research relating to what teachers do in classrooms. Devoting a substantial proportion of the research budget – £10–20 million? – to providing the evidence on effective practice would rapidly change the nature of educational research. Some of the money would be used to fund teachers as researcher–practitioners rather than the objects of the activities of academic researchers. This is one lesson to be learnt from the medical profession. It has to be accepted that, just as it is appropriate to 'buy out' practising teachers to be mentors in teacher training, hard cash is needed to fund teachers to buy time for research. Teacher trainers were slow to yield on the first of these; sadly they may follow rather than lead in the case of the second.

The way money is routed into educational research must be changed. Research councils, especially the ESRC, should have at least their present share, for they have a fine record of funding high quality educational research, as do the various charities. This must continue. Curiosity-driven, long-term 'basic' and 'blue-skies' research is as vital in education as in any other scientific field. What would come to an end is the frankly second-rate educational research that does not make a serious contribution to fundamental theory or knowledge; that is irrelevant to practice; that is unco-ordinated with any preceding or follow-up research; and that clutters up academic journals that virtually nobody reads. It would sharply curtail what Professor Michael Bassey has rightly derived as 'the dilettante tradition' in educational research. From this source a substantial proportion of the research budget can be prised out of the academic community, who currently distribute it to one another as they think fit, and over several years transferred in phases to agencies committed to evidence-based research and to full partnership with teachers in the interests of improving practice.

Some of this research money should be allocated through the Teacher Training Agency. The recent development by the TTA of national standards for teacher 'experts', in subject leadership and in school leadership, as well as qualifications for headteachers, is an exciting development that would make the professional structures and cultures of education and medicine more closely aligned. But there is no virtue in expert teachers and newly qualified heads studying substantial bodies of educational theory and research that is mostly remote from practical application. It is evidence-based research that is particularly relevant here. Expertise *means* not just having relevant experience and knowledge but having *demonstrable* competence and clear *evidence* to justify doing things in one way rather than another. If the expertise claimed by those given the title is to be authoritative, it must be closely related to knowledge of the evidence about practice, otherwise it is no more than a plea for deference to seniority.

Caroline Cox has pointed to four grounds teachers use to justify their practices:

- *tradition* (how it has always been done);
- *prejudice* (how I like it done);
- *dogma* (this is the 'right' way to do it);
- *ideology* (as required by the current orthodoxy).

Doctors have used similar justificatory grounds:

- *tradition* ('we continue to base our clinical decisions on increasingly out-of-date primary training')[6]
- *prejudice* ('most doctors have a very narrow perspective, limiting themselves to their own experience and those of a relatively few colleagues')[7]
- *dogma* ('some operations will continue to be done because they are the fashion')[8]
- *ideology* ('in law, if enough doctors do it, then it is right')[9]

– quotations taken from commentaries on the advantages of evidence-based medicine.

Both professions have the humility to acknowledge that some of their time-honoured practices prove to be worthless or even harmful; teachers must join doctors in seeking to put professional decision-making to evidential test. When educational leaders have evidence for their practices, they may even command the respect of politicians, who advocate their pet ideas in the secure knowledge that the profession lacks convincing evidence to the contrary. The TTA, as its work on expertise develops, must be able to commission evidence-based research to support and justify its endeavours.

And should not OFSTED be allocated some research funding? Without question OFSTED has the most comprehensive database on what teachers do and how it relates to their effectiveness. Would the profession benefit if OFSTED had a research division to analyse the evidence inspectors collect? Would the process of inspection improve if inspectors were better trained in garnering harder evidence about effective practice? Should schools and teachers defined as good by inspectors be funded to investigate further the evidential basis for their success? After all, OFSTED believes in inspection for improvement, but school improvement is currently a largely research-free zone.

Evidence-based medicine is gaining support because the number of variables affecting the selection of the right treatment are so great that no individual doctor can expect to be a constant master of this complexity. It is much the same complexity of variables influencing student attitudes and behaviour that bewilders teachers. In education we too need evidence about what works with whom under what conditions and with what effects. 'The practice of evidence-based medicine' says the journal of that title,

> is a process of life-long, problem-based learning in which caring for our patients creates the need for evidence about diagnosis, prognosis, therapy and other clinical and health-care issues. In the evidence-based medicine process we
>
> - convert these information needs into answerable questions
> - track down with maximum efficiency the best evidence with which to answer them . . .
> - critically appraise that evidence for its validity . . . and usefulness . . .
> - apply the results of this appraisal to our clinical practice, and
> - evaluate our performance.[10]

Can any of you say that a parallel approach in teaching, compatible as it is with the notion of the teacher as reflective practitioner, would not be powerfully beneficial?

Educational researchers may not be enthusiastic about these suggestions, which are perhaps too radical for them. Most academics fear any loss of their autonomy and control over the research process; and they claim practitioner interests are short-termist. There would indeed be some loss of autonomy, and there would be a danger of short-termism that a National Forum would need to take into account. But the end result would be far more research that is closely related to policy and practice, that is carried out by and with users, and that leads to results that are more likely to be applied in practice. There is much to gain and little to lose in moving as soon as possible to an evidence-based teaching profession. The TTA will, I hope, work with the profession and researchers to make the prospects match the exciting possibilities.

Endnotes

1 Pickering, William G. (1996) 'Does medical treatment mean patient benefit?', *Lancet*, **347**, 379–80.
2 Bearn, A. G. (1997) 'The growth of scientific medicine', in McLachlan, G. (ed.), *Medical Education and Medical Care*, Oxford: Oxford University Press.
3 The classic and highly influential statement of this position is that by Nisbet, J. and Broadfoot, P. (1980) *The Impact of Research on Policy and Practice in Education*, Aberdeen: Aberdeen University Press. See also Taylor, William (1973) 'Knowledge and research', in Taylor, W. (ed.) *Research Perspectives in Education*, London: Routledge & Kegan Paul; and Kogan, Maurice (1984) in Husen, T. and Kogan, M. (eds), *Educational Research & Policy*, London: Pergamon Press, 48.
4 See, for example, Glennan, Thomas K. (1994) 'In search of new structures and procedures for organizing government funded education research and development', in *Education Research and Reform: An International Perspective*, OECD/US Department of Education.
5 Husen, T. (1984) in Husen, T. and Kogan, M. (eds), *Educational Research and Policy*, London: Pergamon Press, 31.
6 Rosenberg, William and Donald, Anna (1995) 'Evidence based medicine: an approach to clinical problem solving', *British Medical Journal*, **310**, 1122–5.
7 Quoted from David Grahame-Smith (1995) 'Evidence based medicine: Socratic dissent', *British Medical Journal*, **310**, 1126–8.
8 Pickering, William G. (1996) 'Does medical treatment mean patient benefit?', *Lancet*, **347**, 379–80.
9 ibid.
10 Sackett, D. L. and Haynes, R. B. (1995) 'Notebook', *Evidence-based Medicine*, **1**(1), 5.

Chapter 16

Educational research and teaching: a response to David Hargreaves' TTA lecture

Martyn Hammersley

This is an edited version of an article previously published in *British Educational Research Journal*, **23**(2), April 1997.

Educational research in Britain is currently under threat. There are several causes. External changes and pressures are among the most important factors, especially continuing cuts in resources for both education and academic research, along with the disruption created by multiple government-sponsored reforms at all levels of the education system. But there are also internal problems; for example, the effects of what has been termed the 'crisis of representation', which increasingly afflicts the whole of the humanities and social sciences. This throws doubt on the capacity of research to produce knowledge, in the commonly understood sense of that term (see, for example, Denzin and Lincoln, 1995). One consequence of both external and internal crises has been an increased insistence that research should have a significant impact on professional or political practice. There is by no means universal agreement about exactly what this involves, but commitment to the idea is widespread. Among researchers themselves it is to be found in diverse forms; for example, in greater preoccupation with policy issues, in growing advocacy of action research and in moves towards open partisanship. Similarly, funding agencies insist more and more on policy relevance, on negotiation by researchers with prospective 'users', on explicit plans for dissemination designed to maximise impact, and sometimes on contracts that give funders control over publication.

Against this background, David Hargreaves's recent and controversial lecture on 'Teaching as a Research-based Profession', sponsored by the TTA, has considerable significance (Hargreaves, 1996). In this article I want to assess Hargreaves's criticisms of educational research and the remedies he proposes.

Two main charges seem to be involved. The first is that much educational research is non-cumulative. This first argument leads straight into the second: that research is not found useful by teachers. On this basis, Hargreaves argues that the money allocated to educational research is not well spent.

Educational research as non-cumulative

Criticism of the non-cumulative character of research on education has been a persistent theme in Hargreaves's writings. I have considerable sympathy with Hargreaves's argument. Commitment to one-off studies is an important defect of much educational research, and indeed of social research generally. In addition, I believe that Hargreaves is right to assume the appropriateness of a scientific approach to the study of education, despite the strong trend in the opposite direction in recent times.

Nevertheless, I think that there are also some serious problems with Hargreaves's critique. One is that he is not as clear as he might have been about what criteria he is using to assess educational research. In the early parts of his lecture he stresses its failure to accumulate knowledge by building on earlier work, but the concept of cumulation is not a simple one: there are different forms it can take (see Freese, 1980, pp. 40–9). Moreover, many educational researchers *do* claim that their work has produced theoretical development (see, for example, Woods, 1985, 1987). Hargreaves does not make clear why he would deny these claims. Later in his lecture, this first criticism turns into the charge that educational research is not, or that enough of it is, 'evidence-based'. Again, clarification is required. What is and is not being accepted as evidence here, and what counts as basing claims on evidence? Some specification and justification of the model of research he is employing is necessary. Reference to examples of evidence-based and non-evidence-based educational research might also have been illuminating.

A second problem is that Hargreaves seems to present the failings of current educational research as if they stemmed solely from a lack of commitment on the part of researchers to rigorous and cumulative inquiry. There is no doubt that this commitment has become attenuated. But, to some extent, this is a response to genuine problems. It should be pointed out that the move away from the scientific model, and from a concern with testing the effectiveness of different pedagogic techniques, is relatively recent.

The shift to qualitative method in the 1970s was prompted by powerful criticisms identifying unresolved problems in 'positivist' research.

There can be no denying the serious problems involved in producing conclusive knowledge about causal patterns in social phenomena. At the core of them is precisely the question of the extent to which one can have a science of human behaviour of a kind that models itself, even remotely, on the natural sciences. By failing to mention these problems, Hargreaves implies that the sort of cumulative, well-founded knowledge he wants can be created simply by researchers pulling themselves together and getting back to work (under the direction of teachers). The situation is not so simple; and not so easily remedied.

I can only sketch the problems briefly here. They centre on two areas: the measurement of social phenomena and the validation of causal relationships amongst those phenomena. As regards the former, there are problems involved in identifying distinct and standardised 'treatments' in education. Indeed, there are unresolved measurement problems even in relation to the most specific and concrete aspects of teaching, for example, types of questions asked (Scarth and Hammersley, 1986a, 1986b). The problems are also formidable at the other end of the causal chain, in operationalising the concept of learning. There is room for considerable disagreement about what students *should* learn and what they *actually* learn in any particular situation. More than this, very often what are regarded as the most important kinds of learning – relating to high-level, transferable cognitive skills or personal understanding – are extraordinarily difficult to measure with any degree of validity and reliability; and there are doubts about whether replicable measurement of them is possible, even in principle. In short, in both areas, there are questions about whether it is possible to move beyond sensitising concepts to the definitive concepts that seem to be required for scientific analysis of the kind proposed by Hargreaves.

The problems relating to the establishment of causal patterns are equally severe. Since we are interested in what goes on in real schools and colleges, and because strict experimentation is often ruled out for practical or ethical reasons, this task becomes extremely difficult. How are we to control competing factors in such a way as to assess the relative contribution of each one in what is usually a complex web of relationships? More than this, can we assume that causation in this field involves fixed, universal relationships, rather than local, context-sensitive patterns in which interpretation and decision on the part of teachers and students play an important role? Unlike in most areas of medicine, in education the 'treatments' consist of symbolic interaction, with all the scope for multiple interpretations and responses which that implies. What kind of causal relations are involved here, if they are causal at all? And what kind of knowledge can we have of them?

There is another point too. In my view, one important cause of the unsatisfactory nature of much educational research is that it is too preoccupied with producing information that will shape *current* policy or practice. This seems likely to be one source of the lack of testing and cumulation of knowledge that Hargreaves complains about. The problem, in part, is that while working under the authority of academic disciplines concerned with contributing to theory, researchers have also sought to address the changing political agendas that define pressing educational problems. This is partly a product of sharp competition for funding. But it has also been encouraged by conceptions of research that imply that it is possible simultaneously to contribute to scientific theory and to provide solutions to practical or political problems. However, it seems to me that this view is fallacious, since the production of information of high practical relevance usually depends on a great deal of knowledge that does not have such relevance. In other words, for science to be able to contribute knowledge that is relevant to practice, a division of labour is required: a great deal of co-ordinated work is necessary tackling smaller, more manageable problems that do not have immediate pay-off. Moreover, this requires sustained work over a long period, not short bursts of activity geared to political and practical priorities. In other words, the wrong time schedule has been in control: that of educational policy-making and practice rather than that appropriate to scientific research.

In my view, then, the commitment of educational researchers to addressing the 'big questions' and to producing answers to them in the short rather than the long term, along with parallel expectations on the part of funders, has been a major contributing factor to the weaknesses that Hargreaves identifies. And his call for educational research to be more practically effective will only worsen this problem. He insists that 'curiosity-driven, long-term "basic" and "blue skies" research is as vital in education as in any other scientific field' (p. 7). But he neglects the extent to which the funding for this has already been eroded. Moreover, Hargreaves applauds 'the pressure the ESRC now puts on researchers to demonstrate consultation with, and the involvement of, users as a condition of getting a research grant' (p. 6). Yet it is a feature of basic research that who the users will be and what use they might make of it are largely unknown.

Contributing to practice

Let me turn now to the second complaint in Hargreaves's lecture, to what is indeed its central theme: that educational research has not produced sufficient practically relevant knowledge. I certainly agree that an important ultimate aim (but, for reasons already explained, not an immediate one) of all research should be to produce knowledge that is practically relevant. But there is room for much disagreement about what such relevance amounts to, and about what kinds of knowledge are possible and of value. In his lecture, Hargreaves adopts a narrowly instrumental view of practical relevance: that research should be able to tell practitioners which is the best technique for dealing with a particular kind of problem. In this respect, though his analogy is with medicine, he seems to be committed to what has been referred to as the 'engineering model' of the relationship between research and practice. This portrays research as directed towards finding or evaluating solutions to technical problems.

The question of whether educational research can supply the sort of knowledge assumed by the engineering model has already been dealt with in the previous section, but there is also the issue of whether the problems that teachers face are of a kind that is open to solution by research; in other words, whether they are technical in character. Early on in his lecture, Hargreaves seems to recognise that they may not be. However, his subsequent discussion of the contribution that he would like to see research making to educational practice seems to contradict this; for example, his reference to research needing to 'demonstrate conclusively' that a particular pedagogical approach will produce 'a significant and enduring improvement' (p. 5).

At one time it was widely assumed that educational practice could, and should, be based on scientific theory. However, much recent work on the nature of teaching by philosophers, psychologists and sociologists has emphasised the extent to which it is practical rather than technical in character; in brief, that it is a matter of making judgements rather than following rules. This line of argument throws doubt on the idea that teaching can be *based* on research knowledge. It implies that it necessarily depends on experience, wisdom, local knowledge and judgement. And, I suggest, it is precisely the practical character of teaching, as much as any failing on the part of researchers, which is the main source of the 'yawning gap' between theory and practice.

One of the features of much practical activity, and particularly of teaching, is that goals are multiple, and their meaning are open to debate and difficult to operationalise. In this context, Hargreaves's focus on the 'effectiveness' of pedagogy obscures some of the most important issues. Put into practice, an exclusive focus on effectiveness leads to an overemphasis on those outcomes that can be measured (at the expense of other educational goals), or results in a displacement of goals on to the maximisation of measured output. We see this problem in the currently influential research on 'school effectiveness'. While researchers in this field are usually careful to note that the outcome measures they use do not exhaust or measure all the goals of schooling, their work is sometimes presented and often interpreted as measuring school effectiveness *as such*.

Now, of course, we need to take care not to adopt too sharp a distinction between technical and practical activities. What is involved is more of a continuum, and it seems likely that educational practice is not homogenous in this respect: there may be some educational problems that are open to technical solution, even though many are not. Nevertheless, all teaching beyond that concerned with very elementary skills, seems likely, in general terms, to come close to the practical end of the dimension. And the practical character of most teachers' work is increased by the fact that they deal with batches of pupils, rather than with single clients, one by one, as in the case of medicine. It is this that makes the classroom situation a particularly demanding one in terms of the need for reliance on contextual judgement.

All this is not to suggest that research can make no contribution to teaching. But it may mean that the contribution cannot take the form of indicating what is the appropriate technique to use in a particular situation, or even what are the chances of success of a technique in a particular type of situation. The nature of the contribution may be closer to the enlightenment model, involving the provision of information that corrects assumptions or alters the context in which teachers view some aspect of their situation; for example, by highlighting possible causal relations to which they may not routinely give attention. Equally important is the capacity that research has for illuminating aspects of teachers' practices that are below the normal level of their consciousness. For the most part, such contributions are not dramatic in their consequences. But it is just as much a mistake to try to judge the value of research in terms of its immediate and identifiable practical impact as it is to judge the quality of a school solely by its examination results.

In his lecture, Hargreaves quotes Nisbet and Broadfoot (1980) and Taylor (1973) arguing for the enlightenment view, but he does not explain why he rejects their conclusions. Instead, he simply asserts that this view is a self-fulfilling prophecy.

All this raises questions about Hargreaves's judgement that educational research does not offer value for money. This phrase has become a popular one, but it involves a judgement that is a good deal more complex and uncertain than its use generally suggests. Thus, Hargreaves gives no indication of how he thinks the cost–benefit analysis involved could be carried out. Even measuring the real cost of a particular piece of research would be a formidable task, and measuring the value of its 'impact' would be virtually impossible and always open to debate. Because of their reliance on values, all judgements about cost-effectiveness are likely to be subject to considerable instability across time, circumstances and judges. So the question arises of who is to judge, when and how. Hargreaves relies on the judgements of teachers he has talked to (p. 5). Even apart from the sampling and reactivity problems involved here, we can ask whether teachers are the best judges, given that according to him they have little knowledge of the findings of educational research. Furthermore, teachers are not the only proper audience for such research. Its main function, it seems to me, is to inform public debates about educational issues: to provide information for use by anyone concerned with those issues. How well it does this is an important question, and some assessment of its cost-effectiveness in this respect may be unavoidable; but this can be no more than a speculative and contestable estimate.

Hargreaves's lecture is effectively an evaluation of educational research, and as with all evaluations the conclusions are very sensitive to the standard of evaluation employed. One's attitude to the practical value of current educational research will depend a great deal on one's expectations about the contribution to practice that it *could* make. In my view, researchers have promised – and funders, policy-makers and practitioners have expected – too much: assuming that, in itself, research can provide solutions to practical problems. Disappointment, recriminations and a negative attitude towards research have been the result. Hargreaves's lecture is more of the same in this respect, and as a result it is likely to worsen rather than to improve the situation. By reinforcing the idea that research can provide a scientific foundation for practice, he exaggerates the contribution that it can make, *even in principle*. And the risk is that when it fails in this task, as it almost certainly will, it will be dismissed by even more potential users as worthless.

The parallel with medicine

In his critique of the practical failure of educational research, Hargreaves relies heavily on the analogy with medicine. I have no doubt at all that this comparison can be illuminating, but it ought to be pointed out that implicit in its use is a conception of professionalism that emphasises reliance on an established body of scientific knowledge. And this conception ought not to be taken for granted. We should remember that this has never been a feature of the other occupation whose status as a profession has always been question: the law. Furthermore, as with all analogies, it is important to recognise that there may be significant differences, as well as similarities, between what is being compared. Also, analogies are sometimes based on misconceptions about that which is being used as a comparative standard. We must be very cautious, then, about using medicine as a basis for evaluating educational research and practice. Its appropriateness has to be argued for, not assumed.

In the previous two sections I have discussed aspects of education that mark it off from medicine, in ways that challenge Hargreaves's negative judgements about the relative success of educational research. Certainly, it seems likely that much medical research avoids many of the problems that face educational researchers, in particular those deriving from the peculiarities of the social world. Where it does not, I suggest, we find the same lack of cumulative evidence that Hargreaves bemoans in education. Similarly, medical practice may generally be closer to the technical rather than to the practical end of the spectrum, so that research is able to play a role there which is much closer to that envisaged by the engineering model than is possible in education.

At the same time, it is easy to exaggerate the differences between the two cases. Thus, I think it is misleading to claim that in the case of medicine 'there is little difference between researchers and users; all are practitioners', whereas in educational contexts, 'by contrast, researchers are rarely users' (p. 3). As Hargreaves recognises, much medical research is laboratory-based rather than clinic-based; and is not carried out by practising clinicians. Equally, most educational researchers are also educational practitioners, even though they are often not practitioners in the same type of context as that in which they do research. It is also worth noting that most educational researchers are ex-schoolteachers whose research relates to schools of the same general type to that in which they previously taught. I do not want to deny that there are important differences in the organisation of research and practice in the fields of education and medicine, but the differences are less sharp and more complex than Hargreaves implies.

There are also respects in which the assumptions Hargreaves makes about medical research, and about the way it contributes to medical practice, are open to doubt. One concerns the contrast in quality that he draws between medical and educational research. It is of note that rather similar criticisms to those made by him of educational research have been directed at medical research carried out by doctors. It is worth emphasising the reasons that Altman (1994) puts forward for the poor quality of much medical research, since these relate directly to what Hargreaves claims to be its great strength: the fact that it is carried out by practising doctors. Altman lays the blame on the fact that doctors are expected to engage in research, but are often inadequately prepared for or committed to it. What we may conclude from this is that while there is undoubtedly a great deal more cumulation of well-founded knowledge in medicine than in education, it is not at all clear that this results primarily from the participation of clinicians. And we might reasonably fear that increasing the proportion of educational research that is carried out by practising teachers would not provide a remedy for the methodological ills that Hargreaves has identified.

There are also questions about the assumptions that Hargreaves makes about medical *practice*. There are two closely related aspects of clinical practice that are relevant here. First, clinical decision-making is not based solely, or even primarily, on knowledge drawn directly from research publications. Second, it often does not conform to what we might call the rational model of medical procedure. According to this (rather economistic) model, practice takes the following form: the relevant problem is clearly identified at the start; the full range of possible strategies for dealing with it are assessed in terms of their costs and benefits, on the basis of the best available evidence; and, finally, that strategy is selected and implemented that promises to be the most effective. As has been pointed out in many fields, including economics, for a variety of reasons practical activity deviates substantially from this rationalistic model.

In one way, Hargreaves recognises these features of medical practice. Referring to some comments from Caroline Cox about teachers, he points out how medical practitioners also often rely on 'tradition, prejudice, dogma, and ideology' (pp. 7–8). In adopting this loaded characterisation, he aligns himself with the proponents of evidence-based medicine, who argue that research must play an increased role in clinical practice if the latter's effectiveness is to reach acceptable levels.

What does not come through in Hargreaves's lecture is that evidence-based medicine is by no means an uncontroversial matter (see *The Lancet*, 1995; Grahame-Smith, 1995; Court, 1996). Critics have argued that it places too much emphasis on the role of research findings in clinical decision-making; in fact, that it is a misnomer, since all medicine is evidence-based, even when it does not make the kind of systematic use of the research literature that advocates of evidence-based medicine recommend. What is at issue is not the use of evidence as against reliance on something else ('tradition, prejudice, dogma, and ideology'), but the relative importance of different kinds of evidence. And we should, perhaps, also note that the appropriate balance amongst these will not just vary across medical specialities but also at different stages of treatment. In diagnosis, for example, particular emphasis is likely to be given to evidence from medical histories, physical examinations and/or test results.

Critics also point out some problems in the use of research evidence to inform clinical decision-making. One is that the literature is very variable in quality, and that there is much more research in some areas than others. A consequence of this is that there are significant gaps in knowledge that render the practice of evidence-based medicine problematic in many fields. More significantly, the fact that there may be evidence about some treatments and not others, or better evidence about them, could lead to misleading conclusions being drawn about their relative efficacy. A second point is that there may be biases in the research literature; for example, resulting from the tendency of journals to be less interested in publishing negative than positive findings. A third problem is that the process of summarising the findings and methods of research may itself introduce distortions. Certainly, it makes the critical appraisal of evidence, which advocates of evidence-based medicine emphasise, more difficult and subject to increased threats to validity.

There are also problems surrounding the application of information about aggregates to particular patients. Clinicians are directly responsible for the treatment of individual patients, not primarily concerned with what works in general. Patients always have multiple characteristics, some of which may be such as to render the treatment indicated by the research literature inappropriate; and these characteristics can include patients' preferences.

Even putting aside the problem of applying aggregate data to individual cases, it is not necessarily in a patient's best interests for a clinician to use what is reported in the literature as the most effective treatment. Treatments can demand considerable skills, which a particular practitioner may not have, most obviously (but not exclusively) in the case of surgery. Thus, a formally less effective treatment of which the doctor already has experience may be more advantageous than a less than fully successful attempt at something more ambitious. Using new drugs or surgical techniques can increase the level of uncertainty, and the danger of running into situations that one does not know how to deal with.

It seems unlikely that any clinician would deny the value of research evidence. What is at issue is the degree and nature of its use. The advocates of evidence-based medicine vary in what they recommend. Sometimes, they simply point to the capacity for searching the research literature that is now provided by information management strategies and technology; emphasising that this cannot substitute for experience and clinical judgement. On other occasions, however, more radical proposals seem to be implied, where systematic literature searches are treated as obligatory and as providing benefit/risk ratios that can form the basis not just for clinical decision-making but also for accountability. In this, advocates of evidence-based medicine follow Cochrane's dismissal of clinical *opinion*, and his argument that there is little or no evidence about the effectiveness of many routinely used techniques, where 'evidence' is interpreted as the outcome of randomised controlled trials or as 'immediate and obvious' effects (Cochrane, 1972, p. 30). What is at issue here, then, is not just what is, and is not, to count as adequate evidence, but also the approach to be adopted in clinical decision-making, how it is to be assessed, and by whom.

Sociologists have often noted the role that an emphasis on clinical judgement and uncertainty has played in the power that the medical profession exercises. Evidence-based medicine threatens this, in that there is a close association between it and demands for greater accountability on the part of doctors, in terms not just of efficacy but also of cost-effectiveness. It is this that has led to much of the reaction against evidence-based medicine. However, only if there were good reasons to be confident that research evidence could replace clinical judgement, and that the rational model could be applied, would it be justifiable to dismiss the resistance of doctors as ingrained conservatism or self-interested concern with preserving professional power. And it seems to me that there are no grounds for such coincidence, even though moves towards clearer guidelines for clinicians and increased use of the medical literature may well be desirable.

As in the National Health Service (NHS) so also in the education system there has been growing emphasis on professional accountability, and attempts to set up quasi-markets that maximise efficiency. Moreover, Hargreaves clearly has accountability very much in mind when he argues that: 'expertise *means* not just having relevant experience and knowledge but having *demonstrable* competence and clear *evidence* to justify doing things in one way rather than another' (p. 7). From this point of view, a research-based teaching profession is one that accounts for itself in terms of the details of its practice to those outside by appeal to the following of explicitly formulated procedures backed by research evidence.

However, this move towards evidence-based accountability does not seem likely to enhance the professionalism of teachers, quite the reverse. Just as evidence-based medicine threatens to assist attacks on the professionalism of doctors by managers in the NHS, so Hargreaves's arguments may be used by those who seek to render teachers more accountable. In both areas there are grave doubts about whether this will improve quality of service. It seems more likely further to demoralise and undermine the professional judgement of practitioners, in occupations that have already been seriously damaged in these respects.

Conclusion

Hargreaves's lecture raises very important issues, and some of his criticisms of educational research are sound. It does seem to me that researchers need to be more focused about what their goals are, about the degree of success they have had in achieving them and about the problems they face. Furthermore, we need to try to make our research both build more effectively on earlier work and provide a better foundation for subsequent investigations. We also ought to take more care in disseminating the results of research and to think more clearly about how it is used. Hargreaves's arguments could play a productive role in stimulating developments in these areas. Moreover, the parallel with medicine is surely worth exploring. Indeed, I think we could learn much from examining the role of research in relation to a range of occupations and organisations.

At the same time, I have argued that there are some fundamental problems at the core of Hargreaves's analysis. One is that he is not very explicit about the form he believes educational research should take, in terms of which he evaluates current work negatively. Another is his neglect of the severe methodological problems that educational researchers face. Hargreaves seems to see the task of developing cumulative knowledge about the effectiveness of different pedagogical techniques as much more straightforward than it is. Here, as elsewhere, his reliance on the medical analogy is potentially misleading. Much medical research, while by no means easy or unproblematic, does not involve the distinctive problems associated with studying social phenomena. We might also note that while he stresses the amount of money spent on educational research, this is only a tiny fraction of that allocated to medical research (for which he provides no estimate). Like is not being compared with like here, in either respect.

Another problem concerns the nature of the relationship that is possible between research and practice in the field of education. In my view, Hargreaves uses a standard to judge current educational research that assumes too direct and instrumental a form of that relationship. Even in the field of medicine it is not clear that this model can be closely approximated. And the thoroughly practical character of teaching may mean that research can rarely provide sound information about the relative effectiveness of different techniques that is directly applicable. Furthermore, in my view there is a tension between seeking to improve the rigour of educational inquiry so as to contribute to the cumulation of knowledge, on the one hand, and trying to make its findings of more practical relevance, on the other.

While I disagree with Hargreaves's diagnosis, I do not reject his prescriptions entirely. I have no doubt that practical research carried out by teachers and educational managers in order to further their work can be useful; so long as it is recognised that not every problem needs research to find a solution, and that not every question can be answered by research. However, there are dangers, I think, in this kind of work being required to be scientific. It is designed to serve a different purpose, so that, while there will be some overlap in techniques and relevant considerations, the orientation should be different. Such inquiries are no substitute for academic research, just as the latter is no substitute for them.

I also accept that the establishment of a forum for discussing educational research and its relationship to educational policy-making and practice could be worthwhile. However, I do not believe that giving such a forum a role in planning educational research would be at all helpful. In my view, the currently fashionable view that research can be centrally planned is based on fallacious assumptions about the nature of research and how it can best be co-ordinated and pursued. Moreover, down the road that Hargreaves recommends, and not very far down it at all, lies the extension to the whole of educational research of the contract model recommended by Rothschild for applied research funded by government departments (Rothschild, 1971). That is a destination from which there is probably no return, and not one that is likely to lead to the flourishing of educational research; instead, the latter may become little more than one more public relations tool.

I recognise that the current state of educational research is not healthy, then; but I do not believe that what Hargreaves proposes will remedy it. The diagnosis is mistaken and, taken as a whole, the prescription is likely to be lethal. He emphasises several times the radical nature of what he is proposing, chiding educational researchers for shying at such radicalism. Personally, I have no problem in refusing this fence: radical change is not *necessarily* a good thing (it will often be for the worse rather than for the better); it ought to be adopted only as a last resort, when there is little to be lost (since, at best, it is much more likely to result in unforeseen consequences or unacceptable side effects than less radical change). And I do not accept Hargreaves's judgement that educational research suffers from a '*fatal* flaw' (p. 3, my emphasis) or that '*there is* [. . .] *little to lose* in moving as soon as possible to an evidence-based teaching profession' (p. 8, my emphasis). What could be lost is the substantial researcher and teacher expertise that we currently have.

It is also of significance, though he does not emphasise it, that the evidence-based education that Hargreaves recommends involves a transformation of teaching as well as of research. In particular, it involves extending the accountability of teachers beyond examination league tables and national tests to justifying the details of classroom practice in terms of research evidence. In my view the consequences of his proposals are likely to be as disastrous in this area as they are for educational research.

I would not deny that there is much wrong with the quality of teaching in schools, nor do I believe that research is incapable or providing knowledge that is of practical relevance to improving it. But it seems to me that educational research can only play a fairly limited role in resolving the problems. It can highlight and analyse them, and attempt to provide some understanding. But remedying the failings of schools is a practical business that necessarily depends on professional expertise of a kind that is not reducible to publicly available evidence, even that provided by research. More-over, in part, the problems stem from the same external factors that have affected research in recent years.

There is one further aspect of Hargreaves's lecture that deserves attention. This is to do with its rhetorical form rather than its content. It is not simply a contribution to debate among researchers about how their work should be organised and carried out. The audience for his lecture was wider. There is nothing wrong with this, of course; but what is unfortunate *is* that he engages in pre-emptive dismissal of the arguments of fellow researchers who disagree with him, implying that these are rationalisations. In effect, he addresses what he has to say over the heads of researchers to those who have the power to intervene: he is inviting in the state troopers! In this sense, his lecture is a political intervention, not just a contribution to scholarly debate; and it will be responded to as such.

For me research, like teaching, is a profession. This does not mean that researchers should have total control over their own affairs, but it does mean that they must have considerable autonomy. Hargreaves portrays us as having more than enough of this. And he is quite open that what he is proposing would involve 'some loss of autonomy' (p. 8). He argues that this is justified because educational research is not in a healthy state. But where is the evidence to show that his proposed treatment is the most effective means of curing the illness, and that its side effects will fall within acceptable limits? If we are to have evidence-based practice, surely we should have evidence-based policy-making?

Advocates of evidence-based medicine have often been challenged because they are not able to support their proposals with the kind of evidence that they demand of medical practitioners (see, for example, Norman, 1995). Hargreaves is particularly vulnerable to this challenge, given the admittedly radical character of the surgery proposed. He certainly does not provide evidence that 'demonstrates conclusively that if [researchers] change their practice from x to y there will be a significant and enduring improvement in teaching and learning'. Nor has he 'developed an effective method of convincing [researchers] of the benefits of, and means to, changing from x to y'. The fact that he declares researchers unwilling to change is an admission of failure on his part in this latter respect. Instead of accepting responsibility for this, however, which seems to be what he expects researchers to do if they fail to convince teachers, he blames researchers. Moreover, his view of researchers is in danger of being self-fulfilling. The rhetorical strategy he employs – which is not dissimilar to the anti-professional mode of speech found in many government communications directed at teachers – is likely to lead to political opposition and counter-argument, rather than to reflection and considered discussion. Researchers are not a powerful constituency, of course. However, to the extent that the aim is to improve educational research rather than to save money by eliminating it (and the motives of those who listen to Hargreaves may well differ from his own), little progress can be made without their support. In these terms, his lecture seems likely to inflame the illness rather than to cure it.

References

Altman, D. G. (1994) 'The scandal of poor medical research', *British Medical Journal*, **308**, 283–4.

Cochrane, A. L. (1972) *Effectiveness and Efficiency*, London: Nuffield Provincial Hospitals Trust.

Court, C. (1996) 'NHS Handbook criticises evidence based medicine', *British Medical Journal*, **312**, 439–40.

Denzin, N. K. and Lincoln, Y. (eds) (1995) *Handbook of Qualitative Research*, Thousand Oaks, CA: Sage.

Freese, L. (1980) 'The problem of cumulative knowledge', in Freese, L. (ed.) *Theoretical Methods in Sociology*, Pittsburgh, PA: University of Pittsburgh Press.

Grahame-Smith, D. (1995) 'Evidence based medicine: Socratic dissent', *British Medical Journal*, **310**, 1126–7.

Hargreaves, D. H. (1996) 'Teaching as a research-based profession: possibilities and prospects', Teacher Training Agency Annual Lecture 1996, London: Teacher Training Agency.

The Lancet (1995) Editorial, **346**, 785.

Nisbet, J. and Broadfoot, P. (1980) *The Impact of Research on Policy and Practice in Education*, Aberdeen: Aberdeen University Press.

Norman, G. R. (1995) Letter, *The Lancet*, **346**, 839.

Rothschild, Lord (1971) 'The organisation and management of government R and D', Cmnd 4184, London: HMSO.

Scarth, J. and Hammersley, M. (1986a) 'Some problems in assessing closedness of tasks', in Hammersley, M. (ed.), *Case Studies in Classroom Research*, Milton Keynes: Open University Press.

Scarth, J. and Hammersley, M. (1986b) 'Questioning ORACLE's analysis of teachers' questions', *Educational Research*, **28**, 174–84.

Taylor, W. (1973) 'Knowledge and research', in Taylor, W. (ed.), *Research Perspectives in Education*, London: Routledge & Kegan Paul.

Woods, P. (1985) 'Ethnography and theory construction in educational research', in Burgess, R. G. (ed.), *Field Methods in the Study of Education*, Lewes: Falmer Press.

Woods, P. (1987) 'Ethnography at the crossroads: a reply to Hammersley', *British Educational Research Journal*, B13, 297–307.

Chapter 17

The knowledge-creating school

David H. Hargreaves

This is an edited version of an article previously published in *British Journal of Educational Studies*, **47**(2), June 1999.

The need for professional knowledge creation in education

Expectations of politicians, parents and employers of what schools should accomplish in terms of student achievement have been rising for many years. They will accelerate as we take further steps into the information age or the knowledge society. The world of work is being transformed, particularly by the information and communication technologies (ICT), so schools must prepare students to increasingly higher levels of knowledge and skill, not just in the conventional curriculum or even in ICT, important as these are, but also in the personal qualities that matter in the transformed work place – how to be autonomous, self-organising, networking, entrepreneurial, innovative, with 'the capability constantly to redefine the necessary skills for a given task, and to access the sources for learning these skills' (Castells, 1998).

How schools and classrooms need to change to achieve such aims is an awesome challenge. Teachers will have to decide how to make educational use of the rapidly growing ICT, especially in the form of open, user-friendly, peer-controlled, inter-active, virtual communities, which does not lie within the traditional ways of organising teaching and learning in the school. It is plain that if teachers do not acquire and display this capacity to redefine their skills for the task of teaching, and if they do not model in their own conduct the very qualities – flexibility, networking, creativity – that are now key outcomes for students, then the challenge of schooling in the next millennium will not be met.

An effect of recent educational reforms has been to discourage teachers from engaging in the process of professional knowledge creation by which, in rapidly changing social conditions in schools and society, the profession generates new knowledge to become more effective. Some believe we already possess enough knowledge to make the education service more effective, and the task is to make sure that all teachers and schools, not just the outstanding ones, have access to, and deploy, this knowledge. On this view, the problem is one of the dissemination of existing 'best practice' and/or research evidence. Certainly if the most effective schools and class-rooms were replicated throughout the system, educational standards would indeed rise. But the dissemination of *existing* good practice is an inadequate basis for making a success of schools in the knowledge economy: we need to generate better knowledge and practices. In high technology firms, the importance of knowledge creation, not just its dissemination, is acknowledged, for to be content with current knowledge and practice is to be left behind. My thesis is that the same now applies to schools.

Features of the knowledge-creating school

In the spheres of school management and of effective classroom teaching, schools already engage, to varying degrees and by various means, in professional knowledge creation, though they would probably talk about 'developing good practice' rather than 'knowledge creation'. All professionals depend on working knowledge, or 'the organized body of knowledge that . . . [people] use spontaneously and routinely in the context of their work . . . a special domain of knowledge that is relevant to one's job' (Kennedy, 1983). In professions undergoing changes, such working knowledge needs renewal through the creation of new knowledge. The knowledge creating school, in ideal typical form:

- *audits* its professional working knowledge;
- *manages the process* of creating new professional knowledge';
- *validates* the professional knowledge created;
- *disseminates* the created professional knowledge.

Let us examine each element in turn.

The audit of professional knowledge

Teachers in a school are often collectively ignorant of the knowledge that exists among themselves; in consequence, they cannot share and draw upon that knowledge. At the same time, they do not know what knowledge is lacking, that is, recognise their ignorance, to identify where new knowledge needs to be created. There is a complex social distribution of professional knowledge within a school: no single teacher knows, or could know, the totality of the staff's professional knowledge. Senior staff have managerial knowledge denied to inexperienced teachers; much professional knowledge about teaching and learning is locked in the heads of individual teachers and protected by the privacy of their classrooms. A knowledge audit exposes the social distribution of knowledge so that planned and co-ordinated action on the sharing of existing professional knowledge, and the creation of new knowledge, may be undertaken.

Auditing knowledge is most easily achieved with professional knowledge that is *explicit*, either because it is already codified or because it is easily expressed in words. Much professional knowledge, however, is *tacit*, that is, in the form of practical know-how that is not easily articulated, and so is difficult to audit. A knowledge audit is most easily conducted in a collaborative school culture that encourages frequent and high levels of professional talk and sharing among teachers. Such schools will pioneer methods of *mapping* the nature and extent of their professional knowledge and ignorance. For example, a staff survey could be based on questions such as: Which colleague(s) has helped you improve your teaching – in what ways on what aspects of teaching? What to do you think you know or do that others might find useful or interesting? What aspects of your job do you think you're best at? The results can be used to provide a *Yellow Pages* guide that tells you who to contact if you want help and advice, or just a colleague to talk to about a particular issue. In this way each teacher's cognitive map of the organisation (Goodman, 1968; Weick and Bougon, 1986) is enriched. Mapping is likely to be successful under the following conditions (Kerwin, 1993; McGee and Prusak, 1993; Skyrme and Amidon, 1997; Davenport, 1997):

- the staff select a limited number of areas for knowledge mapping, e.g. one where improvement is needed;
- knowledge is codified into terms and categories that are meaningful for and relevant to current concerns in the teachers' professional practice;
- all the school's skills in information management are used (including the librarian and the ICT co-ordinator);
- the system is devised to promote and support the school's internal networks.

The object of 'knowledge management' (Sveiby and Lloyd, 1987) is to help an organisation to act intelligently to achieve success and realise its 'intellectual capital' – the knowledge and abilities of its staff, not just its material or financial assets. For school leaders, an understanding of the state of the school's overall 'intellectual capital' is important, since the management of professional knowledge creation requires a grasp not only of the capital embedded in individuals and groups among the staff, the students and their families and communities, but also of the 'organisational capital' embedded in the school's structures and culture, the organisational competences and capabilities that underpin the process of knowledge creation and utilisation. Do the school's leaders possess the 'managerial capital' to support knowledge creation and utilisation?

The management of the creation of professional knowledge

It is now a commonplace in reviews of educational research that there is a division between educational researchers and practitioners, and that teachers and policy-makers find too little of what researchers produce to be of practical relevance to, or applicable in, practice. One alternative is to treat practitioners themselves as the main (but not only) source of the creation of professional knowledge. From this perspective, the knowledge-creation process and its management can be analysed from two perspectives – the *characteristics of knowledge-creating schools* and the *process of knowledge-creation.* As yet little is known about either. My hypothesis is that schools that create professional knowledge are likely to display characteristics similar to those of high-technology firms that are demonstrably successful in knowledge creation in response to the dual demand for higher R&D productivity and shorter development lead times (Jelinek and Schoonhoven, 1990; Leonard-Barton, 1995; Dodgson and Besant, 1997; Hussey, 1997; Harryson, 1998). Such pressures are now being exerted on schools; the conditions and factors favouring knowledge creation in schools, to be elaborated in this article, are thus likely to be as follows:

- a culture of, and an enthusiasm for, continual improvement;
- a strong awareness of the external environment, including opportunities (e.g. new initiatives, new funding) and pressures (e.g. requirements that need new knowledge), and a capacity to recognise, assimilate and exploit external knowledge;
- high sensitivity to the preferences of students, parents and governors;
- institutional planning that is coherent (producing a shared organisational state of mind) but flexible (allowing an opportunistic response to events);
- decentralisation and flat hierarchies, groups being given the responsibility for scrutinising ideas and decision-making within their sphere of action;
- recognition by managers of the specialised, expert knowledge held by teachers;
- informality of relationships among staff who value task-relevant expertise rather than organisational status and engage in high volumes of professional talk through intensive internal networking;
- professional knowledge creation not seen as a random, undirected activity of the minority of individual teachers with a creative talent, but as a whole-school process that has to be managed – with the allocation of material and temporal resources, co-ordination of people and activities, regular monitoring and support;
- provision of regular opportunities for reflection, dialogue, enquiry and net-working in relation to professional knowledge and practice;
- internal hybridisation, i.e. cross-functional teams and job rotation;
- the creation of temporary developmental structures that side-step bureaucratic maintenance structures and act as the test-bed for organisational restructuring to meet changing circumstances;
- a readiness to tinker and experiment in an *ad hoc* way with new ideas, or variations on old ideas, in order to do things better, within a culture that does not blame individuals when things prove not to be good enough, mistakes being treated as opportunities for learning;
- encouragement of diversity and toleration of deviant opinion, subversion being a potential seedbed of innovation;
- a readiness to engage in partnerships, alliances and networks to further such work;
- a positive climate with a constant and explicitly maintained tension between liberty and control, freedom and responsibility in professional work.

There is only a limited overlap between these features and what has now become the standard characterisation of the effective school (Sammons *et al.*, 1995) and from which many school improvement schemes derive. Schools that are effective by such criteria will not necessarily success in professional knowledge creation.

As to the *processes of professional knowledge creation*, models developed in industrial firms may apply also to schools with relatively modest variation. Knowledge creation in industry is essential to commercial success, so efforts are made to understand the process. Here I summarise briefly what I believe is the most impressive model of knowledge creation, that of Nonaka and Takeuchi (1995). The basic elements of their model are *explicit knowledge* and *tacit knowledge*, and knowledge creation arises from the interactions between these two forms. Thus four modes of knowledge conversion are postulated: socialisation, internalisation, externalisation and combination. *Socialisation* concerns the shared experience through apprenticeship and on-the-job training that generates tacit knowledge. Dialogue and collective reflection among members of the community trigger *externalisation* by which tacit knowledge is articulated into explicit knowledge. Learning by doing stimulates *internalisation*, by which explicit knowledge is converted into tacit knowledge; as in skill acquisition, what is initially explicit becomes tacit through experience. People with different knowledge coming together through networking results in *combination*, a process of systemisating and elaborating explicit knowledge by combining different bodies of knowledge.

The way Nonaka and Takeuchi claim their model works in industrial setting can serve as no more than a suggestive bridge to the exploration and conceptualisation of professional knowledge creation and its management in schools. We lack sophisticated theories and models of knowledge creation in education simply because such activity has not been seen as a key to educational improvement. The model described above looks promising: can it be usefully applied to educational settings?

The validation of professional knowledge

After knowledge has been created, it needs to be validated. In professional life, knowledge achieves validation when it is turned into a practice that demonstrably and repeatedly works. In the present climate, there is deep confusion about merely a *good idea*, a *good practice*, which implies some kind of validation, and a *best practice*, which implies that it has been shown to be superior to other good practices. All these terms are bandied about in a manner open to criticism (Alexander, 1992).

Knowledge validation may take various forms, including:

- *ipsative.* The teacher makes a personal judgement by comparing present with previous practice or with an alternative practice observed in another teacher or read about in professional papers.
- *social.* A professional group, through analysis, discussion and debate, reaches agreement on what is a better practice than some others.

- *independent.* A consumer, or purported expert, or some one involved in the governance of education has a view of what is a good practice.
- *judicial.* In courts of law, evidence is any material that tends to persuade the court of the truth or probability of some asserted claim. Among educators, evidence of the effectiveness of a practice and its underlying knowledge might be regarded as any material that persuades practitioners of the effectiveness of the practice. Just as in the law, rules have evolved about the admissibility and the weight of evidence and the standard of proof, so educational practitioners might develop rules of evidence to apply to their own circumstances.
- *scientific.* The practice is established as effective or as better than another through formal research that follows scientific rules of procedure.

Self-validation is evidently the most common basis of alleged good practice but on its own it is the least trustworthy. 'It works for me' may be a legitimate claim, but personal, experiential knowledge requires stronger validation if it is to become generalised, professional knowledge. In many schools knowledge validation is in a primitive state, consisting largely of the ipsative form with elements of the social, in which teachers informally exchange experiences but with relatively little analysis or concern to identify and agree upon what might be effective practice. Among teachers

> the recipes are traded on the basis of a validity that is craft embedded and highly experiential. . . . Research evidence is an unlikely source of practitioner infor- mation, not only because it assumes an underlying order but also because the ways in which the theoretical or scientific sources talk and write about instrumental practice are uncongenial: the two frames of reference collide.
>
> (Huberman, 1983)

Knowledge validation is capable of greater sophistication in schools where teachers have themselves undertaken research for a higher degree and are able to apply investigative skills to their practices in a climate of identifying and sharing what works. For example, teachers engaging in some forms of action research attempt to combine the ipsative with the scientific – and sometimes also add social forms of validation. The knowledge-creating school will apply demanding forms of knowledge validation to supply evidence for the effectiveness of its new practices.

The dissemination of professional knowledge

The dissemination of educational knowledge is currently in a poor state. Dissemi- nation has long been seen as a problem by R&D leaders in universities, who claim that better dissemination of their work would lead to improved teaching and learning. However, the evidence from the 1970s (Glaser *et al.*, 1983) was that, in 'centre–periphery' projects even carefully planned dissemination frequently led to low levels of adoption and implementation. some of the traditional models of dissemination are badly discredited. My contention is that wherever possible the old models of dissemination need to be replaced and doing so is a condition of promoting the very knowledge creation on which more effective schooling depends. A new model of knowledge creation in education entails a different model of dissemination. It is not best approached from where there have been most failures, that is, 'centre–periphery' approaches, but from where it might seem to be most simple, namely the dissemination of knowledge or practice within the same school (internal dissemination) or from one school to another, its neighbour perhaps (external dissemination).

A distinction between the *transferability* and the *transposability* of knowledge or practice is in order. Transfer concerns the movement of knowledge or practice between *persons*, and transposition entails movement between *places*. Knowledge or practice is transposable if its 'owner' can deploy it in a new context, e.g. a teacher who finds that a practice works in one classroom and successfully deploys it in a second classroom or even in a different school. Highly experienced teachers moving to a new school can be surprised at the low transposability of the skills they honed in their first school. Knowledge or practice is transferable when a second teacher adopts knowledge or practice from a first and can deploy it successfully in its original context, e.g. both teachers can make the practice work with the same class of students. Thus an experienced teacher successfully advises a novice on 'what works' with students they both teach. School-based initial teacher training involves high levels of such transfer.

Dissemination is difficult because it so often involves the knowledge or practice concerned becoming transposable *and* transferable. Dissemination of practice between schools is more difficult than within schools, because the difference in context and situation (e.g. student intake) may be substantial, thus increasing the complexity of transposability; and differences between the teaching staff of different schools (e.g. their values) increases the complexity of transferability. It is not surprising, then, that a teacher may observe a practice of another teacher with different students in a different school and find that what looks like a very effective practice cannot be transferred and transposed back into his or her own classroom.

It is now evident that the problems of transposition and transfer may make dissemination difficult to achieve even in small-scale, local forms, where the teachers can talk to one another. How much more difficult dissemination will be when it takes the form of the distant, non-interactive, written source that has little credibility with the targeted teachers. An alternative model of dissemination is surely called for.

Knowledge creation in schools

The seeds of professional knowledge creation already lie within the school system, ready to germinate if the right conditions can be provided – by managers or government. There are four principal seeds.

In knowledge-creating schools, the teachers take particular advantage of a ubiquitous feature of classrooms, the readiness of teachers to 'tinker', and elaborate and extend it in the interests of collective knowledge creation. *Tinkering*, the first seed, is widespread among the professions and the crafts, whether the engineer:

> [In the firm focused on knowledge management] much *ad hoc*, inexpensive and unscientific experimentation goes on . . . Employees are experts at cut-and-try. . . . [Engineers] in our sample [high-technology] companies exhibit a recurrent pattern. They are expected to be good enough, enough of the time, to beneficially exploit bootleg ideas and material, equipment and space, for 'horsing around' – whether or not their managers initially agree with their ideas.
>
> (Jelinek and Schoonhoven, 1990)

or the teacher:

> Essentially teachers are artisans working primarily alone, with a variety of new and cobbled together materials, in a personally designed work environment. They gradually develop a repertoire of instructional skills and strategies, corresponding to a progressively denser, more differentiated and well integrated set of mental schemata; they come to read the instructional situation better and faster, and to respond with a greater variety of tools. They develop this repertoire through a somewhat haphazard process of trial and error, usually when one or other segment of the repertoire does not work repeatedly. . . . When things go well, when the routines work smoothly . . . there is a rush of craft pride. . . . When things do not go well . . . cycles of experimentation . . . are intensified. . . . Teachers spontaneously go about *tinkering* with their classrooms.
>
> (Huberman, 1992, italics added)

The 'tinkering' teacher is an individualised embryo of institutional knowledge creation. When such tinkering becomes more systematic, more collective *and explicitly managed*, it is transformed into knowledge creation. Tinkering often precedes knowledge creation, for it provides, in the form of both explicit and tacit knowledge, much of the raw material for knowledge-creation. Tinkering is embedded in the process of professional knowledge creation, since this is the means of testing and modifying an initial 'good idea' into something worth subjecting to more systematic validation. When a group of teachers tinker with ideas emerging from knowledge creation, they are checking the extent to which the emergent practice is both transferable and transposable. In tinkering, knowledge creation and knowledge utilisation are not separate entities that occur in sequence, but an interactive process in which knowledge utilisation becomes part of the creative activity.

Transfer is difficult to achieve for it involves far more than *telling* or simply providing *information*. If one teacher tells a second teacher about a professional practice that the first finds effective, the second teacher has merely acquired some *information*, not knowledge. Transfer occurs only when the knowledge of the first teacher becomes information for the second, who then works on that knowledge in such a way that it is set within, and become part of, his or her context of meaning and purpose and pre-existing knowledge. Transfer is the conversion of information about another person's practice into one's personal knowledge. This is most easily achieved when a teacher tinkers with information derived from another's professional practice. The problem with attempted transfer is that the tinkering element is often overlooked. The dissemination of 'good practice' – whether it be from the DfEE, TTA, QCA, OFSTED or a beacon school – tends to be in the form of the dissemination of *information about* good practice, with inadequate recognition that tinkering – and space and support for it – is essential for the conversion into new professional knowledge to occur. It is when teachers are able to tinker that the transfer of knowledge between them is most likely to succeed.

A second seed of professional knowledge creation is found where a school is heavily involved in initial teacher training. The explanation is simple. When experienced practitioners, or mentors, have to teach novice teachers, or trainees, they are forced to struggle with the tasks of transferring their tacit knowledge (*socialisation* in the Nonaka and Takeuchi model) and of making their tacit knowledge explicit so that mentor and trainee can talk about the relevant knowledge and practice (*externalisation*). Thus mentors typically claim that the act of supervising the trainee is a powerful stimulus to reflection. Through sharing experience and learning by doing under the supervision of the mentor, the trainee acquires professional knowledge (*internalisation*). Trainees often bring new ideas from their work in higher education. When shared with the mentor in a form of internal networking, new ideas from the novice jostle with established ideas in the mentor (*combination*). On-the-job training leads to on-the-job learning, which in turn leads both mentor and trainee to engage in additional tinkering. Yet it is no longer individualised tinkering, but a version that springs out of a form of knowledge creation that uses all four modes of knowledge conversion. All the elements of the Nonaka Takeuchi model of knowledge creation are in place, simply waiting to be managed more actively. An important form of innovation in industry is known as *technology fusion*, in which existing technologies are fused into new combinations of hybrid technologies. To what degree might teacher effectiveness be improved by using combination at school level to create hybrid technologies of teaching?

Teachers engaging in research is a third seed of professional knowledge creation. Again this may be seen as a more systematic form of tinkering. For example, if teachers studying for a professional award undertake an empirical dissertation, their regular dialogue with their university-based supervisor will often draw on the modes of knowledge conversion. Moreover, the knowledge being created is likely to be subjected to validation procedures as an inherent part of the research endeavour. School-based research, and school-based research consortia as pioneered by the Teacher Training Agency, are important here, for there are likely to be several teachers in the one school involved in the research, whereas most teachers reading for a higher degree in a university work alone. TTA-supported research will typically lead to internal and external networking; and such collective tinkering promotes knowledge creation and its effective transposition and transfer.

Some schools make effective use of their middle managers, both curricular and pastoral: this is a fourth seed of professional knowledge creation. In the Nonaka and Takeuchi model, it is claimed that middle managers are critical to successful knowledge creation in industry. Top managers are too far from front-line experience to have the current 'hands-on' knowledge that is crucial to the generation of new knowledge and practices. On the shopfloor, the work is too narrowly conceived or demanding to allow the distancing needed in knowledge creation. Middle managers, however, serve as a 'strategic knot' between top managers and the front-line engineers, a bridge between the company's vision and the chaotic reality of its implementation, between 'what is' and 'what should be'. Here is an insight into the deployment of middle managers in secondary schools as the critical 'knowledge engineers' of educational knowledge creation: and in school-based initial training it is from the ranks of the middle managers that the 'mentors' for the trainees are drawn.

In short, educational knowledge creation is likely to be particularly explicit and effective when schools are engaged in school-based initial teacher training and school-based research, where middle managers become knowledge engineers and professional tinkering of various kinds is encouraged and supported, since these demand and then strengthen the processes that are central to the dynamics of professional knowledge creation and dissemination.

Dissemination: the unsolved problem

To improve the dissemination of the outcomes of educational research, elaborate mediation structures between researchers and user communities have recently been recommended (Hillage *et al.*, 1998). However, past attempts to improve communications, for example by the style and presentation of research reports, have made very little impact on users. Such approaches fail to acknowledge, and do little to close, the gap between the research community and practitioner communities. Something more radical is needed. How do successful high-technology firms solve the problem?

The answer is simple. They bring the researchers and the practitioners into closer contact by closing or reducing R&D departments: to bring the researchers to work alongside those engaged in the manufacturing itself, R&D departments migrated to the factory floor (Jelinek and Schoonhoven, 1990; Fruin, 1997; Harryson, 1998). There is no definite boundary between the production of knowledge and its application and dissemination: the processes are enmeshed in principle and practice (Roos *et al.*, 1997).

That high-technology engineers take radical steps to close the gap between researcher and user communities should be no surprise to educationists. For Huberman has in similar terms advocated a closer linkage in education between researchers and practitioners, between knowledge production and its utilisation. He showed that the most effective utilisation is associated with strong interactions between researchers and practitioners, not only on completion of the research but also during the research and, ideally, from its inception. In short, in effective R&D the separation between university-based researchers and school-based practitioners is reduced to a minimum. He concludes that

> prior links, together with contacts established before and during a given study, are associated with better and more energetic modes of dissemination later on, which then translates into more consequential use of the findings. This is clearly useful, and it points up the fact that stronger linkage is directly related to strength of outcomes.
>
> (Huberman, 1990)

So far so good: here is an evidence-based lesson for more effective educational R&D. But Huberman then continues:

> Still, the effects of a single study, however great, are limited and ephemeral; they decay. In fact, they decay more quickly unless both parties can stay together long enough to bridge from the findings to new or other ideas. In that sense, focusing solely on a replicable technology for disseminating research findings may be, in the long run, short-sighted: a more important concern might be the extent to which dissemination efforts lead later on to increased and more varied collaboration between research units and practitioner settings. For example, a given study which creates ties between these units is not only likely to have a longer half-life, but it is also likely to lead to other fruitful transactions between researchers and practitioners, long after that individual study . . . that brought them into contact has passed into oblivion. Finally, the establishment of stronger links . . . create [*sic*] favourable conditions for disseminating the next piece of research transacted between the two parties, and this, in turn reinforces the bridge between knowledge producers and knowledge users which has long eluded the educational community.

Whilst Huberman is right that such sustained relationships over time between groups of researchers and groups of users would have untold benefits, there are problems. Most researchers cannot maintain long-term contact with the same group of teachers, partly because of changes from project to project in the problem being investigated and the sample of schools required. Furthermore, whilst such sustained relationships assist all kinds of dissemination to the teachers involved, it does nothing to help dissemination to the huge number of schools and teachers who are not, and cannot be, involved in close ties with universities. For the majority of the target audience for educational research, then, inadequate dissemination simply persists, despite the goodwill of the research community.

It is not merely that researchers and users are in different locations, making intensive interaction difficult to achieve, but each side starts from a very different knowledge-base. Sometimes this difference might be of little consequence, but where the focus of professional knowledge creation is teaching and learning, or the management of schools and classrooms, the knowledge gap between researcher and practitioner is sufficiently great to make the researcher-led creation of usable or actionable knowledge especially hazardous. If knowledge creation is primarily concerned, as Nonaka and Takeuchi have suggested, with the mobilisation and conversion of tacit knowledge, then many researchers simply do not share the tacit knowledge of teachers, because either they have never been schoolteachers or it is some years since they were. The tacit knowledge in the researcher's knowledge-base is quite unlike that of the practising teacher. Moreover researchers often lack the specific local knowledge of the schools and classrooms and of the teachers and students involved in the research. In high technology firms, local knowledge plays a vital role in knowledge creation: the companies actively foster local knowledge, for it underpins both the explicit and the tacit knowledge that form the ingredients of the four modes of conversion in knowledge creation (Jelinek and Schoonhoven, 1990). Transfer and transposition of professional knowledge and practice are more complicated between researchers and practitioners than between teachers, so it is not surprising that conventional models of dissemination often fail. Effective dissemination entails a reconstruction of relations between schools and universities, one in which both knowledge creation and its dissemination are reconceptualised.

Towards a different mode of educational R&D

If the objective is the creation of high-quality knowledge about effective teaching and learning that is applicable and actionable in classrooms, then practising teachers must be at the heart of this creation and researchers must get closer to them. It has been painful for university-based teacher trainers to accept that practising teachers have the major role – and two-thirds of the time – in the initial training of teachers. It will be equally painful for them to abandon their tight control over educational research. Many researchers have questioned and progressively abandoned the linear model by which knowledge is created by researchers, then disseminated and finally applied by teachers to their practice. The further steps that must now be taken lead directly into a different mode of educational research.

Two types of knowledge production in science and technology have been distinguished (Gibbons *et al.*, 1994). Mode 1 is university-based, pure, disciplinary, homogeneous, expert-led, supply-driven, hierarchical, peer-reviewed. Out of Mode 1 grows Mode 2 knowledge production, which is applied, problem-focused, trans-disciplinary, heterogeneous, hybrid, demand-driven, entrepreneurial, accountability-tested, embedded in networks. Because Mode 1 is the dominant form, it is more easily understood and recognised. Mode 2 is strongly concerned with knowledge that is useful – to a government or to some kind of user – and does not get produced at all until various groups negotiate its generation from different types of knowledge. Mode 2 knowledge is not created and then applied: it evolves within the context of its application, but then may not fit neatly into Mode 1 knowledge structures. The team generating the knowledge may consist of people of very different backgrounds working together temporarily to solve a problem. The number of sites where such knowledge can be generated is greatly increased; they are linked by functioning networks of communication. The knowledge is then diffused most readily when the participants in its original production move to new situations and communicate through informal channels. Individual creativity is the driving force of Mode 1 knowledge; in Mode 2, creativity is based in the group, which may nevertheless contain members socialised in Mode 1 forms.

It is clear that my argument is that (i) parts of educational research are making a transition from Mode 1 to Mode 2 knowledge production, and that (ii) this shift is desirable since it is a powerful means of creating practical and applicable professional knowledge for teachers. Many educational researchers are still firmly in Mode 1 and may interpret the movement towards Mode 2 as threatening, even though it should not displace high-quality Mode 1 work.

Here are four ways in which university-based researchers can expand Mode 2 educational research in the interests of enhancing professional and institutional effectiveness in education.

(i) Train and support practising teachers in research skills to enable them to carry out more school-based research for professional knowledge creation.
Some university-based teacher educators already do such work, but much remains to be done. The majority of teachers learn research skills not during initial training – a most inappropriate time – but during their studies for a higher degree, usually to carry out an empirical research project. Yet after completing the degree, few of these teachers ever actively use these research skills again, because they are never given the opportunity, or time, to engage in further research. Ways have to be found, building on the work of the Teacher Training Agency, to provide schools with the funding to release teachers to engage in research and professional knowledge creation. Many teachers are ready and able to undertake the work, but they lack a funded infrastructure to provide the time for it.

Most teachers need help with knowledge validation. It is known that the utilisation of new knowledge is likely to flourish under particular conditions – a recommendation by a peer, a demonstration of the practice in operation, and a belief that it could be modified to fit the adopter's circumstances. This peer-based approach to innovation and dissemination, though as yet far from fully developed on a national scale, tends to be much weaker than the previous centre–periphery model in ensuring that any new knowledge is grounded in trustworthy evidence. Research training for teachers should focus on knowledge validation. Unless higher education staff serve as consultants in the design of teacher-led research, validation among teachers will often remain 'soft'.

(ii) Seek opportunities to contribute to the externalisation and combination mode in school-led professional knowledge creation.
According to the Nonaka and Takeuchi (1995) model of knowledge creation, *combination* involves:

> combining different bodies of explicit knowledge. Individuals exchange and combine knowledge through such media as documents, meetings, telephone

conversations, or computerized communication networks. Reconfiguration of existing information through sorting, adding, combining, and categorizing of explicit knowledge (as conducted in computer databases) can lead to new knowledge.

Many university-based courses for teachers provide such activities already. Much continuing professional development of teachers offered by universities works with, not in spite of, the knowledge teachers bring to the encounter. Through their exposure to academic knowledge, teachers enjoy the creativity of combination. Teachers exchanging knowledge with academics should be undertaken as an explicit training in, and contribution to, *the teacher's capacity to engage in continual knowledge production within the school*. But it must be remembered that combination requires the knowledge to be explicit. The experienced teacher's knowledge-base is, in comparison with that of engineers and doctors, far richer in personal and tacit knowledge than in explicit, collective knowledge, which means that teachers need help with externalisation before the most fruitful combination can be achieved. Attending a university-based course should not be seen merely as the individual teacher's short-term opportunity for reflection but as a longer-term investment in learning how externalisation and combination support professional knowledge creation at school level.

It is common to find school teachers seconded to universities for a year. Perhaps it is now time to second university researchers to schools for a year, to contribute to front-line externalisation and combination in relation to how teachers view the agenda for knowledge creation or the fusion of teaching technologies into innovative pedagogies.

(iii) Reconceptualise both professional knowledge creation and its dissemination as the outcome of 'tinkering networks' that need support and co-ordination.
Educational knowledge creation cannot be confined to the idiosyncratic 'tinkerings' of individual teachers, for that does little to change the system. A more deliberate, explicit and collective process of professional knowledge creation at school level is needed by various forms of internal networking among functional and cross-functional teams. What the single school can achieve here is limited, but if a group of schools, either in a local or 'virtual' consortium, works on the same topic of professional knowledge creation and validation through a process of external networking, national progress in advancing the quality of teaching and learning could be rapid and cumulative. ICT provide opportunities for networking for professional knowledge creation, shared tinkering, and concurrent dissemination on a scale and at a rate that has hitherto been unimaginable. Subject-specialist knowledge creation networks should arise, bringing to an end the isolation of teachers specialising in a particular subject of the curriculum, when there are often just one or two such teachers in a single school. Networks are valuable to small or isolated schools whose staff can tap into the experience and knowledge of teachers located elsewhere.

Networks are the key to this different model of dissemination in which *all* schools can now be linked through ICT and so *all* can take part in the activities of professional knowledge creation, application and dissemination. Again, the business world provides a model for education. In industries where the knowledge is both complex and expanding and the sources of expertise are widely dispersed, the locus of innovation is to be found in networks of learning. Innovating companies

> are executing nearly every step in the production process, from discovery to distribution, through some form of external collaboration. These various types of inter-firm alliance take on many forms. . . . The R&D intensity or level of technological sophistication of industries is positively correlated with the intensity and number of alliances. . . . When the locus of innovation is found in an inter-organizational network, access to that network proves critical. R&D alliances are the admission ticket, the foundation for more diverse types of collaboration and the pivot around which firms become more centrally connected. . . . As a result of this reciprocal learning, both *firm-level* and *industry-level* practices are evolving. . . .
> (Powell *et al.*, 1996, italics added; cf. Meyer-Krahmer, 1990)

Here is a vision – one that shatters the stereotype of how things work in industry – of how networks within and between schools could promote professional knowledge creation within the individual school *and in the education service as a whole.* Networks are the crucial feature of high levels of communication and exchange on which professional knowledge creation, dissemination and use so heavily depend.

An intimation of what might be more than the knowledge-creating school, but a knowledge-creating *system* – a web of interlinked knowledge-creating schools – can be found in industry.

> The . . . firm, then, takes on some of the characteristics of a spider's web. Each node is a problem-solving team possessing a unique combination of skills. It is linked to other nodes by a potentially large number of lines of communication. To survive each firm must be permeable to new types of knowledge and *the sector as a whole* becomes increasingly interconnected. The interconnections embrace not only other firms but many other knowledge producing groups, be they in government research laboratories, research institutes, consultancies or universities. . . . This new infrastructure depends upon innovation in the telecommunications and computer industries that will make possible the ever closer interaction of an increasing number of knowledge centres.
> (Gibbons *et al.*, 1994, italics added)

The universities have a potentially powerful role here in initiating, supporting and co-ordinating what we should now call *networks and webs for educational research and professional knowledge creation*, which would include small-scale, preliminary knowledge creation in a consortium of two or three schools to large-scale, multi-site experiments when emergent knowledge has reached the state of requiring sophisticated validation. Indeed, if the universities do not undertake these functions, it is difficult to see how Mode 2 educational research will be a success. A number of universities, each with R&D responsibilities for a region, should take charge of this work in alliance with LEAs. The universities would be a resource to which schools engaged in knowledge creation could turn for advice and help; they would also help to disseminate validated practices to all members of the network. Universities and LEAs should jointly appoint consortium engineers to manage the networks; universities would investigate, and evaluate the effectiveness of, different types of network.

(iv) Make the study of the networked creation, validation and dissemination of professional knowledge a focus of university-led research.
In the field of teaching and learning, new knowledge and new practices cannot normally be transposed to a different context with ease. Part of such contextual differences are the different needs and preferences of the clients involved, and the artistry required by the practitioner to take account of them. The application of knowledge about teaching and learning is constantly adjusted, sometimes to a small degree, sometimes to a larger one, as it is moved from context to context. To strengthen knowledge of 'what works', the adjustments practitioners make in what contexts for what reasons and with what success need to be investigated and reported. The acquisition of such cumulative knowledge requires co-ordinated programmes of R&D involving close alliances between universities and schools.

Advocacy of the knowledge-creating school as a path both to more effective schools and to better educational research should not be confused with a 1960s-type policy of 'letting a thousand flowers bloom' in the education service. Knowledge creation, with its emphasis of knowledge validation, eschews a 'do-as-you-please' philosophy and insists on a tightly focused and disciplined framework for the development and diffusion of high-quality professional practices. Nor should Mode 2 educational research be seen as endangering Mode 1 educational research. The two can and should thrive side by side, feeding off each other. Mode 2 educational research is a constructive addition to the best of past achievements in educational research, a valuable part of the solutions to the problems identified in the recent reviews, and a bridge for teachers, researchers and policy-makers from schools as they now are to the knowledge society and 'schools of the future' on the other side.

References

Alexander, R. (1992) *Policy and Practice in Primary Education*, London: Routledge.
Castells, M. (1998) *End of Millennium*, Oxford: Blackwell.
Davenport, T. H. (1997) *Information Ecology*, Oxford: Oxford University Press.
Dodgson, M. and Besant, J. (1997) *Effective Innovation Policy*, London: International Thomson Business Press.
Fruin, M. (1997) *Knowledge Works*, Oxford: Oxford University Press.
Gibbons, M., Limoges, C., Nowotny, H. S., Scott, P. and Trow, M. (1994) *The New Production of Knowledge*, London: Sage.

Glaser, E. M., Abelson, H. H. and Garrison, K. N. (1983) *Putting Knowledge to Use*, San Francisco: Jossey-Bass.

Goodman, P. S. (1968) 'The measurement of an individual's organization map', *Administrative Science Quarterly*, **13**, 246–65.

Harryson, S. (1998) *Japanese Technology and Innovation Management*, London: Edward Elgar.

Hillage, J., Pearson, R., Anderson, A. and Tamkin, P. (1998) *Excellence in Research in Schools*, London: Department for Education and Employment.

Huberman, M. (1983) 'Recipes for busy kitchens: a situational analysis of routine knowledge use in schools', *Knowledge: Creation, Diffusion, Utilization*, **4**(4), 478–510.

Huberman, M. (1990) 'Linkage between researchers and practitioners: a qualitative study', *American Educational Research Journal*, **27**(2), 363–91.

Huberman, M. (1992) 'Teacher development and instructional mastery', in Hargreaves, A. and Fullan, M. G. (eds), *Understanding Teacher Development*, Cassell/Teachers College Press, italics added.

Hussey, D. E. (ed.) (1997) *The Innovation Challenge*, London: Wiley.

Jelinek, M. and Schoonhoven, C. B. (1990) *The Innovation Marathon*, Oxford: Blackwell.

Kennedy, M. M. (1983) 'Working knowledge', *Knowledge: Creation, Dissemination and Utilization*, **5**(2), 193–211.

Kerwin, A. (1993) 'None too solid: medical ignorance', *Knowledge: Creation, Diffusion, Utilization*, **15**(2), 166–85.

Leonard-Barton, D. (1995) *Wellsprings of Knowledge*, Boston: Harvard Business School Press.

McGee, J. V. and Prusak, L. (1993) *Managing Information Strategically*, London: Wiley.

Meyer-Krahmer, F. (1990) *Science and Technology in the Federal Republic of Germany*, London: Longman.

Nonaka, I. and Takeuchi, H. (1995) *The Knowledge-Creating Company*, Oxford: Oxford University Press.

Powell, W. W., Koput, K. W. and Smith-Doerr, L. (1996) 'Inter-organizational collaboration and the locus of innovation: networks of learning in biotechnology', *Administrative Science Quarterly*, **41**, 116–45.

Roos, R. J., Dragonette, N. C. and Edvinsson, L. (1997) *Intellectual Capital: Navigating the New Business Landscape*, Macmillan.

Sammons, P., Hillman, J. and Mortimore, P. (1995) *Key Characteristics of Effective Schools*, London: University of London Institute of Education/Office for Standards in Education.

Skyrme, D. and Amidon, D. M. (1997) *Creating the Knowledge-based Business*, Business Intelligence.

Sveiby, K. E. and Lloyd, T. (1987) *Managing Knowhow*, London: Bloomsbury.

Weick, K. E. and Bougon, M. G. (1986) 'Organizations as cognitive maps', in Sims, H. P. and Giola, D. A. (eds), *The Thinking Organization*, San Francisco: Jossey-Bass.

Chapter 18

The experience of evidence-based healthcare

Alison Hill

Commissioned for this volume (2000).

What is evidence based healthcare?

There is an email discussion group called the Evidence-Based Health mailbase,[1] which has nearly two thousand list members. On 10 February 2000 someone posted the following questions:

1 What is the *raison d'être* of evidence-based healthcare?
2 Why is evidence-based healthcare so important?
3 How does evidence-based anything contribute to the research process?
4 Does conducting evidence-based research necessarily mean using an RCT (*randomised controlled trial*)?

This request generated a flurry of correspondence.[2] Responders gave answers ranging from the practical technical solutions to problems, making clinical decision-making more explicit, managing pressure groups, challenging experts, avoiding harm, through to a new paradigm and a philosophy, with the patient at the centre of decision-making. These wide-ranging comments show that evidence-based health-care means many things to many people. There is, however, a fundamental principle underlying all those comments: that healthcare workers should seek to base their actions on the best evidence available.

Although the example above suggests that there are a number of perspectives on evidence-based healthcare, it is still possible to define it. There are several definitions in the literature (Critical Appraisal Skills Programme, 1999), which are all variations on a theme. One of these does seem to encapsulate the meaning for decision-makers in healthcare whether clinicians, managers or policy makers and this is:

> Evidence-based clinical practice is an approach to decision making in which the clinician uses the best evidence available, in consultation with the patient, to decide the option which suits the patient best.

> (Gray, 1977)

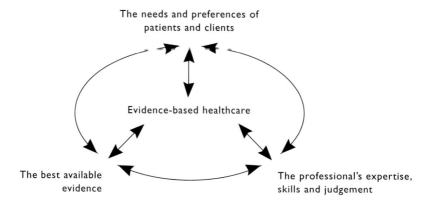

The needs and preferences of
patients and clients

Evidence-based healthcare

The best available
evidence

The professional's expertise,
skills and judgement

Figure 18.1 **The three elements of evidence-based healthcare**

The central feature of any of the definitions of evidence-based healthcare is to ensure decisions are based on sound evidence, derived, where possible, from rigorous research. The above definition also emphasises the role of the patient in decision-making and the clinician's ability to draw on their own clinical experience and professional judgement.

Although the principles go back to last century, the term 'evidence-based' was used to describe a movement initiated at McMaster University in Hamilton, Ontario, where a pioneering medical curriculum was introduced. This required medical students to keep up to date with the medical literature in order to inform their decision-making and so equip them with the skills to find and appraise evidence. The movement was given impetus in the early 1990s when it spread to the UK, with the setting up of the first UK Centre for Evidence-based Medicine in Oxford. It is now an international movement as interest in it from both clinicians and policy-makers grows.

The term 'evidence-based' was used deliberately to challenge established practice and as the movement gained momentum, it met with negative reactions from the medical establishment (Grahame-Smith, 1995; *Lancet*, 1995a, 1995b), and continues to generate gentle ridicule and controversy (Molesworth, 1998; Isaacs and Fitzgerald, 1999). Criticism ranges from evidence-based medicine being 'old hat' (the usual response being 'Of course I've always based my practice on evidence') to it being a dangerous innovation, aimed at rationing healthcare and suppressing clinical freedom through cookbook medicine (Sackett *et al.*, 1996). Increasingly though it is being adopted within the healthcare community, through Department of Health policy (Dept. of Health, 1998), and through medical

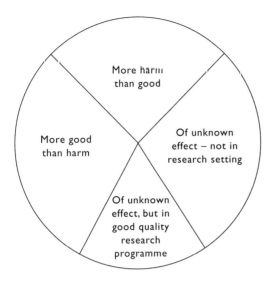

Figure 18.2 Present distribution of the various types of interventions in healthcare. (Source: Gray, 1997, p. 21)

and other health care professional curricula (Green, 1999; Norman and Shannon, 1998).

Why must health services be based on evidence?

Healthcare decision-making is complex. For example an observation of some hospital doctors found that in a half day each needed about 16 pieces of new, clinically important information (about two questions for every three patients), and four clinical decisions would have been altered if clinically useful information had been available and used (Covell *et al.*, 1985).

It has been estimated that only 15 per cent of medical practice is based on solid scientific evidence (Smith, 1991). This though is a rather too black-and-white approach as all healthcare has both benefits and harms and the key is to ensure the balance tilts towards benefit. Benefit means interventions that are effective, safe and acceptable. Harm is often more difficult to identify but there is almost no intervention that is without harm. Muir Gray suggests that the current distribution of interventions in healthcare probably follow that in Figure 18.2. The information to inform judgements on benefits and harms have to come from good quality research and for any one decision this may require information from a variety of different sources.

Figure 18.2 is one person's speculation on the distribution of intervention, but this estimate is not being widely disputed by healthcare professionals. This diagram indicates there is still much to do to close the gap between research and practice.

Gaps between research and practice

A major tenet of Hippocratic medicine was 'First do no harm (*primum non nocere*)' (Porter, 1997). And yet there are numerous examples in the biomedical literature of healthcare that is not based on evidence and that almost certainly caused harm. Some examples are given below:

- Steroids in preterm labour. In the 1980s a number of research studies suggested that steroids given to pregnant women in premature labour might reduce the death rate in babies but none of the studies by themselves were large enough to show a difference. As a result there was no consensus about whether or not to give steroids. It was not until the study results were combined that it became apparent that there was a strong effect. If bigger and better studies had been done thousands of babies might have been saved (Crowley, 1996). But not only was there a delay in generating the research evidence, there was also a delay in incorporating this knowledge into practice of several years (OSIRIS Collaborative Group, 1990).
- Thrombolytic (clot busting) therapy in heart attack. Had researchers and practitioners searched, the evidence was available in the 1970s that clot-busting drugs improved the outlook in people with heart attacks (Antman *et al.*, 1992). And yet as late as 1987 the *Oxford Textbook of Medicine* was stating 'The clinical value of thrombolysis . . . remains uncertain.'
- Dilatation and curettage (D&C). The commonest operation in the UK in the 1980s was dilatation and curettage for women with heavy periods. In 1993 a paper was published that showed that there was no evidence to suggest that D&Cs had any benefit on women's symptoms other than in the very short term (Coulter *et al.*, 1993).

This gap between evidence and practice at first glance appears remarkable given that healthcare is supposed to have been built around the scientific process. But there are several steps between the requirement for knowledge to inform practice and the implementation of that knowledge, which are described in the section below.

Why we do not always practise evidence-based healthcare?

The three stages of evidence-based healthcare are producing evidence, making evidence available and using evidence (i.e. getting research into practice) (Gray, 1997). Within these three components there are a vast number of steps and it is

Table 18.1 Index of interest in various diagnoses (number of papers listed in Index Medicus 1986 in English/discharges and deaths (D&D) from hospital in-patient enquiry ($\times$ 1000)

Diagnoses	Discharges and deaths	Index of interest Papers/D&D $\times$ 1000
Slow virus CNS disease	40	2000
Myaesthenia Gravis	930	156
Crohn's disease	6670	44
Carcinoma of the breast	41,220	33
Cerebrovascular disease	111,250	7.7
Hip replacement	37,400	5.0
Inguinal hernia	64,400	0.8
Varicose veins	47,160	0.6

Source: Frankel and West, 1993

inevitable therefore there will be a gap between the need for knowledge and the implementation of evidence-based healthcare.

Producing the evidence

Ideally research commissioned should reflect the requirements of the health service. However, researchers often determine the research agenda without seeking a clear direction either from health service decision-makers or from consumers. For example, Table 18.1 shows that some of the commonest conditions treated in English hospitals are the least researched. In some ways this table demonstrates the need for researchers to determine the agenda. This table was produced before the BSE (bovine spongiform encephalopathy) crisis hit Britain; clearly the research done then has been enormously helpful in enhancing knowledge about BSE and Creutzfeldt-Jacob disease. The table also demonstrates that common diseases do not receive the research interest they need partly because they are not pushing the frontiers of science and do not generate the profile and glamour of some of the rarer diseases.

Making evidence available

Even when research is completed it does not necessarily get into the public domain. Publication bias is a well-recognised phenomenon. This comes from both authors and journal editors. Submission bias is the tendency of authors only to publish papers that have a statistically significant result. Acceptance bias is the tendency of editors only to accept papers of trials in which a new treatment is shown to be superior to a standard treatment. Retrieval bias is the tendency for research with significant results to be published in more widely read journals. These biases all promote new treatments at the expense of long-standing, more traditional interventions.

Using evidence: getting research into practice

Finding the evidence

Unpublished 'grey' literature presents major problems for the researcher wanting to access comprehensive research on a subject. But even when research is published there is still a major problem in finding evidence. There are a number of different bibliographic databases available but the two principal ones are MEDLINE and EMBASE (Excerpta Medica database). MEDLINE is a database prepared and maintained by the US National Library of Medicine and has referenced information from 3,700 journals worldwide since 1966. EMBASE has better coverage of European literature, covering references from 1974. Indexing of references on these databases has not been comprehensive and as a result key references cannot be retrieved. Even the best and most experienced of electronic searchers find only about half the references that a detailed hand search will find, and an inexperienced searcher will find only about 15 per cent of the relevant papers (Adams *et al.*, 1994).

English language bias is also a problem. For example, the papers contributing to a systematic review of the effectiveness of the herbal remedy St Johns Wort for depression (Linde *et al.*, 1996) were all published in German. The searchers would have looked in vain if they done a search for English language publications.

Appraising the evidence

In order to make sense of the evidence from scientific papers, readers of papers need to be able to interpret them. The skill to do this is called 'critical appraisal'. Critical appraisal is about applying a systematic approach to assessing a research paper.

The innovative educational programme for medical students in McMaster University described in Section 1 was exceptional. Acquisition of critical appraisal skills has not been a component of the education of healthcare professionals, and has been slowly creeping in through continuing professional development programmes. Dunn *et al.* (Dunn *et al.*, 1998) undertook a survey in nurses of the barriers to evidence-based practice and found that 75 per cent could not understand the statistics and 70 per cent could not critically appraise a research paper.

Implementing evidence

The final and perhaps the biggest gap is the problem of implementing research evidence. There are innumerable examples of both omission and commission, of delays in acting on the evidence and of introducing new techniques not supported by evidence. Barriers to change and ways of overcoming these move us into change management, educational and behavioural theory. Barriers exist at an individual and at an organisational level, and the culture of an organisation is critical for determining whether an individual can be enabled to change.

Ensuring research can inform practice

The reason we need research is to minimise both the bias and the play of chance in our observations. In healthcare too many studies have been too small to have the power to show a difference, and often they have inherent biases. Over the last ten years the focus of research has begun to shift to synthesising what is already known, and indeed the major research funders usually demand now that systematic reviews of the literature are undertaken before decisions are made to fund a specific piece of research. Secondary research in the form of systematic reviews of the literature is, though only slowly, becoming accepted as quality research that will attract appropriate research ratings. There are a number of sources of research syntheses now (Critical Appraisal Skills Programme, 1999), but the first port of call in any search for evidence has to be the Cochrane Collaboration.[3] This is a large international movement that is gaining more and more momentum. It brings together onto one database, the Cochrane Library,[4] the results of painstaking synthesis of research studies, using rigorous standard protocols. Maintenance of the reviews has to be a lifelong commitment. Systematic reviews on the Cochrane Library are regarded as the most trustworthy source of evidence on healthcare. (A similar movement called the Campbell Collaboration is starting for social and educational policies and practice.[5])

The randomised controlled trial is regarded as the 'gold standard' evidence as its design means that bias can be avoided. Evidence-based healthcare has therefore developed a reputation for focusing solely on randomised controlled trials, and dismissing other forms of research methods, such as observational, cross-sectional or qualitative. There is some truth in this, but the value of other types of research is increasingly recognised for its contribution to healthcare knowledge.

In addition to the development of a number of sources of synthesised studies, there are considerable efforts being made internationally to improve the indexing of the major bibliographic databases. For instance the Cochrane Collaboration requires hand searching of journals to find randomised controlled trials. Those not indexed are incorporated in MEDLINE. In addition medical journals are increasingly attempting to reduce publication bias by accepting studies on the basis of their rigour rather than on their results.

Evidence-based clinical practice

An evidence-based approach to decision-making can be broken down into five key steps set out in Figure 18.3 below.

Asking a question, searching and critically appraising are addressed below. Acting on the evidence is a subject in its own right and is not addressed in this article. For those who are interested there are some excellent references on this topic, which are as relevant in the field of education as in medicine (Haines and Donald, 1998; University of York, 1999; Dunning et al., 1999).

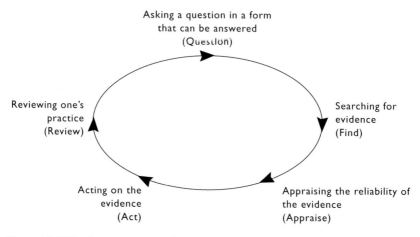

Figure 18.3 The five steps in evidence-based healthcare

Asking a question in a form that can be answered (Question)

Defining the question is the starting point of evidence-based healthcare. Arguably this is the most significant stage in evidence-based practice, for two reasons. First, identifying the knowledge gap is a skill in itself particularly if it goes counter to custom and practice. Second, framing the question is crucial, as it helps: to clarify the problem and the information needed to solve it; to define the kind of evidence needed to answer the question; and to formulate the strategy for the literature search.

A well-built question contains three or four elements (Richardson *et al.*, 1995).

P   The problem – the patient or client, population, or condition you are dealing with.
I   The intervention you are considering.
C   A comparison (if appropriate and relevant) – an alternative intervention with which you would like to compare your information.
O   The outcome or outcomes you are interested in.

For example, an 80-year-old man is found to have mild hypertension (raised blood pressure) at his annual health check. His GP needs to decide whether or not to put him on antihypertensive treatment. The clinical question would be as follows:

> For 80-year-old men with mild hypertension (P) would antihypertensive treatment (I) compared to no treatment (C) reduce the risk of stroke and heart disease and other complications of raised blood pressure (O)?

This question helps determine the type of study to look for and the terms to be used in the search. There is an additional element to this question that reflects back to the discussion in Section 2. This is the issue of harm. In this case study the need to weigh up the benefits versus the harm for the individual is essential.

Searching for evidence (Find)

There is an overwhelming volume of published evidence from a huge variety of sources. About 25,000 biomedical journals and about 17,000 new biomedical books are published annually, MEDLINE holds more than 7 million articles, and the web is resulting in an explosion of additional information. Developments in information technology have linked personal computers to vast databases, and practitioners need to find their way round this morass of data in order to capture the relevant articles, and exclude the irrelevant. Increasingly summarised and synthesised evidence sources are being made available. But even so to get the best out of these sources practitioners need to know how to access them and how to search them using evidence-based protocols and search strategies.[6] Librarians are a key expert support in finding the evidence and these skills are being increasingly taught at undergraduate and postgraduate level.

Appraising the reliability of the evidence (Appraise)

Critical appraisal skills are at the heart of evidence-based practice. Experience in the health service has shown that everyone – consumers, managers, clinicians and policy-makers – can learn and apply critical appraisal skills. There are well-established programmes for teaching critical appraisal that can make it relevant and non-threatening to people who do not have a scientific background.

Research evidence to inform practice comes in a variety of forms, from large-scale randomised controlled trials to small qualitative studies of patient experience. Whatever the evidence, critical appraisal helps the reader decide three things:

- whether the reader can trust the results,
- what the results mean,
- whether they are relevant to the reader's situation.

In order to assess these three areas requires an appraisal of the research methods, the quality of the data, and the analysis and interpretation placed on the findings. Within this framework each type of research requires different questions. An example of checklists for a systematic review and a qualitative study is set out in Tables 18.2 and 18.3 below.

There is not space here to set out all the different appraisal checklists – these are available on the Critical Appraisal Skills Programme web site.[7] This site also has examples of appraisals of different types of research studies.

Table 18.2 A critical appraisal checklist for a systematic review

A Are the results of the review valid
1 Screening Question. Did the review address a clearly focused issue?
2 Screening Question. Did the authors look for the appropriate sort of papers?

You need to decide here if it is worth continuing

B Detailed Questions
3 Do you think the important, relevant studies were included?
4 Did the review's authors do enough to assess the quality of the included studies?
5 If the results of the review have been combined, was it reasonable to do so?

C What are the results?
6 What is the overall result of the review?
7 How precise are the results?

D Will the results help locally?
8 Can the results be applied to the local population?
9 Were all-important outcomes considered?
10 Are the benefits worth the harms and costs?

© Critical Appraisal Skills Programme (CASP) 2000

Table 18.3 Checklist for appraising a qualitative study

A Screening Questions
1 Was there a clear statement of the aims of the research?
2 Is a qualitative methodology appropriate?

B Detailed Questions
3 Was the sampling strategy appropriate to address the aims?
4 Were the data collected in a way that addresses the research issue?
5 Was the data analysis sufficiently rigorous?
6 Has the relationship between researchers and participants been adequately considered?

C Findings
7 Is there a clear statement of the findings?
8 Do the researchers indicate links between data presented and their own findings on what the data contain?

D Will the results help locally?
9 Are the findings of this study transferable to a wider population?
10 How relevant is the research?
11 How important are these findings to practice?

© Critical Appraisal Skills Programme (CASP) 2000

Evidence-based practice: a new movement

To go back to the mailbase discussion group mentioned in the introduction, a quote from Toby Lipman[8] is a fitting finale to this article:

> Evidence-based medicine is more than a set of techniques – it is a different way of looking at the world, a new paradigm. It gave me a new direction – really a new philosophy. Part of this is in the explicit use of scientific evidence, in critical appraisal and in the application of clinical epidemiology to the care of individual patients. All these are valuable, but seem to many reductionist, reaffirming positivist approaches to health (classifying disease, applying the 'correct' treatment). However, there is much more to it than that.
>
> By developing our ability to identify the most important questions – those most relevant to patients – we will often find that we don't need RCTs or systematic reviews, but human understanding, often backed up by evidence from qualitative research or even literature and the arts. This is one of the most exciting aspects of evidence-based medicine for me – we are able not only to avoid unnecessary medicalisation, but have a process whereby we can expand our understanding of patients' predicaments beyond our personal experience and think of some useful ways they can be helped.

Endnotes

1 http://www.mailbase.ac.uk/lists/evidence-based-health/
2 http://www.mailbase.ac.uk/lists/evidence-based-health/2000-02/thread.html
3 The Cochrane Collaboration. http://www.cochrane.org/
4 The Cochrane Library, Update Software, Oxford. Email info@update.co.uk
5 The Campbell Collaboration web site. http://campbell.gse.upenn.edu/intro.html
6 Health Care Libraries Unit. CASPfew. http://libsun1.jr2.ox.ac.uk/caspfew/
7 Critical Appraisal Skills Programme web site. www.casp.org.uk
8 http://www.mailbase.ac.uk/lists/evidence-based-health/2000-02/0076.html

References

Adams, C. E., Power, A., Frederick, K. and Lefebvre, C. (1994) 'An investigation of the adequacy of MEDLINE searches for randomised controlled trials (RCTs) of the effects of mental health care', *Psychol. Med.*, **24**, 741–8.

Antman, E. M., Lau, J., Kupelnick, B., Mosteller, F. and Chalmers, T. (1992) 'A comparison of results of meta-analyses of randomised controlled trials and recommendations of clinical experts. Treatments for myocardial infarction', *JAMA*, **268**, 240–8.

Coulter, A., Klassen, A., MacKenzie, I. Z. and McPherson, K. (1993) 'Diagnostic dilatation and curettage: is it used appropriately?', *BMJ*, **306**, 236–9.

Covell, D. G., Uman, G. C. and Manning, P. R. (1985) 'Information needs in office practice: are they being met?', *Ann. Intern. Med.*, **103**, 596–9.

Critical Appraisal Skills Programme (1999) *Evidence-based Health Care: An Open Learning Resource for Health Care Practitioners*, Oxford: Update Software Ltd.

Crowley, P. (1996) 'Corticosteroids prior to pre-term delivery', in Enkin, M. W., Keirse, M. J. N. C., Renfrew, M. J. and Neilson, J. P. (eds), *Pregnancy and Childbirth Module of the Cochrane Database of Systematic Reviews*, Oxford: Update Software.

Department of Health (1998) *A First Class Service. Quality in the new NHS.*

Dunn, V., Crichton, N., Roe, B., Seers, K. and Williams, K. (1998) 'Using research for practice: a UK experience of the BARRIERS scale', *J. Adv. Nursing*, **27**, 1203–10.

Dunning, M., Abi-Aad, G., Gilbert, D., Hutton, H. and Brown, C. (1999) *Experience, Evidence and Everyday Practice. Creating Systems for Delivering Effective Health Care*, London: King's Fund.

Frankel, S. and West, R. (1993) *Rationing and Rationality in the National Health Service*, Basingstoke: Macmillan, 11.

Grahame-Smith, D. (1995) 'Evidence based medicine: Socratic dissent', *BMJ*, **310**, 1126–7.

Gray, J. A. M. (1997) *Evidence-based Healthcare: How to Make Health Policy and Management Decisions*, Edinburgh: Churchill Livingston.

Green, M. L. (1999) 'Graduate medical education training in clinical epidemiology, critical appraisal, and evidence-based medicine: a critical review of curricula', *Academic Medicine*, **74**, 686–94

Haines, A. and Donald, A. (1998) *Getting Research Findings into Practice*, BMJ Books.

Isaacs, D. and Fitzgerald, D. (1999) 'Seven alternatives to evidence based medicine', *BMJ*, **319**, 1618.

Lancet (1995a) 'Evidence based medicine; in its place' [editorial], **346**, 785.

Lancet (1995b) 'Correspondence. Evidence based medicine', **346**, 1171–2.

Linde, K., Ramirez, G., Mulrow, C. D., Pauls, A., Weidenhammer, W. and Melchart, D. (1996) 'St John's wort for depression – an overview and meta-analysis of randomised clinical trials', *BMJ*, **313**, 253–8.

Molesworth, N. (1998) 'Sacred cows: to the abattoir! Down with EBM!', *BMJ*, **317**, 1720–1.

Norman, G. R. and Shannon, S. I. (1998) 'Effectiveness of instruction in critical appraisal (evidence-based medicine) skills: a critical appraisal', *CMAJ*, **158**, 177–81.

OSIRIS Collaborative Group (1990) 'Early versus delayed neonatal administration of a synthetic surfactant – the judgement of OSIRIS (Open Study of Infants at high risk of or with Respiratory Insufficiency – the role of Surfactant)', *Lancet*, **340**, 1363–9.

Porter, R. (1997) *The Greatest Benefit to Mankind. A Medical History of Humanity from Antiquity to the Present*, London: Fontana Press.

Richardson, W. S., Wilson, M. C., Nishikawa, J. and Hayward, R. S. A. (1995) 'The well-built clinical question: a key to evidence-based decisions' (editorial), *ACP Journal Club*, Nov–Dec, **123**, A12–13.

Sackett, D. L., Rosenberg, W. M. C., Gray J. A., Haynes, R. B. and Richardson, W. S. (1996) 'Editorial: Evidence based medicine: what it is and what it isn't', *BMJ*, **312**, 71–2.

Smith, R. (1991) 'Where is the wisdom . . . ? The poverty of medical evidence', *BMJ*, **313**, 798–9.

University of York (1999) 'Getting evidence into practice', *Effective Healthcare Bulletin*, **5**(1).

Chapter 19

What is evidence-based education?

Philip Davies

This is an edited version of an article previously published in *British Journal of Educational Studies*, **47**(2), June 1999.

Introduction

In most societies education is constantly being asked to do more and more things, to higher and higher standards, with greater accountability and finite (if not diminishing) resources. Its agenda is often driven by political ideology, conventional wisdom, folklore and wishful thinking as it strives to meet the needs and interests of the economy, business, employers, law and order, civil society, parental choice and, at least rhetorically, the children, young people and adults who make up the learning community (Apple, 1982; Apple and Weis, 1983; Ball, 1990, 1993; Bowles and Gintis, 1976; Giroux, 1983, 1992, Willis, 1997). Much of this impetus represents the triumph of hope over reason, sentiment over demonstrated effectiveness, intuition over evidence. Increasingly, the direction of change in educational thinking and practice is top-down from central governments, think tanks, opinion formers, educational regulators (such as OFSTED), the media and academic departments whose research is often selective, unsystematic and prone to political or scientific bias (or both). Some recent examples from the United Kingdom include: the form and content of the National Curriculum; the introduction of standardised tests and league tables as a means of 'raising standards' and supposedly increasing parental choice; the substitution of 'trendy' teaching methods based on activity-based, student-centred, self-directed learning and problem solving, with whole-class teaching based on 'rows' and 'columns' classroom organisation, didactic instruction and a more passive approach to learning, often by rote.

It is often unclear whether these developments in educational thinking and practice are better, or worse, than the regimes they replace. This is in part because educational activity is often inadequately evaluated by means of carefully designed and executed controlled trials, quasi-experiments, surveys, before-and-after studies, high-quality observational studies, ethnographic studies that look at outcomes as well as processes, or conversation and discourse analytic studies that link micro structures and actions to macro level issues. Moreover, the research and evaluation studies that do exist are seldom searched for systematically, retrieved and read, critically appraised for quality, validity and relevance, and organised and graded for power of evidence. This is the task of evidence-based education.

Using *vs* establishing evidence

Evidence-based education operates at two levels. The first is to utilise existing evidence from worldwide research and literature on education and associated subjects. Educationalists at all levels need to be able to:

- pose an answerable question about education;
- know where and how to find evidence systematically and comprehensively using the electronic (computer-based) and non-electronic (print) media;
- retrieve and read such evidence competently and undertake critical appraisal and analysis of that evidence according to agreed professional and scientific standards;
- organise and grade the power of this evidence;
- determine its relevance to *their* educational needs and environments.

The second level is to *establish* sound evidence where existing evidence is lacking or of a questionable, uncertain, or weak nature. Practitioners of evidence-based education working at this level need to be able to plan, carry out and publish studies that meet the highest standards of scientific research and evaluation, incorporating the methods of the social sciences, the natural sciences and the humanistic and interpretive disciplines. The objective of evidence-based education at this level is to ensure that future research on education meets the criteria of scientific validity, high-quality, and practical relevance that is sometimes lacking in existing evidence on educational activities, processes and outcomes (Hargreaves, 1996, 1997; Hillage *et al.*, 1998; Tooley and Darby, 1998).

This view of evidence-based education is derived quite explicitly from the University of Oxford Master's programme in Evidence-Based Health Care. This programme offers health professionals of all types the opportunity to develop their professional skills whilst maintaining full-time professional practice. A central feature of the Oxford programme in Evidence-Based Health Care is that students learn by attempting to solve clinical and population-based problems that *they* bring to the course. This approach to learning, and teaching, is explicitly based on the problem-solving, self-directed model of adult education developed by Knowles (1990) and derived from the learning theory of Piaget, Bruner, Vygotsky and the 'constructivist' school of learning (Davies, 1999).

The need for both levels of evidence-based practice in education seems clear. There have been a number of recent criticisms about the gap between the teaching and the research communities, the relevance, applicability and quality of educational research, the non-cumulative nature of good educational research, and its effective dissemination (Hargreaves, 1996, 1997; Hillage *et al.*, 1998; Tooley and Darby, 1998). Hargreaves (1996, p. 7), for instance, has called for an end to:

> second-rate educational research which does not make a serious contribution to fundamental theory or knowledge; which is irrelevant to practice; which is uncoordinated with any preceding or follow-up research; and which clutters up academic journals that virtually nobody reads.

Such broad-brush characterisations of educational research have, not surprisingly, received a strong and critical response from the educational research community (Norris, 1996; Gray, 1996; Edwards, 1996; Hammersley, 1997), and a debate that has often shed more heat than light. There is a risk that observations such as those of Hargreaves may promote a narrowly utilitarian and philistine approach to research and intellectual life. What constitutes the relevance of research, for instance, depends to a large extent on what questions are being asked, in what context and for what practical ends. The demands of practice in one context may make a seemingly narrow and esoteric piece of research highly relevant and very enlightening for those who use it. Similarly, research that is apparently more generalisable, cumulative and based on highly representative samples for some purposes may be of little value to those with different practice needs and in quite different contexts from those in which the research took place. There is no such thing as context-free evidence.

Some of the criticisms of educational research, however, do have some validity. Hammersley, who has responded most critically to Hargreaves's 1996 lecture, acknowledges, with apparent sincerity, that educational research does lack a cumulative character and that it needs 'to move to a situation where new research builds more effectively on earlier work, and where greater attention is given to testing competing interpretations of data, whether descriptive or explanatory' (Hammersley, 1997, p. 144). Also, the claim that there is a gap between educational research and teachers (Hargreaves, 1996; Hillage *et al.*, 1998) is undoubtedly true, though perhaps in different ways to those suggested by these critics. The problem is not so much that teachers do not undertake research, or that they are often excluded from determining the research agenda (both of which may be true), but that there is often not a culture of teachers using research to inform their everyday school practice. Contrary to Hargreaves's claim about medicine, the same situation prevails in many areas of clinical practice. One of the ways in which evidence-based healthcare has had some influence in recent years is in getting clinicians to be clearer about the clinical problems for which they require solutions, and utilising existing evidence effectively and critically to help them solve these problems. There is no question of evidence replacing clinical judgement or experience, but of uniting these two dimensions of knowledge to provide a sound basis for action. Evidence-based practice can provide a similar basis for professional knowledge and action in education. It can also ensure that those who undertake educational research are properly trained in research methods, and understand its underlying theoretical and methodological principles, thereby enhancing its quality.

Some objections

Some objections from the educational community to such a model of evidence-based education can be anticipated, and have been expressed by respondents to Hargreaves's (1996) call for teaching to be a research-based profession (Norris, 1996; Gray, 1996; Edwards, 1996; Hammersley, 1997). It is claimed that education is unlike healthcare, and medicine especially, because its activities, processes, and outcomes are complex and culturally, or contextually, specific. Consequently, it is argued, there are problems of measurement and causation in educational research that are not found in medicine and healthcare. Medicine and healthcare, however, face very similar, if not identical, problems of complexity, context-specificity, measurement and causation that Hammersley (1997) has identified in education. The activities, processes and outcomes of healthcare are also highly complex, often indeterminate and context/culture specific, making their measurement both difficult and controversial (Le Grand and Illsley, 1986; Wilkinson, 1986; Samphier et al., 1988; MacBeth, 1996). The generalisability of evidence-based healthcare is one of its major concerns, as it is of all epidemiology and clinical practice. The uncertain relationship between how people behave in hospitals and in their own and other environments (i.e. ecological validity) is a well documented problem in the medical and healthcare literature (Christmas et al., 1974; Andrews and Stewart, 1979; Newcombe and Ratcliff, 1979; Davies and Mehan, 1988; Davies 1996), with clear parallels with students'; educational performances in schools and colleges on the one hand and in the 'real world' on the other. Greenhalgh and Worrall (1997) have recently argued that the concept of context-sensitive medicine is appropriate to describe the skill of applying the findings of research to the demands of everyday clinical practice.

So far as the measurement of outcomes is concerned, the only discrete and (usually) uncontroversial outcome of healthcare is death (or survival). Almost every other outcome of healthcare depends on whether one is concerned with objective or subjective dimensions of health and illness, the contexts within which health and illness occur, or the improvement, maintenance, or deterioration of people's health status. Central to these problems is the interaction of signs and symptoms on the one hand and variations in health and illness behaviour according to social class, gender, ethnicity and cultural practices on the other. For Hammersley to claim that 'unlike in most areas of medicine, in education the "treatments" consist of symbolic interaction, with all the scope for multiple interpretations and responses which that implies', is to ignore his own detailed knowledge of both medical practice and the extensive sociological work on health and illness that has been inspired by symbolic interactionists such as Goffman (1959, 1963, 1964), Glaser and Strauss (1965, 1967), Davis (1963), Fagerhaugh and Strauss (1977) and Strong (1979).

The claim that medicine and healthcare are based on the natural sciences and their methodologies, whereas education is much more firmly embedded in social science and its approaches to research and evaluation, is also unsustainable. The rejection of natural science as the only basis of modern healthcare has come from such diverse sources as Balint (1957), Capra (1982), Laing (1965) and Sacks (1990), and the professional training and accreditation bodies of nursing and almost all allied professions, including medicine. Similarly, educational research draws upon the methodological principles and practices of the natural and the social sciences. Whilst it is undoubtedly the case that experimental and quasi-experimental research is harder to achieve in many aspects of education than it is in some aspects of healthcare, it is not unknown in educational research and other areas of social scientific inquiry (Oakley, 1998). Randomised controlled trials are difficult to undertake in evaluations of teaching or learning effectiveness, though their potential has been recognised by some researchers (Boruch *et al.*, 1978; Oakley and Roberts, 1996; Oakley, 1998). Consequently, researchers who evaluate educational methods or initiatives tend to rely more heavily on controlled comparisons of matched schools, classrooms, or communities, and to develop models of the effects of extraneous variables (Anderson, 1998).

An associated problem, often mentioned by people in the educational community, is that education is, and must be, concerned with *qualitative* research whereas healthcare is much more concerned with *quantitative* research and evaluation. This is also a false polemic, and one that is unsustainable when one examines research studies in education and healthcare. A recent review article on research methods in American educational research concluded that

> results are consistent with those of other studies in that the most commonly used methods were ANOVA and ANCOVA, multiple regression, bivariate correlation, descriptive statistics, multivariate analysis, non-parametric statistics and t-tests. The major difference in current methodology is the increase in the use of qualitative methods.
>
> (Elmore and Woehlke, 1996)

The journals reviewed by Elmore and Woehlke represent the more positivistic tradition of American educational research. Other journals, such as the *Harvard Educational Review, Anthropology and Education Quarterly, Qualitative Studies in Education, Social Psychology of Education* and *Linguistics and Education* have a tradition of publishing more qualitative research, and the proliferation of articles using qualitative methods and discourse analysis confirms the increase in these types of research in the educational field. This trend is also evident in the British educational research literature.

Another common feature of educational and healthcare research is the use of systematic reviews and meta-analyses. Indeed, meta-analysis and systematic reviews have their origins in educational research following the pioneering work of Glass (Glass *et al.*, 1980). Glass's work on meta-analysis, like that of Kulik and Kulik (1989), has been described as 'a form of literature review [that] is not meant to test a hypothesis but to summarise features and outcomes of a body of research' (Bangert-Drowns, 1985). Others in the educational research field (Hunter and Schmidt, 1995; Hedges, 1992; Rosenthal, 1995) have used meta-analysis in a way that is more akin to that found in healthcare research, as a way of data-pooling and 'the use of

statistical methods to combine the results of independent empirical research studies'
(Hedges, 1992). Meta-analysis in educational research has the same problems as in
healthcare research, such as ensuring the comparability of different samples, research
designs, outcome and process measures, identifying confounding factors and bias
and determining the attributable effects of the intervention(s) being assessed. As
Preiss (1988) points out 'the researcher will have several options when cumulating
empirical studies and readers will have questions regarding judgment calls made
during meta-analysis'.

What is evidence?

A key issue in developing evidence-based education, and evidence-based healthcare,
is the uncertainty as to what counts as evidence. For those who ask questions such as
'does educational method (or healthcare intervention) x have a better outcome than
educational method (or healthcare intervention) y in terms of achieving outcome z',
evidence consists of the results of randomised controlled trials or other experimental
and quasi-experimental studies. Other types of question, for which valid and reliable
evidence is sought in both educational and healthcare research, require evidence
about the strength and pattern of relationships between different variables that effect
the processes and outcomes of education (and healthcare). These are best provided
by survey and correlational research using methods such as simple and multiple
correlation, regression analysis and analysis of variance.

Yet other questions are more concerned about the *processes* by which educational
and healthcare activities are undertaken and the *meanings* that education or healthcare have for different people (e.g. learners/patients, teachers/healthcare professionals,
school governors, healthcare executives, purchasers, etc.). The ways in which teachers
and doctors typify students and patients, and use categories and practices that open
up, and close down, opportunities for advancement in education (Cicourel and
Kitsuse, 1963; cicourel and Mehan, 1985; Mehan *et al.*, 1996) or healthcare (Strong,
1979; Davies, 1979) are important topics about which high-quality evidence is
needed. Evidence is also required about the *consequences* of educational and healthcare activities on students' and parents' sense of self and their sense of social worth and
identity. These types of question require more qualitative and 'naturalistic' research
methods such as ethnography, detailed observations and face-to-face interviews.

Other evidence may be sought about the patterns and structures of interaction,
conversation and discourse by means of which both educational and healthcare
activities are accomplished. Such questions focus on naturally occurring activities
between teachers and students, health professionals and patients, and between
professionals. Studies such as those by Button and Lee (1987), Fisher and Todd
(1983), Silverman (1987) in health care and by Cazden (1988), Mehan (1977),
Mehan *et al.* (1996) and Spindler (1982) in education represent types of research and
evidence from within the conversation analysis and discourse analysis tradition.

Evidence is also required about ethical issues of educational or healthcare practice,
such as whether or not it is right or warrantable to undertake a particular educational

activity or healthcare intervention. Each of the methodological approaches mentioned above may inform these issues, but none will resolve them without additional considerations about the moral and ethical issues of universal versus selective action, informed choices, social inequalities and social justice, resource allocation and prioritisation, and the values underlying education and healthcare. There is a considerable literature on the ethics of research and professional practice in healthcare (Brazier, 1987; Fulford, 1990; Gillon, 1985; Veatch, 1989; Weiss, 1982) and education (Adair *et al.*, 1985; Frankel, 1987; Kimmel, 1988) that the competent practitioner needs to include in his or her considerations of appropriate evidence for best practice.

Bibliographic and database problems

A third objection to evidence-based education is that the databases that serve educational research are less developed, and contain lower-quality filters, than those found in medical and healthcare research. It does seem that the ERIC Clearing House for educational research is less universal, comprehensive and systematically indexed than MEDLINE and other databases in healthcare (e.g. CINAHL), social science (SOCIOFILE, PSYCLIT, ECONLIT) and biological sciences (BIOLOGICAL ABSTRACTS), and that many studies in education fail to appear on it. This is an issue of improving the reporting and indexing of educational research and changing its reporting practices.

Educational research has also lacked a centralised database for the preparation, maintenance and dissemination of systemic reviews of education such as the Cochrane Collaboration, Best Evidence and the Centre for NHS Reviews and Dissemination. The Cochrane Collaboration has already begun to assemble a database of reviews and meta-analysis of social and educational research. The Social, Psychological and Educational Controlled Trials Register (SPECTR) is an extension of The Cochrane Controlled Trials Register in healthcare (Milwain, 1998; Petrosino *et al.*, 1999). To date, hand searching, electronic database searching and the searching of reference lists have identified over 5000 references to studies in education, criminology and psychosocial-learning research. These studies do not include research that uses methodologies other than experimental or quasi-experimental designs. Such studies also need systematic identification, review and critical appraisal if the full range of educational research is to be used in the ways suggested in this article.

This indicates an urgent need for the development of such infrastructural arrangements in education (see Hillage *et al.*, 1998, p. 53), and the financial support of central governments and the major research councils to develop and maintain them. The existence of many high-quality educational research centres throughout the world that can undertake systematic reviews and meta-analyses on different aspects of education suggests that a similar network of collaboration in educational research is feasible.

In short, the inadequacy of databases and bibliographic sources in education is a real problem, but one that is surmountable with appropriate effort and resources. The need for the continuing professional development of teachers, educational researchers, policy-makers and school governors, so that the principles and practices of evidence-based education can be nurtured and introduced into everyday educational life, is also clearly indicated.

Evidence and professional judgement

Establishing best practice, in both education and healthcare, is more than a matter of simply accessing, critically appraising and implementing research findings. It also involves integrating such knowledge with professional judgement and experience. Much professional practice in education and healthcare is undertaken on the basis that things have always been done in a certain way, or they carry the authority and legitimacy of some charismatic, highly valued practitioner. The role of 'common-sense' and 'back to basics' is also favoured by politicians and those charged with developing national educational practice.

Whilst tradition, charismatic authority and experience can work against change and the development of best practice, they do have some merit. A teacher's experience and judgement can be much more sensitive to the important nuances of contextual and cultural factors than the findings of research alone, however thorough and valid that research may be. The question of the *relevance* of high-quality research to more local issues of teaching and learning (or treatment and change of health status) has already been noted, and is one that demands the highest levels of professional skill, judgement, and experience. Just as evidence-based healthcare means 'integrating individual clinical expertise with the best available external evidence from systematic research' (Sackett *et al.*, 1996), so evidence-based education means integrating individual teaching and learning expertise with the best available external evidence from systematic research. Indeed, a central feature of evidence-based education must be the two-way process of broadening the basis of individuals' experience and judgement by locating it within the available evidence, and generating research studies and evidence that explore and test the professional experience of teachers, students and other constituents of learning communities.

Conclusion

Education seems to be in a position remarkably similar to that of medicine and healthcare five or ten years ago. There are many research journals that contain a broad range of reports on research using different methodologies and addressing a diverse range of educational issues. Some of this research is of a high quality, some less so. The demands being made upon teachers and others who provide education call out for educational practice to be based on the best available evidence as well as the professional skills, experience and competence of teachers. To do this, the educational research literature needs to be better registered, indexed, classified, appraised and made accessible to researchers and teachers alike. Educators need access to this research and to be able to search and critically appraise it in order to determine its relevance (or lack of relevance) to *their* schools, students and educational needs. Whether this is called evidence-based education, research-based education (Hargreaves, 1996), literature-based education (Hammersley, 1997), or context-sensitive practice (Greenhalgh and Worrall, 1997) is immaterial.

Evidence-based education, like evidence-based healthcare, is not a panacea, a quick fix, cookbook practice or the provider of ready-made solutions to the demands of modern education. It is a set of principles and practices that can alter the way people think about education, the way they go about educational policy and practice, and the basis upon which they make professional judgements and deploy their expertise.

References

Adair, J. G., Dushenko, T. W. and Lindsay, R. C. L. (1985) 'Ethical regulations and their impact on research practices', *American Psychologist*, **40**, 59–72.

Anderson, G. (1998) *Fundamentals of Educational Research*, London: The Falmer Press.

Andrews, K. and Stewart, J. (1979) 'Stroke recovery: he can but does he?', *Rheumatology and Rehabilitation*, **18**, 43–8.

Apple, M. W. (1982) *Education and Power*, Boston: Routledge and Kegan Paul.

Apple, M. W. and Weis, L. (1983) *Ideology and Practice in Education: A Political and Conceptual Introduction*, Philadelphia: Temple University Press.

Balint, M. (1957) *The Doctor, His Patient, and the Illness*, London: Tavistock.

Ball, S. J. (1990) *Politics and Policy Making in Education*, London: Routledge.

Ball, S. J. (1993) Market Forces in Education, *Education Revue*, **7**(1), 8–11.

Bangert-Drowns, R. L. (1985) 'The meta-analysis debate', paper presented at the *Annual Meeting of the American Educational Research Association*, Chicago, 4 April 1985.

Boruch, R. F., McSweeney, A. J. and Sonderstrom, E. J. (1978) 'Randomised field experiments for program planning, development and evaluation, *Evaluation Quarterly*, **2**, 655–95.

Bowles, S. and Gintis, H. I. (1976) *Schooling in Capitalist America*, New York: Basic Books.

Brazier, M. (1987) *Medicine, Patients and the Law*, Harmondsworth: Penguin Books.

Button, G. and Lee, J. R. E. (1987) *Talk and Social Organisation*, Clevedon and Philadelphia: Multilingual Matters.

Capra, F. (1982) *The Turning Point: Science, Society and the Rising Culture*, London: Wildwood House.

Cazden, C. B. (1988) *Classroom Discourse*, New York: Heinemann.

Christmas, E. M., Humphrey, M. E., Richardson, A. E. and Smith, E. M. (1974) 'The response of brain damage patients to a rehabilitation regime', *Rheumatology and Rehabilitation*, **13**, 92–7.

Cicourel, A. V. and Kitsuse, J. I. (1963) *Educational Decision Makers*, Indianapolis: Bobbs-Merrill.

Cicourel, A. V. and Mehan, H. (1985) 'Universal development, stratifying practices, and status attainment', *Research in Social Stratification and Mobility*, **4**, 3–27.

Davies, P. T. and Mehan, H. (1988) 'Professional and family understanding of impaired communication', *British Journal of Disorders of Communication*, **23**, 141–55.

Davies, P. T. (1979) 'Motivation, sickness and responsibility in the psychiatric treatment of alcohol problems', *British Journal of Psychiatry*, **134**(1), 449–59.

Davies, P. T. (1996) 'Sociological approaches to health outcomes', in Macbeth, H. (ed.), *Health Outcomes Reviewed: Biological and Sociological Aspects*, Oxford University Press.

Davies, P. T. (1999) 'Teaching evidence-based health care', in Dawes, M. G., Davies, P. T., Gray, A., Mant, J., Seers, K. and Snowball, R. (1999) *Evidence-based Practice: A Primer for Health Professionals*, Edinburgh: Churchill Livingstone.

Davis, F. (1963) *Passage Through Crisis: Polio Victims and Their Families*, Indianapolis: Bobbs-Merrill.

Edwards, T. (1996) 'The research base of effective teacher education', *British Educational Research Association Newsletter*, Research Intelligence, Number 57, July, 7–12.

Elmore, P. B. and Woehlke, P. L. (1996) 'Research methods employed in *American Educational Research Journal, Educational Researcher* and *Review of Educational Research*, 1978–1995', paper presented at the *Annual Meeting of the American Educational Research Association*, New York, 8 April 1996.

Fagerhaugh, S. Y. and Strauss, A. L. (1977) *Politics of Pain Management: Staff–Patient Interaction*, Menlo Park: Addison-Wesley Publishing Company.

Fisher, S. and Todd, A. (eds) (1983) *The Social Organisation of Doctor–Patient Communication*, Washington, DC: Centre for Applied Linguistics.

Frankel, M. S. (ed.) (1987) *Values and Ethics in Organisation and Human Systems Department: An Annotated Bibliography*, Washington, DC: American Association for the Advancement of Science.

Fulford, K. W. M. (1990) *Moral Theory and Medical Practice*, Cambridge: Cambridge University Press.

Gillon, R. (1985) *Philosophical and Medical Ethics*, New York: John Wiley.

Giroux, H. (1983) *Theory and Resistance in Education*, London: Heinemann Education Books.

Giroux, H. (1992) *Border Crossing: Cultural Workers and the Politics of Education*, London: Routledge and Kegan Paul.

Glaser, B. and Strauss, A. (1965) *Awareness of Dying*, Chicago: Aldine Publishing Co.

Glaser, B. and Strauss, A. (1967) *The Discovery of Grounded Theory: Strategies for Qualitative Research*, Chicago: Aldine Publishing Co.

Glass, G., Mcgaw, B. and Lee Smith, M. (1980) *Meta-Analysis in Social Research*, Beverly Hills: Saga Publications.

Goffman, E. (1959) *The Presentation of Self in Everyday Life*, Harmondsworth: Penguin.

Goffman, E. (1963) *Stigma: Notes on the Management of Spoiled Identity*, Harmondsworth: Penguin.

Goffman, E. (1964) *Asylums: Essays on the Social Situation of Mental Patients and Other Inmates*, Harmondsworth: Penguin.

Gray, J. (1996) 'Track record of peer review: a reply to some remarks by David Hargreaves', *British Educational Research Association Newsletter*, Research Intelligence, Number 57, 5–6 July.

Greenhalgh, T. and Worrall, J. G. (1997) 'From EBM to CSM: the evolution of context-sensitive medicine', *Journal of Education in Clinical Practice*, **3**(2), 105–8.

Hammersley, M. (1997) 'Educational research and a response to David Hargreaves', *British Educational Research Journal*, **23**(2), 141–61.

Hargreaves, D. H. (1996) *Teaching as a Research-Based Profession: Possibilities and Prospects*, Cambridge: Teacher Training Agency Annual Lecture.

Hargreaves, D. H. (1997) 'In defence of research for evidence-based teaching: a rejoinder to Martyn Hammersley', *British Educational Research Journal*, **23**(4), 405–19.

Hedges, L. V. (1992) 'Meta-analysis', *Journal of Educational Statistics*, **17**(4), 279–96.

Hillage, J., Pearson, R., Anderson, A. and Tamkin, P. (1998) *Excellence in Research on Schools, Research Report RR74*, Department for Education and Employment, Sudbury: DfEE Publications.

Hunter, J. E. and Schmidt, F. L. (1995) 'The impact of data-analysis methods on cumulative research knowledge: statistical significance testing, confidence intervals and meta-analysis', *Evaluation and the Health Professions*, **18**(4), 408–27.

Kimmel, A. J. (1988) *Ethics and Values in Applied Social Research*, Beverly Hills: Saga Publications.

Knowles, M. (1990) *The Adult Learner: A Neglected Species*, Houston: Gulf Publishing Company.

Kulik, J. and Kulik, C. C. (1989) 'Meta-analysis in education', *International Journal of Educational Research*, **13**(3), 220.

Laing, R. D. (1965) *The Divided Self*, Harmondsworth: Penguin.

Le Grand, J. and Illsley, R. (1986) 'The measurement of inequality in health', paper presented to a meeting of the *British Association for the Advancement of Science*, Bristol, 1–5 September 1986.

Macbeth, H. (ed.) (1996) *Health Outcomes Reviewed: Biological and Sociological Aspects*, Oxford: Oxford University Press.

Mehan, H. (1977) *Learning Lessons*, Cambridge, MA: Harvard University Press.

Mehan, H., Villanueva, I., Hubbard, L. and Lintz, A. (1996) *Constructing School Success*, Cambridge: Cambridge University Press.

Milwain, C. (1998) *Assembling, Maintaining and Disseminating a Social and Educational Controlled Trials Register (SECTR): A Collaborative Endeavour*, Oxford: UK Cochrane Centre.

Newcombe, F. and Ratcliff, G. (1979) 'Long term psychological consequences of cerebral lesions', in Gazzangia, M. (ed.), *Handbook of Behavioural Neurobiology*, **2**, Chapter 16, New York: Plenum Press.

Norris, N. (1996) 'Professor Hargreaves, the TTA and evidence-based practice', *British Educational Research Association Newsletter*, Research Intelligence, Number 57, 2–4 July.

Oakley, A. and Roberts, H. (eds) (1996) *Evaluating Social Interventions*, Ilford, Essex: Barnardos.

Oakley, A. (1998) 'Experimentation in social science: the case of health promotion', *Social Sciences in Health*, **4**(2), 73–88.

Petrosino, A. J., Rounding, C., McDonald, S. and Chalmers, I. (1999) 'Improving Systematic Reviews of Evaluations: Preliminary Efforts to Assemble a Social, Psychological and Educational Controlled Trials Register (SPECTR)', paper prepared for the meeting on Research Synthesis and Public Policy, University College, London, 15–16 July 1999.

Preiss, R. W. (1988) *Meta-Analysis: A Bibliography of Conceptual Issues and Statistical Methods*, Annandale, VA: Speech Communication Association.

Rosenthal, R. (1995) 'Interpreting and evaluating meta-analysis', *Evaluation and the Health Professions*, **18**(4), 393–407.

Sackett, D. L., Rosenberg, W., Gray, J. A. M., Haynes, R. B. and Richardson, W. (1996) 'Evidence-based medicine: what it is and what it isn't', *British Medical Journal*, **312**, 71–2.

Sacks, O. (1990) 'Neurology and the soul', *New York Review of Books*, **37**(18), 44–50.

Samphier, M. L., Robertson, C. and Bloor, M. J. (1988) 'A possible artefactual component in specific cause mortality gradients. Social class variations in the clinical accuracy of death certificates', *Journal of Epidemiology and Community Health*, **42**(2), 138–43.

Silverman, D. (1987) *Communication and Medical Practice: Social Relations in the Clinic*, London and Newbury Park: Sage Publications.

Spindler, D. (ed.) (1982) *Doing the Ethnography of Schooling*, New York: Rinehart and Winston.

Strong, P. M. (1979) *The Ceremonial Order of the Clinic: Parents, Doctors and Medical Bureaucracies*, London: Routledge and Kegan Paul.

Tooley, J. and Darby, D. (1998) *Education Research: An Ofsted Critique*, London: OFSTED.

Veatch, R. M. (1989) *Medical Ethics*, London: Jones and Bartlett.

Weiss, B. D. (1982) 'Confidentiality expectations of patients, physicians and medical students', *Journal of the American Medical Association*, **247**(19), 2695–7.

Wilkinson, R. G. (1986) 'Socio-economic differences in morality: interpreting the data on their size and trends', in Wilkinson, R. G. (ed.), *Class and Health: Research and Longitudinal Data*, London: Tavistock.

Willis, P. (1977) *Learning to Labour: How Working Class Kids Get Working Class Jobs*, Westmead: Saxon House.

Chapter 20

Accessing the evidence: towards the research-informed age

Elizabeth Bird

Commissioned for this volume (2000).

> The essence of professional development, and especially of its education component, is that it involves the learning of an independent, evidence-informed and constructively critical approach to practice within a public framework of professional values and accountability.
>
> (Bolam, 1999, p. 3)

> Educationalists at all levels need to be able to . . . know where and how to find evidence systematically and comprehensively using the electronic (computer-based) and non-electronic (print) media.
>
> (Davies, 1999, p. 109)

Introduction

Calls have been made for teaching to move towards evidence-based or research-based practice. A review of educational research *Excellence in Research on Schools* (Hillage *et al.*, 1998) commissioned in England by the Department for Education and Employment (DfEE) concluded that 'the actions and decisions of policy-makers and practitioners are insufficiently informed by research'. The DfEE stated (Sebba, 2000) that within five years they wished to be in a position in which:

- Research evidence will be central to the development of policy and practice.
- Teachers are able to draw readily on the findings of research.

Discussions on evidence-based practice have highlighted particular issues, most particularly the quality of educational research, and what are seen as its failings – in particular the lack of cumulative evidence (Hargreaves, 1996) and a failure of researchers to disseminate their findings.

There is also considerable debate about the extent to which research studies and research findings can provide solutions for problems in classroom practice, or point towards changes in practice that will produce improvement. There are robust and coherent arguments in terms of the highly context specific nature of teaching and learning that contend that solutions that are found to work in one situation may have

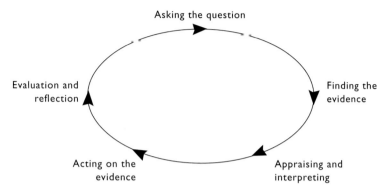

Figure 20.1 Steps in evidence-based healthcare

little or no applicability to others. Hargreaves's (1999) discussion of the transferability (between persons) and transposability (between places) of knowledge or practice is useful here. In policy terms, however, there seems general agreement in many countries that it is desirable for practice in education to be, in some way, evidence- or research-based.

Starting from this premise, a major consideration is how practitioners are to access the research and other evidence. How can they find out about the whole range of options that are suggested by different research studies (including those whose findings run contrary to the political agenda, since these may be less vigorously promoted and less enthusiastically disseminated) in order to identify those that may be most applicable to their own situations?

I suggest that it is useful to consider two different ways that teachers may wish to encounter and to use research evidence, and that require different (but overlapping) approaches to collecting information; I shall refer to these as *search* and *monitoring*.

The *search* approach reflects the view the University of Oxford's Master's programme in Evidence-based healthcare, which represents evidence-based practice as shown above (Critical Skills Appraisal Programme, 1999; see also Alison Hill's chapter in this book, Figure 18.3).

Although this is represented as a cyclic process, their approach clearly states that the starting point is the identification of a problem that leads to defining a question. This produces a need for a *search* for research evidence that may be helpful in answering that question.

The *monitoring* approach to evidence-based practice has a different starting point: that of research information, which leads to the identification of a problem or suggests an innovation in practice. This requires practitioner awareness of current research, some of which may throw new light on their practice or suggest changes even where a problem (or information gap) had not been identified. This level

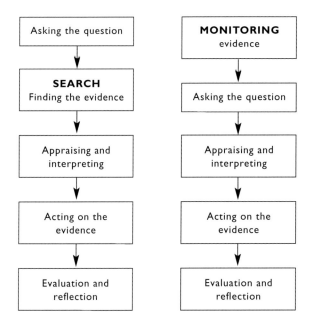

Figure 20.2 Search and monitoring patterns in evidence-based practice

of 'keeping in touch' with research requires a different approach to evidence – an ongoing monitoring of research publications.

The two approaches can be contrasted as being *problem-led* in the case of the search model, and as *research-led* in the monitoring approach. They can be represented as shown above.

These two patterns are inter-related: in particular, the identification of a question within the monitoring pattern may lead to the adoption of a search pattern as further research evidence is sought. Nevertheless, the distinction is a useful one in terms of the types of access to research materials that are required.

Search

Consider first the *search* for research findings in response to a specific question. This may be a question identified by an individual teacher, by a department or faculty, or by senior management within the school. Little evidence is likely to be found within the school itself. There are very large numbers of educational research journals, with many different foci, and it is unlikely, given the budgetary restraints, that any school would subscribe to many of these. Furthermore, the majority of these periodicals are not available in most public libraries. Even if there are links with academic libraries in which research journals can be consulted, the time and travel considerations posed by hand searching research journals within a university library do not encourage frequent consultation of the research literature.

On-line databases

It is more efficient, in terms of time and of breadth of access, if initial searches for research evidence can be carried out electronically, from within the school itself, or by an individual from home. Although, in many cases, searching of on-line databases is not available without subscription, increasing amounts of research information are freely available via the Internet.

BIDS (Bath Information and Data Services,[1] password required) is the best known and most widely used bibliographic service for the academic community in the UK, providing academic institutions with access to bibliographic data, scholarly publications and research data. BIDS provides access to key databases. BIDS Education gives access to the British Education Index (BEI) and the Educational Resources Information Centre (ERIC). The BEI describes itself as 'the authoritative index to the contents of UK education journals'. At the beginning of 1998, the Index database contained 89,000 references to journal articles, with about 5000 references being added each year. It is straightforward to search the BEI for references on a particular topic, to limit and combine searches. From this, a list of journal articles can be selected. In some cases, but by no means all, abstracts of the journal articles are available. This is invaluable in choosing articles that have direct relevance to the posed problem, or to the particular context. Selected articles can be saved to disk or emailed.

The Social Sciences Citation Index available from the Web of Science site[2] (password required), may also be of use although it does not have a specific educational focus. This database provides a helpful addition to subject searches: citations searches provide a useful method of searching forward from a particular article. A citation search lists articles within a database that have quoted the particular article within their references. This makes it possible to follow up on a particular piece of research: to look for subsequent developments in related areas. The EBSCO database Academic Services Elite[3] covers a wide range of fields, including education, and provides the full text of some articles.

These databases are available on a site licence that provides unlimited access to staff and students at academic institutions. But controlled access is a disadvantage for teachers in schools or colleges: in order to make use of these databases teachers need full access to a higher education institution (HEI) library. Some academic libraries may give reading or borrowing rights to local teachers, but this is unlikely to include access to on-line resources. The UK higher education and research libraries site[4] can be used to find information about individual academic libraries and access to them. For example, linking to the University of Bristol library web pages indicates that local teachers are entitled to borrow books from the education library on payment of a fee. However, there is no indication that this arrangement would give access to on-line databases. De Montfort University libraries indicate that non-members of the university may register as library users, but that the 'PC and other computer facilities provided by the Library are for use only by DMU students, staff and research students'.

The Online Computer Library Center (OCLC) First Search service[5] (password required) also provides access to a number of databases. WorldCat provides a world-wide catalogue of publications, mainly books, while Article First is a database of journal articles; neither of these databases has an education focus. This service has the advantage that it provides links to a number of commercial ways in which to 'get' the articles, including mail and fax.

Another option is the ERA database (Educational Research Abstracts),[6] which, on its introduction in 2000, scanned over 700 journals. This database contains hypertext links to full-text articles and to document delivery services. However, like the BEI and OCLC, ERA is available only on subscription.

Free on-line databases

Other databases, for which subscription is not required, are available. Of particular importance is the Educational Resources Information Centre (ERIC), which is a national (USA) information system. Although access to ERIC is provided via BIDS, it can also be freely accessed via the Internet.[7] The ERIC database is the world's largest source of education information and contains more than a million abstracts of documents and journal articles on education research and practice. ERIC enables searches to be mapped to subject headings, and exploded, so that related articles are more likely to be found. Despite coverage of many UK journals, the majority of research papers do reflect the USA context, and may be of less obvious immediate relevance to UK teachers. Obtaining copies of ERIC documents in libraries in the UK may also prove more difficult, although the use of international document delivery services may be an option. Publications with an ERIC Document (ED) number can be ordered on-line: this, of course, has cost implications.

COPAC[8] is an internationally accessible catalogue that provides free access to the merged On-line Public Access Catalogues (OPACs) of a number of large research libraries in the UK and Ireland. The majority of COPAC records are for books. The database can be searched for title words, author and organisation names, subject words, date, language and library, and records can be downloaded directly into Personal Bibliographic Software. The British Library OPAC[9] can also be searched free of charge, in order to find materials held in the major reference and document supply collections of the British Library.

The Ingenta journals database[10] provides access to over a million articles from professional and specialist publications linked to full-text articles in Ingenta Journals. Ingenta can be searched free, and links for document delivery of full text are provided. Subscribers can download the full text of articles.

Another useful source of information that has free access, and the valuable attribute of providing full text free of charge, is Education-line. Set up in the UK under the national Electronic Libraries programme, Education-line was launched in early 1997. It provides an indexed, full-text electronic archive of conference and working papers, reports, policy and discussion documents and early research results in the field of education and training.[11]

This is particularly useful in providing access to unpublished, 'grey' literature that may otherwise be difficult to locate. Education Line is now supported by the BEI and Education Line documents are listed in the BEI database.

Quality

Apart from the issue of access to educational databases, Davies has raised the issue of quality:

> the data bases which serve educational research are less developed, and contain lower-quality filters, than those found in medical and health care research. . . . There is an issue of improving the reporting and indexing of educational research and changing its reporting practices.
>
> (Davies, 1999, p. 115)

While this may indeed be the case (although we should note that even in the case of medicine less than a third of the world's medical journals are routinely indexed in the major electronic databases),[12] we should be aware that this is a situation that can change rapidly. It is likely, given the current climate, that significant improvements in the provision of educational databases will occur within a short time-scale. The DfEE (Sebba, 1999; Blunkett, 2000) has commissioned a new Centre for Evidence Informed Policy and Practice to establish a research database that is accessible to all education practitioners and policy-makers.

Other sources of research information

Searches for research information related to a specific question may also make use of a number of other sources of research information that are freely available through the world wide web. The *Times Educational Supplement* web site,[13] which can be accessed free of charge, has an archive section that can be searched to find references to any particular topic. (The Times Higher Education Supplement Internet Service,[14] however, requires a subscription in order to access its archives.)

The Key Information and Statistics pages of the Department of Education for Northern Ireland (DENI)[15] contain three sections of useful information: a statistical press release library, research briefings and a compendium of Northern Ireland Educational statistics. In Scotland, the Scottish Executive Education Department (SEED) Research unit has set up the server 'Educational Research in Scotland',[16] which is designed as an information point on educational research in Scotland, giving access to detailed summaries of research.

For England and Wales, the DfEE web site provides reports on commissioned research.[17] The Teacher Training Agency web-site has a research section that reports on research findings: these are likely to be in areas of national concern. For example, at the time of writing, the research section of the TTA web site[18] carries reports on large-scale studies commissioned by the TTA to consider effective teaching of literacy and numeracy. Summaries of report findings are available on the site, together with contact details of researchers from whom the complete report can be obtained. This provides rapid, free access to research findings – however, there is the caveat that such research may reflect the current political agenda. Ofsted[19] and the Qualifications and Curriculum Authority (QCA)[20] web sites may also be useful, and the National Grid for Learning[21] may provide links to helpful research.

The National Foundation for Educational Research (NFER) describes itself as

> an independent body undertaking research and development projects in all sectors of the public education system. It aims to gather, analyse and disseminate research-based information with a view to improving education and training.[22]

This site provides a catalogue of publications for purchase, but also contains summaries of research reports and conference papers that can be downloaded. These reports include reviews of research and annotated bibliographies. At the time of writing, for example, the publications include reviews of 'Streaming, Setting and Grouping by Ability' and 'Factors affecting the take-up of post-16 options'.

The NFER site also provides the Focus on Educational Research database that 'seeks to include all recently completed and ongoing research in the United Kingdom, in education and related fields'. In order to compile this register, the NFER collects information annually from research institutions, including universities, specialised institutes and government agencies. On-line searches of this database are not possible, but NFER library staff will carry out searches on specific topics. Requests for searches can be sent by telephone, letter or email.[23] It may be possible to obtain photocopies of journal articles from this source. At the time of writing, a nominal charge of £5.00 is made for each search, and each record produced costs 25p. Focus on Educational Research is also available in printed form. REGARD[24] is a bibliographic database of UK research funded by the Economic and Social Research Council, which can be freely accessed and provides brief summaries of funded research.

Searching for information

For those searching the web for information beyond that available in the main databases, sites that include a web directory, such as Education 2000,[25] are useful in providing links to many education sites, for example to teachers' union and subject organisation web sites, which may contain useful research evidence.

The use of Internet gateways is especially helpful. Two UK gateways that are likely to be of help in the field of education are National Information Systems and Services (NISS)[26] and the Social Sciences Information Gateway (SOSIG). SOSIG 'aims to offer social scientists a quick and easy way of finding quality networked information that can support their work'.[27] The SOSIG Internet Catalogue offers users the chance to read descriptions of resources available over the Internet and to access those resources directly. The Catalogue provides links to many resource types including articles, books, government publications, discussion groups, organisations, research projects, etc.

Accessing primary research

In the search for research information, the use of on-line databases is only the first step, and the subsequent task of consulting those documents selected as being the most relevant is much more problematic for the school-based researcher, as it requires access to the publications themselves. This problem is greatly reduced where journal articles and other publications can be accessed on-line in full text. Many journal articles are available on-line although there is generally a charge. For example, a selection of peer-reviewed education journals is available on-line from the Catchword service.[28] The database can be searched and documents purchased on-line, and electronic subscriptions to individual periodicals may be taken out. A few on-line journals are available free of charge (see, for example, the USA National Forum site[29]), but these have no guarantee of quality, and frequently do not provide an archive.

Library access

Many other publications are not available electronically, and access to library and document delivery services is an essential. Use of local academic libraries is one way of accessing journal articles or books; it may be possible to borrow books, but journals will generally need to be consulted in the library, or photocopies made of the relevant article. It is possible, if an academic library is to be used, to save time by consulting the library OPAC to establish in advance whether the library holds the material. Most academic library catalogues can be consulted in this way.[30]

If a local library does not hold the required book or periodical, these can be obtained through document delivery services. Academic libraries will provide document delivery services for staff and students, but less often for other users. However, public libraries provide document delivery services that are usually very low cost, although it may take some time to obtain the publication. Information about those public libraries with a web presence in the UK is freely available.[31] In some cases, as already noted, document delivery can be used through on-line access but the fees charged for these services can be high. Commercial services are highly priced because of the need to pay both copyright fees and VAT. For example, at the time of writing, the British Library Lexicon service[32] charges £9.50 per item, plus an additional copyright fee depending on the item ordered. For an article from *Educational Review*, for example, the copyright charge is an additional £9.00. VAT is charged on top of this.

Monitoring

Monitoring of research can take place in a number of ways. The following quotation from a teacher in a study by Hannan *et al.* illustrates one of these:

> I am most likely to read about and be influenced by findings in the publications to which I subscribe, rather than in books. The former are received regularly, easily accessible and often relevant. Articles are useful – sometimes because they point out things of which I was previously unaware, sometimes because they highlight tendencies which I myself have observed (it helps to know you're not the only one!) and I can be challenged to adapt my own practice. This may only be in a small way but the regular reminders from the *Times Educational Supplement*, etc do assist the 'ordinary classroom teacher' in keeping informed, flexible, more in tune with the needs of pupils and more able to denounce some of the myths prevalent amongst those less involved in education.
>
> (Hannan *et al.*, 1998, p. 21)

The regular reading of journals and the *TES* by individual teachers constitutes a form of monitoring. In a large school, the total number of journals monitored in this way may be considerable. The knowledge of research evidence acquired through monitoring of this sort may be largely confined to the individuals reading the publications, but this need not be the case. Monitoring of this sort can be given a more formal status and be made more systematic, also the research findings can be disseminated *within the school*. Individual staff can be responsible for monitoring particular publications on a regular basis (whether their own subscription or a school subscription), and for reporting back to other members of staff. Whether this takes place within the whole school, year team, faculty, or other group will depend on the school itself. There is an important leadership role in organising this systematic monitoring and in allocating time for feedback to group(s) of staff. However, even systematic monitoring of this sort is unlikely to provide the sort of coverage of the research literature that is required if a staff is to remain fully informed of current research findings. In particular, in secondary schools, Hannan's work suggests that most of the journals to which teachers or departments subscribe are likely to be subject related rather than general education publications (Hannan *et al.*, 1998, pp. 4–5), so that a whole body of evidence may be missed.

An additional way of monitoring, but one that may involve greater time commitment from an individual, or from all individuals within a staff team, is to use alerting services. An example of a journal alerting service is Scholarly Articles Research Alerting (SARA).[33] This service is free and provides a useful tool for monitoring research publications by delivering contents pages by email in advance of the printed edition. It is possible to receive contents pages for selected individual journals or for all those within particular subject clusters (e.g. *Education Research, Teacher Education,*

Medical Education, etc.). Some other organisations provide alerting services; for example, the NFER will email details of new reports as these are produced. Book shops, for example, Blackwells Online Bookshop[34] will also email information about new books in chosen subject categories. Publishers' catalogues may also be useful in this respect.

There are organisational and leadership decisions to be made here. Are contents pages to be emailed to a school address that can be accessed by all members of staff? Are all staff expected to check through this information, or is one (or more) individual member of staff to be responsible for regular scanning of new contents pages, and for selecting relevant materials? Who is to obtain full-text copies of relevant research, and how are these to be paid for? Who will critically read and appraise the published research articles and disseminate their findings to the staff?

In some cases, this sort of monitoring already takes place in a highly organised fashion. In one infant school:

> recent and relevant research was apparently reviewed by the staff as a whole on a regular basis, with meetings of the staff and in-service events focused on research findings.
>
> (Hannan *et al.*, 1998, p. 11)

Activities at this school included books being 'dished out' to staff for them to read and to offer critiques at staff meetings. All members of staff were involved, including NNEB and support staff. Staff co-ordinators had a role in reading incoming materials and in disseminating relevant information to staff, both in written form and at staff meetings.

Attendance at conferences may be another way of keeping in touch with the research evidence or of searching for the answer to particular questions. Conferences used by researchers to disseminate their findings are likely to become an increasing source of practitioner information given that

> Funding agencies insist more and more on policy relevance, on negotiation by researchers with prospective 'users', on explicit plans for dissemination designed to maximise impact.
>
> (Hammersley, 1997, p. 141)

Yet again, however, conference attendance has cost implications, especially when supply cover has to be paid for, and this may severely restrict this type of activity.

A further possibility worth mentioning here is the use of networks, and especially of electronic networks, in monitoring. National or local teacher networks could provide a forum for teachers to share the research evidence of which they have become aware. Facilities of this sort could be especially valuable in sharing the findings of school-based action research.

Systematic reviews

Thus far, we have considered practitioner access to the primary evidence – to the research itself. In terms of the constraints of time and access under which teachers practise, accessing primary research evidence need not be an initial step in the search for evidence. Rather, reviews, syntheses and meta-analyses[35] of primary research should provide teachers with rapid access to the evidence they require. The Hillage report identified, as an issue in dissemination, the 'absence of time and intermediary support available to both policy-makers and practitioners to help them access research' (Hillage *et al.*, 1998, p. xi).

There are approaches that can be used that avoid going straight to the primary research: in particular to look at reviews published in periodicals and research reviews such as those produced by the NFER, mentioned above. A particularly helpful feature of ERIC is the existence of ERIC Digests, which are two-page research syntheses. There are currently more than 1600 Digests, and approximately 100 new titles are produced each year. These digests provide useful summaries of research, and can be downloaded free of charge. However, useful though existing reviews may be, it has been claimed that many of the existing published reviews are not systematic.

Over the last ten years, the medical profession has developed systematic reviews that track down large volumes of relevant evidence and appraise them using robust and explicit methods. This kind of research can be accessed by the medical profession through the international Cochrane Collaboration[36] and the United Kingdom NHS Centre for reviews and dissemination.[37] The Cochrane Collaboration prepares, maintains and provides access to systematic reviews of the effects of healthcare interventions. Reviews are prepared by international collaborative review groups, which are responsible for identifying as high a proportion as possible of all the studies relevant to their particular focus. This includes hand searching through medical journals for accounts that are not indexed in the major electronic databases such as MEDLINE and EMBASE. The reviewers then assemble, appraise and sometimes synthesise the data. They are supported in this by groups of methodologists that have been formed to work on improving the validity and precision of systematic reviews.

As Davies rightly points out,

> Educational research has also lacked a centralised data-base for preparation, maintenance and dissemination of systematic reviews of education such as the Cochrane collaboration.
>
> (Davies, 1999, p. 16)

An increase in the number of available research syntheses is an important element in the establishment of a research-informed teaching culture. However, there is a caveat here. The body responsible for compiling such syntheses must not be seen to be acting in self-interest, or pursuing its own agenda, but must have clear and transparent methods that can be seen to be systematic and, in so far as it is possible, objective.

The Campbell Collection, formally established in February 2000,

> is an emerging international effort that aims to help people make well-informed decisions by preparing, maintaining and promoting access to systematic reviews of studies on the effects of social and educational policies and practices.[38]

In England, the DfEE's commissioned Centre for Evidence-Informed Policy and Practice in Education has responsibility not only for an education database, but also for registering review groups of researchers and users to undertake systematic reviews of educational research. 'The aim of the centre is to make the key lessons from research much more accessible to and usable by policy makers and practitioners such as teachers' (Wicks, 1999). In her paper presented to the British Educational Research Association in 1999, Sebba stated that the Centre would make evidence available in a variety of ways, suggestions being:

- Comprehensive list of references on a topic
- Full systematic review of evidence where each study has been subjected to quality criteria by the review group
- Half a page of key points arising from the systematic review that might be used as a basis for discussion in a school staff meeting.

(Sebba, 1999, p. 2)

This type of provision should enable teachers to access evidence in a particular area of concern without having to find and read large numbers of original papers and reports. Where time is of considerable significance, this approach is of enormous value.

This article has outlined some routes to accessing evidence that may inform practice in education. Learning how to access evidence may be considered as a first step in practitioner professional development towards a research-informed age.

Endnotes

1 http://www.bids.ac.uk/
2 http://wos.mimas.ac.uk/
3 http://search.global.epnet.com
4 http://www.ex.ac.uk/library/uklibs.html
5 http://firstsearch.uk.oclc.org/
6 http://www.tandf.co.uk/era
7 For example at http://ericir.syr.edu/Eric/index.html
8 http://copac.ac.uk/copac/
9 http://www.bl.uk
10 http://www.ingenta.com
11 http://www.leeds.ac.uk/educol
12 Figure quoted on the Cochrane Collaboration web site http://www.cochrane.org/

13 http://www.tes.co.uk
14 http://thesis.co.uk
15 http://www.deni.gov.uk
16 http://www.hmis.scotoff.gov.uk/riu/index.html
17 http://www.dfee.gov.uk/research/originalindex.htm
18 http://www.teach-tta.gov.uk/research
19 http://www.ofsted.gov.uk/ofsted.htm
20 http://www.qca.org.uk.
21 http://vtc.ngfl.gov.uk/
22 http://www.nfer.ac.uk
23 enquiries@nfer.ac.uk
24 http://www.regard.ac.uk/
25 http://www.education2000.co.uk/index.html
26 http://www.niss.ac.uk
27 http://sosig.ac.uk
28 http://www.catchword.com
29 http://www.nationalforum.com
30 http://www.niss.ac.uk/lis/opacs.html
31 http://dspace.dial.pipex.com/town/square/ac940/weblibs.html
32 http://www.bl.uk/services/bsds/dsc/lexicon.html
33 http://www.tandf.co.uk/sara
34 http://bookshop.blackwell.co.uk
35 Meta analysis: technique in systematic reviews of experimental and quasi-experimental studies that involves combining the original data generated by different but very similar studies, and using statistical techniques to create a single estimate of the results.
36 http://www.cochrane.org/
37 http://nhscrd.york.ac.uk/
38 http://campbell.gse.upenn.edu/

References

Blunkett, D. (2000) ESRC Lecture, 2 February. Reported at: http://dfee.gov.uk/news/00/043. htm (accessed 25 April 2000).

Bolam, R. (1999) 'The emerging conceptualisation of INSET: does this constitute professional development?', paper presented at SCETT annual conference, 26–28 November, Dunchurch, Rugby, 3.

Critical Skills Appraisal Programme (CASP) and Health Care Libraries Unit (HCLU) (1999) *Evidence-based Health Care. An Open Learning Resource for Health Care Practitioners, Unit 2*, Luton: Chiltern Press, 2.

Davies, P. (1999) 'What is evidence-based education?', *British Journal of Educational Studies*, **47**(2), 109.

Hammersley, M. (1997) 'Educational research and teaching: a response to David Hargreaves' TTA lecture', *British Educational Research Journal*, **23**(2), 141.

Hannan, A., Enright, H. and Ballard, P. (1998) *Using Research: The Results of a Pilot Study Comparing Teachers, General Practitioners and Surgeons*, Education-line, http://www.leeds. ac.uk/educol, 21 (accessed 25 April 2000).

Hargreaves, D. (1996) *Teaching as a Research-based Profession: Possibilities and Prospects*, TTA Lecture.

Hargreaves, D. (1999) 'The knowledge-creating school', *British Journal of Educational Studies*, **47**(2), 129.

Hillage, J., Pearson, R., Anderson, A. and Tamkin, P. (1998) *Excellence in Research on Schools*, London: DfEE, xi.

Sebba, J. (1999) 'Developing evidence-informed policy and practice in education', paper presented at the British Educational Research Association Conference, University of Sussex at Brighton, 2–5 September.

Sebba, J. (2000) 'Educational research and the role of central government', paper presented at the conference Diversity or Control in Educational Research?, London: City University, 27 January, slide 12.

Wicks, M. (1999) Address to the Further Education Research Network Conference, 9 December. Reported at http://www.dfee.gov.uk/news/99/582.htm (accessed 25 April 2000).

Section 5

Education, communication, information and the future of professional development

Chapter 21

New technologies for teacher professional development

Ronald W. Marx, Phyllis C. Blumenfeld, Joseph S. Krajcik and Elliot Soloway

This is an edited version of an article previously published in *Teaching and Teacher Education*, **14**(1), January 1998.

Recent research on learning in classrooms (Newman *et al.*, 1989) and other settings (Lave and Wenger, 1991) suggests that learning is far more contextual, social and distributed than earlier models had proposed. Since teachers are also learners, these new models require that researchers and teacher educators reconsider their approaches to helping teachers rethink their teaching. Rather than focusing on delivering prescribed sets of behaviours or methods of instruction, efforts to foster teacher change and teacher learning should be more appropriately construed as social collaborations. By capitalising on participants' different capacities and expertise, teachers can construct understandings of innovation, situate problems of enactment within their own classrooms and develop a range of practices that are congruent with theory.

In this article, we briefly examine literature on teacher knowledge and professional development. We discuss how this literature can inform the design of three types of technology that can support teacher learning and professional development efforts, including multimedia, productivity tools, and telecommunication information systems, and we consider how these technologies can contribute to innovation efforts. Finally, we identify questions that remain to be addressed and speculate on possibilities for technology that are likely to arise in the near future.

Teacher knowledge

Borko and Putnam (1996) suggest that four central features of knowledge – that it is constructed, situated, social and distributed – should inform efforts to change teaching. What teachers take away from professional development efforts is based on their existing knowledge and beliefs. Rather than having information delivered to them, teachers need to examine their beliefs about subject matter, student learning and instruction in the light of innovation. Efforts to help teachers examine assumptions include teacher journals (Calderhead, 1993); teacher autobiographies

(Knowles, 1992) action research (Feldman, 1996); and teachers' written case reports of their teaching (Scott, 1994). Other approaches rely on a knowledgeable other as a way to help teachers examine their beliefs and practice and the congruence between them (Fenstermacher and Richardson, 1993).

Teacher knowledge is situated in the context of classrooms and the events and activities of teaching. Much of teachers' knowledge is stored in terms of classroom events and how to enact tasks that teachers accomplish in classroom settings (Carter and Doyle, 1989), not in terms of abstract principles. Its genre is much more like a narrative or story than an expository essay (Carter, 1993). Knowledge about teaching and practices related to this knowledge cannot be learned independently of the situation in which it will be used. Teachers cannot merely apply a set of predefined prescriptions, they need to plan and teach in order to tailor innovation to fit their unique circumstance, anticipating possible problems and devising strategies to deal with them.

Many prior instructional innovations have not considered the problems of classroom enactment or other impediments to the teacher's ability to make change. There are a myriad of reasons for this lacuna (Cohen and Barnes, 1993). One obvious set of barriers concerns cost and availability of models that illustrate new ways to teach and solve accompanying problems. If the knowledge held by researchers or expert teachers cannot simply be depicted as a set of abstract principles, as we argue above, then alternative forms of representation are needed. One form is the live enactment of teaching, accompanied by discussion and analysis of the events. It will be far too costly for widespread professional development to rely on this approach, even though some efforts do incorporate visits to other classrooms. However, as we illustrate below, new technologies can provide visions of enactments of innovations along with teachers' reflections and researchers' analyses to help their colleagues develop robust understanding of the innovation and its enactment.

Social elements, cultural practices and norms affect what we learn and know. To combat the isolation of teaching, many scholars have argued for increased interaction and collaboration among teachers (Lieberman, 1990) as ways of adding important social elements to professional development. Collaboration among teacher colleagues and others provides several benefits. The cognitive benefits include the opportunity for teachers to gain access to new information, clarify their ideas and beliefs, examine different ways of thinking about teaching, and reflect on their own practice (Bruer, 1995). The emotional benefits of collaboration include support for teachers' struggles with new approaches, their willingness to experiment with ways of teaching for which they may not be very skilled, and the courage to take risks in the face of organisational or community pressures against experimentation (Firestone and Pennell, 1997).

In addition, collaborative efforts between researchers and teachers can contribute to the learning of both groups (Bickel and Hattrup, 1995). Researchers bring new knowledge to inform teachers of new practices, along with concepts and language from research that can help propel conversation. Teachers bring experience with students and contexts, knowledge of the limits imposed by curriculum frameworks and craft knowledge of the daily rhythm and flow of life in schools. Collaboration in this vein is not a top-down model of what constitutes good practice. Rather, it is a process of group design and problem solving constructed by the participants.

A corollary to the claim that knowledge is social is that it is distributed among group members. Certainly, teachers need to master a repertoire of understandings and practices, but professional development must balance a focus on individual competence and on socially shared, collaborative activities that can support individual proficiency. The aim is to develop teachers who are adaptive learners and who have skills to attain competence and information when need arises rather than have everyone learn the same things at the same time. In operation, this might result in a division of efforts and roles that vary across time, but with the goal that all participants enhance their competence and knowledge. Because knowledge and competence are distributed far wider than any individual teacher's professional or social network, access to widely distributed knowledge is essential. Traditionally, this access has been limited by time, resources and technology. Resource limitations restrict access because teachers rarely have the time or money to visit other schools or to attend enough teacher conferences and workshops in order to learn new practices. Similarly, until recently, the predominant medium to access distributed expertise has been print publications, such as teacher magazines and journals. New technologies, including the world wide web, electronic mail and multiple user domains hold the promise of gaining access to distributed expertise that has been unavailable.

We used these ideas about teacher learning and results of our own experience to develop a set of interpersonal experiences to help teachers learn project-based science (PBS). PBS is an approach to curriculum and instruction based on constructivist views of learning that is consistent with recent reform efforts in science education. Our approach relies on cycles of collaboration, enactment, reflection and adaptation that extend over time. The goal is for teachers to construct new possibilities for instruction, better conceptual understanding of the subject matter, new under-standings of the premises underlying the innovation, recognition of challenges and dilemmas, and practical knowledge of strategies for meeting challenges in the classroom. Fidelity to a particular set of instructional behaviours is not the desired result of professional development. Instead, our approach draws on Richardson's (1990) position regarding the development of 'warranted practice' where teachers meld practical concerns with theoretical knowledge. Ultimately, the aim is for teachers to use a range of practices that are congruent with the principles of innovation and that are tailored to their own situational constraints and personal preferences.

We have designed and developed technologies for teachers based on the principles of learner-centred design (Soloway et al., 1994). Learner-centred design recognises the fact that learners differ from experienced users of new technologies and from knowledgeable experts. It also is based on constructivist philosophies of learning; rather than respond to didactic presentations, the technology needs to engage learners in generative learning activities. Software needs to scaffold complex cognition such as organising, synthesising, problem solving and applying new understanding. Also, technology needs to adjust and grow with the teacher as it addresses different levels of proficiency with technology and supports changing levels of content understanding.

Designing multimedia

Multimedia systems have many potential benefits for teachers. A number of systems that portray the difficult nature of teaching through video-based cases have been designed. These systems differ in the amount of structure the developers impose to the cases, ranging from relatively unstructured to tightly structured; the length of time that is portrayed in the case, ranging from a single lesson to an eight-week project; and the purpose of the case, such as illustrating a teaching philosophy or a particular teaching technique. Several issues need to be addressed in the design of multimedia systems that consider what is known about teacher learning. Using these principles, we have designed an application called CaPPs (Casebook of Project Practices) to introduce teachers to our PBS innovation. Five design principles guided our work.

First, the use of cases has been advocated as a way to convey the rich and complex nature of teaching (Shulman, 1992). Cases are productive means of effectively conveying issues in teaching because they capture the richness and complexity in classroom situations. Cases are accessible to teachers because they represent teaching as contextualised events (Carter, 1993) and they provide concrete examples for teachers, not just abstract theory (Shulman, 1992). Technology can be organised around cases that illustrate how teachers resolved challenges of the innovation's features. In addition, because multiple instances are important if teachers are to understand and develop a range of practices congruent with the premises of the innovation, several different cases of how teachers meet the same challenges need to be included.

Second, because teachers learn from realistic portrayals (Carter, 1993), video clips should come from actual classrooms and cases should describe real teaching situations, not fabricated ones. Video should depict teachers from a variety of backgrounds and contexts in terms of class composition and size, school resources and locations. Technology should contain overviews and commentary that address the background of teachers, classrooms and curriculum portrayed in video.

Third, teacher knowledge is represented in the language of classroom activities and events, rather than as a set of propositions and prescriptions (Carter, 1993; Richardson, 1990). Thus, the premises of an innovation need to be cast as illustrations of practice. In the development of CaPPs, we approached this issue by describing features and associated challenges that serve as the basis of conversation. In technology, these features are concretised through video that illustrate how teachers meet the challenges. The video helps create visions of alternative practice that are more powerful than text alone.

Fourth, teachers are highly influenced by their own and others' stories (Carter, 1993; Shulman, 1992). Teachers need reassurance to support continued risk taking as they try to change practice to accommodate an innovation. Therefore, technology should contain commentary by teachers about their intents, constraints, rationales and understandings. Seeing video and reading case reports of how others have struggled and how they resolved dilemmas and overcame challenges, encourages teachers as they face the difficult task of altering practice.

Fifth, teachers need to be thoughtful as they consider cases and watch video. Commentary and prompts associated with video help focus attention on issues of particular relevance in the video and also raise more general issues that teachers can consider as they think about enactment in their own classroom.

Teachers' experiences with CaPPs

We have studied teachers using CaPPs and have encountered a number of useful findings. Teachers' conceptual and technological backgrounds influence how they interpret and use information in CaPPs. More able users and more knowledgeable teachers can do more with CaPPs and participate in different kinds of conversations. Teachers who are more familiar with instruction similar to PBS draw on this experience and knowledge to interpret the video and text. Teachers who have more experience using computers have less initial difficulty understanding and using the system. However, after three or four sessions with CaPPs, most teachers are able to navigate among the screens.

CaPPs creates opportunities for teachers to collaborate. Viewing clips and reading text often prompt teachers to share strategies to enact a feature. After viewing a clip, teachers frequently interpret the clip, focusing on important aspects of what was occurring. Then they consider what they might do in their own classroom, focusing on strategies they might use. Viewing clips prompts teachers to discuss the meaning of a particular feature, exploring whether what they observed was a good example of PBS pedagogy.

It takes teachers time to determine where in the system they can get information concerning questions posed in the task. Generally, teachers emphasise analysis of individual clips rather than thinking about several simultaneously. We have seldom observed teachers synthesising how a series of clips provided insight into a particular challenge. For instance, we have not seen teachers synthesising how the individual clips of getting started, working in small groups, and sharing in large groups provided insight into the challenge 'How to help students design investigations'. In addition, participants seldom considered how the particular challenge was related to other challenges posed by the feature around which the case was written.

The way professional development tasks are defined influences how teachers use and understand CaPPs. We have created tasks to help teachers explore the components of CaPPs so that they could navigate the system and examine what the video and text fields contain.

New directions in multimedia

If they are to capitalise on the potential of the new technologies, developers must confront questions concerning design, use patterns, evaluation and pedagogy. For what instructional purposes are multimedia cases most appropriate and what are some of the possible limitations of using them? We believe that multimedia cases are good vehicles for presenting teachers with visions of what innovative teaching might look like. How can multimedia cases be constructed so that they grow with the development of teacher expertise? Is it possible that they become less useful as teachers' experience with enactment grows? Perhaps teachers need to move from an examination of existing cases to the creation of their own and the examination and discussion of colleagues' cases, so that the challenges and their possible solutions become real examples of professional problem solving and exchange.

In addition, there are questions about how to show change over time and what level of teacher proficiency to exhibit.

Other questions concern how to support learning. What structures and scaffolds are necessary? CaPPs offers written commentary by teachers in the video to help viewers interpret events and provide insight into teachers' intents, reactions and quandaries. It also provides workspace for writing. In CaPPs, teachers can create a personal journal that includes comments about cases, video imported from cases, or video of themselves and their own reactions. While there is evidence that teachers can profit from the reflection that comes from writing about practice, how teachers use the functionality and benefit from it in multimedia systems is not known. Finally, effective means have to be researched for helping teachers organise, store and retrieve their thoughts in order to help them in their inquiry about teaching.

At this time, there is not a sufficiently robust body of research findings about what teachers learn from different multimedia designs. Horserace comparisons among different systems are not likely to be productive. Rather, careful analyses of how teachers learn from multimedia and how they incorporate their learning into their daily practices will enable designers to create systems tailored to different teacher learning needs.

Designing productivity tools

Productivity tools based on new technologies have been developed for all professions. With respect to new computer-based technologies, productivity tools are software applications that enable professionals to do the routine, everyday tasks of their work more effectively and efficiently. However, tools designed specifically for teachers have been notoriously absent, aside from simple tools like classroom test authoring applications and lesson planning applications based on linear (i.e. objectives, methods, testing, reinforcement) approaches to lesson design. We have designed the Project Integration Visualisation Tool (PIViT) to aid in teacher planning. In contrast to more linear, narrow models of planning that emphasise objectives and methods, planning for innovation is an iterative design problem. The problem is how, as teachers work within particular conditions and constraints, they design experiences to help their students develop content understanding. The benefit of planning is not merely that teachers can implement the plan; rather teachers learn by thinking through what to teach and how to teach it, anticipating and solving potential difficulties (Clark, 1988). Expert teachers' plans are explicit and rich in inter-connections; they include details about teaching activities and possible alternatives, expected student understanding and behaviour and explicit routines for managing common classroom tasks and circumventing potential difficulties (Clark and Yinger, 1987). During planning, teachers create mental representations that can be changed during enactment based on classroom conditions, student reactions and their own evaluations of how their aims are being accomplished.

Productivity tools are not specific to any particular content. PIViT can be used to plan projects for any grade level and any subject in science (with minor adjust-ments, it can also be used for subjects other than science). Because it can be used in different science classes across different grades, teachers can become proficient users of the tool and knowledgeable about the innovation it supports. It has been revised several times based on studies of how teachers use it and the supports they need.

There are several reasons why a planning tool is an appropriate productivity technology for professional development. First, planning helps teachers understand the innovation as they attempt to contextualise it to their specific situation and as they provide warrants for their decisions. Through planning, particularly group planning that involves presentations of plans to other teachers in a professional development programme, teachers provide reasoned and argued justification for their decisions in light of various forms of knowledge (e.g. knowledge about students, classrooms, subject matter and curriculum frameworks). Second, planning helps teachers instantiate the innovation in practice and adapt it to their circumstances – planning makes learning about innovation real in teachers' professional lives. Third, planning is an authentic task for teachers; they have to plan in order to teach. Thus, planning is motivating. Teachers become intensely involved in professional development when it provides them with useful products (i.e. instructional plans for their classrooms). Fourth, a technological planning tool can serve as a common template that can be used by other teachers, not just the original planners, to think about the innovation. Presentations of plans to others capitalises on distributed knowledge – teachers learn from others. A fifth and related advantage is that the common template of planning tools like PIViT can be used to create communities of practice that share models of how innovation works in the rough and tumble of schools. For teachers who are newly introduced to an innovation, examining PIViT documents helps them understand how the innovation can be instantiated. The planning tool thus becomes a learning tool. As teachers gain expertise, libraries of planning documents, complete with annotations and extensions, constitute the lingua franca for the community of practice.

New directions productivity tools

PIViT can serve as the vehicle for enabling curriculum materials to be truly educative for teachers. Ball and Cohen (1996) argue that reform efforts driven by policy, including curriculum policy, will not take root unless the new curriculum is educative for teachers. But what does it mean to have educative policy and curriculum?

One answer to this question is that educative policy provides opportunities for directed learning on the part of teachers. By using PIViT, the curriculum plans might be set up so that they link to particular web sites or other material that can help teachers develop and learn new content knowledge. For example, concept maps show teachers' understanding of particular ideas. Referencing concept maps to other material and sharing both the maps and the reference material can serve to engage communities of teachers in discussing and learning new content. It is likely that 'knowledgeable others', that is, experts in new pedagogy, technology, science content and classroom instruction, will need to monitor and guide the discussion so that the teachers' new content learning conforms to accepted understanding in scientific (or other) fields and leads to the design of instructionally powerful projects for learners. In this manner, teachers' content learning develops hand-in-hand with their developing pedagogical content knowledge.

The planning document grows and changes based on teachers' use. As teachers try the plan in different contexts, they can annotate the plan based on what happened in their class by adding examples of student work, video of their students as they work and examples of artifacts and other assessments. Thus, teachers get the opportunity to compare and contrast plans and enactments that are situated and contextualised. We are not suggesting that teachers ought to be curriculum developers, but they need to be curriculum modifiers. To the extent that instructional activities that they have already used are theoretically compatible with a project framework, teachers can modify them for inclusion in a project design. Thus, in the best sense of adaptation, teachers become modifiers of curriculum materials. This provides real meaning to our argument that it is not a prescription that is needed for teachers to enact innovation, but profiles of enactment that are consistent with the philosophy of the reform.

Using information and telecommunication systems

Professional development is often limited because teachers rarely have the time or money to visit other schools or attend enough high-quality teacher conferences and workshops. The predominant technology to gain access to distributed expertise has been through print publications, such as teacher magazines and journals or through face-to-face interactions at institutes or workshops. The information and tele-communications environment for education has changed dramatically in recent years. With the advent of the world wide web as an easily accessible resource complete with chat groups, forums, and MOOs (multi-user, object-oriented applications) and with the development of new forms of information storage and retrieval such as digital libraries, teachers now have access to distributed expertise that has hitherto been inaccessible due to limitations of cost and time (Levin and Thurston, 1996). However, these forms of communication and information storage and retrieval are not likely to be helpful to teachers unless they can relate to teachers' work, have relatively low opportunity costs in relation to other forms of information access (such as library books or the teacher's filing cabinet full of previously used materials), and have fairly short learning curves so that the initial investment in learning results in useful material for instruction.

Telecommunications can help teachers and university researchers engage in substantive conversations and share teaching artifacts (e.g. video clips, PIViT documents). However, experience with teacher use of telecommunications (Roup *et al.*, 1992) has shown that conversations may not be particularly substantive. The challenge is to help teachers engage in productive conversations.

Electronic conversations must revolve around a framework for considering an innovation with a focus on issues of practice (Peterson *et al.*, 1996). In addition, databases of classroom-relevant and useful ideas, materials and resources need to be accessible by teachers. In our case, we created the Project Support Network (http://www.umich.edu/ ~ pbsgroup/psnet/) where teachers can download a PIViT plan or send their PIViT project plans to be indexed and added to the database. This database of plans serves as a form of community memory; more experienced teachers upload their plans, annotated with suggestions for how to implement them, while new participants can benefit from the project plans created by more experienced teachers. Preferably, creators of the plans should be available for on-line discussion with downloaders of the plans.

It is important that adequate attention is paid to scaffolding teacher learning. This is particularly important when web materials are specific to an innovation. Because innovations invariably require teachers to engage learners in different ways and to design instruction differently than in the past, materials need to help teachers learn to understand the innovation and translate it into teaching and learning activities for their context. If lesson plans published on a site are sketchy and lack the elaborations to scaffold teacher learning, it is less likely that the plans will help teachers teach differently than in the past.

If networking is to help develop communities of practice, teachers need guidance and support to engage in the kinds of conversations we have described. Although teachers may be energised by a desire to improve student learning and motivation, they initially can be hesitant about change in practice. It takes time for them to grapple with the real issues underlying the innovation. Fenstermacher and Richardson (1993) have noted that knowledgeable others help to promote change. Hence, mentors are critical for the success of network-based communication. Mentors, whose role is to facilitate and scaffold the conversation (Roup *et al.*, 1992), can initiate and sustain the conversation when the network first starts and provide information and resources, raise questions or offer ideas, direct inquiries, and connect groups with similar interests and needs as the network becomes better established.

It is important for the development of a community of practice that a critical mass of teachers participate in telecommunication-mediated conversations to discuss teaching practices and share artifacts on a routine basis (Markus, 1987). While other professional groups have reached such critical mass, the literature on teacher telecommunications does not report major successes in this regard. While hard-to-use, expensive technology and time constraints are cited as the major barriers for teachers not using telecommunications, the deeper reason is that teachers likely do not find much through telecommunications that is useful to their professional lives. In order to engage teachers, an essential feature of new information and tele-communications technologies is that they must be useful.

New directions for designing software for teachers

As technology for professional development expands, software designers need to be sensitive to the needs of teachers as learners. We have been exploring three types of scaffolds based on the principles of learner-centred design: (a) functional scaffolds that hide the cognitive complexities of the task, making the simplest level of functionality available to the novice learner, but allowing learners to access advanced features as their capability grows; (b) guidance scaffolds that help learners navigate and understand the technology itself by guiding them through the process; and (c) metacognitive scaffolds that help the learner in the metacognitive elements of planning, monitoring and evaluating their thinking as they learn.

In learning an innovation, teachers need to understand the model of student learning upon which it is based and its implications for classroom management and instruction. By itself, this places substantial cognitive demands on teachers. When technologies are used, such as those we describe here, at the same time they must understand how the software represents the innovation. Initially scaffolding can mask some functionality of complex tools so that the software is simplified and novice users are not overwhelmed. Later the user can decide to introduce more functionality as their knowledge of the tool increases. For instance, multimedia programs may be more or less organised to illustrate issues in the innovation or show different facets, such as teacher–student interaction, issues of content representation, or management of group work.

Many teachers are not sophisticated technology users. Even for the proficient, learning a new piece of software can be quite time consuming and confusing. There-fore designers need to help new users master the programs easily if teachers are to be willing to use them. One way to do this is to tailor the tools to different levels of user expertise. In addition, providing navigational support is important since keeping track of where one has been can be quite difficult in hypermedia systems. Providing image maps or other ways for the user to understand the different aspects of the software can also be helpful, especially when it is not obvious that there are a variety of sources of information or functions available. Scaffolding is necessary to guide teachers through the conceptual tasks in the software. For instance, as teachers use multimedia, prompts can remind them to read commentary or background information about what they are viewing. Moreover, guidelines for new users that take them step-by-step through a program might be helpful. Planning programs could have lists of what steps need to be accomplished and different ways to accomplish them. Multimedia programs might have lists of various things one might view or consider.

Finally, scaffolding can be designed to promote reflection. It is very likely that new teachers may be so involved in mastering the technology and trying to figure out aspects of the innovation, that ways to enhance thoughtfulness are required. For this purpose, oral and written questions as teachers view media can help teachers focus on important issues. For instance, to promote reflection CaPPs has a field called 'Issues to Consider' that asks teachers to reflect on various issues of the video clips they observed. In PIViT, we have fields that allow teachers to reflect back on the plan they created.

Conclusions

Work on technology for teachers is quite new. To date, the focus has been on preservice teachers. The literature on in-service teachers and technology is more meagre. It does not deal primarily with how to use technology for professional development. Instead, most of this literature is focused on how to help teachers use technology with their students and how to help teachers overcome the difficulties they face when technology is introduced into classrooms.

There are, however, issues to consider regarding when and how technology for professional development is introduced and used. Schofield *et al.* (1994) argue that the effects of technology are inextricably bound to the social system in which technology is used. Generally software, such as multimedia cases or productivity tools, is developed with a particular theoretical approach in mind. Copley (1992) argues that if professional development is aimed to promote constructivist teaching, then technology should be compatible with the theoretical tenets of constructivism. Technology should not be used if it was designed with a more skills-based, information transmission point of view. Similarly, an obvious but important point is that the philosophy of staff developers needs to mesh with that of the software and of the innovation itself; otherwise the technology is not likely to be an effective aid. Additionally, care must be given to the design of the tasks that teachers are asked to perform as they initially work with the technology. As with scaffolding in the software itself, initial tasks must help teachers understand the nature of the tool, how it reflects the innovation, and what its affordances are to help teachers understand and enact the innovation. Moreover, the interplay of technology and interpersonal interaction merits attention. We see technology as a way to supplement interpersonal professional development efforts, not as a means to supplant them. Thus, whereas many commercial software packages are designed to be used by themselves, the systems we have described are not used in isolation, but are part of a larger instructional effort used by groups working together.

Another set of issues is the development of an infrastructure that supports teachers' continuing use of technology for professional development after its introduction during in-service work sessions. Teachers will not profit from the technology nor will it be self-sustaining unless infrastructure capacity is developed, including attention to resources and maintenance. Some issues that need to be considered include where the technology will be located, how teachers will be given the time to use it and what support will be provided to help teachers continue to upgrade their skills and understanding. For example, productivity tools for planning require that teachers have access to technology at home or at work; the tools have to be available when teachers are not with their students. Computers that are only available in a lab or that are locked into closets for security after school hours will not be available when and where teachers need them for planning. Moreover, as they gain expertise and have questions about functionality or when they encounter problems with the technology, timely and easily accessible help needs to be provided.

References

Ball, D. L. and Cohen, D. K. (1996) 'Reform by the book: what is – or might be – the role of curriculum materials in teacher learning and instructional reform?', *Educational Researcher*, **25**, 6–8.

Bickel, W. E. and Hattrup, R. A. (1995) 'Teachers and researchers in collaboration: reflections on the process', *American Educational Research Journal*, **32**, 35–62.

Borko, H. and Putnam, R. T. (1996) 'Learning to teach', in Berliner, D. C. and Calfee, R. C. (eds), *Handbook of Educational Psychology*, New York: Macmillan, 673–708.

Bruer, J. (1995) 'Classroom problems, school culture, and cognitive research', in McGilly, K. (ed.), *Classroom Lessons: Integrating Cognitive Theory and Classroom Practice*, Cambridge, MA: MIT Press, 273–90.

Calderhead, J. (1993) 'The contribution of research on teachers' thinking to the professional development of teachers', in Day, C., Calderhead, J. and Denicolo, P. (eds), *Research on Teacher Thinking: Understanding for Professional Development*, Washington, DC: Falmer, 11–18.

Carter, K. (1993) 'The place of story in the study of teaching and teacher education', *Educational Researcher*, **22**, 5–12, 18.

Carter, K. and Doyle, W. (1989) 'Classroom research as a resource for the graduate education of teachers', in Woolfolk, A. E. (ed.), *Research perspectives on the graduate education of teachers*, Englewood Cliffs, NJ: Prentice-Hall, 51–68.

Clark, C. M. (1988) 'Asking the right questions about teacher preparation: contributions of research on teacher thinking', *Educational Researcher*, **17**(2), 5–12.

Clark, C. M. and Yinger, R. J. (1987) 'Teacher planning', in Calderhead, J. (ed.), *Exploring Teachers' Thinking*, London: Cassell, 84–103.

Cohen, D. K. and Barnes, C. A. (1993) 'Pedagogy and policy', in Cohen, D. K., McLaughon, M. W. and Talbert, J. E. (eds), *Teaching for Understanding: Challenges for Policy and Practice*, San Francisco: Jossey-Bass, 207–39.

Copley, J. (1992) 'The integration of teacher education and technology: a constructivist model', in Carey, D., Carey, R., Willis, D. and Willis, J. (eds), *Technology and Teacher Education Annual*, Association for the Advancement of Computing in Education, 617–22.

Feldman, A. (1996) 'Enhancing the practice of physics teachers: mechanisms for the generation and sharing of knowledge and understanding in collaborative action research', *Journal of Research in Science Teaching*, **33**, 513–40.

Fenstermacher, G. D. and Richardson, V. (1993) 'The elicitation and reconstruction of practical arguments in teaching', *Journal of Curriculum Studies*, **25**, 101–14.

Firestone, W. and Pennell, J. (1997) 'Designing state-sponsored teacher networks: a comparison of two cases', *American Educational Research Journal*, **34**, 237–66.

Knowles, J. G. (1992) 'Models for teachers' biographies', in Goodson, I. (ed.), *Studying Teachers' Lives*, New York: Teachers College Press, 99–152.

Lave, J. and Wenger, E. (1991) *Situated Learning: Legitimate Peripheral Participation*, Cambridge: Cambridge University Press.

Levin, J. and Thurston, C. (1996) 'Educational electronic networks: a review of research and development', *Educational Leadership*, **54**(3), 46–50.

Lieberman, A. (ed.) (1990) *Schools as Collaborative Cultures: Creating the Future Now*, New York: Falmer.

Markus, M. L. (1987) 'Toward a "critical mass" theory of interactive media: universal access, interdependence, and diffusion', *Communication Research*, **14**, 491–511.

Newman, D., Griffin, P. and Cole (1989) *The Construction Zone: Working for Cognitive Change in School*, Cambridge: Cambridge University Press.

Peterson, P. L. *et al.* (1996) 'Learning from school restructuring', *American Educational Research Journal*, **33**, 119–54.

Richardson, V. (1990) 'Significant and worthwhile change and teaching practice', *Educational Researcher*, **16**(9), 13–20.

Roup, R., Gal, S., Drayton, B. and Pfister, M. (eds) (1992) *LabNet: Toward a Community of Practice*, Hillsdale, NJ: Erlbaum.

Schofield, J. W., Eurich-Fulcer, R. and Britt, C. L. (1994) 'Teachers, computer tutors, and teaching: the artificially intelligent tutor as an agent for classroom change', *American Educational Research Journal*, **31**, 597–607.

Scott, C. (1994) 'Project-based science: reflections of a middle school teacher', *Elementary School Journal*, **95**, 75–94.

Shulman, L. S. (1992) 'Toward a pedagogy of cases', in Shulman, J. H. (ed.), *Case Methods in Teacher Education*, New York: Teachers College Press, 1–30.

Soloway, E., Guzdial, M. and Hay, K. E. (1994) 'Learner-centered design: the challenge for human computer interaction in the 21st century', *Interactions*, **1**(2), 36–48.

Chapter 22

Using networks to support the professional development of teachers

Bert Moonen and Joke Voogt

This is an edited version of an article previously published in *Journal of In-service Education*, **24**(1), February 1998.

Integration of technology in the classroom

Since the early 1980s, efforts to integrate technology in education have been carried out by the Dutch government (for an overview, see Plomp *et al.*, 1996). Yet despite these efforts, in practice the integration of Information and Communication Technologies (ICT) in Dutch education is still limited (Brummelhuis, 1995; Moonen and Kommers, 1995; Janssen Reinen, 1996). International comparative research (Pelgrum and Plomp, 1993) shows that the situation in The Netherlands does not differ much from other industrialised countries. While lack of hardware and appropriate software appeared to be the major problem of technology integration in the 1980s, in the 1990s insufficiently trained teachers and not enough time for teachers to prepare for using computers in their lessons seem to have become the primary problems (Pelgrum and Plomp, 1993). This shift, that started after the biggest problems concerning the availability of hardware and software were solved, illustrates that the integration of technology cannot only be perceived as a technical issue, but should also be considered as a complex endeavour from a social viewpoint as well. Particularly, the changing demands on teachers makes technology integration in the curriculum a complicated innovation.

Fullan (1991) synthesised findings from many studies in order to understand the meaning of change for individuals and organisations involved in it. He argues that innovation in education is a multi-dimensional process that not only implies the use of different materials, but also often presupposes changes in beliefs and behaviour.

Doyle and Ponder (1977–78) introduced the term 'particality ethic' for the way teachers react to innovations. They pointed out three dimensions – instrumentally, congruence and cost – of a change proposal, which determine whether an innovation is seen as practical by teachers. Instrumentality refers to the clarity and specificity of the innovation, congruence to the extent the innovation is aligned with the teacher's teaching philosophy, and practices and cost to the teacher's estimate of the extra time and effort the innovation requires compared with the benefits the innovation is likely to yield.

From the studies of Olson (1988) and Voogt (1993) on computer integration in education, it can be inferred that the way teachers use software is strongly influenced by their prior practices and routines. Veen (1994) describes routines as the inter-relationship between beliefs and skills. In his study he found that teacher beliefs seemed to influence skills such as competence in managing classroom-related activities, pedagogical skills and – less importantly – computer-handling technical skills. Janssen Reinen (1996) discovered that the intensity of computer use is influenced by the perception of the teacher towards possible changes in the educational process as a result of the use of technology. Communication with other teachers about ICT use is a second critical factor that evidently determines the amount of computer use in education (Moonen, 1995). It can be concluded that in order to improve the implementation of ICT in education the focus should nowadays be on the teacher.

The potential of teacher networks

In response to the problems teachers are facing when integrating complex innovations in the classroom, various efforts have been undertaken to facilitate their tasks. For example, in The Netherlands, Voogt (1993) and Keursten (1994) studied the role of curriculum materials within ICT implementation in education and Berg (1996) and Roes (1997) looked closely as in-service training in general (not specifically with respect to ICT). The conclusion of Collis and Moonen (1995) to a two-year national study of teachers' use of ICT was that teacher networks can offer interesting possibilities for the integration of ICT innovations. These studies will be described successively in the paragraphs that follow.

The design and use of curriculum materials

Akker *et al.* (1992) concluded after an extensive literature research on the integration of ICT in education that teachers have many problems when having to implement ICT. Teachers have difficulties selecting suitable software, often lack technical skills in using ICT and experience problems with this new teaching role. Akker and his colleagues (1992) concluded that some implementation problems can be foreseen, so in consequence solutions can be integrated in advance in the teacher materials that support ICT use, for example by adding procedural specifications. Teacher materials that were developed from this starting point turned out to be useful in the classroom (Keursten, 1994; Voogt, 1993).

Based on her study, Voogt (1993) also concluded that it is very helpful for teachers to use a teacher manual. A teacher manual, containing procedural specifications (very concrete how-to-do specifications for teachers focused on essential, but vulnerable elements of the innovation) should always be part of the learning materials. Procedural specifications relate to suggestions for guidance of the learners and information about possible problems that can occur during the lessons. However, Voogt also discovered that despite its benefits, teachers very often do not use the teacher manual. Voogt concluded, after evaluation, that the teacher manual and thus also the procedural specifications can best be integrated within the learner materials.

Akker and Nies (1992) described the essential characteristics of exemplary lesson materials. Exemplary lesson materials should:

- be a series of lessons about a certain theme or topic, with a clearly described starting point and end;
- be a clear operationalisation of the essential curriculum ideas;
- contain student material, teacher material and assessment aids;
- be carefully evaluated and optimised.

The studies of Voogt (1993) and Keursten (1994), which were aimed at improving the integration of ICT in education, showed that exemplary lesson materials that contain procedural specifications are very useful for the teacher, especially for lesson preparation and execution. These exemplary lesson materials can function as an example, containing technical and instructional guidelines, and should be detailed and ready to use. When exemplary lesson materials are used by teachers as an example, teachers are most likely to undergo a successful first experience when using ICT in their practice.

From an implementation perspective, Voogt (1993) and Keursten (1994) also concluded that these sorts of exemplary lesson materials, which can be seen as learning materials for teachers (cf. Akker, 1998), do help, but are in themselves not sufficient to integrate the use of ICT in the classroom to a satisfactory level. As said before, the problem is not the materials (teacher manuals) themselves, but the teachers who very often do not use the manuals. In turn, teachers do not use the manuals because of their beliefs and their behaviours (Fullan, 1991). It is often assumed that in-service training can contribute to a change in these beliefs and behaviours.

The use of in-service training

The combination of exemplary lesson materials (containing procedural specifications) for the teacher combined with in-service education looks promising for solving problems faced in implementing complex innovations as the integration of ICT in education (Voogt, 1993; Keursten, 1994). From a meta-analysis of effective in-service education, Joyce and Showers (1995) concluded that in-service education should consist of five components: theory, demonstration, practice, feedback and coaching.

Berg (1996) sees interesting opportunities for using ICT with in-service activities. For example, the use of a CD-ROM to offer a number of exemplary lessons captured with video. It should also be more interesting to use ICT to support the analysis of exemplary lessons as part of the component demonstration than to only have teachers analysing written summaries of lessons.

The following assertions for further research were drawn by Berg (1996). First, in-service training might have a negative influence on the teacher's attitudes towards the educational innovation, if the ideas of this innovation are not the same as those of the teacher. Besides this, the effect of in-service training on this attitude change is partly based upon the reactions of other teachers in the school. Finally, Berg (1996) stated that a positive attitude change caused by in-service training is, among other aspects, connected with joint exploration of the implications of the innovation with other participating teachers.

Roes (1997) found that exemplary lesson materials are useful in fulfilling the demonstration and practice components of in-service training. In addition, demonstrations can show teachers what the curriculum designers expect to see in terms of observable teacher behaviours (Akker and Voogt, 1994).

According to Roes (1997), in an in-service course teachers expect to get practical pedagogical clues to use within their educational activities. Teachers also hope to obtain lesson materials and to get skilled in applying a new teaching method. Based on her research that consisted of a series of in-service training activities she concluded that:

1   Presentations and written background materials can explain the starting points of an innovation.
2   Exemplary lesson material combined with procedural specifications (and a video showing a 'real' lesson) can be very effective in explaining the use of the innovation and, by that, in creating a first positive experience.
3   Teachers should carry out some exemplary lessons in their own classrooms. This is one of the most powerful components of in-service education because teachers experience whether or not they can use the innovation and how their students react to it.
4   The components (peer) coaching and feedback remained under-examined, but Roes (1997) advises that ICT should also be used to overcome this problem.

It is especially the components (peer) coaching and feedback, which up until now have often been under-examined, that can easily be integrated in teacher networks. Research (Collis and Moonen, 1995; Moonen, 1995; Janssen Reinen, 1996) has shown that communication between teachers is of paramount importance to implement ICT effectively in education. This communication can be stimulated by teacher networks.

The use of teacher networks

In order for educational technology infusion to occur in education, teachers need more than just knowledge about educational technology, they need practical examples and ideas; and they need coaching and mentoring as they try new techniques in their classrooms (Zachariades *et al.*, 1995). Collis and Moonen (1995) concluded that teacher networks can offer interesting possibilities in in-service training settings (for example, on the integration of ICT). Based on definitions given by Galesloot (1994), A. J. Jansen (1996) and Leenheer (1995), a teacher network is defined as a group of teachers from different schools who co-operate for a longer period of time on the implementation process of a certain innovation in education.

All networks should be based upon some essential components. Lieberman and Grolnick (1996) cited Parker (1977) who performed an important early study of networks. He described five key components of networks, which he drew up after studying over 60 networks for educational improvement. These five key components are that members of networks should have:

1   a strong sense of commitment to the innovation;
2   a sense of shared purpose;
3   a mixture of information sharing and psychological support;
4   an effective facilitator;
5   voluntary participation and equal treatment.

These general components have been made concrete for the Dutch situation by Galesloot (1994), A. J. Jansen (1996) and Leenheer (1995). They formulated the following recommendations:

1   A teacher network should not be too big or too small. Ten to fifteen teachers, preferably two teachers from each participating school, and four to seven schools per network is the optimum.
2   Teachers in the network should be teaching the same subject.
3   Start a network with a narrow topic that is important to the participants (a so-called 'hot item').
4   Make sure that the participants not only get information, but also bring some.
5   Teachers in the network must learn to believe that they can learn from each other.
6   An open environment must be created during the network workshops, so that the participants are willing to take risks.
7   Accept differences between participants in experience, knowledge and learning-methods and make these differences productive.
8   Do not just start organising in-service activities, but develop them based on questions that arise.
9   Teachers in the network should have a lot to say about the topics, working-method, location, time and frequency of the network meetings.

Design of a TINTIN network

In the TINTIN project, teacher networks to support teachers in the process of ICT implementation have been established, following the above recommendations. To lower the communication barriers with other participating teachers, an electronic component has been added to the teacher networks. In the next paragraph the design of the TINTIN research will be explained.

Bos *et al.* (1995) indicate that an electronic teacher network for in-service training is extremely well suited for reflection among the teachers about what the teachers have tried. An electronic teacher network turns out to be a crucial step in the process of the implementation of innovations, because teacher networks create a supportive audience (the other network participants) for feedback and develop into sources for new ideas. The added value of (electronic) teacher networks is, according to Bos *et al.* (1995):

1   Teachers can easily reflect on their practice and share these reflections with other teachers.
2   Teachers can benefit from moral support, curriculum guidance and the opportunity for joint reflection.
3   Teachers undertaking new innovations have need for ongoing contact and support.
4   Rural isolation increases the need for teachers to have contact with other teachers and content experts.

In the previous section we concluded that the integration of technology in the classroom is a complex issue because of the tremendous task laid upon the teacher. The combination of curriculum materials and in-service training cannot solve all implementation problems. In the TINTIN research this combination is situated within a teacher-network environment. The general research question is:

> How can social and electronic teacher networks as a method of in-service education contribute to the professional development of teachers?

In the TINTIN research the aim of this professional development relates to the use of ICT (mostly Internet) in secondary education.

Within the TINTIN research, three teacher networks (two on foreign languages and one on social studies) are set up, but starting at different points in time. The first one, started in March 1997, is organised around the topic 'French and the use of ICT' and has 15 participants. The second one started in September 1997 and has 'German and the use of ICT' as the topic.

Essential characteristics of TINTIN teacher networks

Based upon the literature discussed earlier (for example, Galesloot, 1994; Leenheer, 1995; A. J. Jansen, 1996) the following essential characteristics of TINTIN teacher networks have been defined:

1   Long lasting in-service activities so the teachers will have the time to try the innovation in their classroom and thereby are able to reflect upon it. The TINTIN networks will exist for at least two years.

2   Occasional face-to-face meetings in addition to electronic communication since network participants should know each other before they can provide professional collaboration most effectively at a distance. These meetings will be held approximately every 3 months.

3   Exemplary lesson materials (which contain procedural specifications) and a demonstration video should be used. These lesson materials are based upon the needs of the participating teachers.

4   Stimulation of electronic communication by providing some sort of 'homework', for example, preparatory activities for ICT projects, implementation instructions and sharing experiences on the use of ICT.

5   An active moderator, responsible for the organisation of the network.

6   A content expert (on ICT and the school subject involved) is part of the teacher network.

7   Easy communication, information exchange, (peer-)coaching activities performance and feedback possibilities for the teachers.

The (electronic) and social) teacher networks within the TINTIN teacher networks are divided into three phases: familiarisation, practice and reflection and self-support. Because most of the teachers participating do not have (sufficient) knowledge on the most basic uses of ICT, the in-service activities start with an introduction to the windows operating system, Internet browsers, email programs, etc. The second phase starts with the actual use of ICT in education. In this phase teachers get information, exemplary lesson materials, and as much feedback and coaching possibilities as needed, in order to stimulate the teachers to use ICT in their classrooms. In this phase the use of the electronic communication possibilities can be very helpful, since it facilitates feedback and coaching activities. In the third and final phase the network organiser and content expert will reduce the amount of input and stimulation. Appointments will be made so that the teachers will support the network themselves by providing sufficient information based on their experiences and products relating to the use of ICT in their classrooms.

Reflection and perspectives

In summary, the results that have been achieved during the start of the TINTIN project are positive. The teachers are enthusiastic and are eager to learn more about ICT. The combination of exemplary learning materials (with procedural specifications) and in-service training in a teacher network looks very promising. It is, however, in the future to determine the effects the teacher networks will have in the classroom.

References

Akker, J. J. H. van den (1998) 'The teacher as learner in curriculum implementation', *Journal of Curriculum Studies*, **20**, 47–55.

Akker, J. J. H. van den and Nies, A. C. M. (1992) 'Handreikingen voor het ontwikkelen van lesvoorbeelden: basiskatern & bronnenboek [Assistance for the development of exemplary lessons]', Enschede: SLO (internal publication).

Akker, J. J. H. van den and Voogt, J. M. (1994) 'The use of innovation and practice profiles in the evaluation of curriculum implementation', *Studies in Educational Evaluation*, **20**, 503–12.

Akker, J. J. H. van den, Keursten, P. and Plomp, Tj. (1992) 'The integration of computer use in education', *International Journal of Educational Research*, **1**(17), 65–75.

Berg, E. van den (1996) *Effects of In-service Education on Implementation of Elementary Science*, Enschede: Universiteit Twente.

Bos, N. D., Krajcik, J. S. and Patrick, H. (1995) 'Telecommunication for teachers: Supporting reflection and collaboration among teaching professionals', *Journal of Computers in Mathematics and Science Teaching*, **14**(1/2), 187–202.

Brummelhuis, A. C. A. ten (1995) *Models of Educational Change: The Introduction of Computers in Dutch Secondary Education*, Enschede: Universiteit Twente.

Collis, B. A. and Moonen, B. H. (1995) 'Teacher networking: a nationwide approach to supporting the instructional use of computers in the Netherlands', *Australian Educational Computing*, **10**(2), 4–9.

Doyle, W. and Ponder, G. A. (1977–78) 'The practicality ethic in teacher decision making', *Interchange*, **8**(3), 1–12.

Fullan, M. (1991) *The New Meaning of Educational Change*, New York: Teachers College Press.

Galesloot, L. (1994) *Collegiale netwerken van ervaren docenten en schoolleiders* [Networks of experienced teachers and school managers]', Utrecht: Academisch Boeken Centrum, De Lier.

Jansen, A. J. (1996) *Docentennetwerken begeleiden. Een Praktijk handleiding voor begeleiders en deelnemers* [Guiding teacher networks], Appeldoorn: Grant.

Janssen Reinen, I. A. M. (1996) *Teachers and Computer Use: The Process of Integrating IT in the Curriculum*, Enschede: Universiteit Twente.

Joyce, B. and Showers, B. (1995) *Student Achievement Through Staff Development. Fundamentals of School Renewal* (2nd edn), New York: Longman.

Keursten, P. (1994) *Courseware-ontwikkeling met het oog op implementatie: de docent centraal* [Courseware development for implementation: the teacher is central], Enschede: Universiteit Twente.

Leenheer, P. (1995) *Ervaringen in netwerken* [Experiences in networks], Tilburg: MesoConsult.

Lieberman, A. and Grolnick, M. (1996) 'Networks and reform in American education', *Teachers College Record*, **98**(1), 7–45.

Moonen, B. H. (1995) *Een onderzoek naar de factoren die het gebruik van informatietechnologie in de klas veroorzaken* [Research into the factors that influence the use of computer software in instruction], Enschede: Universiteit Twente.

Moonen, J. C. M. M. and Kommers, P. A. M. (1995) *Implementatie van communicatie-en informatietechnologieën (CIT) in het onderwijs* [Implementation of communication and information technology in education], Enschede: Universiteit Twente.

Olson, J. (1988) *Schoolworlds – Microworlds, Computers and the Culture of the Classroom*, Oxford: Pergamon Press.

Parker, A. (1997) 'Networks for innovation and problem solving and their use for improving education: a comparative overview', unpublished manuscript, Washington, DC: School Capacity for Problem Solving Group, National Institute of Education.

Pelgrum, W. J. and Plomp, Tj. (1993) *The IEA Study of Computers in Education: Implementation of an Innovation in 21 Education Systems*, Oxford: Pergamon Press.

Plomp, Tj., Scholtes, E. and Brummelhuis, A. ten (1996) 'Policies on computers in education in the Netherlands', in Plomp, Tj., Anderson, R. E. and Kontogiannopoulou-Polydoudes, G. (eds), *Cross National Policies and Practices on Computers in Education*, Dordrecht: Kluwer Academic Publishers, 359–80.

Roes, M. G. (1997) *Nascholing op basis van lesvoorbeelden: in de context van curriculmvernieuwing* [In-service education based on exemplary lessons], Enschede: Universiteit Twente.

Veen, W. (1994) *Computerondersteunde docenten: de rol van de docent bij de invoering van computers in de klaspraktijk* [Computer supported teachers: the role of the teacher during the implementation of computers in the class], De Lier: Academisch Boeken Centrum.

Voogt, J. M. (1993) *Courseware for an Inquiry-based Science Curriculum: An Implementation Perspective*, Enschede: Universiteit Twente.

Zachariades, E., Jensen, S. and Thompson, A. (1995) 'One-to-one collaboration with a teacher educator: an approach to integrate technology in teacher education', *Journal of Computing in Teacher Education*, **12**, 11–14.

Chapter 23

Breaking the silence: the role of technology and community in leading professional development

Jenny Leach

Commissioned for this volume (2000).

> If human beings had not become capable of choosing, deciding, breaking away, and projecting, capable of remaking themselves as they remake the world . . . if they had not become capable of valuation, of dedication to the point of sacrifice to the dream they fight for, of singing and praising the world, of admiring beauty, there would be no reason for talking about the possibility of neutrality in education. But there would not be any reason to talk about education.
>
> (Freire, 1999)

Introduction

This article is about the potential role for new information and communications technologies in professional development. It is also about the communities in which such development takes place. In this opening decade of the twenty-first century we are witnesses, many have argued, to a time of global transformations (Giddens, 1999). The combined impact of a revolution in Information and Communications Technology (ICT), the formation of a global economy and widespread cultural changes, it is widely suggested, call into question traditional patterns of communication, as well as the structures upon which institutional and national cultures have been built. Knowledge generation and information processing have become central dimensions of a 'new sociotechnical paradigm' (Porat, 1997). In seeking to emphasise the social dimension of these new information generation and information processing processes, Castells (1999) dubs this the new 'information-al society'. As this so-called new world order emerges, grandiose claims about the potential for new technologies to change our lives radically, including education, have become commonplace.

Given such spin and media hype, it is important to find fresh metaphors through which to interpret the current context. Metaphors that allow for different perspectives and which challenge all-pervasive common-sense images and folk beliefs. I will suggest in this article that far from technology shaping educational communities, technology (or the lack of it) embodies the capacity of such communities to transform themselves. I hope to show that communities generally cannot be understood or represented without account being taken of the technologies, as well as related skills and meaning-making activities, intrinsic to them. In this sense technological change is as located in the particular communities in which it takes place and by which it is shaped, as it is in the broader systems of societal and global relations. It is people and the uses to which we put technology, not simply technology itself, that have the power to transform education. From this perspective then, technology *is* community. Technology is the expression of communities – their values, their goals and the activities through which we come to know them. The purpose of this chapter is to analyse and explore the meaning of community and technology for education, and the way in which new technologies can be used to support, extend and indeed transform professional practice.

New metaphors – changing world views

Many current models of learning and professional development conceptualise the professional task as a solo endeavour – be it carried out in classroom, head teacher's study, doctor's consulting room or architect's studio. Notions of reflective practice (Schon, 1987), personal growth theories, experiential learning (Kolb, 1984), traits and style theories of leadership (Adair, 1983; Yukl, 1994), for example, are all characterised as processes of development, or the acquisition of skills and competences, that take place in the mind of the individual. All these models are based on a view of learning as an essentially individual activity, a process by which knowledge is internalised, whether it be 'discovered', 'transmitted' from others, or 'experienced in interaction' with others. Bruner (1996) characterises this as the 'computational' view of mind and learning, Bredo (1994) calls it the 'symbol processing' view. Whatever terminology is used, the main focus is the individual mind, the process by which we sort, store, memorise, collate, 'digest' and reformulate information and ideas, be it through discovery, transmission or a process of reflection. There are of course very different accounts of this process. At one end of the spectrum the learner is seen as a passive processor of information. The more widely accepted view, as exemplified by the 'reflective practitioner' tradition for example (Schon, 1987), sees the individual learner as actively engaged in the construction of knowledge through reflection and action. At whichever end of this spectrum, however, the development of knowledge and understanding is conceived as a largely cerebral process. The person is the unit of analysis. This traditional view of mind currently dominates the way in which learning is viewed within many educational institutions worldwide. It permeates everyday language, informs how we teach and dictates the way in which a good deal of professional development practice is both conceived and implemented. Sfard (1998) has called it the *acquisition* metaphor of learning. It leads educational development into a cul-de-sac, I would argue, since it assumes a false dichotomy between person and world.

The advert for new recruits into teaching in England and Wales shown in Figure 23.1 appeared in a national newspaper in 1999. It illustrates for me the dead-end into which teacher development walks when preoccupied with the individual's acquisition of discrete skills and abstract standards. The young man presented through this 'cool'

I couldn't decide between becoming a manager, an actor or a diplomat.

So I became them all.

No one forgets a good teacher

Figure 23.1 Teaching recruitment advert. (Reprinted with permission of the TTA. Photographer: Henrik Knudsen.)

media image, reminiscent of David Hockney's Ossie Clarke, sits alone aspiring, the reader is informed, to be an actor, manager and diplomat. The advert implies that he will draw on a variety of skills belonging to different professions, but he is solitary, removed from the people, activities and technologies of a particular practice. He identifies with no particular community. His goal is empty. This individual view of the developing teacher paradoxically promotes a non-personal view of the knowledge and skills that this individual must acquire and the tasks and activities to be carried out. From this perspective, professional knowledge is a commodity to be acquired and professional practice is the accumulation of technical skills unrelated to context and values; devoid of vision, empty of passion for specific kinds of knowledge and forms of understanding.

But human activity is neither solo nor conducted unassisted, even when it would appear to go on 'in the head'. Learning and professional development at whatever stage never takes place as the result of the acquisition of a set of decontextualised, abstract skills or competences. Mental life is lived with others, is shaped to be communicated and unfolds in activity with others (Bruner, 1996). This 'situated' (Bredo, 1994) or 'cultural' (Bruner, 1996) perspective, Sfard (1998) calls the '*participation*' metaphor of mind and development. From this point of view knowing and communicating are inseparable. For individual learning is not shaped *by* specific cultures or situated *in* particular practices, somehow like water poured into and moulded by differently sized and shaped containers. Rather participation *creates* culture: learning *is* practice. Rogoff (1999) puts it this way: an individual's actions and skills cannot be understood out of the context of the immediate practical goals being sought and the enveloping socio-cultural goals into which they fit. It is the communities to which they belong that provide the communicative tools for organising and understanding experience and generating knowledge. Without such tools Bruner (1996) argues, humans are themselves empty abstractions.

From this situated perspective, the unit of analysis embraces *both* individual and community. And, paradoxically, if we start from social practices and take participation within these practices, rather than individual cognition, to be the crucial process, then an explicit focus on the individual is demanded. But individual *in* the world, individual as a member *of* a particular community. This involves seeing that community as integral to one's identity; it necessitates the sharing of the vision, goals and purposes of the group. In this sense too, some commentators argue, and perhaps most radically, there is no individual notion of an idea or concept, but a distributed one. Cognition is always distributed within and across communities:

> stretched over, not divided among – mind, body, activity and culturally organised settings (which include other actors), across persons, activity and setting.
>
> (Lave, 1988)

Bruner has argued that Western educational traditions get in the way of our understanding of the importance of such intersubjectivity in educational development. Even when we attempt to tamper with the *acquisition* model, more often than not we remain loyal to its unspoken precepts. Yet only a very small part of educating takes place on such a one way street – and it is probably one of the least successful parts. We need, he suggests, to ask the innocent but fundamental question: 'how best to conceive of a sub community that specializes in learning amongst its members?' (Bruner, 1996, p. 21). This question is crucial to this article. The intention is not to deny the subtle and complex process of human mind and development (Gardner, 1993; Bredo, 1994, Sachs, 1999). Rather, it is to raise questions about the equally subtle and complex process of community of which such development is an integral part. For whilst it may appear obvious that human development, including adult professional learning, takes place in social situations, and that human tools and representational media support, extend and re-organise mental functioning, nevertheless there continues to be a silence about such relationships in educational development at almost every level. The section that follows explores aspects of community, the role of technologies in their development and dimensions through which they might be analysed and thus evaluated. Two case studies of professional development communities are used by way of illustrations.

Aspects of community: identity, participation and change

The origins of *community* in contemporary English can be traced from *communis* (Latin), *comuneté* (Middle French) through to the fourteenth-century *comunete* (Middle English). Across cultures and time the word has gathered a variety of connotations which Roget (1971), has classified according to three main clusters of ideas and meaning – Mankind, Participation and Antagonism. These broad classifications provide a useful frame within which to analyse the term. I will call these three themes:

- identity
- participation
- conflict and change.

Identity

In the first classification, *Mankind*, community is grouped with collective nouns (e.g. people, folk, population, society, civilisation, world, race) and singular terms (e.g. human being, individual, fellow creature, living soul, earthling, etc.). Taken as a whole, these words encompass both individual and collective identity. Community from this perspective expresses the essence of what it means to be human: the integration of individual-*in*-world, person *of* culture, actor *and* acted on. Technology is an integral part of this dialectic between individual consciousness and world, since it both embodies and executes human action in and on the world. Thus communities and their development cannot be understood or represented without technological tools (Braudal in Castells, 1996). The visual leap frog shown in Figures 23.2–6, providing a brief cartoon of this assertion, depicts five diverse communications technologies as used in differing historical, geographical and social settings. At one and the same time they can be seen to signify some of the goals, activities, roles, relationships and discourse of individuals and their communities, the types of skills and knowledge demanded and valued by these communities, as well indicating the process of human change and transformation of societies more generally.

Clay tablets such as those depicted in Figure 23.2 illustrate one of the oldest forms of communication technologies on record. Dating from 4000 BCE they are said to carry the legend 'ten goats here' 'ten sheep there' (Manguel, 1997). Though historians can only speculate on the specific knowledge it represented for a community living in the fertile valley of Tel Brak (was it a personal record or a shared database?) the tablet has been used to help construct accounts of daily life and work. Such artefacts have also provided the starting point for conjecture about the social and political culture of the times. As new ways of recording economic data emerged

Figure 23.2 Clay tablet: Syria 4000 BCE. (Source: Manguel, A., *A History of Reading*. Reproduced with permission of HarperCollins Publishers Ltd.)

(Schmandt-Besserat, 1996), so did new socio-political structures, deriving from new agricultural and urban settlements and the rise of an elite. A single act of communications technology thus enables us to reflect on the knowledge and identity of the farmer who fashioned it, as well as on the role such a token might have played in the transformation of agricultural communities.

Rather more complex skills and materials were required to produce a codex some five and a half thousand years later.

Codex Mendosa (Figure 23.3) eloquently articulates a leap in human technological development, including the making of paper and fine paints. It is also a detailed historic, economic and ethnographic document, widely used as the basis for understanding the development of the Nahuatl way of life. The codex depicts parents educating their children, matrimony rituals, artisans and craftsmen, merchants (*pochteca*) who travelled to remote locations, warriors, dignitaries, judges, priests and other public figures ranging from ambassadors to executioners. Produced by native scribes (*tlacuilos*) at the request of Mexico's Viceroy, Mendoza, when the country was a Spanish colony, it was shipped to Spain in 1542. Actually, the codex never reached its destination, for the galleon carrying it fell into the hands of French pirates. In contrast with the clay tablet, the producers of this codex displayed the lived practices, the knowledge, values and beliefs of their community, through the technology belonging to – and at the behest of – their colonisers.

Samuel Morse's historic telegraphic message (Figure 23.4) 'What hath God wrought?' was transmitted three hundred years later from the Capitol to Morse's assistant in Baltimore. History is largely silent about the distributed knowledge of Morse's close colleagues, and the wider scientific community, on which this technological breakthrough depended. The product does, however, mark Morse's much

Figure 23.3 Codex Mendosa, Mexico City, 1541–2. (Source: MS. Arch. Selden. A. 1, fol. 2r, Bodleian Library, University of Oxford. Reproduced with permission)

Figure 23.4 First telegraphic message, United States, 1844

desired personal transformation to acclaimed inventor. It also pays tribute to his home community. A personal inscription can be made out on the telegraph print out 'and was indited by my much loved friend Annie Ellsworth'. Ann Ellsworth was the young daughter of Morse's friend, she had suggested the message, drawing it from her reading of the Bible, Numbers 23:23.

The broadside shown in Figure 23.5 was created less than a decade after Morse's historic telegraph and would have been widely displayed in his home city. Like television adverts, broadsides were usually produced for some commercial or political purposes and were a standard form of communication in the 1850s in Europe and the Americas. As a political activist said to be convinced of the benefits of slavery, it is probable that Morse would have opposed the values of the Boston community that created this poster.

The producers of this broadside were utilising the long established technology of printing, believed to have been used in China at the end of the second century AD but first used in Europe around 1450. Due to the technological limitations of many print shops in North America in the mid-nineteenth century, large print and brief text were used to gain the attention of readers. The broadside, printed one year after the controversial Fugitive Slave Act, demonstrates how low cost, simple technology was effectively used by abolitionists in their historic movement against slavery. It expresses the struggle of communities in conflict. It speaks of the determination of a group of people with diverse interests and backgrounds but a shared goal. A common knowledge of, and a commitment to, social justice.

The screens shown in Figure 23.6 depict a discussion mediated through Internet-enabled computers. It is only within the last decade that professionals have had the opportunity to develop the skills required to send an email or take part in a 'virtual' discussion group. This specific electronic environment engages educationists from across the United Kingdom in a discussion about how teachers might be supported in using information and communications technology (ICT) as part of their professional development. The discussion takes place against the background of government legislation requiring teachers to develop competence in ICT-related

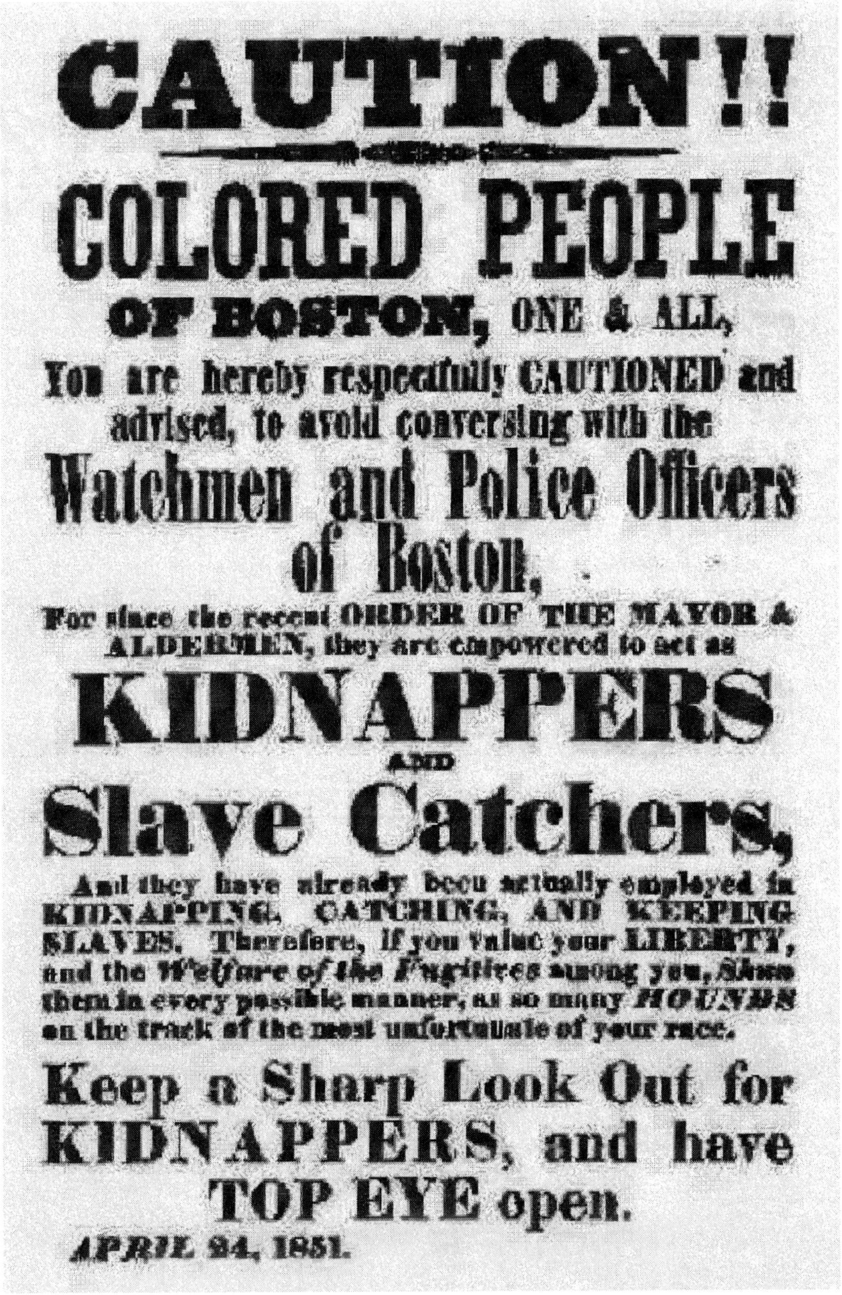

CAUTION!!

COLORED PEOPLE

OF BOSTON, ONE & ALL,

You are hereby respectfully CAUTIONED and advised, to avoid conversing with the

Watchmen and Police Officers of Boston,

For since the recent ORDER OF THE MAYOR & ALDERMEN, they are empowered to act as

KIDNAPPERS

AND

Slave Catchers,

And they have already been actually employed in KIDNAPPING, CATCHING, AND KEEPING SLAVES. Therefore, if you value your LIBERTY, and the *Welfare of the Fugitives* among you, *Shun* them in every possible manner, as so many *HOUNDS* on the track of the most unfortunate of your race.

Keep a Sharp Look Out for KIDNAPPERS, and have TOP EYE open.

APRIL 24, 1851.

Figure 23.5 Abolitionists Broadside, United States, 24 April 1851

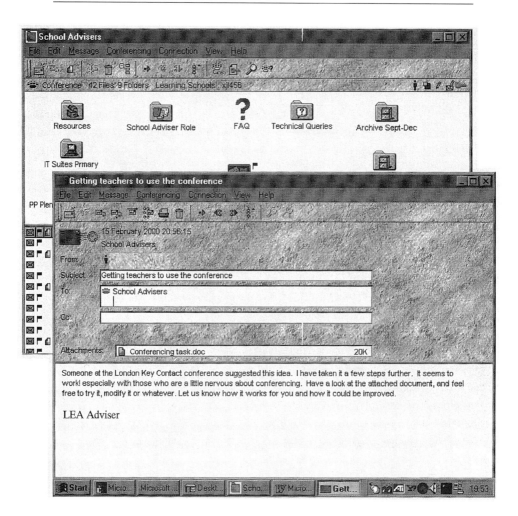

Figure 23.6 Computer-mediated conference of school advisers, United
Kingdom, 2000. (Source: Windows ®98. Screen shot reprinted by
permission of Microsoft Corporation. First Class is a registered
trademark of SoftArc Inc., a wholly owned subsidary of Centrinity
Inc.)

standards, as well as the more global developments outlined in the introduction to
this article.

This leap frog symbolises the transformations that have taken place in human
development in six millennia – from the stick in the sand, to the email linking groups
across the world in a matter of seconds. Despite diverse technologies and widely

varied products, across different times and locations, these images enable us to locate some enduring dimensions of community (Leach and Moon, 1999):

- *goals and purposes*;
- *knowledge* (required and valued);
- *activities* (including the use made of technologies);
- *differing roles and relationships*;
- *discourse*.

Each setting can be said to constitute a series of interconnected nested boxes, simultaneously suggestive of these dimensions at a personal, institutional and societal level. They speak of individuals' participation, by choice and otherwise, in one or more communities. They hint at a complex history of infinite networks and social relationships stretching through time.

Participation

Roget's second classification is *Participation* (Joint Possession). Here 'community' is grouped with words and phrases such as *partnership, co-operation, communion, possession in common.* Participation in any community assumes activity is directed towards common goals, whether explicit, implied or emergent. An essential characteristic of authentic communities is the provision of both formal and informal structures that enables members' participation. Such participation structures ensure joint collaboration and the utilisation and development of different knowledge and skills, interests and expertise towards common goals. Be the shared situation a family, religious sect, football club, community hospital, or teenage band, each is itself a 'form of life' (Wittgenstein, 1958). Each community depends on group activities demanding participation structures with a common and unique discourse (e.g. religious *liturgy*, rules of the *game*, hospital *protocols*, and band *performances*). Each depends on common as well as distributed knowledge (e.g. communicant, server, priest, altar boy; referee, right back, centre forward, managing director; anaesthetist, porter, surgeon, nurse; saxophonist, drummer, guitarist, singer, songwriter). Each demands differing roles and relationships (e.g. father, son, granddaughter, sister; coach, manager, team player).

Recent developments in communications technologies provide participation structures that are enabling new communities to develop in hitherto unimagined ways. Graddol (1997) argues that the development of the Internet is allowing dispersed communities to emerge based on shared interests such as hobbies, mutual support, or even criminality with diasporic cultural and linguistic groups sharing concerns, ideas and decision-making as never before. Research (Joo, 1998) carried out with over 500 primary headteachers and secondary heads of department in British schools found that leading professionals are strongly aware of the implications of this new context for their own educational communities. The majority (87 per cent) were *personally* interested in using the Internet to access on-line resources for professional development. When asked to indicate which would be the most important of four 'on-line resources',[1] priorities were clear. Over half of primary school heads (52 per cent), and over two-thirds of secondary school heads of department (68 per cent) selected *material for classroom use* as the most important. *Resources for updating subject knowledge* was the second most important, and *exchanging ideas with teachers in other schools* was third. This research confirms the high interest of professional leaders in the opportunity that new technologies offer for 'access to a wide range of ongoing activity, other members of their teaching community; and to information, resources and opportunities for participation' (Lave and Wenger, 1991).

Similar findings emerged from data collected over a four-year period within the Open University (e.g. Leach, 1997). Annual surveys carried out over a four-year period (1996–99) into the use of information and communication technologies on an initial teacher education programme (1000 trainees per year) showed high use of the medium by trainees. Some 77 per cent of respondents used computer-mediated conferences twice a week or more, 44 per cent logged on daily. Electronic environments focusing on trainees' subject specialism or phase were rated most highly. In relation to the purposes given for using these conferences, 'exchange of teaching ideas/resources' was rated most highly, closely followed by 'contact with other specialists' and 'social support'. Whilst valuing personal contact most highly, this particular research suggests, the majority of trainees sought it amongst the subject communities of which they aspired to be members. Electronic conferencing provided the opportunity for close contact with both experienced practitioners and aspiring subject specialists: what they thought and said, how they said it, what they admired, what they disliked. Such research seems to confirm that where identity in a particular community is both the goal sought and the knowledge valued, the community itself becomes the 'learning curriculum'.

Jean Lave and Etienne Wenger (1991) have formulated the notion of a 'learning' curriculum quite precisely; this they distinguish from what they term a 'teaching' curriculum'. The former, they argue, has the characteristics of a community.

Learning curriculum	Teaching curriculum
• Strong goals for learning and overview of purposes shared by learners.	• Teaching goals are implicit.
• Basic phenomenon is learning, little observable 'teaching'.	• Teaching is the focus of activity (external view of what 'knowing' is about).
• Engagement in practice the condition for learning.	• Engagement in practice is the 'object' of the learning.
• The practice of the community itself creates the potential curriculum.	• The curriculum is constructed for the instruction of newcomers and can be considered in isolation, manipulated in arbitrary, didactic terms.

- Extensive participation between learners, masters, old-timers, advanced apprentices (both symmetrical and asymmetrical).
- Learners learn mostly in relationships with other learners.
- Learning resources are viewed from the perspective of learners.

- Discourse takes place 'within' as well as about the practice.

- Asymmetrical master/apprentice relationships.

- Teacher is locus of authority deciding 'dictates for proper practice'.
- Resources for learning are supplied and controlled, mediated through an external view of what knowing is about.
- Discourse is about practice; didactic use of language has an existence of its own.

An analysis of the learning curriculum of two professional communities follows. The way in which new technologies were used to facilitate innovative participation structures in these communities is explored.

Case study 1: The 'Grammar Room'

Imagine the following setting. From a large cohort of trainee teachers, over one hundred (mainly primary and secondary modern foreign language and English specialists) have signed up for an optional, two-month seminar on Language and Grammar. A room has been allocated for this seminar, open 24 hours a day and housing a resources area for relevant materials (e.g. books, research papers and model lessons). A lecture by a national expert in the field sets the agenda, subsequent discussion is facilitated by tutors. Across the two-month period there is vigorous exchange of theoretical debate, exploration of lesson models and approaches to teaching, resources and analysis of classroom observation and practice. This room is always in use, one or other participant always there to make a contribution. A core group of 19 lead discussion, some students visit the seminar daily, others once a week. There is no pressure to participate. There is no interruption. Individual contributions vary in length from one minute to ten. Most of the time the discussion is intense and serious, there are disagreements, but also frequent bursts of humour. Some contributors are asked to repeat arguments several times for clarification. Participants leave to read/reflect on particular ideas or to compose a response to an argument, returning several days later to make their point. Pairs or small groups continue the discussion elsewhere. Across the two-month period the resource area grows, with books, materials, lesson plans and other teaching materials brought in from homes, libraries and schools.

We are only beginning to find a language to describe and analyse new electronic environments or to understand the potential of the participation structures they facilitate. We often struggle to compare them with face-to-face scenarios. This account was constructed from data drawn from a two-month electronic seminar, questionnaires to participants, follow-up interviews and a transcribed group discussion with six participants. The account does not translate neatly into traditional, face-to-face professional development activity, since there are opportunities afforded by e-conferencing (e.g. asynchronous communication) that cannot be so interpreted. Here is a summary of the data (Leach, 1997) from which the account was drawn:

- 110 regular Participants (defined as regular readers) across an eight-week period (May–June).
- Participation optional. Core group of 19 contributors (defined as posting between 3–10+ messages each).
- Selective reading of message 'threads' by individual participants (message postings unopened).
- Messages read on as many as three separate occasions by some participants.
- Response time (i.e. from time message read to time replied to) between one and ten days.
- Participants articulated intentions to reflect, check information, search for a resource, compose a reply (actioning of intentions varied from one hour to one week), e.g.:

  - 'Just had the "—— paper" through the post . . . will do a mini summary over the weekend.'
  - 'Is this what you mean? I'll attach the other ones I designed tomorrow, but they are a little harder.'
  - 'Having scanned the first couple of sentences, I know I need to read this closely off line.'
  - 'Wow! S——, talk about taking the horse by the bit! I will get back to you when I have time to digest this – there is a lot of food for thought there. . .'

- Resources taken up by participants:

  - 'Sounds brilliant I will scour the library tomorrow.'
  - 'I've read everyone's comments with interest. I've also made a note of the book you recommend, A——.'

- Message postings varied in length from one line of text to fifty lines of closely argued prose.
- Personal email exchange about the seminar took place between participants.
- Time of postings widely varied across the 24-hour period from 7 a.m. to 2 a.m. (8.30–10.30 the most frequent time):

  - 'At last a few minutes to share my experiences with you. I enjoyed reading all the comments about "cette question epineuse".'

- Two participants read and then contributed to the seminar on a regular basis two-thirds of the way through (i.e. week 6 of 8):

    - 'First apologies for joining the debate so late . . . Your ideas and comments have made fascinating reading.' (12 June)

Additional data drawn from messages, interviews and questionnaires suggest the following were significant elements of the emerging learning curriculum.

Authentic professional task

The question 'How do you teach grammar?' was fundamental for participants, raising important and controversial issues about teaching and learning in their specialisms. Many were attending job interviews during this period and knowledge about language was a topic under scrutiny. The initial 'e-lecture' emphasised a variety of ways of looking at and resolving the question under discussion. It encouraged a climate of critical debate, analysis and understanding of the theme.

Distributed knowledge

Resumés[2] revealed a variety of expertise, illustrating joint practice at its richest. Contributors included native speakers of French, linguists fluent in Spanish, German, Ibo, Russian; trainees with specialisms in literature or special needs, provided complementary knowledge in discussion. The knowledge of numerous 'others' was also woven into the discussion: mentors, other teachers, course texts, tutors, texts about the teaching of grammar, theoretical texts about language, quotes from children's literature and novels. Over 30 explicit examples were documented and many more implicit references served to illustrate the complexity of the concept of 'distributed' cognition.

Varied roles and relationships

Old timers (the tutor-moderators), novices (the trainees), aspiring experts (some of the trainees and recently qualified teachers) and other experts (guest speakers, other course tutors) worked alongside each other (Lave and Wenger, 1991). Moderators raised key points, new questions and ideas, checked for misunderstandings, selected and posted relevant electronic resources. A variety of other roles were taken on at various times by contributors, including facilitator, coach, enthusiast, modeller, assessor, friend, critic, opponent, expert. One contributor had expertise in linguistics. Whilst she had taken a low-key role in a previous e-discussion on literature, an area of subject knowledge identified as needing development, in this e-seminar she vocalised her exceptional knowledge in this element of subject knowledge. In interview she confirmed the increased self-confidence she developed by her participation as an 'aspiring expert'.

Creation of a 'joint oeuvre'

Meyerson has argued that community activity creates joint 'oeuvres', and that these '. . . produce and sustain solidarity, help to make a community of learners . . . promote the sense of division of labour that goes into such a product' (Bruner, 1996, p. 22). This seminar was of itself a significant oevre, a joint work that allowed for explicit sharing and negotiable ways of thinking as a group, as well as providing a public record of individual effort involved as well as the joint knowledge being developed.

> There were great ideas but it sort of didn't matter who they came from . . . these were messages . . . I feel . . . the fact that somebody said it before you or said it in a different way . . . these were important points . . . it's almost as if anyone could have made them.
>
> (from participant interview)

Use of the discourse of practice

Trainees frequently related anecdotes – references to school placements, stories about mentors, pupils and their own classrooms, allusions to their own school day experiences and those of their own children. Lave (1988) distinguishes 'talking about' and 'talking within' a practice. Talking within, she argues, embraces both talking within (e.g. exchanging information, discussing concepts) and talking about (e.g. stories, community lore). In a community both forms of talk fulfil important functions, they include engaging and focusing attention but also supporting communal forms of memory and reflection. Stories signal membership of the community 'acquiring' a store of appropriate stories and, more importantly, knowing the appropriate occasions for telling them.

Group reflection

Thinking aloud was characterised by tentative discourse not dissimilar to face-to-face conversation ('it occurs to me that'; 'presumably if'; 'I'm finding my feelings to be ambiguous') frequently leading into new angles or further problems to be solved.

Conflict

There were frequent disagreements about concepts and practice ('I'm not sure how I should put this but . . .'; 'Yes I agree . . . but'; 'I think your comment is interesting . . . but'). Some contributors deliberately invited argument ('I would love someone to enter the fray . . . HAVE I PUT EVERYONE OFF? I DIDN'T MEAN TO?').

Change of identity

It can be argued that the group activity transformed the identity of some individual contributors as well as the group as a whole. Over the two-month period data show:

An increased willingness to formulate and ask questions

> any other suggestions?; . . . do you have this for each class?; . . . but how does he introduce clauses and phrases . . . this is an area of the NC I've never seen taught and it is an area that the new test will focus on?; . . .what texts are used in MFL teaching?; . . . how could we apply this strategy to younger pupils? There lies the challenge?

A growing acknowledgement of complexity

> I'm finding my feelings about grammar to be ambiguous

> One of my targets is to improve the way I keep tabs on such things. I will invest in a notebook

An increased assurance, confidence and knowledge of the subject

> Oh . . . what a good idea . . . ; Interesting, L——! ; Sounds brilliant!

> I now have the courage to try out all sorts of things I was absolutely terrified of. I'm amazed. If you had told me last year that I would have been doing [those things] I would have laughed at the inanity of the suggestion . . .

Individuals developed as subject experts, and as more confident, critical professionals, ready for work within new communities of practice:

> Just to let you know that as a result of this conference, I have begun to liaise with our MFL department at my placement school (where I have a job for September). In the hope that we can produce some kind of unified approach to language.
>
> (19 June – one of the final messages from an English specialist)

Case study 2: Moving Words

Moving Words (Leach *et al.*, 2000) is a web site for the professional development of English teachers, created by a group of teachers, web designers, teacher trainers and computer technologists. It is part of an Open University research project being used to explore three key questions:

- Can the web make professional learning more accessible?
- Can the web promote improved learning?
- What kind of innovations are possible?

The Literature of Different Cultures and Traditions was chosen as the focus of the site, because it is a compulsory element of the National Curriculum for English and part of the school exam syllabus in England and Wales. Moreover, many teachers find this area a challenging one to teach and supporting resources are limited. The site seeks to suggest new possibilities for pedagogy, a better understanding of the subject and innovative uses of ICT. The Home Page uses language and image that immediately reflects the discourse of the 'subject' community. A Background Section provides information about the purpose of the site, its relation to the National Curriculum and National Literacy strategy, as well as the nature of the research project as a whole.

Guiding questions, models of practice and group tasks

The site has six main areas, each presenting a two-hour INSET session for English faculties. Individual sections focus a single text or theme dealing with a generative issue such as identity, human rights and creativity, as well as playful and humorous content. Each area consists of multimedia presentations, resources (including linked texts and web sites) and collaborative Activities. These Activities incorporate:

- *key questions* – three guiding questions (see Figure 23.7) are used for each session, with hyperlinks to further text that scaffold understanding and discussion if required;
- *models* of practice – e.g. lesson outlines, completed storyboards; a worked hypertext exploration of a short story and exemplar e-DARTs activities;
- *artefacts and resources* – these include kinetic poems and video collages; Shockwave Flash text mapping presentations and useful web links. The resources include authentic work by pupils and presentations intended to stimulate classroom discussion and group activities (e.g. a kinetic, poem created by two 15-year-old pupils using Powerpoint software; a video collage made by pupils focusing Macbeth's soliloquy 'Tomorrow and Tomorrow and Tomorrow.');
- *group tasks* – new texts are provided to be worked on collaboratively, based on new models; a gallery allows for the sharing of new artefacts by teachers and pupils; numerous pair and group activities are suggested for departmental use.

Forums for on-line collaboration

A discussion area is integral to the site, users can move into this from any of the group Activities. It enables communication across geographic space, independent of the time and space restrictions inherent in face-to-face INSET. Thus professionals with diverse interests, backgrounds and expertise are provided with an opportunity to share materials and resources, discuss models, collaborate on projects and explore the

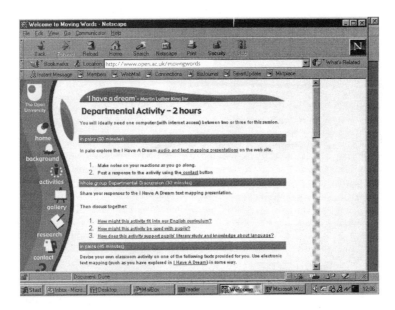

Figure 23.7 Moving Words (1)

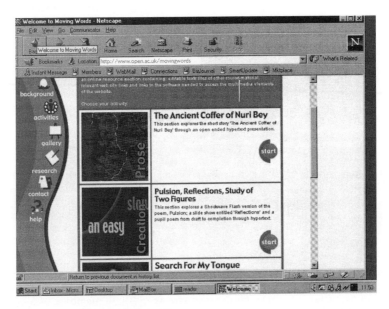

Figure 23.8 Moving Words (2)

(Source: Windows ®98. Screen shots reprinted by permission of Microsoft Corporation. Netscape Navigator is a trademark of the Netscape Communications Corporation)

Table 23.1 Dimensions of community

Dimension of community	Grammar room	Moving Words
Goals • Strong goals and overview of purposes	Purposes of conference publicly posted and permanently displayed	• Background page with explicit aims and purposes • 3 core questions in each activity
Knowledge • The practice of the community creates the potential curriculum • Knowledge always distributed	• Authentic task • Seminar depends on variety of knowledge and expertise	• Authentic task • Image and discourse of site reflects concerns of community • Creation/ construction and implementation of site dependent on distributed knowledge (computer tech-nology specialists; teacher educators; web designers; writers; teachers, etc.
Activities (including use of technology) • Engagement in practice the condition for learning; • A field of learning resources viewed from the perspective of learners	• Arises out of expressed student need • Requirement to act as a group • Sharing of resources, lesson plans, practice and outcomes • Discourse central to activity	• Joint departmental activity with requirement to plan and act as a group • Models and solutions offered • Gallery-production of joint oeuvres • Free, non-linear navigation • Additional text files for creation of new products • Related web sites and other texts • Talk Boards
Roles and relationships • Basic phenomenon is learning; little observable teaching	• Collaboration between 'experts' and novices • Moderator acts as facilitator	• Open access • Designed to be of interest to all members of a subject community

Dimension of community	Grammar room	Moving Words
• Participation between learners, masters, old-timers, advanced apprentices	• Specialist input provided	(e.g. student, teacher, head of department, subject adviser, researcher, teacher trainer, etc.) • Democratic space • Variety of roles taken • On-line peer evaluation of products/processes
Discourse • Discourse takes place within as well as about practice	• Discourse central to activity • Exchange of the 'stories of practice'	• Talk boards integral to activities • Exchange of resources and new forms • Collaborative gallery

potential of the medium generally. As the forum is used, the Moving Words site is transformed from a collection of resources suspended on the web into an authentic learning curriculum. Such environments provide what have been called 'tools for learning communities', enabling professionals on-line to move 'beyond forums for exchanging titbits and opinions, to structures which rapidly capture knowledge value and foster rapid accumulation and growth of a community's capabilities. Ideally the infrastructure for a learning community should be so designed that each contribution spawns far greater value than the contribution itself costs to produce' (Roschelle and Pea, 1999).

Table 23.1 maps the five dimensions of 'community' (goals; knowledge; activities, roles and relationships; and discourse) to elements of the case studies. It illustrates the way in which computer-mediated conferencing and web technology can be intentionally orientated towards the facilitation of a learning curriculum.

The case studies highlight the following features of innovate, leading professional development communities:

- Explicit, shared goals;
- Authentic tasks;
- The requirement to plan and act as a group;
- The use of technology to make thinking explicit;
- The modelling of practices and solutions;
- A requirement to talk within (as well as about) practice;
- Collaboration on a product [s];
- Participants with range of expertise;

- Participants taking a variety of roles at different times (e.g. expert, coach, facilitator, learner, novice, collaborator, aspiring expert, evaluator, leader).

(based on Murphy, 1999)

In both communities there is the expectation that participants will know different things and speak from different experiences. It is this element of community that is often least explored and to which we turn in the final section.

Conflict and change

Roget's third classification of community is *Antagonism*; it is subsumed, in common with Participation, under the more general heading 'Volition'. This classification yields the most numerous words of the three (e.g. party, faction, side, crew, band, horde, posse, phalanx; family, clan; team; tong, familistere, brotherhood, sisterhood, knot, gang, clique, circle; coterie, club) and challenges any notion of community as a feel-good term. This third classification also gestures to the inherently conflictual nature of communities. From this perspective communities are never homogenous frameworks, they are inherently multi-voiced, constitutive of individuals who view their worlds from differing positions, identifying more or less with a variety of overlapping communities (e.g. family, work, national, linguistic, ethnic, etc.). Communities work because, as Eagleton remarks of cultures, 'they are porous, fuzzy edged, indeterminate, intrinsically inconsistent, never quite identical with themselves, their boundaries modulating into horizons' (Eagleton, 2000, p. 96). And since communities are not only what we live, but also what we live for, in reality these blurred boundaries present complex and competing demands on individuals' identities. Community, however, must be carefully distinguished from culture. Eagleton (2000) rightly argues that the 'primary problems we face in the new millennium' – conflict, poverty, the displacement of peoples – are not especially cultural at all, and that cultural theory has precious little to contribute to their resolution. This is not the case, however, of communities. Communities can be – and many are – displaced, poor, riven with conflict, subject to racism as the leap frog across technologies in the first part showed. But such communities, like any other, also have the potential to transform themselves – and to be transformed in collaboration with others.

Acquisition models of development fail to account successfully for the process of transformation and change. *Participation* models explain much more effectively how learning and development is created and transformed through dialogue between people, their collective knowledge and experiences. Engestrom (1996) has suggested that significant change is impelled by 'collective invention in the face of felt dilemmas and contradictions that impede ongoing activity' (Chaiklin and Lave, 1993, p. 13). Freire (1972) argues that authentic transformation and change arises from a dialectic embedded in two inter-related contexts – *authentic dialogue* between people and the *social reality* in which people exist. 'Without dialogue there is no communication, and without communication there can be no true education. The educators' role is to create "pedagogical spaces", posing dilemmas in order that learners can analyse experience and arrive at a critical understanding of their [and others'] reality.'

The changing context outlined in the introduction provides educators with significant dilemmas, contradictions and conflict. Many teachers in the United Kingdom, for example, see new technologies as imposed on them by an alien world or a controlling government; others are frustrated at the lack of adequate resources, the funding to support demands made upon them. Still others fear the impact an uncontrolled Internet might have on their pupils, the demise of 'The Book' and libraries more generally, the loss of expertise. Issues of access to new and changing technologies also bring existing inequities into sharp relief, raising issues of equality. Research (Castells, 1996) shows that communities within as well as across nations have increasing differential access to new technologies, new literacies and new possibilities for communication, blurring the traditional North/South geographical divide. These concerns are not to be swept away and one scenario might be that we watch silently as computational media radically reshape the frontiers of our educational communities. For communities can respond to their lived experience in silence, creating participation structures that demand muteness not dialogue, indeed Davies (2000) has argued that such a silence currently prevails within educational communities in Britain. Goals that embrace 'big' ideas such as democracy, equity and social justice, and that acknowledge some pupils' daily experiences of failure, poverty and racism, have ceased to be fashionable, he argues, largely because the politics that kept such questions alive have been marginalised (Davies, 2000).

This article has suggested another scenario – that leading professional development communities can utilise technologies in order to ensure renewed professional dialogue. Dialogue that engages with real life concerns that the majority of educators care deeply about. Concern about how every student in our education system might equally and successfully participate in schooling. Concern for the development of young people's self-esteem and achievement, rather than for the grading of their minds. Concern with how teachers develop their subject and pedagogic knowledge, developing shared values that can support, extend and transform educational settings. Such dialogue is risky, for it challenges silence. Such dialogue will certainly involve conflict and – inevitably – change:

> Education is risky, for it fuels the sense of possibility. But a failure to equip minds with the skills for understanding and feeling and acting in the . . . world is not simply scoring a pedagogical zero. It risks creating alienation, defiance and practical incompetence. And all of these undermine the viability of a [community].
>
> (Bruner, 1996, p. 43)

Endnotes

1 They were (1) material for classroom use, (2) resources or training for professional development or INSET, (3) resources for updating subject knowledge, and (4) exchanging ideas with teachers in other schools.

2 Students are asked to prepare an introductory resumé as one of their first tasks when they come on-line. They can be read by double clicking on the name.

References

Adair, J. (1983) *Effective Leadership*, London: Gower.

Bredo, E. (1994) 'Reconstructing Educational Psychology', in Murphy, P. (ed.), *Learners, Learning and Assessment*, London: Paul Chapman.

Bruner, J. (1996) *The Culture of Education*, Cambridge: Harvard University Press.

Castells, M. (1996) *The Rise of the Network Society*, Oxford: Blackwell.

Castells, M. (1999) 'Flows, Networks, Identities', in Castells, M., Flesh, R., Freire, P., Giroux, H. A., Macedo, D. and Willis, P. (eds), *Critical Education in the New Information Age*, Oxford: Rowan and Littlefield.

Chaiklin, S. and Lave, J. (eds) (1993) *Understanding Practice*, Cambridge: Cambridge University Press.

Cobb, P. (1999) 'Where is the mind?', in Murphy, P. (ed.), *Learners, Learning and Assessment*, London: Paul Chapman.

Davies, N. (2000) 'Schools in crisis', *The Guardian*, Wednesday, 8 March 2000.

Eagleton, T. (2000) *The Idea of Culture*, London: Blackwells.

Engestrom, Y. (1996) 'Non scola sed vitae discimus: Towards overcoming the encapsulation of school learning', in Daniels, H. (ed.), *An Introduction to Vygotsky*, London: Routledge.

Freire, P. (1972) *Pedagogy of the Oppressed*, Harmondsworth: Penguin.

Freire, P. (1999) 'Education and community involvement', in Castells, M., Flecha, R., Freire, P., Giroux, H. A., Macedo, D. and Willis, P. *Critical Education in the New Information Age*, Oxford: Rowman and Littlefield.

Gardner, H. (1993) *Multiple Intelligences: The Theory in Practice*, New York: Basic Books.

Giddens, A. (1999) 'Globalisation – Lecture 1 Runaway World', BBC Reith Lectures, 1999. http://news.bbc.co.uk/hi/english/static/events/reith_99/week1

Graddol, D. J. (1997) *The Future of English*, London: The British Council.

Joo, J. (1998) *Schools On-Line*, Centre for Research and Development in Teacher Education, The Open University.

Kolb, D. (1984) *Experiential Learning*, Englewood Cliffs, NJ: Prentice Hall Inc.

Lave, J. (1988) *Cognition in Practice*, Cambridge: Cambridge University Press.

Lave, J. and Wenger, E. (1991) 'Participation, learning curricula, communities of practice', in Lave J. and Wenger, E. (eds.), *Situated Learning*, Cambridge: Cambridge University Press.

Leach, J. (1997) 'Changing discourse, transforming pedagogy: developing on-line community for teacher education', paper presented at the 3rd Conference of the European Conference of Educational Research, Frankfurt, 24–27 September 1997.

Leach, J. and Moon, R. E. (1999) *Learners & Pedagogy*, London: Paul Chapman.

Leach, J., Stannard, R., Jones, M. and O'Hear, S. (2000) 'Moving Words: a web site for English teachers', *English and Media Magazine*.

Manguel, A. (1997) *A History of Reading*, London: Flamingo.

Murphy, P. (1999) 'Supporting collaborative learning', in Murphy, P. (ed.), *Learners, Learning and Assessment*, London: Paul Chapman.

Porat, M. (1999) *The Information Economy*, Washington DC: Department of Commerce, Office of Telecommunications.

Roget, P. (1971; revision 1991) *The Everyman Roget's Thesaurus*, London: Chancellor Press.

Rogoff, B. (1999) 'Cognitive development through social interaction', in Murphy, P. (ed.), *Learners, Learning and Assessment*, London: Paul Chapman.

Roschelle, J. and Pea, R. (1999) 'Trajectories from today's WWW to a powerful educational infrastructure', *Educational Researcher*, June July, **28**(5).

Sachs, O. (1999) 'Making up the mind', in Murphy, P. (ed.), *Learners, Learning and Assessment*, London: Paul Chapman.

Schmandt-Besserat, A. (1996) *How Writing Came About*, Austin, Texas: University of Texas Press.

Schon, D. (1987) *Educating the Reflective Practitioner*, San Francisco: Jossey Bass.

Sfard, A. (1998) 'On two metaphors for learning and the dangers of choosing just one', *Educational Researcher*, **27**(2), 4–13.

Shulman, L. (1986) 'Those who understand; knowledge and growth in teaching', *Educational Researcher*, February.

Wittgenstein, L. (1958) *Philosophical Investigations*, London: Macmillan.

Yukl, G. (1994) *Leadership in Organizations*, Englewod Cliffs, NJ: Prentice-Hall.

Index